TEACHING CLASSICS WITH

TEACHING CLASSICS WITH TECHNOLOGY

Edited by Bartolo Natoli and Steven Hunt

BLOOMSBURY ACADEMIC
LONDON • NEW YORK • OXFORD • NEW DELHI • SYDNEY

BLOOMSBURY ACADEMIC
Bloomsbury Publishing Plc
50 Bedford Square, London, WC1B 3DP, UK
1385 Broadway, New York, NY 10018, USA

BLOOMSBURY, BLOOMSBURY ACADEMIC and the Diana logo are trademarks of
Bloomsbury Publishing Plc

First published in Great Britain 2019
Reprinted 2019

A catalogue record for this book is available from the British Library.

Library of Congress Cataloging-in-Publication Data
Names: Natoli, Bartolo, editor. | Hunt, Steven (Classicist), editor.
Title: Teaching classics with technology / edited by Bartolo Natoli and Steven Hunt.
Description: London, UK ; New York, NY : Bloomsbury Academic, 2019. |
Includes bibliographical references and index.
Identifiers: LCCN 2018056515 (print) | LCCN 2019011305 (ebook) |
ISBN 9781350086272 (epub) | ISBN 9781350086265 (epdf) |
ISBN 9781350086258 (hb :alk. paper) | ISBN 9781350110939(pb :alk. paper)
Subjects: LCSH: Classical literature–Study and teaching–Technological innovations. |
Classical education–Technological innovations. | Educational technology.
Classification: LCC PA76 (ebook) | LCC PA76 .T43 2019 (print) | DDC 478/.00785–dc23
LC record available at https://lccn.loc.gov/2018056515

ISBN: HB: 978-1-3500-8625-8
       PB: 978-1-3501-1093-9
       ePDF: 978-1-3500-8626-5
       eBook: 978-1-3500-8627-2

Typeset by RefineCatch Limited, Bungay, Suffolk
Printed and bound in Great Britain

To find out more about our authors and books visit www.bloomsbury.com
and sign up for our newsletters.

CONTENTS

Contents

FIGURES

Figures

EDITORS AND CONTRIBUTORS

Scott Arcenas is a lecturer in the Classics Department at Dartmouth College, USA.

Kevin Ballestrini (@kballestrini) teaches Latin at Mansfield Middle School in Storrs, Connecticut, USA.

Alan Chadwick has been teaching Classics in schools since 1997 and is currently Head of Classics at the City of London Freemen's School, UK.

Jessie Craft (@MagisterCraft) is an educator in Latin/Classics at the secondary level in Winston-Salem, North Carolina, USA.

Caron Downes is a teacher of Classics at the secondary level in York, UK.

Kate Gilliver is a senior lecturer in Ancient History at Cardiff University, UK.

Lisa Hay is a secondary school teacher of Classics at Hitchin Girls' School in Hertfordshire, UK.

Steven Hunt is Subject Leader for the Postgraduate Certificate of Education course in Latin/ Classics at the University of Cambridge, UK.

Kenneth Kitchell taught two years in the high school classroom, 22 years at LSU and 16 at UMass, Amherst, USA, before retiring in 2014.

Ray Laurence is Professor of Ancient History at Macquarie University, Australia.

Elizabeth Lewis teaches Latin and Greek at secondary level in London, UK.

Mair E. Lloyd (@MairLloyd) is Senior Project Assistant at the Cambridge School Classics Project, UK.

Helen Lovatt is Professor of Classics at the University of Nottingham, UK.

Bartolo Natoli (@banatoli) is an assistant professor of Classics at Randolph-Macon College, USA.

Sonya Nevin (@SonyaNevin) is a researcher on the ERC project, *Our Mythical Childhood . . . The Reception of Classical Antiquity in Children's and Young Adults' Culture in Response to Regional and Global Challenges.*

Matthew Nicholls is Professor of Classics at the University of Reading, UK.

James Robson is Professor of Classical Studies at the Open University, UK.

Justin M. Schwamm, Jr, taught high school Latin in a large, very diverse school district in south-eastern North Carolina, USA, from 1992 to 2014.

Emma Searle (@EmmaCESearle) is writing her doctoral thesis on domestic art consumption in Roman Italy at the Faculty of Classics, University of Oxford, UK.

Editors and Contributors

Stephen T. Slota (@steveslota) is an assistant professor-in-residence of Educational Technology at the University of Connecticut, USA.

Roger Travis is an associate professor in the Departments of Literatures, Cultures and Languages and of Digital Media and Design in the University of Connecticut, USA.

Verity Walden worked as a teacher on distance-learning courses for the Cambridge School Classics Project, UK, from 2006 to 2018.

FOREWORD
Kenneth Kitchell

"A slow sort of country!" said the Queen, "Now, here, you see, it takes all the running you can do, to keep in the same place. If you want to get somewhere else, you must run at least twice as fast as that!"

Lewis Carroll (Charles Dodgson), *Through the Looking Glass*, Chapter 2

It is an honour to be asked to write a preface to a volume such as this, which is, when one gets down to it, a rallying cry for adaptive activism. Latin and Greek, it proclaims, are worth fighting for. They have far too much to offer students of any generation to be allowed to be pushed to the sidelines by the whims of bureaucrats or the pressures of changing technology. As one who began his teaching career using mimeograph machines, film strips, slide shows and cassette recorders, only to end it using student-centred learning in a specially designed, multimedia flipped classroom, I am enthusiastic for the need this book will fill, offering teachers of all age groups new ideas and techniques for immediate classroom use, and setting the stage for how we will adapt to the inevitable next wave of digital wizardry around the corner.

The time is long gone when a teacher can cling to outmoded ideas and methods. We must all admit the fact that our students have changed rapidly and profoundly in the last decade or so. These are young learners for whom telephones and cameras have been always been the same device. Skills such as cursive writing, using capital letters and writing in complete sentences have all been profoundly impacted by media, as any teacher will attest. The grammar and vocabulary of Latin may not have changed, but the consumers on the other side of our desks are quite different indeed. We must meet them on their ground.

The current work takes its place in a history of volumes created to address specific problems besetting Classics. Like its predecessors, it demonstrates that, ever since Latin and Greek were declared no longer mandatory in our curricula, teachers of the classics have been at the forefront of those who have learned the wisdom of the widespread aphorism 'Adapt, or die.' For a complex set of reasons, Latin, especially, and Greek, to a lesser extent, lay at the core of curricula for centuries. They offered the best job opportunities to and served as the clearest marker of an educated (and thus upper-class) male. Such was their power that women often had to fight their way into their study and, in nineteenth-century America, the study of the classics lay at the heart of arguments over how to educate newly freed slaves.

During the difficult 60s and 70s, the restless American youth of my generation rose up against such a mossy education, demanding a more 'practical' one. Soon enough other countries followed suit, and over the last 40–50 years Latin has been repeatedly pushed to the 'irrelevant' section of curricula, joining former cornerstones of the liberal arts (such as music, philosophy and art) as the first soft targets to be put in the sights of budget hawks and educational reformers alike.

This is not the place or the space within which to discuss what 'practical' should mean, but some statistics will help us trace the history of classicists' attempts to retain their place in the curriculum. I am best acquainted with American educational trends and I thus take my examples from my own side of the Atlantic. Others will undoubtedly be able to find parallels in their own countries. The works of Bob Lister (2008) and Christopher Stray (2003, 2007), for example, are very useful for the fate of Classics in British schools and universities.

The fall, ironically, coincided with my personal story as a classicist. I was born in 1947, and statistics for the next year, 1948, show that 13.7 per cent of high school students (aged 13–18) took a foreign language. Latin was taken by 7.9 per cent of high school students and 37 per cent of high school students taking a foreign language took Latin. By the time I graduated college and entered graduate school, Latin was studied by only 2 per cent of high school students. The number would eventually fall as low as 1.1 per cent. Enrolment figures are notoriously hard to come by (or trust), but a recent collaborative study issued by the American Councils for International Education in 2017 shows a total of 210,306 students taking Latin in the United States in grades K–12, roughly 1.8 per cent of students studying a foreign language. This is a decrease of 95.14 per cent since 1948.

Many factors contributed to this decline, of course, but the most central one seems to be a question of utility: 'What is he going to *do* with Latin? No one speaks it any more. It is a dead language!' Governmental programs like No Child Left Behind or an emphasis on STEM (Science, Technology, Engineering and Mathematics)-based curricula increasingly jam pragmatic courses in one end of the curriculum, squeezing out 'frills' like Latin at the other end. Online discussion groups routinely request letter-writing campaigns when a school district decides not to replace a retiring Latin teacher, intending to hire an Arabic or Chinese teacher instead.

Classicists saw the writing on the educational bulldozer and decided to fight back with what I have called elsewhere 'The Great Counter-Offensive'. New textbooks were devised. Classical organizations ran advertisements in educational journals touting Latin's merits, and collections of essays appeared addressing the problem. Most major classical organizations created committees or task forces charged with identifying the major issues and with devising practical ways to address them. It was a rare conference at the local, state or national level that did not feature papers on new ways to teach elementary classical languages in an all-out attempt to retain our slim place in the curriculum.

One conference, funded by the National Endowment for the Humanities and jointly run by our two major national classics groups, met in 1986. It published its findings and implemented them over the next two years, eventually leading to the National Committee for Latin and Greek, which remains active today (Burns and O'Connor 1987, Davis 1991).

In the face of our efforts, enrolments began to climb a bit, ironically leading to a new crisis – a shortage of properly trained Latin teachers. Two books of essays edited by Rick LaFleur (1987, 1998) pointed out the problem and offered solutions to it. The second of these volumes, published twenty years ago, sought to establish best practice for teachers and programmes and, for the first time, addressed emerging topics such as oral Latin, distance learning, Latin and Spanish and the effect of the rapidly emerging field of educational computing. One article, written by myself, seems quite antiquated as it encourages use of things like slide projectors, cassette recorders and filmstrips. I even encouraged teachers to 'not forget the power of the World Wide Web' and gave a single paragraph of possible uses (LaFleur 1998: 288).

How inadequate those words seem today. Classics conferences and discussion groups abound with practical suggestions on how to use technology to reach today's students. But it is, one fears, rather a hodgepodge. For some time there has been a need for a single volume written by leading educators in the field and offering a guide to the best practices. Within the pages to follow we are offered thoughtful and tested ways to meet students where they live – in a world inhabited by iPads, social media, online resources, videos and, yes, *Minecraft*. Any teacher of Latin and Greek who does not wish to be left behind in the dustbin of mimeograph machines and VCRs owes it to his or her students to contemplate what this book has to offer.

Other collections have followed (such as Farrell 2001, Gruber-Miller 2006, Archibald et al. 2015) and even the current volume, fulfilling such a vital need as it does, will not be the final word. Technology will continue to evolve. Programmes will continue to be threatened and a disquieting tendency to eliminate the study of Latin in government-funded schools is not going to go away on its own. We will once more have to decide what the goal of teaching Latin is. Is it to offer cultural insights? Is it merely a form of language arts? If oral Latin and total comprehension become the norm, what will happen to the goal of reading Cicero and Virgil?

To answer these and many more questions will be the task of future essay collections. They would do well to follow the model of the current volume so that, as stated so well in a saying misattributed to Ovid, 'omnia mutantur, et nos mutantur in illis': 'All things change and we are changed along with them.'

References

American Councils for International Education. (2017), *The National K-12 Foreign Language Enrollment Survey Report June 2017*. Available online: www.americancouncils.org.

Archibald, E., Brockliss, W., and Gnoza, J. (2015), *Learning Latin and Greek from Antiquity to the Present*, Cambridge: Cambridge University Press.

Burns, M. and O'Connor, J. (1987), *The Classics in American Schools: Teaching the Ancient World*, Atlanta, GA: Scholars Press.

Davis, S. (1991), *Latin in American Schools*, Atlanta, GA: Scholars Press.

Farrell J. (2001), *Latin Language and Latin Culture: From Ancient to Modern Times*, Cambridge: Cambridge University Press.

Gruber-Miller, J. (2006), *When Dead Tongues Speak: Teaching Beginning Greek and Latin*, Oxford: Oxford University Press.

Kitchell, K. (1998), 'Teaching Resources for the Latin Classroom', in R. LaFleur (ed.) *Latin for the 21st Century: From Concept to Classroom*, Glenview, IL: Scott-Foresman- Addison Wesley.

LaFleur, R. (ed.) (1987), *The Teaching of Latin in American Schools: A Profession in Crisis*, Decatur, GA: Scholars Press.

LaFleur, R. (ed.) (1998), *Latin for the 21st Century: From Concept to Classroom*, Glenview, IL: Scott Foresman-Addison Wesley.

Lister, B. (ed.) (2008), *Meeting the Challenge: International Perspectives on the Teaching of Latin*, Cambridge: Cambridge University Press.

Stray, C. (2003), *The Classical Association: the First Century, 1903–2003*, Oxford: Oxford University Press.

Stray, C. (2007), *Oxford Classics: Teaching and Learning, 1800–2000*, London: Duckworth.

ACKNOWLEDGEMENTS

This volume has been a long time coming. It has its roots in a 2014 panel at the Classical Association Annual Meeting entitled 'New Approaches to eLearning in Classics'. Many of the contributors to this current volume participated in the panel and, more importantly, the two editors met for the first time. Shortly after the conference, the idea was hatched for a trans-Atlantic volume to assess the state of the field of Classics and Technology. Thus began the nearly four-year journey from concept to product.

As is natural for an edited volume of this sort, there are numerous individuals to thank. First and foremost, our deepest appreciation goes to our contributors. Throughout the process of compiling this work, we both have been amazed by the expertise, innovation and enthusiasm of each and every one of them. They are the true heroes of this volume, and we hope that you, as readers, draw as much knowledge and inspiration from their insights as we have.

Likewise, thanks are owed to the tremendous institutional support each of us has enjoyed for the duration of this process. Bartolo would like to recognize his outstanding colleagues at Randolph-Macon College, particularly Gregory Daugherty and Elizabeth Fisher, whose steadfast support afforded him the opportunity to work on the manuscript amid other departmental duties. Moreover, to Randolph-Macon as a whole, Bartolo gives thanks for awarding him a Walter Williams Craigie Grant to fund the completion of this manuscript. Steven would like to thank all the teachers and teacher trainees he has had the endless pleasure of observing in the classroom, and his colleagues at the Faculty of Education, University of Cambridge and at other universities across the UK for help in developing the ideas and contacts for this book.

At the Bloomsbury Academic Press, we were lucky to be the beneficiaries of a tremendous team of editors, all of whom helped us fine-tune the scope of this manuscript into its current form. We especially thank Alice Wright and Emma Payne for their tireless efforts and their patience with the endless emails and corrections that accompany edited volumes. Likewise, we owe a great debt of gratitude to the anonymous readers who reviewed our proposal and who helped push us to consider alternative approaches and to improve our arguments. Any shortcomings that remain in the volume are due either to our own collective stubbornness or oversight.

Finally, we would like to thank our families, without whom this entire project would not have been possible. Individually, Bartolo would like to thank his wife, Morgan, to whom he is indebted for her unwavering confidence and patience throughout the many editions of this work. Steve would like to thank family and friends who gave their support through the final illness of his wife, Jane. She would have liked this book. We both would like to recognize our children, Luca, Olivia, Mira and Robi, for their boundless energy and love of learning. This volume is dedicated to them: may they grow up with a love for the ancient world, one stoked by inspiring instructors who constantly strive to make their learning relevant and fun.

B.N.

S.H.

October 2018

INTRODUCTION

Bartolo Natoli and Steven Hunt

Twenty years ago, the field of Latin pedagogy welcomed a new publication that would provide direction for the coming decades. Richard LaFleur's *Latin for the 21st Century: From Concept to Classroom* (1998) was the first comprehensive Latin methods and resource text published since the 1960s, and it sought to expand the pedagogical horizons of Latin teachers by exposing them to the different approaches being taken in the Latin classroom. The premise of the book was simple yet profound: a progression from general chapters beginning with conceptual and theoretical foundations of Latin pedagogy, to specific chapters detailing case studies and practical applications of these foundations. The result was a pedagogical resource that became required reading for all those interested in Latin instruction in the United States.

On the heels of *Latin for the 21st Century* came another publication on teaching Latin with a similar scope and impact. John Gruber-Miller's *When Dead Tongues Speak: Teaching Beginning Greek and Latin* (2006) aimed at familiarizing prospective teachers of Latin and Greek with the research undertaken by linguists, psychologists and language professionals during the second half of the twentieth century, as well as providing concrete examples of the application of this research in the Latin and Greek classroom. Whereas *Latin for the 21st Century* had a broad audience of educators, administrators and teacher-trainers in mind, *When Dead Tongues Speak* aimed directly at the classroom teacher, seeking to get them up to date with the latest scholarship and pedagogical models.

What links these two publications together – and also what made them so profoundly influential to the field of Latin pedagogy – is twofold. First, in both works there is a clear and intentional attempt to connect theory to practice, to explain the 'why' behind the newest methodologies of language teaching. Such connections help educators root the day-to-day classroom activities in a larger theoretical framework and gain confidence in their lesson plans. Second, both LaFleur (1998) and Gruber-Miller (2006) turned outward to the collective experience and expertise of the Classics community and recruited some of the most distinguished professionals in the field of Latin pedagogy to share their wisdom. As a result, these two works paint a picture of the landscape of Latin teaching that is both remarkably broad and detailed, allowing readers to see theoretical concepts and classroom practices on a variety of instructional levels and for learners of all ages and ability levels.

In the nearly two decades that have passed since the publication of these books, however, much has changed in the field of Latin pedagogy. Natoli (2018) points out two of the most major shifts in practice:

> First, there has been a noticeable shift away from passive learning techniques and towards active learning methods that emphasize critical thinking and collaboration

(i.e., 21st century skills). Second, in Classical languages (and particularly in Latin), there has been a growth in the variety of methodological approaches to teaching language, with grammar-translation and reading approaches being joined by linguistic, spoken, and comprehensible input (CI) methods.

Natoli 2018: 5

Alongside these seismic shifts in methodological approaches has been the rise of the use of technology. The development of new and faster technological innovations – from smartphones and tablets, to broadband and cloud computing, to virtual and augmented reality (VR and AR) – puts increased pressure on educators to keep up with the times and to keep their instruction fresh, engaging and relevant to learners. However, at times these pressures – oftentimes from administrators – push educators to adopt technology for the sake of technology and not for any instructional benefit. Such *technologia gratia technologiae* runs the risk of becoming completely unrooted in pedagogical theory and unevaluated for its effectiveness, a situation succinctly crystallized in one of my favourite quotes from Diane Ratvich, a former US Assistant Secretary of Education: 'In the land of American pedagogy, innovation is frequently confused with progress, and whatever is through to be new is always embraced more readily than what is known to be true' (Ratvich 2010: 12).

Moreover, these shifts in methodological approaches and the simultaneous pressures of technology are not limited to Latin in the United States. In the UK, the use of digital resources has grown enormously in the last twenty years. This has been spurred on by the investment of millions of pounds by successive governments in equipment such as interactive whiteboards and, more recently, personal laptops and tablet computers in state schools for all students. Teachers have been encouraged to experiment with the technologies and it has now become normalized for students in primary schools upwards to learn how to use basic computer applications such as word processing, PowerPoint presentations and video making. By the time they reach secondary school at age eleven, they are often now ahead of their teachers in knowledge and use of computers.

But the provision of hardware is only one thing. The award of a government grant towards the development of digital materials for the teaching of Latin in the Cambridge School Classics Project (CSCP) gave teachers of the Cambridge Latin Course (and other courses too) more than just a new way of delivering old materials: it has given them opportunities to update and improve their pedagogies. In today's world, where students are surrounded by technology in almost every other classroom subject and in their daily lives, Latin needs to show that it is not being left behind or let enrolments suffer.

Originally designed for students who did not have a specialist Latin teacher, the digital resources developed for the Cambridge Latin Course are often now most used by the teachers themselves to supplement the traditional paper-based resources, to provide extra resources for students to use on different digital platforms (such as smartphones) outside the classroom, and even for non-specialist teachers to learn from. The adoption of some of the CSCP software by the WJEC examinations board, the Eton Greek Project[1] and even the Open University shows its adaptability and effectiveness. Meanwhile, a thriving online community of classicists has arisen through the Classics Library[2] and the Journal of Classics Teaching Facebook Group[3] in the face of few opportunities for traditional (but expensive) continuing professional development. A number of universities – such as Oxford with its Oxford

Classics Outreach site,[4] Cambridge with The Greeks, the Romans and Us[5] and Warwick with its Warwick Classics Network[6] – have set up their own outreach websites to encourage students to engage with the broader field and to provide them with advice, and teachers with resources.

Therefore, it is these dueling issues of methodological shifts and the successful incorporation of technology into the Latin classroom that this book seeks to address. Taking its cue from LaFleur (1998) and Gruber-Miller (2006), this book has attempted to utilize the collective wisdom of some of the most distinguished scholars and practitioners of Latin pedagogy and technology to provide a handbook to assist classicists in mobilizing technology in their classrooms and connecting their technological practice to pedagogical theory. However, this book differs from its predecessors in two major respects. First, it is not limited to language instruction. Although the instruction of Latin and Greek has been reimagined by the use of technology, it is not the only type of instruction affected. Undergraduate courses in translation, ancient history and art, as well as primary- and secondary-level courses on culture and mythology, have begun to be restructured with technology. Therefore, a broader scope is provided here. Second, whereas LaFleur (1998) and Gruber-Miller (2006) focused their attention on the instruction of Latin and Greek in the United States, this book takes a more global approach. Instructors from the United States, the United Kingdom and Australia, and from primary, secondary and undergraduate levels, have been brought together to contribute to this work as a means of providing a synoptic view of how instructional technology is changing the Classics classroom across the globe.

The book itself is divided, as it were, *in partes tres*. The first section, 'Blended and distance models', provides an explicitly theoretical and big-picture view of the question of how to use instructional technology in Classics. In Chapter 1, Kate Gilliver provides an overview of the renaissance of the flipped classroom model, beginning with the theoretical underpinnings and ending with specific advice for implementing the model in the Latin classroom. Chapters 2 and 3, by Justin Schwamm and Verity Walden, discuss the theory and practice of teaching Latin online in both the United States and the UK, rooting their discussions in the Vygotskian theories of cooperative and social learning. In Chapter 4, Mair Lloyd and James Robson give a glimpse into the world of teaching Latin online at the Open University, paying particular attention to the digital resources available and the issues surrounding the assessment of student learning outcomes. In Chapter 5, Elizabeth Lewis explores the pedagogical theory behind virtual learning environments (VLEs) and the application of that theory through the use of Microsoft OneDrive to facilitate online discussions in her A-level Latin courses. In Chapter 6, Alan Chadwick introduces us to the theories behind the SAMR model and its application in his fully online Latin course entitled CyberCaesar. Finally, this section concludes with Chapter 7, in which Stephen Slota and Kevin Ballestrini bring Latin instruction into the world of practomimetics, online role-playing and cultural competency with their discussion of *Operation LAPIS*, a multi-year, text-based, alternate-reality role-playing game for learning Latin and Roman culture.

The second section, 'Classics without language: Literature, culture and outreach models', builds upon this theoretical section by providing more specific examples of technology in action and bringing together contributions dealing with using instructional technology in classes without original Latin or Greek. These chapters are more practical in nature and serve as case studies rooted in pedagogical theory. In Chapter 8, Emma Searle returns to the question of VLEs first explored by Lewis in Chapter 5 within the context of Latin instruction. Here, however, Searle calls attention to the ways in which VLEs can also be leveraged as vehicles for Classics outreach through a case study of OxLAT, a branch of the outreach programme used by the Faculty of Classics at the University of Oxford. Chapter 9 builds upon the theme of outreach in Chapter 8, as Ray Laurence explains how two of his animated films, *A Glimpse of Teenage Life in Ancient Rome* and *Four Sisters in Ancient Rome,* became YouTube sensations, while exploring how the power of such social media can be harnessed as an outreach tool for Classics. Chapters 10 through 14 return the reader to the classroom setting and discuss how technology can be used to provide transformative and engaging instruction in Classics courses at all levels. In Chapters 10 and 11, Sonya Nevin and Matthew Nicholls provide case studies of how digital animations of Greek vases and student creation of digital modelling of Roman architecture and urban planning at both the primary and secondary levels have succeeded in bringing the ancient world to life for their students. Likewise, in Chapter 12, Caron Downes discusses the use of a 1:1 iPad scheme to teach Greek theatre and tragedy to her Year 10 and 12 students as a means of increasing student engagement and appreciation of the visual elements of theatrical performance. Finally, in Chapters 13 and 14, Helen Lovatt and Scott Arcenas explore the ways in which instructional technology and digital tools can, indeed, make lectures great again through the use of just-in-time learning devices (e.g. clickers, Socrative and Kahoot!) and interactive mapping software through ORBIS: The Stanford Geospatial Network Model of the Roman World.

The final section, 'Using technology in the ancient language classroom', provides a collection of case studies focused on the use of instructional technology in the ancient language classroom. Although the focus of these models is on Latin, any and all of these models could be employed with equal success in the ancient Greek classroom as well. In Chapter 15, Jessie Craft provides a how-to guide for using Comprehensible Input (CI) and Teaching Proficiency through Reading and Storytelling (TPRS) methodologies in the ancient language classroom via a case study on using the digital gaming platform *Minecraft* to teach Latin. In Chapter 16, Steven Hunt explores the ways in which the e-CLC digital resources for the Cambridge Latin Course can be paired successfully with interactive whiteboards (IWB) to create a socio-collaborative, dialogic education environment through a case study involving UK students at the secondary level. In Chapter 17, Roger Travis reviews how the online document sharing software Google Docs fostered authentic learning opportunities and allowed students to create their own community of classicists through the students' construction of critical annotations on a text in Latin or Greek. Chapter 18 provides another example of authentic learning for students, as Bartolo Natoli describes the use of digital commentary creation in his advanced undergraduate Latin class as a means of Project-Based Learning. Finally, in Chapter 19, Lisa Hay pulls many of the theories and practices outlined in the preceding chapters through the creation of a multi-modal lesson plan for Latin, one that shows the flexibility of instructional technology and its ability to integrate seamlessly into existing curricula.

Taken together, these chapters hope not only to shine the spotlight on the tremendous and innovative uses of instructional technology occurring in Classics classrooms across the globe, but also to provide fodder for inspiration and debate, for collaboration and networking, and – ultimately – for teaching and learning. For, as Kenneth Kitchell so rightly points out in the preface to this volume, the time is, indeed, long gone when a teacher can cling to outmoded ideas and methods. We, as a profession, must adapt and embrace the changing landscapes of technology and pedagogy as an opportunity to better the field, not as an obstacle to be overcome or begrudgingly accepted. Therefore, we conclude this introduction whence it began, with a quotation from LaFleur's (1998) landmark collection; for like that collection, this one has the same aim:

> This is a book for teachers, and for those who teach teachers, at all levels, from grade school to graduate seminar. My hope is that it will enable this to teach not solely as they were taught, and to learn new lessons not only 'the hard way'. If you are a teacher, make this little book your *vade mecum*: it will not tell you everything you need to know, but it will tell you a great deal and . . . it will point you in most of the right directions.
>
> LaFleur 1998: xiii

Notes

1. See https://www.etoncollege.com/GreekProject.aspx?nid=e19484e6-707c-44d4-a3d7-f8b93df8751f for details.
2. See https://www.theclassicslibrary.com/ for details.
3. See https://www.facebook.com/groups/568931393210000/ for details.
4. See https://clasoutreach.web.ox.ac.uk/ for details.
5. See https://www.greeksromansus.classics.cam.ac.uk/ for details.
6. See https://warwick.ac.uk/fac/arts/classics/research/outreach/warwickclassicsnetwork/ for details.

References

Gruber-Miller, J. (2006), *When Dead Tongues Speak: Teaching Beginning Greek and Latin,* New York: Oxford University Press.

LaFleur, R. (1998), *Latin for the 21st Century: From Concept to Classroom*, Glenview, IL: Scott Foresman-Addison Wesley.

Natoli, B. (2018), 'From Standards for Classical Learning to World-Readiness Standards: What's New and How it can Improve Classroom Instruction', *Teaching Classical Languages*, 9(1): 1–18.

Ratvitch, D. (2010), 'A Century of Skills Movements', *American Educator*. Spring. Available online: https://irvingtonparentsforum.files.wordpress.com/2015/05/ravitch-on-21st-century-skills-american-educator-annotated3.pdf (accessed 30 September 2018).

PART I
BLENDED AND DISTANCE MODELS

CHAPTER 1
FLIPPING ROMANS: EXPERIMENTS IN USING TECHNOLOGY FOR TEACHING IN HIGHER EDUCATION
Kate Gilliver

Introduction

The experiments in teaching outlined in this chapter arose from an invitation to join an interdisciplinary group at Cardiff University during the 2016–17 academic year, which was investigating student preferences for different media used to present the 'taught' element of a course that had been flipped (e.g. PowerPoint presentation, Prezi, podcast, transcript or recording of lecture). Like several others involved in the project, I had little previous experience of flipped learning, so the learning curve in implementing this method of teaching was as steep for me as it was for my students. I chose to flip an entire course rather than just to trial a few lectures, but I intended to do so in a way that would allow a reversion to traditional lecturing should the experiment not prove a success. The class I chose was a course on the Roman Army that was taught almost entirely by myself, which has traditionally been very popular with students. The content was delivered in the form of pre-recorded lectures, produced using the Panopto recording and streaming program,[1] that students were required to watch in advance of the weekly class. The success of this experiment, from the experience of both the students and myself, led me to employ a similar approach the following year on another course, but with some adjustments to the way the taught content was provided.[2]

Flipped learning has been used as a teaching technique in both schools and tertiary education for some time now. Mazur developed a form of flipped learning to teach physics undergraduates at Harvard in the early 90s (Crouch and Mazur 2001, Mazur 2009), and a similar approach was developed by Bergmann and Sams, two Colorado chemistry schoolteachers who helped to popularize the teaching method, including the terms 'flipped learning' and 'the flipped classroom' (Bergmann and Sams 2012). Many published examples of flipped learning relate to the teaching of sciences, including mathematics, or of economics (Lage et al. 2000, Gavrin 2006, Mazur 2009); few relate to the teaching of humanities. However, in humanities higher education, we have been using flipped learning for a long time, possibly without actually realizing it or giving it a particular name. It is standard practice in many humanities subjects to set our students work to read before coming to seminars. This might include assigning modern scholarship so that students have an understanding of different theoretical approaches to the theme to be discussed, or expecting students to come to seminars having not just read a range of set primary sources, but having considered various pre-circulated questions relating to the materials read. Nonetheless, outside the seminar, the formal lecture remains a central aspect of teaching humanities at many universities. Lectures may be more or less interactive, perhaps with some form of discussion or dialogue taking place within the context of a lecture, or a pause in the lecture to watch a video clip, but many courses still revolve around the long-established tradition of an expert standing up and speaking to an audience. In the flipped learning model, instead of students listening to an academic standing at the front of the room lecturing, the timetabled classroom session is used for active learning and builds on materials reviewed and studied by students in advance of the class.

Bishop and Verleger (2013) discussed the pedagogic theories behind flipped learning, stressing that the point of it is not so much rearranging teaching activities and using technology to capture lectures, but the active learning, and in particular the group-based activities that students in flipped classes are engaged in. Active learning incorporates peer-assisted learning (encompassing cooperative and collaborative learning as well as peer tutoring) along with problem-based learning (Foot and Howe 1998). The latter appears to have a positive effect on skills rather than knowledge (Dochy et al. 2003). However, peer-assisted learning underpins flipped learning: Topping and Ehly (1998) posit that this is a broad enough term to encompass both Piaget's theory of cognitive development and Vygotsky's zone of proximal development. Though the two forays into flipped learning described here found peer-assisted learning to be an effective, engaging and exciting approach to teaching, technology was central to the success of the courses and to student achievement and satisfaction, because having the full set of recorded lectures which had formed almost the entirety of the formal teaching for previous cohorts gave students the confidence to embrace a new way of learning.

Lecturing to the webcam

Panopto is a lecture capture system used by many universities and it will be familiar to many colleagues working in higher education. The software provides a means of recording lectures in either video or audio format, editing them and streaming them, usually through Virtual Learning Environment (VLE) hosts. When replaying a lecture, the programme simultaneously displays PowerPoint slides or other audio-visual (AV) resources, such as film clips or output from a digital whiteboard or writing pad, and video of the lecturer if a webcam is being employed. Preview panes allow the viewer to navigate to a particular section of the lecture, should they wish. The program is regularly used for recording live lectures, but can also be used for personal capture by using any networked computer with a webcam or microphone. Opting for personal capture allowed considerable flexibility, including the ability to record lectures outside the university, and meant it was not necessary to book a lecture theatre; the office or home study became the lecture theatre. Using a webcam instead of the wider angle of cameras in a lecture theatre set-up also allowed for a more personal interface for those watching, as they could see the lecturer's facial expression rather than just a distant figure.

I recorded each fifty-minute lecture in sections, each approximately twenty minutes long, in case a technical problem resulted in the loss of a recording (this only happened once, with an irreconcilable lack of synchronicity between audio and video). These lecture sections were considerably longer than the six-minute optimum recommended by Guo (2013), but I wanted time to develop complex arguments and felt that shorter sections would have broken up the flow. I also aimed to give the students a 'normal' lecture experience through the recordings, should they choose to revert to traditional teaching when given the option. As discussed below, the students gave themselves pauses when watching the lectures. Dividing up lectures also meant I would be able to refresh lecture notes further and edit the PowerPoint slides between recording each section of the lecture. In addition, I would be able to replace a whole section of a lecture to reflect new developments and interpretations for future iterations of the course, rather than having to rerecord an entire fifty-minute lecture.

Lecturing to a webcam rather than live to a group of students took some adjustment. Being able to pause, rephrase material to ensure greater clarity (particularly necessary given that there was no audience reaction to provide a cue if the explanation was not clear) and edit slides even during the course of a recording were positives, but the spontaneity of a live lecture was sorely missed, resulting in fewer digressions and less wit. However, without the need to interact with students or rephrase material as in a live lecture, there was more time to explore the material: on average seven to eight minutes more in a fifty-minute lecture. Post-recording editing was relatively straightforward, particularly as there was no attempt to get a flawless recording. The following year, for a new course that required lectures written from scratch, partly in response to student feedback from the previous year I chose to record 'lecture shorts' of twenty to thirty minutes for each class, rather than a full fifty-minute lecture. Students still fulfilled the learning outcomes of the module, but those who tended to rely too heavily on lecture content rather than on a balance of lectures and library work did not perform as well. Time pressures also led me to record as podcasts, with just voice accompanying the AV aids, rather than video; this was considerably quicker, as I could work much more extensively from full notes since maintaining eye contact with the webcam was not necessary.

As with any new technology, it took a while to become confident with editing recordings and publishing them to the university's VLE (Blackboard) with the correct permissions. I did not attempt to produce a flawless lecture, however; the audience was restricted only to the students on the course and I continued lecturing from notes in my usual style. One of the advantages of editing the lecture was being able to splice in video clips taken either from YouTube or from Box of Broadcasts (BoB), a shared off-air media-recording and archive service for educational institutions in the UK.[3] Clips from movies, television series and re-enactment groups helped to bring liveliness to the lectures, in addition to illustrating points being made. As I grew increasingly familiar with both the technology and its potential, I took to directing students to pause the recording either to think about a question that I had posed, or to read a key article or some sources before continuing the lecture with the material fresh in their minds. Thus, despite not having a live audience, the recorded lectures were still interactive. Students were given pointers that a particular question I posed would be discussed in class subsequently and so could they prepare more effectively for upcoming classes.

The recorded lectures were made available several days before the timetabled class via Blackboard, along with additional resources: the PowerPoint slides from the lecture, any handouts, an additional bibliography including PDFs of key articles and book reviews, and a word list. The latter was popular with students, and it was their suggestion to include it to make up for the lack of a physical board on which I would write unfamiliar words during traditional lectures.

The flipped . . . lecture theatre

Limitations in the teaching estate at my institution and the size of the cohort (over sixty students) meant the teaching room was a traditional raked lecture theatre, not ideal for active learning; however, the 150-seat lecture theatre provided some room for flexibility simply by virtue of its size, and the acoustics were good for interaction across the whole student cohort. The following year, the smaller class size allowed for use of a teaching space designed and organized for flipped learning, a space far more conducive to effective discussion and group activities. Such an arrangement would potentially be less practicable with a class size of over fifty. Each fifty-minute class started with question time, a standard feature of the flipped classroom (Lage et al. 2000), to ensure that students had understood the recorded lecture and to provide an opportunity to explore a topic in more depth, and it was normally during this part of the class that students were asked to discuss any questions posed during the recorded lecture. This was not intended to become a series of mini-lectures, however, and this part of the class was never more than a few minutes long.

To facilitate in-class discussion, and in an attempt to address the general reticence of undergraduates to speak in front of a large class, students were divided into groups of five or six. Each group appointed, on a rotational basis, a 'centurion' to lead the discussion and a 'scribe' to present the group's views to the rest of the class, the idea being that no-one was required to speak individually, but on behalf of their group. Once familiar with this approach, most students adjusted and were happy to present to the full class when their group was called each week. General discussion might ensue, with individual students joining in, but the format was deliberately kept flexible. Whilst groups were in discussion, I would circulate to ask and prompt questions as appropriate. The questions the groups discussed provided a stepped increase in the complexity of the tasks over the course of a class: factual and observational questions led into discussion of theoretical approaches, different interpretations and key themes relating to the content of the recorded lecture they had watched. Students were recommended to bring laptops and tablets to the class and encouraged to make use of the internet to research topics and find appropriate evidence to contribute to discussions; researching in class enhanced the corpus of evidence that students had access to for the course, and helped them to develop critical skills in selecting and employing evidence. The result was 'like a giant seminar', according to one student who found this mode of learning very engaging. Ideas were swapped amongst the cohort, and instant confirmation or correction was available from other students or myself, so feedback was constant, and might be followed up with a mini-lecture on something that needed clarification.

More active learning, literally, accompanied these class discussions. Using mocked-up equipment, students explored the practicalities of Roman military equipment and differing modern views on legionary fighting stance and style; a scale model catapult formed the basis for discussing the effectiveness of ancient artillery, as well as the value of modern reconstructions. Inevitably, given the subject of the course, a mock decimation took place as part of the class's exploration of military discipline. An optional visit to a pair of well-preserved marching camps in the Brecon Beacons had already provided for hands-on study of the defences and layout of campaign camps, including intervisibility within the camp and the practicalities of communicating between different corners of the camp. This study also drew on animated reconstructions of the encampments, the production of which I have been involved with for a phone app produced by the Brecon Beacons National Park Authority aimed at enhancing visitor experience to the site. Together, the visit and the animations brought to life very effectively the descriptions and information in ancient texts. But one of the most revealing examples of active learning came with the classes on pitched battle.

In the recorded lecture on pitched battle, I discussed battlefield orations, a key feature of the ancient battle description. Within the additional resources for this class the students were given some examples of pre-battle speeches, an overview of modern studies of the genre, and video clips from *Gladiator* and other movies. They were also each asked to select an account of a pitched battle from the ancient sources that interested them and to extract key information from the narrative, both from an historical or a literary perspective. In the ensuing class, each group selected one battle and presented an analysis of it to the rest of the class, leading to a broad discussion of both the circumstances of pitched battles and literary representations of them. Each group then composed an oration for the battle they had chosen and selected one member of the group to give the oration to whole class, which highlighted some of the issues relating to the practicality of giving a speech. This exercise showed how well the students had understood both the historical and literary contexts: the speeches were directly relevant to their specific battle and showed an unexpectedly deep understanding of the Roman military psyche.

In the second year of flipped teaching, on the course on life in Rome, class activities included studying articles on finding one's way round an ancient city and then employing Roman methods to give directions round Cardiff, and a public inquiry into the Neronian fire in Rome, drawing on accounts and analysis of ancient fires and on the public inquiry into the Grenfell Tower fire, which was taking place at the time.[4] Because of the accelerated learning of foundational material provided through the recorded lectures, students were able to develop more critical engagement with ancient and contemporary sources to achieve a more nuanced understanding of the subject.

Student experience

Students were advised when they selected the courses how they would be taught and were promised a reversion to the traditional lecture format at the end of the first semester, if they wished. When teaching started, there was initially a mixed response; students were generally very positive about the pre-recorded lectures, though some noted that they found listening to them very time-consuming. Given that the pre-recorded lectures were not substantially different from the live lectures I had given previously on the module, this probably indicates that students were being more conscientious about note taking. Nevertheless, initial student feedback did encourage the change to 'lecture shorts' in the second year, which received a more mixed response: some were happy with the change, whilst a few who had not done the course in the previous year felt they were being 'short-changed' on lecture time. Flipped learning requires the student to take greater responsibility for their own learning (Educause 2012, Talbert 2014) and there were students on the course in the second year who were less willing or able to undertake this task.

Some students were uncomfortable with the group discussions, or lacked confidence in them. However, this was generally overcome through reassurance and reinforcement of the role of centurion and scribe. 'I pay to sit and listen to lecturers, not discuss things with other students' was one response, which suggests more a lack of understanding of higher education than specifically flipped learning. As is the case with seminars, there were some groups where not all students were willing to engage fully in the activities. Two students transferred to another course early on, both citing the teaching methods as the reason: one was unwilling to take a risk with non-traditional teaching, despite reassurances to the whole class that I was confident this would not impact on student performance; I told them that the vast majority of studies indicated an improvement in student attainment (Crouch and Mazur 2001, DesLauriers et al. 2011). The main negative feedback from the students in the end-of-year questionnaire related to the physical space: as mentioned earlier, the traditional raked lecture theatre was not ideal for this form of teaching.

But the vast majority of students were enthused from the very start, as much about the methods of teaching as the subject matter, and by the second year of flipped learning, students were choosing to take a course specifically *because* it was being delivered in this way. Feedback came from mid-course and end-of-course surveys, from informal comments and from student interviews (Cardiff University Learning Hub 2017). The pre-recorded lectures were almost universally a major hit. Students loved the flexibility provided by the pre-recorded lectures, the ability to replay a section, or to pause to research key points. Students felt the format encouraged them to undertake more of their own research into the subject, and to carry out more independent work. Some students watched the lecture together, and would pause the recording whilst discussing things amongst themselves, with the result that the active learning began even before the class. Whilst a few students noted dissatisfaction with the workload implications of watching a lecture before class each week, many more were much more positive about the extra contact time and felt that they were learning more and retaining more from the recorded lecture than in a normal lecture. They were also aware that the lectures would be very helpful for revision for an end-of-year exam.

The group work in class encouraged students to be more thoughtful and analytical in studying the subject, and ensured they considered alternative perspectives in addition to their own. The active learning enhanced students' interest in the subject, with one student noting that 'coming to the lecture to discuss with like-minded people in groups really made the classes stimulating'. As in other flipped learning classes (Brame 2013), students were also aware that they were getting instant feedback, both from their peers and from the course tutor, and they were able to confirm or revise their interpretations with confidence.

In the first year, when given the option of reverting to traditional lecturing halfway through the course, 95 per cent of the 65 students opted to continue with flipped learning. In the second year, given the same option, only one student of the 45 strong cohort voted for traditional lectures. Surveys showed a very high level of satisfaction with the teaching, including 81 per cent of students reporting high confidence in communicating the knowledge they had gained on the course. This almost certainly relates to the class activities and the rotation of responsibilities for disseminating the small groups' discussions to the rest of the class. Colleagues noted better group organization and initiative on other courses, aspects partly accounted for by the work done in the flipped classes.

Viewing statistics generated by the Panopto program revealed good engagement with the lecture recordings throughout the year. There was a slight drop off towards the end of the academic year (−13 per cent of average viewing figures), particularly after coursework essays had been submitted (−19 per cent of average viewing figures), but the majority of students continued watching throughout the year, with a notable spike in the revision period (+300 per cent of average viewing figures). In the second year the drop-off was more noticeable (−18 per cent of average viewing figures), but no more so than in other courses in an academic year disrupted by industrial action;[5] again, students made significant use of the lectures for revision (−36 per cent of average viewing figures after coursework submission, but +270 per cent in the revision period).

In the first year, the average grades for the Roman Army course increased by 2 per cent over the grades of previous cohorts (60 per cent, compared with an average of 58 per cent for the previous two cohorts). With a new course in the second year of flipped learning, comparisons with previous cohorts were not possible. This increase was not as high as increases reported elsewhere (Crouch and Mazur 2001, DesLauriers et al. 2011), but nonetheless there was a clear improvement in attainment, particularly in the use of and engagement with scholarly debate in both coursework and exam essays. With the expectation of using the recorded material in future, more time will be available for adjusting and refining the class activities, so there is the potential for further improvements in marks in future. However, the transferable skills developed by the students during the courses – hard to quantify in terms of grades – are of considerable importance: cooperative skills, communication (which the students themselves recognized), questioning, debating and research skills improved for the vast majority of students on the courses.

Teacher experience

The experiences reported from these experiments with flipped learning do not differ substantially from many other reported studies. There is no doubt that establishing a flipped learning course can be very demanding on time (Millard 2012, Taylor 2015: 61). Without additional resources, such as teaching relief or easily accessible IT support, flipping a course wholesale – rather than just a discrete section of course – may not be feasible. However, as well as ensuring lectures do not become dated, there will be significant time-saving with future iterations of the course. Lecturing to the webcam is an easy adjustment, particularly if perfection is not an aim and lecturing is done in a natural style. Being able to splice videos into the lectures and ask the audience to pause a lecture in order to read something was a huge benefit, and a great time-saver compared to a live lecture. The technology used for these experiments was relatively intuitive, and valuable assistance was provided in the form of instructional videos from learning technologists within the university who were keen to help, another factor that could make a big difference to the success – and time investment – of setting up flipped teaching.

After only a few weeks of flipped classes it became apparent that the students were already at a more advanced stage than previous years, both in terms of depth of understanding and engagement with evidence (Hamdan et al. 2013). Student collaboration and cooperation was superior to previous years; even when the lecturer was unable to make the class because of illness, a very large number of students turned up regardless, organized themselves into groups, and got on with work themselves. The lecturer was more aware of students' knowledge and misconceptions than in the more passive environment of a traditional lecture. Perhaps most importantly, from my perspective, is that this is teaching, not lecturing, and it is enormous fun. Students are clearly thinking and being challenged, and being encouraged to be more adventurous; but so too is the lecturer, because of the interaction with students in class, and because of the time freed up for active learning. This is the most stimulating and rewarding teaching I have been involved with.

Lage et al. (2000) suggested that the flipped teaching model might require lower student numbers because it is resource heavy, or that it could be effective with larger class sizes through the employment of additional tutors to help facilitate sessions. Many university lecturers in the current educational climate would be happy with smaller class sizes, but whilst working with smaller classes may be easier and the students might have more direct engagement with the teacher, the method of class teaching employed on these two courses – using small group work within the context of the flipped learning environment – has proved successful with groups of fifty to seventy students and is likely to be employed with larger classes in future. One of the primary limiting factors is the physical environment: traditional fixed-seat lecture theatres still dominate many university estates, and it can be very difficult, expensive and time-consuming to have space redesignated and made suitable for more flexible teaching needs.

Where next?

Whilst not having as significant an impact on student grades as some other examples of flipped learning, and not satisfying all students (particularly those who, regardless of their intellectual ability, perhaps struggle with taking responsibility for their learning), this is a form of teaching in which I have considerable confidence. The vast majority of students have benefitted from the flipped format in terms of their academic and employability skills, and have enjoyed the format as much as the teacher. It has had a positive effect for the students going on to other courses as well, encouraging initiative and exploration of their subjects. Future iterations of the courses will bring refinements in class activities and organization, though the latter depends to an extent on cohort size and room allocation. In terms of technology, the lecture capture system employed, Panopto, allows for the inclusion of in-lecture quizzes, either at time of recording or retrospectively, through which students can check their understanding of the lecture material; this could allow the lecturer to monitor how students engage with pre-recorded lectures, as opposed to merely viewing them. And as technology advances, who knows what other opportunities there will be to develop teaching materials for flipped learning?

Notes

1. See https://www.panopto.com.
2. Thanks are due to Cardiff University students on the Roman Army (2016–17) and Life in Ancient Rome (2017–18) courses for being enthusiastic guinea pigs in my exploration of flipped learning, for their thoughtful and helpful feedback and for helping to create a positive learning community in classes. Thanks also to Steve Rutherford of Cardiff University School of Biosciences for leading the flipped learning project funded by the university's Centre for Education Innovation, and to Dewi Parry, Learning Technology Officer, and Karl Luke, Business Change Officer, for their ready and valuable support with the technology.
3. See https://learningonscreen.ac.uk/ondemand.
4. See https://en.wikipedia.org/wiki/Grenfell_Tower_fire.
5. Universities in the UK were affected by academic staff striking in the spring of 2018 in an industrial dispute over employee pensions. There was a noticeable drop-off in student engagement even in courses unaffected by the industrial action.

References

Bergmann, J. and Sams, A. (2012), *Flip Your Classroom: Reach Every Student in Every Class Every Day*, Eugene, OR: Institute of Science for Technology in Education.

Bishop, J. and Verleger, M. (2013), 'The Flipped Classroom: A Survey of the Research', *American Society for Engineering Education*, ASEE National Conference Proceedings, Atlanta, GA.

Brame, C. (2013), 'Flipping the Classroom', *Vanderbilt University Center for Teaching*. Available online: https://cft.vanderbilt.edu//cft/guides-sub-pages/flipping-the-classroom/ (accessed 26 June 2018).

Crouch, C. and Mazur E. (2001), 'Peer Instruction: Ten Years of Experience and Results', *American Journal of Physics*, 69 (9): 970–977.

DesLauriers, L., Schelew, E. and Wieman, C. (2011), 'Improved Learning in a Large-Enrollment Physics Class', *Science*, 6031 (332): 862–864. Available online: http://science.sciencemag.org/content/332/6031/862.full (accessed 28 June 2018).

Dochy, F., Segers, M., Van den Bossche, P. and Gijbels, D. (2003), 'Effects of Problem-based Learning: A Meta-analysis', *Learning and Instruction*, 13 (5): 533–568.

Educause. (2012), '7 Things You Should Know About Flipped Classrooms', Educause Learning Initiative. Available online: https://library.educause.edu/resources/2012/2/7-things-you-should-know-about-flipped-classrooms (accessed 26 June 2018).

Foot, H. and Howe, C. (1998), 'The Psychoeducational Basis of Peer-assisted Learning', in K. Topping and S. Ehly, eds. *Peer-Assisted Learning*, Mahwah, NJ: Lawrence Erlbaum Associates, 27–43.

Gavrin, A. (2006), 'Just-in-Time Teaching', *STEM Innovation and Dissemination: Improving Teaching and Learning in Science, Technology, Engineering and Mathematics*, Metropolitan Universities, 17 (4): 9–18.

Gilliver, K. (2017), Cardiff University Learning Hub Flipped Learning Case Study. Available online: https://www.cardiff.ac.uk/learning-hub/view/using-personal-capture-for-flipped-learning (accessed 26 June 2018).

Guo, P. (2013), 'Optimal Video Length for Student Engagement', edX Blog, 13/11/2013. Available online: https://blog.edx.org/optimal-video-length-student-engagement#.U-Qs-vldV8F (accessed 13 January 2019).

Hamdan, N., McKnight, P., McKnight, K. and Arfstrom, K. (2013), *A Review of Flipped Learning*. London: Flipped Learning Network, Pearson. Available online: https://flippedlearning.org/wp-content/uploads/2016/07/Extension-of-FLipped-Learning-LIt-Review-June-2014.pdf (accessed 28 June 2018).

Higher Education Academy. (2017), 'Flipped Learning', Higher Education Academy Knowledge Hub. Available online: https://www.heacademy.ac.uk/knowledge-hub/flipped-learning-0 (accessed 11 June 2018).

Lage, M.J., Platt, G. and Treglia, M. (2000), 'Inverting the Classroom: A Gateway to Creating an Inclusive Learning Environment', *The Journal of Economic Education*, 31 (1): 30–44.

Mazur, E. (2009), 'Farewell, Lecture?', *Science*, 323: 50–51.

Millard, E. (2012), '5 Reasons Why Flipped Classrooms Work'. Available online: https://www.universitybusiness.com/article/5-reasons-flipped-classrooms-work (accessed 20 September 2018).

Talbert, R. (2014), 'Flipped Learning Scepticism: Do Students Want to Have Lectures?', *The Chronicle of Higher Education*, May 5, 2014. Available online: http://www.chronicle.com/blognetwork/castingoutnines/2014/04/28/flipped-learning-skepticism-is-flipped-learning-just-self-teaching/ (accessed 11 June 2018).

Taylor, A. (2015), 'Flipping Great or Flipping Useless? A Review of the Flipped Classroom Experiment at Coventry University London Campus', *Journal of Pedagogic Development*, 5 (3): 57–65.

Topping, K. and Ehly, S. (1998), *Peer-Assisted Learning*, Mahwah, NJ: Lawrence Erlbaum Associates.

CHAPTER 2

AUREAM QUISQUIS MEDIOCRITATEM DILIGIT: THE JOYFUL LEARNING COMMUNITY MODEL FOR LEARNING LATIN ONLINE

Justin M. Schwamm, Jr

Introduction

All too often, the phrase 'online language learning' connotes unfortunate extremes: a 'chalk and talk', textbook-focused physical classroom reproduced online; a dreary set of drill-and-practice exercises with automated feedback at best; or perhaps an uncomfortable combination of the two. But language emerges from culture and community; it is difficult, if not impossible, to learn a language (and the culture and history embodied by that language) in technologically imposed isolation. In this chapter, we explore the theoretical foundations of the joyful learning community model of language learning used by the Tres Columnae Project, which aims to be the *aurea mediocritas* (or perhaps the *via media*) between the unfortunate extremes. We move from theory to practice with extensive examples of how this approach has been used in both blended and purely online settings, with learners of widely different ages, socio-economic backgrounds and learning profiles. We conclude with observations and suggestions for teachers who would like to employ the joyful learning community approach in their own teaching contexts.

First impressions: learning and teaching

What does it mean to learn online or to teach online? And what, in particular, might it mean to learn Latin online – or, for that matter, any other language? As a reader of this chapter (and of this volume), you almost certainly have your own images and experiences of online teaching and online learning, and those images may not be entirely favourable. 'You mean online *cheating*, don't you?' more than one colleague has asked me. 'All those translations of every possible textbook, all out there on the internet, just waiting to be copied and pasted. Don't even get me started on the websites that will conjugate verbs and decline nouns for you!'

Where some see danger and woe, others see profound opportunity. My work over the past decade or so, building what I've come to call 'joyful learning communities' in many different learning environments and with many 'unconventional' learners of Latin, has made it clear that such an approach is not only possible, but profoundly *more effective* than the typical textbook-based approach or the default 'throw out the textbook and make up everything from scratch' response. A learning community that creates its own learning materials – and shares them with other communities, who in turn make their own contributions – can and should be the golden mean that unites, and simultaneously transcends, seemingly irreconcilable adversaries. This chapter will show how community, story and questions can function together as powerful tools, producing and sustaining a coherent story-world or 'mythocosm' in which seemingly irreconcilable approaches and theories find a happy, productive synthesis.

Online learning and teaching?

As this chapter was being written in the early summer of 2018, a quick Google search revealed some six billion results for 'online learning' and nearly three billion more for 'online teaching'. As one might expect, most of the early search results for 'online teaching' lead to job listings (or job search advice) for those who wish to become 'online teachers' of various subjects. The results for 'online learning', while slightly more varied, include paid advertisements for a variety of 'online course' providers, as well as a Wikipedia 'disambiguation page' that leads to articles about: e-learning in education; e-learning theory; online learning in higher education; massive open online courses (MOOCs); and online machine learning in computer science and statistics.[1] The 'e-learning in education' article,[2] in turn, contains discussion of theories of 'behaviorism, cognitivism and constructivism' and practices ranging from 'synchronous and asynchronous' to 'linear learning', 'collaborative learning' and, of course, the 'flipped classroom'. After an extensive list of media (incorporating everything from the obvious 'computers, tablets and mobile devices' through 'whiteboards' to 'learning objects'), the article goes on to address topics including settings, advantages and disadvantages, teacher training, analytics and careers. Most of these topics are treated thoroughly and at length in other chapters in this volume.

Both in theory and in practice, online language teaching and online language learning follow the contours of the broader online teaching and online learning fields that one might infer from the headings of the Wikipedia article. One can find online courses, both live and pre-recorded, that use a variety of textbooks and teaching methodologies, as well as online tutoring in both individual and small group settings. One can also find online study groups, both free and paid for, in which Latin learners and teachers help each other through challenges or, in some cases, work together to complete a given textbook or perhaps to read, translate or discuss a particular work of Roman literature. Again, other chapters in this volume address these models of online learning, both in general and in specific application, in detail.

A personal (and yet universal) story

In reflecting on my own career as both teacher and learner, I realized that I had experienced all of these formats from both the teacher and the learner sides of the (metaphorical and virtual) desk – and that my perceptions of the advantages and disadvantages of each, both from my own perspective and from those of students, had deeply shaped the joyful learning community model or Three Column Way of learning Latin (and other languages) that I developed in partnership with them. My first experiences with online learning came in the days when 'online' meant 'by email'. In 1998 or so, despite some misgivings and concerns, I first went online and joined the then-new, now-lamented Latinteach email list in its daily digest format. How exciting it was to receive an email each day (!) with a few – or a few dozen – postings from Latin teachers all over the world, and to participate in what was variously described as a never-ending conference or an online teachers' lounge! By the mid-2000s, other email lists for Latin teachers had arrived: textbook-specific ones, for example, and those focused on a particular methodology or teaching approach. By 2004, when I was a candidate for certification by the National Board for Professional Teaching Standards, I was able to be part of a virtual study group, exchanging emails (with attachments!) with a fellow Latin teacher in Florida who was also working through the process. Along the way, I found myself joining more and more asynchronous, never-ending virtual conferences by Twitter chat and, eventually, Facebook groups.

By 2011, I had also become both a teacher and a learner in more formal online courses. I took, and eventually taught, asynchronous online professional development courses offered by the large American school district where I had worked from 1992 to 2014, in which participants worked through a series of modules housed in the Moodle learning management system. As a participant, one would read or watch the 'module content' and then make an open-ended response – perhaps on a discussion thread, perhaps with an online submission form, perhaps with an uploaded document – to which the instructor would respond with some narrative feedback and a score of either 'Satisfactory' or 'Needs Improvement'. As an instructor, I read the responses, wrote the feedback and chose between 'Satisfactory' (almost always) and 'Needs Improvement' (in the rare cases when participants had totally misunderstood the question or, more often, uploaded the wrong file). Then came the era of the MOOC, in which I was an early and enthusiastic participant, watching recorded lectures (and responding to the occasional multiple-choice question or 'peer-graded' longer response) on topics ranging from Roman archaeology to 'design thinking' to a framework for becoming a more effective 'leader of learning'.

What, I wondered, were the common threads that made effective and enjoyable learning experiences, both in physical and online settings? Active involvement was certainly key, as was the presence (whether intended or accidental) of a genuine community of learners rather than a group 'going through the motions'. In an especially effective and enjoyable learning community, participants felt free and comfortable to share stories and questions with each other. Ineffective, unpleasant learning experiences, whether in the physical world or online, tended to lack one or more of these essential features, and truly tedious or horrible experiences lacked all three.

And that realization brings us to a story about questions and community. On a dreary, rainy April Friday, my Latin students were struggling to read a passage in their textbook and answer some questions about it, after which I had planned a discussion of some important ideas in the passage and, perhaps, a quick review of the 'almost new' grammatical element of future and future perfect tense verbs. But the level of pain and frustration in the room was palpable. 'What's wrong?' I finally asked, and the answers came in a rush: 'We just hate this textbook. Actually, we hate all textbooks, and here's why.'

Their list of 'why we hate textbooks' fell into the very same categories that I had been grappling with: problems with story, questions and community. 'At least there are some stories', they said, 'but the characters are flat and superficial, the situations are contrived and there's no continuity. You don't really care what will happen to the characters, and they really don't seem very Roman. At least there are some grammatical explanations, but they're obviously superficial as well. At least there are readings about Roman culture and history, but they're obviously contrived and artificial, too.'

'And yet you all signed up to take more Latin classes next year!' I noted. 'Yes,' they replied. 'We like you, and we like the class. We just hate the textbook. We like going deeper, and we like it when we make up our own stories or improve on the ones in the book.' And then a girl (whom I've referred to as B in blog posts) asked the most powerful question of all: 'Why couldn't we just do that?'

Suggestions followed quickly. Obviously we wouldn't use the flat and superficial (and copyright-protected) characters or the contrived situations and settings of the textbook. We could incorporate characters from all different strata of Roman society, at various time periods in Roman history, in all different parts of the Roman world. We could endeavour to make 'truly Roman' characters who were motivated by Roman values and did 'Roman things in Roman ways'. There could be strong, rounded, complex characters – including 'women who don't just sit there', as B suggested – who were rich or poor, free or enslaved, citizens and non-citizens alike. There could be (should be!) a central plot or set of plots, but there also could be (should be!) subplots or 'eddies in the river', and there could be (should be! *must* be!) 'gaps' and 'branches' left undeveloped at first. There could be (must be, obviously, they said) a logical progression of vocabulary development, beginning with more common and immediately useful words and gradually expanding to others. 'Don't introduce multiple verb tenses at once like that one textbook', we decided. Pay attention to what, if anything, is known about the 'natural order' of the acquisition of grammatical features in inflected languages – which turned out to be a much more complex issue than we had initially realized.[3] Have lots and lots of stories from which to choose, and don't necessarily expect the kind of class where everyone reads (or laboriously translates) everything together, word by painful word. The writing and creation of the stories need not be one person's job (although 'obviously you'll have to do the first ones', they admitted), and the goal should be a phrase I had used that had resonated deeply with this group: to 'try to see things with Roman eyes and hear with Roman ears and understand with Roman hearts', but also to realize that we are always using lenses and cannot ever fully inhabit the native-speaker mind of a language whose native speakers have died.

I went home that Friday with a truly delightful homework assignment – and the notion that 'this won't be that hard; we should have something ready by fall; and we should have the basics done within six months to a year'.

Aurea mediocritas, via media and mythocosm

That rainy Friday afternoon was in April of 2008. Ten years later, the 'mythocosm' or story-world we envisioned is very much alive and growing, and additional mythocosmic story-worlds in other languages are under development. Although one could argue that even the basics are far from done, the power of story, questions and community has proven itself in both live and recorded courses, synchronous and asynchronous study groups, and even synchronous and asynchronous private lesson settings. To quote again from the Wikipedia article referenced above, we have borrowed elements from the behaviourists, the cognitivists and the constructivists, along with their colleagues the design thinkers and developmental theorists and social learning theorists; we've combined linear learning and collaborative learning and even a dose of the flipped classroom, with a wide variety of media and settings included. Advantages (and a few disadvantages) have become apparent, along with some principles for teacher training and analytics and even careers, which we will explore below. We have certainly discovered that, properly understood and implemented, a mythocosmic approach can be the *aurea mediocritas* or *via media* that takes the best features of seemingly contradictory methods and recombines them into something qualitatively different from those apparently conflicting roots.

Building a mythocosm

Within a few weeks of that rainy Friday afternoon, my students and I had a rudimentary outline for the main river of our plot and had developed the first set of important characters. There would be three core families, we decided: the very wealthy (and sometime senatorial) Caelii, the equestrian Valerii and the poor (but mysterious) Lollii. We would situate our first stories immediately after the Year of Four Emperors, as Vespasian is consolidating his power in the early 70s CE. Initial stories would take place in Campania, in and around Herculaneum; the Caelii would actually live in a *villa rustica* on the slopes of Vesuvius itself. Each family would have an eight-year-old son who would be a young adult by the time of the eruption of Vesuvius in 79, and each would have at least one intelligent, determined daughter with a significant role in the plot. There would be animal characters as well as humans – and before we knew it, Rīdiculus mūs had made his first appearance, declaring that, unlike uncivilized animals, he and his family dwelt *in cēnāculō, nōn in cavō!* Ridiculus would have a bitter enemy in Sabina the weasel, and unlikely allies in Ferox and Medusa, the Valerius family dogs. Meanwhile, on the Caelius family farm, young Cnaeus would have strangely symbolic dreams about Fortunata the cow, her husband Maximus the bull and their daughter Io. There would be wolves, sheep, goats, chickens, snakes and a full complement of Aesopic animals, all (more or less) true to their characterization in the fable tradition. We would publish online, using a simple platform (we eventually settled on Wordpress), because simple online platforms make it easy to add, revise and even eliminate stories and storylines when necessary. We would incorporate images and audio as much as possible, building on the affordances of an online platform that cannot be found in a conventional codex or scroll. We would sneak in references to important cultural practices and ideas, leaving trails for others to follow as the interest struck them. We began to realize this was a larger job than we had initially anticipated, and were very glad when other teachers (and their students) discovered the project and began to contribute.

As the mythocosm expanded, we discovered the need for other dreams and other dreamers. There would be all sorts of quests, mistaken identities and mysterious letters hidden in the most unlikely places. Weasels, mice and hedgehogs would become powerful symbols, and characters would be involved in all manner of political intrigue. The backstories of the three primary mythocosmic families (and the backstories of other characters and families associated with them) would take us deep into early Roman history, and in spring of 2018 a group would begin working on an 'alternative ancient future' in which descendants of the Valerii and Caelii contend to become emperor. In the process of building the stories, members of the joyful learning community would take deep dives into areas of Roman culture and history that they found fascinating – in some cases, areas that they never expected to explore. As early as 2012, when I was still using the characters and stories in a blended learning approach in a fairly traditional physical classroom, two girls (whom I will call F and G) happened to notice the hairstyle of one character – a hairstyle we had adapted from depictions of Vespasian's wife, Flavia Domitilla. 'How', they asked, 'could Roman women style their hair that way, given the technologies and resources available to them?' I referred them to Janet Stephens's work[4] and, having made a profound and passionate personal connection (and, in F's case, a connection to a career in which she was strongly interested), both F and G went from potential failure to solid success in a matter of weeks.

An ever-expanding (and never-ending) story-world can be a powerful motivator for students. But can it really deliver on the promise I made above, the promise of creating a synthesis among seemingly opposed educational theories and practices? Based on my students' experiences – and my own observations, along with theirs, over the past decade or so – I would argue that the answer is yes, whether the seeming opposition is as profound as theories of learning or as down to earth as daily classroom practices.

Disparate learning theories?

To oversimplify matters significantly, behaviourists hold that, whatever happens 'on the inside' when anyone learns anything, those interior processes are a 'black box' that cannot be opened or directly observed. What matters to a behaviourist, therefore, is that which can be observed: the external behaviours that are evidence of learning, and the various forms of stimuli which can be observed to enhance or induce such behaviours. By contrast, cognitivists hold that the 'black box' can and should be opened and examined, and that the internal processes of learning can and should be observed and explained. Constructivists maintain that those internal processes largely depend on the learner's own discoveries and *construction* of knowledge from experience, while design thinkers focus on specific processes for the design and construction of learning experiences, and developmental theorists, including proponents of andragogy, focus on optimal forms of learning for different ages or stages of learning. Significant among developmental theorists, especially for Latin instruction in the United States, are proponents of what is known as the 'Classical model' or 'Trivium model', who contend that grammar, logic and rhetoric or dialectic are not only branches of the liberal arts, but developmental stages through which all learners must progress in sequence.

Are these approaches in conflict, or are they metaphorically represented by the old tale of the blind men inspecting the elephant, each describing it as 'like a tree' or 'like a rope' or 'like a fan' or 'like a spear', depending on which part of the elephant he had encountered? Given the mythocosmic foundation of story, questions and community, the reader is likely to anticipate my answer of 'yes' or 'it depends' to a seemingly binary choice.

In any case, from the behaviourists we have taken an emphasis on that which can be observed and experienced, both by the language learner and, secondarily, by the teacher. 'How comfortably,' we might ask, 'does this language learner appear to read and understand an unfamiliar text? How comfortably and confidently does she participate in writing or story-creation activities? What sorts of questions does he ask about cultural or historical topics? How confidently does she use a given set of vocabulary or grammatical patterns? What sorts of observations about such patterns does he make?' But in a mythocosmic approach to language learning, the primary 'customer' for observable, experiential evidence is the individual learner; the teacher's role is to observe, to guide and to confirm, not to play the role of distant evaluator or judge. Borrowing from the cognitivists, a mythocosmic language teacher invites the learner to inspect and examine not only the 'what and how' of the target language and culture, but also the 'what and how' of the learning process itself. Again, the primary 'customer' for this inspection and examination is the individual learner, not the teacher – an emphasis partly borrowed from the constructivists. From them, as well, comes the emphasis on learning by doing – for example, developing one's understanding of cultural practices and perspectives by attempting to build, and then presenting to others, an increasingly 'authentic' character, interaction among characters, or a fully fledged story or sequence of stories. In the iterative cycle of developing and refining such characters, we have learned much from the design thinkers, and in using the process with learners from age seven to adult learners, we have learned much from the developmental theorists.

For example, in the fall of 2014, after twenty-two years of mostly physical world and blended teaching experiences, I found myself using a mythocosmic approach to teach live online classes from my home, then in North Carolina, to high school students in two different cities in New Jersey and to a small group of nine- to twelve-year-old homeschoolers. I quickly discovered that the younger learners were much more willing, even eager, to engage with the process of story, questions and community than their older peers, and that the two groups in New Jersey – though barely twenty miles from each other geographically – were from different worlds as well when it came to their willingness to embrace these *tres columnae* of mythocosmic language learning. The students in District Q, as I referred to them in blog posts at the time, had from their prior teacher, whom I had known personally, a strong sense of community and story: their transition to the approach was relatively painless. The beginning group in District Y, with a strong sense of community and no experience of other approaches to language learning, mostly embraced mythocosmic learning with gusto. Their counterparts in intermediate and advanced classes, having never experienced story or questions in their prior Latin classes, struggled to adapt at first, but were upheld and sustained by their strong sense of community. The administration of District Y was able to find a physical world teacher in 2015. In communication with her, I was glad to discover that, while she created her own materials and stories with and for her students, she continued to build on that foundation of story, questions and community. By contrast, the administration of District Q desired what one might call 'death with dignity' for a Latin programme that they saw as unsustainable. The mythocosmic approach allowed for that, while also providing a meaningful and enjoyable experience for the students who finished up their Latin learning experiences during the two academic years that we provided classes to District Q, before the 'dignified death' of that Latin programme.

The success of a mythocosmic approach in a conventional school such as those in District Y and District Q depends, to a large extent, on the learning and teaching culture of the school and community and, to an even larger extent, on the teacher's ability to 'sell people what they want while giving them what they need', as the old saying goes. Story, questions and community can – and generally will – create a challenging but supportive environment for language acquisition, but are unlikely to create a perfectly orderly classroom environment with perfectly orderly rows of desks and so-called perfect numerical data to represent students' mastery of discrete points of vocabulary or grammar. To the extent that the teaching and learning culture of a given school is focused on standardized process, that school is likely to be a poor fit for a mythocosmic approach.

Disparate learning approaches?

As we have seen above, a mythocosmic approach synthesizes the seemingly disparate insights of behaviourists, cognitivists, constructivists, design thinkers and developmental theorists. It also pulls together important features of other apparently opposite approaches of linear learning (perhaps best defined as 'what textbooks do', with a specified set of steps leading to a desired outcome) with non-linear or serendipitous learning, along with the various forms of collaborative learning that occur when a learning community establishes its own goals, and when individual learners establish goals for themselves. In a formal setting, whether a class or a programme or a study group or even a set of private lessons, some specific set of desired outcomes is always present, whether expressed or unexpressed. Through the power of story, questions and community, a mythocosmic learning experience can bring those unexpressed but desired outcomes to consciousness and reveal a path (or a series of possible pathways) from present reality to desired goal. For example, when I meet a new potential participant (or group of participants) for the first time, I normally begin by asking everyone to share his or her short version of their language learning story, because stories build community, and because they enable a group of strangers to get to know, like and trust each other quickly, and because stories tend to reveal purposes and desired results that a person may not be able to verbalize in other ways.

After sharing our stories, I tend to ask a version of question known as the Dan Sullivan Question, drawn from a book with the same title:[5] 'Imagine that it is a year from today and we are having this conversation again. As you think about that year, what would need to happen for you to be *absolutely delighted* with your progress as a learner of Latin?' Often there's a very specific goal, such as 'I'd like to be able to read this author or text' or 'I'd like to be able to look at an English word and break it apart and see why it means what it means' or 'I want to know everything I can about this given period of Roman history, or this aspect of Roman culture.' At other times, students state their desired outcomes more broadly: 'I want to be much better at Latin and enjoy it deeply' or 'I want to be a better Latin reader.' No matter how broadly or how narrowly stated the goals are, the learner, parent and teacher can observe progress (or, in a few cases, lack of progress) and respond appropriately. From the individual goals (and from any mandates imposed by the school, school district or state in which the learning community forms), and from an assessment of current reality ('Where are we now in terms of these goals?'), learners and teacher can usually reach an agreement on how to bridge the gap from current reality to desired results. With that agreement in place, it is rarely difficult to make connections between overarching goals, desired results and specific learning activities. Cries of 'But why are we doing this?' may not be entirely absent, but they are significantly less frequent than in a learning environment where 'Because I said so' or 'Because the powers that be are making us do it' are the default responses.

To borrow or to build?

Readers of this chapter may now be wondering about the application of mythocosmic learning. Is it better to *borrow* an existing mythocosmic framework, or to *build* one's own from scratch with students and – as we quickly began to do – with other teachers and their students? My short response would be 'It depends'. Many teachers, especially in schools with overwhelmingly large class sizes, may wish to *borrow and adapt* or to *join in on* building that which has already begun – and if that is your reality, I invite you to contact me at the address below to discuss the many possibilities for collaboration. Others, due to the needs of their students or their own areas of greatest interest, may wish to *build* a mythocosm of their own. For example, you might want or need a late antique setting, or one that takes place primarily during the Punic Wars or the chaos of the first century B C. Someone might build an Attic Greek or Hellenistic mythocosm, or perhaps even a Sanskrit one. Someone else might yearn for a mythocosmic setting for Medieval Latin or Patristic Greek.

It depends – but the underlying principles of mythocosmic language teaching and learning are becoming clear. Start with a place or time that you (teacher and learners) find fascinating and intriguing. Make some characters, and make them representative of many different voices of the place and time. Be sensitive to issues of cultural representation, misrepresentation and appropriation. Be willing, even eager, to revise and expand, even to eliminate stories or characters that become problematic or unpleasant. Seek *gaps* and *eddies* as well as a *broad stream* (or many broad streams) of interconnected stories. Be sensitive to students' interests, and help them discover how to create a meaningful, engaging story that uses *words we know* and *forms we know*. Always be mindful of the power of story, questions and community – and remember that without community, there is no venue for either stories or questions. When faced with seemingly irreconcilable goals or ideas, seek that higher-level *aurea mediocritas* or *via media*. And never be afraid to learn online or teach online in new, unexpected ways.

Notes

1. See https://en.wikipedia.org/wiki/Online_learning.
2. See https://en.wikipedia.org/wiki/Educational_technology.
3. The 'natural order' of acquisition is the notion, developed by Steven Krashen and other researchers in the field of second language acquisition, 'that children learning their first language acquire grammatical structures in a pre-determined, "natural" order, and that some are acquired earlier than others'. See, for example, https://www.teachingenglish.org.uk/article/natural-order. Unfortunately, very little is known about the natural order of acquisition even in commonly spoken languages; for a language such as Latin, without a living community of native speakers, it may not be possible to reconstruct the true natural order.
4. Janet Stephens's historical hairdressing tutorials based on archaeological research and primary sources. See www.youtube.com/channel/UCboS0faGVeMi3n5_2LsVazw.
5. Sullivan, D. (2009), *The Dan Sullivan Question.* City unknown: The Strategic Coach, Inc.

CHAPTER 3
DISTANCE LEARNING AND TECHNOLOGY: TEACHING LATIN, GREEK AND CLASSICAL CIVILIZATION AT A DISTANCE FROM THE UK
Verity Walden

Introduction

In this chapter, the author's experiences of teaching distance learning courses for Latin and Classical Greek and non-linguistic courses in Classical Civilization are discussed. These include both asynchronous courses, which are primarily based online using a message board and email, and synchronous teaching by means of video conferencing. I will discuss the advantages and disadvantages for both provider and learners of both types of distance learning course, including the technologies and pedagogies involved, with a focus on the importance of the visual element of the presentation of Latin sentences. I want to show that, despite the distance, it is possible to build empathy and strong relationships with learners, and show how important these are for motivation.

Reasons for distance learning

The shortage of specialist Classics teachers has been relentlessly catalogued (see Hunt 2018, 2016, 2012, 2011, Lister 2007 and Partington 2011) and can have the effect of forcing schools and individuals to use distance learning courses and video conferencing. In 1999, Lister, then director of the Cambridge School Classics Project (CSCP), set up a division within the Cambridge to develop distance learning courses. It was well placed to do so as it already had a mature, developed Latin course (CLC) with which to work, and the technology and specialist staff to operate it. Since then attendance on the programme's Latin and Classical Civilization courses has grown to around 200 students each year. CSCP is a not-for-profit organization and students pay for the courses to cover the operating costs.

There are courses for beginners in Latin starting with CLC Book 1,[1] intermediate students with Books 2 and 3, and more advanced students in preparation for GCSE with Books 4 and 5. There are also courses based on the specifications for A-level Latin, and there have been courses for A-level Classical Civilization. Many people also do the courses simply for pleasure and personal fulfilment. On the programme we also offer courses which are based on reading original literature and are not for a particular qualification. Distance learning courses usually comprise resources which include information, translations (where appropriate), details of activities and tasks for learners to carry out, as well as assignments to send to a tutor for marking. The asynchronous distance learning courses incorporate a message board for distributing materials and the facility for email correspondence. These types of course are convenient and relatively cheap. The disadvantages are that the students can be isolated from each other, miss out on the collegiality of a group, and lack the speed of feedback and personalized teaching and learning which face-to-face learning in a classroom with a teacher present promotes. The materials also have to be prepared by the provider in advance in a one-size-fits-all fashion, even though the learners range greatly in age, from about eight to eighty (!), and also vary in background, maturity, ability, location, attitude, learning style and motivation. Nevertheless, the success rate in public examinations is high for students on these kinds of CSCP distance learning courses in Latin and Classical Civilization. Unfortunately, we cannot be sure of accurate figures on this as we are reliant on the students to tell us the results (examination boards issue results only to the institutions who enter them and to the individuals; CSCP provides the courses, but the students enter for examinations independently). Many do tell us of their success, but others do not; whether this is because they did not get the grade they wanted or because they simply forgot or were too busy, we do not know. Thus, the number of successful results that we know about may be much lower than the actual amount. This is one of the frustrations for the providers of distance learning. Nevertheless, I can report that in one typical year the results recorded, out of 24 students, 21 students gaining top grades (A* or A). One factor which contributes to the success of the students is that the marking of their work is individual and highly detailed, so that any misunderstandings can be caught and dealt with. Usually these are issues concerning grammar and syntax, but sometimes there can be misunderstandings about the subject matter itself. For example, when the set text for A-level examination was an excerpt from Catullus 63 about the castration of Attis and the recommended textbook was coy, some of the younger students were totally perplexed and asked for an explanation as to exactly what Attis had done. This seemed beyond my brief as a teacher of Latin and caused me some anxiety. It seemed best to give a straight definition.

Who, then, signs up to study an ancient language or culture, intending to spend several hours a week on a course which lasts one or even two years, but where they may never meet their teacher either visually or in person? For some students the experience of learning on a distance learning course now is not very different from that of the people who received postcards on Sir Isaac Pitman's shorthand correspondence courses in 1840 and sent them off for marking. The students need to know that the quality of the product and of the teaching can be assured. CSCP provides this. But what motivates them in the first place? We ask our students this question on the enrolment form, so I will let some of them tell you in their own words why they chose to do the courses. Here are some of the most common reasons:

- interest in Latin;
- passion for Latin;
- to continue to the next step in learning;
- interest in Roman history and I would like to read Latin literature in Latin;
- I need another A-level for my university application;
- my school does not have a Latin teacher;
- regretted never studying Latin at school;
- now I'm retired I have more time;
- to keep my brain active;
- personal enjoyment;
- to become a teacher of Classics.

Some students just sign up and send their work without further comment. Others send an introductory email:

> I am just writing to introduce myself as I've just joined the AS classics course. I was based in the USA, and I've just moved to Belgium today. I am 15 years old and go to a tennis academy, and I took all my GCSEs last year, including Class[ical] Civ[ilization] so I'm looking forward to the course.

In reply to such introductory emails, it's good to refer to something mentioned in order to establish a firm student–tutor relationship. I see it as analogous to responding to the body language and tone of voice in a face-to-face counselling session.

Here are three more of these initial emails. They seem to exemplify a yearning to return to childhood, to pick up their schooling and take up learning again for its own sake.

> I'm honoured to have you as my tutor and I look forward to working with you. A few details about myself – I am 66 years of age, a retired HR Manager and I live in Dublin, Rep. of Ireland. I did Latin in Secondary School in the sixties but had the misfortune do it through Irish! In 1st Year I missed a lot of time through illness and never really got a proper handle on the grammer [sic.] although I managed to scrape a pass in the Irish Leaving Certificate. I did Books 1–3 in the last year and I hope to progress further.

> Last year – aged 27 – I made the decision to take up studying in my spare time. This was firstly to satisfy a love of learning, but also as part of a longer term plan to apply for an undergraduate course in Law at university. I made the decision not to go to university directly from school because there were many other things I wanted to do first & knew that I wasn't ready to give my full attention to studying. Having travelled extensively & had various enjoyable jobs, I began to long for the opportunity to learn again and take the time to do something in-depth and sustained, rather than fleetingly dipping in and out of genial jobs. I concluded that I was ready for university.

> I don't know if it's important but I thought I'd tell you a little about myself. I passed Latin O level[2] in 1965 and left the subject alone for about forty years and then I came across the Cambridge Latin Course books which I really enjoyed working through. I worked through all five books and then stopped, not really knowing what else to do. I've now retired from teaching English to 11–18 year olds and I'd like to take my Latin study further.

Sometimes small details about the students' lives are revealed during the course through the assignments. For example, one student apologized for his tardiness in submitting his assignment with the news that he had been accompanying his daughter to Guatemala to adopt a baby. Students have sent pictures of their new babies, their dogs and even the model of a tram which they have made.

When self-motivation becomes weak, a strong relationship between tutor and student can help the student to persevere. Picking up on what the students reveal about themselves makes it possible to create this even by email. It makes it easier for students to send work and receive criticism. It is difficult to submit work to someone you have not met, seen or heard, and a clue that reveals the tutor as human and compassionate makes it easier. There is the physical isolation of distance learners and the absence of classmates and the social experience that normal classroom-based learning offers. The lack of these things can be alleviated by communication between learners via a message board or forum which all those on a course can use. There can be safeguarding issues with this, especially if some students are adults and some are children. Also, many students are simply unwilling to take part in class discussions via a forum, even if a specific task suitable for collaboration is set.

Although some students receive information about tasks from an online message board, they will still print out the session material and complete the tasks on paper. I think this is because it can simply be more convenient, and not just because they are practicing handwriting for timing in examinations, where it is still necessary. Sometimes students even work in an exercise book with a pencil – old technology that still works! Some students will combine the old with the new: they will photograph the paper or the page of the exercise book on a mobile phone or scan it to send by email. Of course, they do not have to do it in that way; they can just do it all digitally.

Students on the CSCP email courses do achieve personal fulfilment and high grades in public examinations. This is a pleasing message from a student:

> I understand that CSCP likes students to send in their results, so I wanted to let you know that I got an A in A2 Latin and will be taking up a place at Oxford University to study a BA Classics in October. Thank you for your help.

Distance learning by video conference can – or at least, should – counter the disadvantages to which I have referred about distance learning via email. Through video conferencing the teacher and student(s) can communicate face to face in the virtual classroom, except that they see and hear each other via a screen and speakers. Because both parties can see and hear each other in real time, teaching and learning can be done in almost the same way as in a real classroom. Text and pictures can be shown to the students instantly on screen or whiteboard. Feedback is instantaneous. The teacher and pupils can see and hear each other in real time just as if they are in the same room, so lecturing is possible and so is dialogic teaching and learning (see Hunt's chapter in this volume). Sometimes there can be a slight delay in a response being received – similar to that which used to be experienced on a long-distance telephone call. There can be a problem of people talking over each other in order to fill the gaps, and so teacher and students must learn good habits of turn-taking.

CSCP began teaching by video conference in 1999 and is still providing personalized courses to schools in Latin and other classical subjects up to A-level. Sometimes the video conference lessons are held in usual school hours, but more often they are early morning sessions before school starts, or afternoon sessions when school has finished for the day. Early morning sessions are in some ways better as the students are fresh and there is less absenteeism: sporting fixtures occupy a lot of afternoons! The inflexibility of the school bus timetable can sometimes cause difficulties and often the goodwill of parents is necessary to provide transport the children at odd hours. Lessons for sixth form students are easier to arrange as they often have more flexible lesson timetables.

For Latin and Greek, CSCP suggests that two years is the minimum time to get beginners to GCSE. Three years is more comfortable, but it depends on the number of hours for lessons and the age of the students. What usually happens is that a non-specialist in a school begins teaching

Latin as a club off timetable and takes the students as far as they can. At some point the teacher decides they cannot manage any more: the class has passed their level of knowledge, or they lack confidence in more advanced work, or they run out of available time in busy schedules. This last occurs very often when a second group has started and the first group wants to continue. In these cases they call CSCP for video conference lessons. Sometimes schools have been let down by someone they have employed, usually not a trained teacher, who leaves around March to get another position elsewhere, and they turn to video conferencing because no other local teacher can be found at that time of the year.

Video conferencing is a good medium for teaching the Cambridge Latin Course, as it suits the philosophy and pedagogical methods of the course. Text or pictures can be shown on the students' screens at the press of a button and then switched back to the teacher's face. While the students see text, the teacher continues to see the students and so can still keep control. The teacher can show text prepared in advance or invented on the spot, or highlight features by colour or font and thus illustrate a language feature while talking about it.

Early research into video conferencing was concerned with comparing it with face-to-face teaching or audio. Greenberg's 2004 review of research into teaching by video conferencing suggested that it was expensive but effective, reporting, 'What does this research tell us? Unequivocally, that two-way, interactive videoconferencing technology can be an extremely effective medium for delivering quality education to a broad, geographically dispersed student population' (Greenberg 2004). Gradually, equipment for video conferencing has both improved and become cheaper, and the ability to use the internet rather than telephone ISDN[3] meant that using it became even cheaper.

It is possible to achieve good results through video conferencing with a range of students. I have had students with dyslexia, ADHD and severe visual difficulties, sometimes all in the same class. Students with visual difficulties can be assisted with the help of a device called an i-loview, which allows them to magnify text in print, on a computer screen and on the whiteboard. With the help of specialized staff within the school from the Special Educational Needs and Disabilities department, most students can be successful. All of one such class with three statemented pupils recently passed GCSE Latin.

Despite students' success in public examinations and enthusiasm for subjects such as Latin and Greek, to which they would otherwise not have access because of a shortage of specialist teachers, UK schools are still not using video conferencing to the extent that had been envisioned a decade ago. Most do not have suitable equipment, and those which do tend to use it for one-off lessons, such as those provided by museums, rather than for courses. Lawson and Comber (2014) identified several key factors critical to the sustainability of video conference teaching in UK schools. The first of these is 'policy frameworks', such as government policy and its lack of investment in technology:

> Despite the positive learning outcomes associated with the *Videoconferencing in the Classroom Project* (Comber *et al.* 2004), the Education Department shifted its priorities away from videoconferencing and towards other forms of educational technology, such as interactive whiteboards. It would seem reasonable to conclude that the almost ubiquitous integration of the latter in UK schools, and the patchy distribution of the former, is at least the partial outcome of this policy position.
>
> Lawson and Comber 2014: 73

Another key factor is the enthusiasm and knowledge of staff in schools, the 'key personnel syndrome' (Comber and Lawson 2012: 21). Whether students in schools or colleges are on email distance learning courses or video conferences, there are some things that need to be done in school: enrolling and preparing students for lessons, motivating and supporting them, liaising with tutors and reporting to others within the school. For video conferencing, they also need to arrange sessions and manage the equipment. In the schools which I have been involved with, the people who coordinated the video conferences or supervised the lessons included teachers, head teachers, deputies, modern foreign languages assistants, librarians, IT technicians, special educational needs staff and pastoral staff.

It is natural that school staff and parents will worry about students' discipline and learning by video conferencing. Before they have experienced video conferencing, parents and students sometimes ask for a 'real teacher'. I am sometimes asked how it is possible to keep the students in order when I am not there with them physically, but most of the usual techniques are still available and still work: the disapproving look, warning remark and even raising of the voice are all still effective. Also effective is the reminder that, at a click, I can instantly take a photograph or video record their misbehaviour and send it to the head teacher or appropriate person. This has only once been necessary, mostly because most of my students have been willing participants. On the occasion on which it was necessary to take action of this kind, the misbehaviour was shown by other students on their way home, who thought it would be fun to make faces through the window, open the door and shout rude things. I threatened to take a photograph of them. Meanwhile, in fact, my class was so annoyed at this and so eager to learn Latin, that they moved a grand piano across the room to block the door. In this case, despite our requests, there had been no adult in the room at the time – neither the video conference coordinator nor any other supervisor. The Year 9 class had been left to turn on the equipment and fend for themselves for the whole lesson. The lack of a responsible adult in the room shows that the coordinator of enrichment for those students had not been taking his role seriously and indicates a tick box attitude to providing distance learning. His decision to hold the Latin sessions in the music rooms at the end of the school day had not been a good one either, apart from the availability of the grand piano as a barricade. The practice rooms were still available for other students to use for playing, and the sound of drumming in particular had been rather a distraction to the Latin class.

The success of teaching by video conferencing depends primarily on the goodwill and understanding of the staff in the school. There is quite often a failure in schools to appreciate the importance of finding a suitable place to site video conference sessions and equipment. In one school in which I was teaching by video conference, the students were in a lecture room which had six large servers humming and buzzing at one end, a sound readily picked up by the immovable wall-mounted microphone. This same room had immovable tiered seating, and the screen for the students to look at was at the front of the room but the camera was on the side, so I could only see the students in profile and thus missed the expressions on their faces. In another school there was regularly a problem turning with on the camera, as the switch was on the ceiling beyond the reach of the facilitator. She usually asked me to teach the students even though I could not see them. This resulted in my looking at a completely blue screen and asking pathetically whether the students were there yet. The equipment can now enable good eye contact and a view of body language. Slovak wrote: 'Unfortunately, none of the systems created so far has reached the common goal of supplying the participants with an environment that allows natural interaction' (Slovák 2007). Now, when the equipment actually *can* do this, if it is not being used properly, teaching and learning continue to be compromised.

Good-quality sound is more important than good-quality vision – especially for language teaching. Being able to hear the teacher is essential, and so a school should invest in effective speakers; however, it is even more important for the teacher to hear the students' responses. It is easier for the students to hear the single voice of the teacher who is endeavouring to speak clearly than for the teacher to understand the voices of several students who may at times not speak clearly, or may speak to or over each other. Microphones vary in quality. The need to spend on good microphones and indeed *enough* microphones is sometimes resisted by schools because of the expense. Of course, people in the classroom do not get to experience what the teacher at the other end is hearing via the equipment; they assume that the teacher hears what they do. It is not so.

Understandably, schools usually wish to have the largest possible number of students in the room for a session. A good 'boundary' microphone in a classroom will cover about twelve people. Several might be needed for larger groups. No school at which I have taught has ever addressed this problem adequately. I have taught a group moving a microphone intended for use by a single individual from hand to hand among five people. I have taught a group of twenty-eight in a room using one microphone which was suitable for a group of twelve. The one microphone, in that case, was on one table – only the group of six at the front near the microphone could be heard. When the school had asked if I could teach more than the twelve, which was our usual stated maximum, they were told that they would need at least four microphones and they had promised that they would get more. But it did not happen. For several sessions the facilitator passed the microphone from one table to another. Even when it became obvious that this was not going to work, the school did not acquire more microphones.

It might seem unnecessary to say that it is essential for the school's equipment and the students to be in the same room. It is not helpful for the equipment to be in a room to which students do not have access. In one school, the video conference equipment was in a room which is used once a month for a governors' meeting – not because the governors were video conferencing, but because the school judged it necessary for the governors to meet in an impressive room, a room with the most up-to-date electronic gear. Every month a lesson would be cancelled. Apparently less of a consideration was the detriment to the exam success of the students who were missing a quarter of their lessons. Greenberg again:

> Like any technology, it can be abused, misused, inappropriately applied, or fall into neglect if not deployed with proper planning and training. A distance education program is only as good as the people who stand behind it, the planning and programs that go into it, and the ultimate content that results. There are plenty of cases of technology that sits idle because its acquisition was viewed as the hard part, when in fact the real work that needed to be done had nothing to do with buying, and everything to do with planning and training.
>
> Greenberg 2004

There is still resistance to and misunderstanding about distance learning and video conferencing among network managers and IT teams, either because they regard it as not being in their province or because it is out of their experience. One IT team advised a school to stay with ISDN, despite the expense, because of a fear that there would be too much strain on the broadband. This fear is still prevalent, but it has not ever happened in my experience. Sometimes people, especially network managers and technicians, assume that video conferencing means Skype. There can indeed be problems with Skype. The typical camera and microphone used for calls to family or friends on Skype will only be effective for one or two people and so can only be suitable for a very small group, such as an A-level group of three, but not for a whole class. When schools have tried ordinary Skype, they have found that it is generally not adequate or even available: some schools have banned the connection to Skype because of misuse by some of their students. The free version of Skype is not an advanced system. Schools need high-definition cameras, good microphones and connection by a dedicated bridge (portal) such as Vscene (formerly Janet, now Ajenta). Without this, often the school's firewall or a local gatekeeper will prevent connection.

With the right equipment, a secure, quality portal connection service and the willingness of all the people involved, video conferencing can be used successfully for the teaching of classical subjects. Initial setbacks can be overcome, as can be seen form the following set of emails:

IT person in a school, to a provider: Would it be possible to arrange a test call to you? We've been provided a software solution which should be able to dial your video conferencing unit, and our tests have been promising.

Provider's office: Yes. If you are still around, I will turn on the machine so that you may call through.

IT: I'm afraid I was kicked out rather early yesterday. If you wouldn't mind doing the same today so that I can test, I'd appreciate it.

Provider: Thank you. I'll turn on the machine now. If you come on, just shout as I may not hear you being down the hall.

IT: Thank you for this. I'm having some trouble getting through. Could you please confirm the number for the unit?

Provider: It's [11-digit number] or [13-digit number].

IT: Having some trouble connecting to you, and our LGFL support are having the same issue. When convenient, would it be possible for you to attempt a call to us? I have our end permanently turned on at the moment. Our number is [8-digit number] or you may need to use our full 17-digit number: [17-digit number].

Provider: I tried calling – it seemed to work somewhat when I dialled [14-digit number] or [18-digit number]. The message came up as 'call cleared', but a second later 'call disconnected'. Sorry it didn't work on our end.

IT: Thank you for trying.

The conclusion that I can draw from the research and my experiences is that distance courses in classical subjects – both asynchronous, such as by email, and synchronous, by video conferencing – can be fulfilling for students and can lead to examination success. For teacher and students to be physically in a room with one another can bring about a very valuable dynamic, but it is not essential for learning to take place. At a distance, both teachers and learners need to adopt strategies for creating relationships and motivation. Technologies can enable communication and rapport. But it would be so much easier if there was more coordination between people involved in education and those involved in the provision of equipment and services for distance learning.

Notes

1. UK Book 1 is equivalent to US Unit 1. The US Unit series does not quite match the content of the UK series: thus the UK series runs from Books 1–5, whereas the US series runs from Units 1–4.
2. Latin O-level was the UK national qualification taken by sixteen-year-olds from 1951 (when it took over from the School Certificate) until 1988 (when the GCSE took over). It was hardly ever offered to students who attended non-selective schools, and it acted as one of a number of matriculation requirements for entry to selective universities, as well as preparing the foundations for further academic study.
3. ISDN: International Services Digital Network is a set of communication standards for simultaneous digital transmission of voice, video, data and other network services over the traditional circuits of the public switched telephone network.

References

Anderson, T. (2008), 'Is Videoconferencing the Killer App for K-12 Distance Education?', *Journal of Distance Education*, 22: 109–123.

Castro, M., López-Rey, A., Pérez-Molina, C., Colmenar, A., de Mora, C., Yeves, F., Carpio, J., Peire, J. and Daniel, J. (2001), 'Examples of Distance Learning Projects in the European Community', *IEEE TRANSACTIONS ON EDUCATION*, 44 (4). Available online: www.academia.edu/29540736/Examples_of_distance_learning_projects_in_the_European_Community (accessed 7 October 2018).

Comber, C., Lawson, T., Gage, J., Cullum-Hanshaw, A., Allen, T., Hingley, P. and Boggon, J. (2004), *Evaluation for the DfES Videoconferencing in the Classroom Project*, London: DfES Research Project.

Comber, C. and Lawson, T. (2012), 'Sustaining Technological Innovation: The Example of Videoconferencing in English Schools', *Education and Information Technologies*, 18 (4): 641–659.

Greenberg, A. (2004), 'Navigating the Sea of Research on Videoconferencing-Based Distance Education: A Platform for Understanding Research into the Technology's Effectiveness and Value', *Polycom/Wainhouse Research*. Available online: https://pdfs.semanticscholar.org/e7a8/34af7c79fc67f81098a56 410b68befa8842d.pdf (accessed 7 October 2018).

Hunt, S. (2011), 'Training Classics Teachers', *Journal of Classics Teaching*, 24: 2–3.

Hunt, S. (2012), 'Classics Teacher Vacancies 2010–11: Not Meeting the Demand', *Journal of Classics Teaching*, 25: 2–6.

Hunt, S. (2016), *Starting to Teach Latin*, London: Bloomsbury.

Hunt, S. (2018), 'Getting Classics into Schools? Classics and the Social Justice Agenda of The UK Coalition Government, 2010–2015', in Holmes-Henderson, A., Hunt, S., and Musié, M., eds, *Forward with Classics!*, London: Bloomsbury, 9–26.

Lawson, T. and Comber, C. (2014), 'Videoconferencing and Learning in the Classroom: The Effects of Being an Orphan Technology?', *The International Journal of Technologies in Learning*, 20 (1): 69–79.

Lister, B. (2007), *Changing Classics in Schools*, Cambridge: Cambridge University Press.

Partington, R. (2011), 'The Threat to Latin Posed by Teacher Shortages', *Journal of Classics Teaching*, 23: 12–13.

Slovák, P. (2007), 'Effect of Videoconferencing Environments on Perception of Communication', *Cyberpsychology: Journal of Psychosocial Research on Cyberspace*, 1 (1): article 8. Available online: https://cyberpsychology.eu/article/view/4205/3246 (accessed 7 October 2018).

CHAPTER 4

MAKING IT COUNT: MEASURING STUDENT ENGAGEMENT WITH ONLINE LATIN RESOURCES AT THE OPEN UNIVERSITY

Mair E. Lloyd and James Robson

Introduction

Over 5,000 students have studied beginner's Latin at the Open University since the module *Reading Classical Latin* was launched in 2000. But while many students successfully completed this book-based grammar-translation module, a significant proportion withdrew from study or failed. October 2015 saw the launch of a new module, *Classical Latin: The Language of Ancient Rome*, incorporating entirely new pedagogy and technology. This chapter outlines some of the innovations introduced in the new module – such as its bespoke interactive websites, online vocabulary and grammar testers and interactive reading aid – grounding them in theories drawn from the field of modern foreign languages (MFL). Student retention and success rates, satisfaction statistics and comments on online learning (gathered in surveys and interviews) are used to assess the effectiveness of the use of new technology in this module. The conclusion reflects on the lessons learnt and outlines plans for future research and enhancement.

As a distance learning institution, the Open University (OU) has been at the forefront of teaching Classics with technology ever since its foundation in 1969. In the early days, the OU was the 'University of the Air' (to use Harold Wilson's memorable phrase), innovatively harnessing the power of television to broadcast lectures on the BBC. The OU's relationship with the BBC has evolved since these early days (the OU now 'co-produces' mainstream BBC documentary series), but other OU traditions have been slower to change: Classical Studies undergraduates still receive specially prepared printed books as part of their course materials, for example, just as Arts students did in the university's early days. Where learning technology is concerned, it is, of course, the advent of the internet that has altered our students' relationship with the university most dramatically. Some of the changes enabled by new technology are very familiar to those in 'brick' institutions (e.g. the posting of learning resources on the virtual learning environment (VLE), and the electronic submission of assignments), but the internet is also used at the OU to deliver a very different learning experience from that offered in conventional institutions (while our undergraduate students are usually given the option to attend some face-to-face tutorials, for example, online tutorials are far more common). The reliance on technology is particularly pronounced at master's level, with the OU's MA in Classical Studies being taught exclusively online. Thus MA students rarely, if ever, meet their tutors in person, and the study materials – a mixture of print, audio, video and interactive resources – are all accessed by students remotely. OU undergraduate modules, too, are increasingly foregrounding online learning, with OU academics overseeing the development of interactive resources for each new course they produce. And it is the rich mixture of interactive resources produced for the module *Classical Latin: The Language of Ancient Rome* – a combined language and literature module designed for beginners in Latin – that forms the subject of this chapter.

One of the purposes of what follows is to provide an overview of the online resources available to students of Latin at the OU: or in other words, a geeky 'show and tell'. These resources range from an open-access site aimed at complete beginners, Introducing Classical Latin, to tools such as a Vocabulary Tester, Principal Parts Tester, and Story Explorer, all designed to allow leaners to build, review and extend their knowledge of Latin during their studies. However, the bulk of the discussion that follows will be given over to an analysis of how students interacted with these resources in 2015, the first year that the *Classical Latin* module was taught.

OU-based researchers find themselves in a privileged position when it comes to exploring students' engagement with technology, since the sheer number and diversity of those studying Latin at the university – typically 150–200 students each year, of varying ages – make statistical analysis of learners' online behaviour a particularly meaningful proposition. In this chapter, we have focused on the collection and analysis of data for the purpose of mapping not only the changing patterns of use of the interactive resources as the student cohort progressed through the course, but also of judging differing levels of engagement with technology according to factors such as the students' age and sex. The quantitative data captured in our study raise important questions about the OU's interactive resources in particular, but importantly, too, about students' use of technology in general, such as why some resources are used more than others and how students can be encouraged to engage with technology more consistently. Qualitative data from student feedback go some of the way to answering these questions, while simultaneously providing useful insights into how the resources were regarded by learners. But throughout the chapter we also provide suggestions (as well as raise questions) as to how resources might be presented more effectively and be made more meaningful to student users.

A further, important aim of this chapter is to demonstrate the power and possibilities of using data to examine students' use of technology. Not that this chapter in any way seeks to provide an exhaustive analysis of the data we have assembled at the OU; rather, we have selected a number of variables and techniques to demonstrate what can be achieved. The purpose of showing the potential of such investigations, of course, is to help to inform and direct the development of technology for ancient language learning in the future by outlining methodology that instructors and researchers might use and build on to evaluate their own online tools.

Interactive Latin resources

The development of a new module opens up significant financial resources at the OU, and so the advent of *Classical Latin: The Language of Ancient Rome* in 2015 provided OU academics with an opportunity to design a whole new suite of interactive resources for Latin learners ahead of its launch. Central to the pedagogical design of *Classical Latin* is its dual language and culture focus, with students studying beginner's language alongside the culture and history of ancient Rome and Latin literature in translation. But when planning the online components, the team working on this course nevertheless chose to prioritize the linguistic side of the module. This is where the team thought that learners were more likely to struggle and where IT could be used to best effect.

Having reflected on our prior experience of teaching classical languages at a distance, and having analysed student retention and performance data on our previous beginner's Latin and Greek modules, the team agreed that a key priority should be to support learners' first steps in Latin, since historically it was at the beginning of the modules that many students had either got into difficulties or dropped out. One aim of the IT resources, then, would be to help students to negotiate the initial challenges of Latin learning and to build their confidence. The team also made the decision to develop tools for students to consolidate their learning throughout the module, providing informal test and review opportunities, in addition to their formal tutor-marked assignments (TMAs) and final examination. A further ambition was to use IT where it could make the most difference for the least outlay. One way to achieve this was to develop resources incorporating scalable and repeatable tasks, such as vocabulary drilling and accidence testing, since these would potentially remain useful to students for the whole length of the module.

The principal resource developed to support learners engaging with the language in the early stages of study was Introducing Classical Latin.[1] This is a freely available, open-access site where students are introduced to the pronunciation of the language, acquire a basic vocabulary and engage with some of the fundamental ways in which Latin grammar differs from that of English.

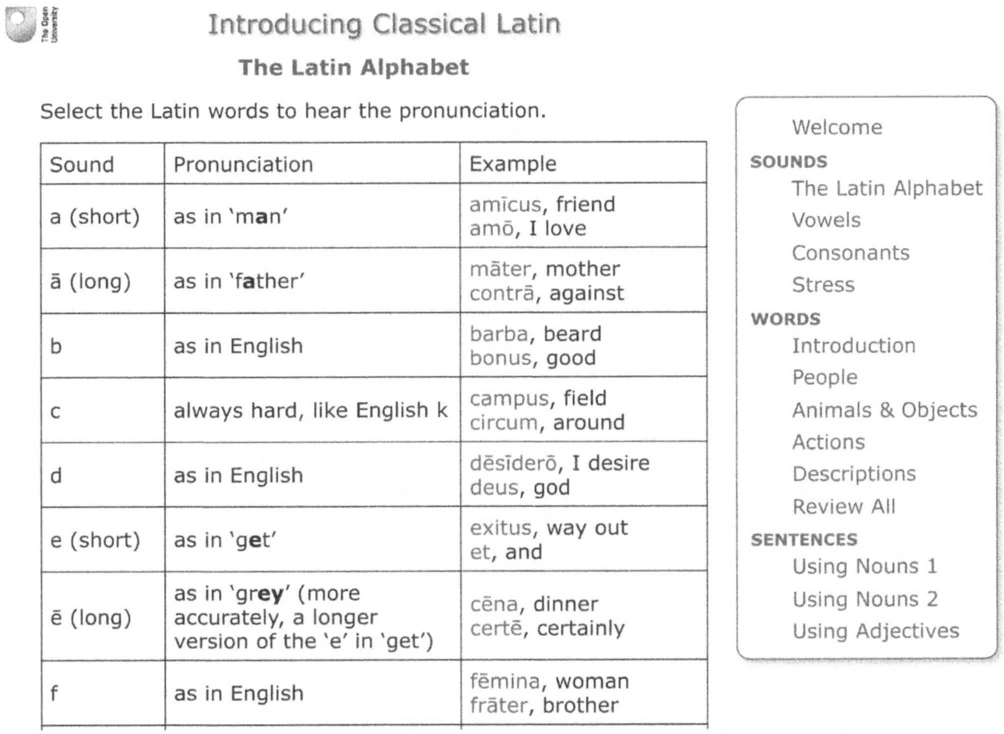

Introducing Classical Latin

The Latin Alphabet

Select the Latin words to hear the pronunciation.

Sound	Pronunciation	Example
a (short)	as in 'man'	amīcus, friend amō, I love
ā (long)	as in 'father'	māter, mother contrā, against
b	as in English	barba, beard bonus, good
c	always hard, like English k	campus, field circum, around
d	as in English	dēsīderō, I desire deus, god
e (short)	as in 'get'	exitus, way out et, and
ē (long)	as in 'grey' (more accurately, a longer version of the 'e' in 'get')	cēna, dinner certē, certainly
f	as in English	fēmina, woman frāter, brother

Welcome

SOUNDS
The Latin Alphabet
Vowels
Consonants
Stress

WORDS
Introduction
People
Animals & Objects
Actions
Descriptions
Review All

SENTENCES
Using Nouns 1
Using Nouns 2
Using Adjectives

Figure 4.1 Screenshot of Introducing Classical Latin: The Latin Alphabet. © The Open University.

Introducing Classical Latin is structured as follows. In the 'Sounds' section, students learn about the pronunciation of Latin with the aid of an alphabetic list of clickable words. In the 'Words' section, students get to master a total of twenty-four vocabulary items, broken down into four sections covering nouns ('people', 'animals'), verbs ('actions') and adjectives ('descriptions'). The 'Sentences' section draws on this vocabulary to introduce the basic concepts both of inflection (through simple sentences comprising subject-object-verb) and of the agreement of nouns and adjectives on the basis of gender. At each stage there are short, interactive exercises which allow students to practise their understanding. The 'Words' section is also enlivened by cartoon flashcards, while the 'Sentences' section includes both images and animation (in pedagogical terms, the use of images allows learners to experience concepts in a concrete form before moving on to the abstract, a technique often employed in Latin school textbooks; see Gay 2003: 83). The site's uncluttered and user-friendly design helps students to get to grips with the basics of Latin in a fun and unthreatening way, boosting motivation and self-confidence (see Krashen 1982: 29–31 for the importance of these affective factors).

A suite of online testers was also developed to support students' learning throughout the course. These include a Latin Vocabulary Tester (which users can customize to test themselves on different units of the course book) and a Latin Grammar Tester (testing noun, adjective and verb endings and similarly adaptable to cover such forms as have been met at any given stage in the course). In a similar vein, the Principal Parts Tester (recommended for use after week sixteen of the course, i.e. once the past participle/supine has been met) is essentially a set of online flash cards which students can click to flip round, thereby revealing the four principal parts of the verb in question. These resources were also conceived as useful tools to aid consolidation ahead of the final examination, where students would be required to demonstrate recall of language components drilled in the testers; that is, the testers rehearsed content aligned with the end-of-course assessment.

A further resource which students were encouraged to use throughout their studies is the Story Explorer (which is based on the same technology as the Explorer tool developed for use with the *Cambridge Latin Course*). So, while tech-shy students can choose to read the synthetic Latin stories which form the spine of the course in the traditional way in their printed books, the Story Explorer provides an interactive way to work through these texts online. Key here is the 'click and look up' feature, which provides students with instant help on vocabulary and grammar, making continuous reading less arduous and potentially more enjoyable.

Two further online resources were available to students in 2015. The first of these was the collection of audio recordings of the first ten sets of synthetic Latin stories which students read in the opening weeks of the course (readings of Latin poetry were also available to students in later weeks). In a distance learning context it is particularly important to be able to hear the sounds of Latin, of course, since students do not have regular access to a teacher reading Latin aloud and/or assisting with pronunciation. These recordings proved so popular with some learners that the module team later recorded the rest of the stories for student use in subsequent years (on the importance of hearing spoken Latin, see also Lloyd and Robson, forthcoming).

Lastly, we come to the five online quizzes. These are designed as formative assessment points, allowing students to consolidate their learning in a low-risk way by testing themselves between formal assignments. Typically, the quizzes test the grammar and vocabulary met in recent study weeks, with students asked to perform a variety of tasks over the course of ten questions. So, students might use drop-down lists to choose nouns, adjectives or verbs with appropriate endings to fit into a given sentence, for example; or match a Latin description with the name of an historical or mythical character; or they might complete a grammatical table. When users get questions wrong, they are given hints, with the right answers eventually revealed after three unsuccessful attempts. To aid consolidation and revision, quizzes can be repeated multiple times.

Methods

Having provided our students with the opportunity to use these innovative resources, we wanted to assess how valuable they had been. Previously, we had been able to use student data routinely gathered in the Learning and Teaching Innovation (LTI) unit, including student demographic and module results data, as well as the results of an end-of-module survey, to explore the effectiveness of changes introduced in this new module (Lloyd and Robson, forthcoming). In 2016, inspired by an idea originating in the OU's Centre for Research in Education and Educational Technology (CREET), we also accessed the university archive of student activity generated from the OU Moodle VLE. This archive preserves a daily record of the number of times a particular component of the VLE (for instance, an audio recording or online quiz) has been accessed in a particular way (e.g. viewed, attempted, etc.) by each individual student. This meant that we could analyse how many students had accessed each resource or activity, and also give a profile over time of patterns of usage. In addition, because each of the datasets we used (demographic and results data, end-of-module survey data and VLE activity data) uses the same student identifier within each record, we had the opportunity to pull together information across datasets to explore connections between factors such as demographics and VLE activity.

The datasets we used are summarized in Figure 4.2.

(For the technically minded, data was provided to us by LTI in MS Excel format, and we also exported VLE activity into Excel before merging all three datasets in MS Access. A master file of all data was re-exported to Excel and analysed using pivot tables.)

	Demographic and results data	Student end-of-module survey data	Student VLE activity data
Source	Provided by OU LTI unit	Provided by OU LTI unit	VLE archive accessed via Statistical Analysis System (SAS) Enterprise
2015 course	182 students	65 responses	181 students*

* One student did not use any of the resources or activities on the VLE.

Figure 4.2 Sources of quantitative data used in this chapter. © Mair Lloyd and James Robson, The Open University.

In addition, we designed our own technology-focused questionnaire (using Survey Monkey), which a small group of students completed. The data we gathered offer a wealth of opportunities to explore factors influencing student outcomes. In this chapter we have chosen to focus on usage data relating to the resources and activities identified in the previous section:

- Introducing Classical Latin;
- Latin Vocabulary Tester;
- Latin Grammar Tester;
- Principal Parts Tester;
- Story Explorer;
- Audio recordings;
- Online quizzes.

We have also used quantitative data from the demographics and results and survey databases, as well as qualitative data from the end-of-module survey and our own independent survey, to extend our understanding of student perceptions of the technology we introduced. Triangulating findings across different datasets and mixing quantitative and qualitative methods has allowed us to paint a rich picture of Latin students' use of, and their attitudes towards, the online resources available to them in 2015.

Findings

Discovery of resources/activities

We first turn to investigate how many of the 182 students taking *Classical Latin* in 2015 made any attempt to use particular resources and activities provided via the VLE.

Figure 4.3 shows the number of students who accessed each resource or activity at least once in any way at all. Under Story Explorer, for example, a student is counted as using this resource if they accessed any one of the available Story Explorer texts. Similarly, counting a student as having used the audio recordings means that they visited the audio player page and

Resource	Students using resource at least once (out of 182)	Proportion of students using resource at least once
Introducing Classical Latin	163	90%
Vocabulary Tester	163	90%
Audio Recordings	163	90%
Story Explorer	161	88%
Grammar Tester	156	86%
Online Quizzes	128	70%
Principal Parts Tester	103	57%

Figure 4.3 Frequency of use of online resources by students. © Mair Lloyd and James Robson, The Open University.

opened at least one of the ten recordings, and they are counted as having used the online quizzes if they viewed at least one of the five quizzes. Figure 4.3 therefore gives an indication both of how easy it was to find these resources and of whether students judged them important or attractive enough to explore when they saw them signposted. The statistics show that while a high proportion of students visited Introducing Classical Latin, the Vocabulary Tester, an audio recording or the Story Explorer, relatively few (57 per cent) ever visited the Principal Parts Tester.

What could explain this difference in the level of student engagement with the resources? One factor here seems to be the point in the course at which the resources are introduced. Those initially signposted to students in the first few weeks of study have far higher take-up rates than the online quizzes (the first of which comes in week 11) and the Principal Parts Tester (first flagged up formally to students in week 16). This pattern of usage may partly reflect the fall in student numbers as the course progressed (26 per cent of students who began the module failed to complete it). But it may also indicate that students get set in their study patterns early on and become less experimental as they progress through the course. Furthermore, mastering principal parts and completing non-assessed quizzes may plausibly feel like less of a core activity to students than learning vocabulary or word endings (for which the Vocabulary Tester and Grammar Tester provide constant reinforcement). Lastly, the way in which the resources were presented to students may also have been a factor. The links to the three testers were provided on the module website as shown in Figure 4.4.

The order of listing may have influenced the extent to which students explored the resources available to them, and the lack of an explanation of the importance of the Principal Parts Tester may also go some way towards explaining why so few students clicked on the link (had they landed on the Principal Parts Tester page, this would have registered as a 'view'). This discussion highlights the importance of providing both encouragement and compelling reasons to explore online resources – a situation which might be improved in a distance learning environment by providing more references to the resources in the study materials, several different ways of navigating to the same resource at different points in the course, and a better account of their utility and value. In a face-to-face context this might translate into frequent reminders and encouragement to use the technology, as well as patient explanation of the benefits that interactive resources can offer.

Using a combination of demographic and activity data, we can also explore variation across (for example) age or sex in visiting particular resources (or combinations of resources). For the Introducing Classical Latin resource we obtained the results shown in Figures 4.5 and 4.6.

Vocabulary and grammar testers

<> Latin Vocabulary Tester

<> Latin Grammar Tester

Testing yourself on your understanding of new grammar will really help your progress and confidence. This Latin Grammar Tester, designed specifically for A276, will help you to do just that. You can start using the Grammar tester from Section 3 onwards. Use it to test yourself on the endings of the nouns, adjectives and verbs you meet as learning vocabulary in this module.

<> Principal Parts Tester

© The Open University

Figure 4.4 Section of the module website. © The Open University.

Age group	Total students in each age group	Number visiting Introducing Classical Latin	Proportion visiting Introducing Classical Latin
Under 25	18	13	72%
26–35	41	34	83%
36–45	44	39	89%
46–55	33	32	97%
56 and over	46	45	98%

Figure 4.5 Students visiting Introducing Classical Latin by age. © Mair Lloyd and James Robson, The Open University.

Sex	Total students	Number visiting Introducing Classical Latin	Proportion visiting Introducing Classical Latin
Female	123	111	90%
Male	59	52	88%

Figure 4.6 Students visiting Introducing Classical Latin by sex. © Mair Lloyd and James Robson, The Open University.

These cross-tabulations of data suggest that, while there is little difference between male and female students in terms of the proportions who visited Introducing Classical Latin, our younger age group may need more guidance and encouragement to make them aware of and engage with the resources available. It is also worth saying at this point that OU policy dictated that all the interactive Latin resources could only be accessed online (and were not, say, available as apps): consequently, we have no way of assessing the extent to which the platform might influence the level of engagement displayed by different age groups. Certainly it would be interesting to know whether the availability of apps would lead to a greater engagement by students in general, and this younger demographic in particular.

While there are, of course, other relationships and resources that could be investigated in this way, we now turn to exploring how the number of students visiting a particular resource changed over time.

Students visiting resources throughout the course

Because student activity was recorded with a date for each day of the course, it was possible to plot usage against time. We used this technique (aggregating data on a weekly basis) to explore usage of a number of different resources. Figure 4.7, for example, shows the usage data pertaining to the three testers (Vocabulary Tester, Grammar Tester and Principal Parts Tester), all of which are designed for continuous use throughout the course once they have been introduced.

Weeks '–4' to '–1' comprise the time before the course officially opened but within which the VLE could be accessed by registered students. Weeks 11b and 11c were designated

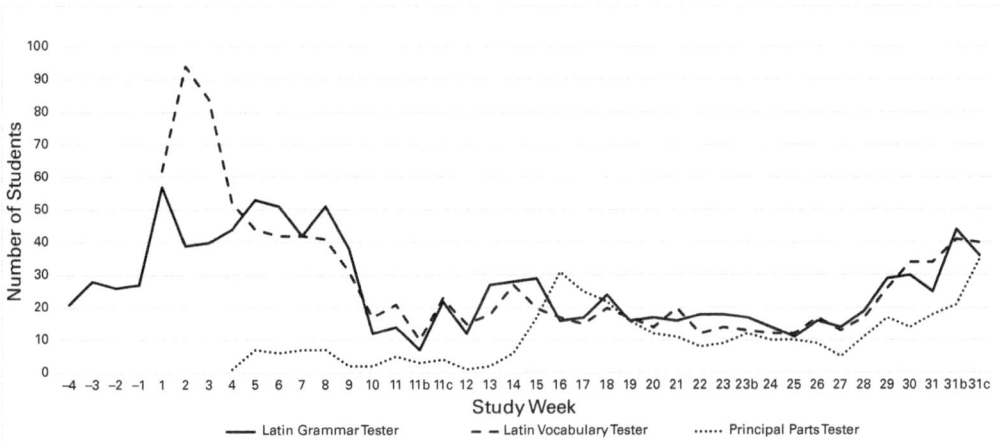

Figure 4.7 Number of students using testers each week. © Mair Lloyd and James Robson, The Open University.

Christmas break and 23b Easter break. The course officially finished at week 31, but there were two further weeks, 31b and 31c, before the final examination.

Figure 4.7 shows that, after an initial period where many students were using the Vocabulary Tester and Grammar Tester, usage fell mostly to under 30 students per week, but then picked up again in the period leading up to the final examination. Vocabulary, grammar and principal parts can be looked up by students when completing their in-course assignments, but not in the final examination, and this pattern suggests that students were either leaving learning until late in the day and/or becoming more focused on memorization and testing as the day of the examination approached. There were also a significant number of students not using the testers each week even in the run up to the examination.

As for other factors affecting the use of these resources, it is worth stating that there were various teething problems with the Vocabulary Tester (resolved after the end of the year) which may have had an impact on student engagement (indeed, some disgruntled and tech-savvy students even developed their own vocabulary testers for the course using freeware). This said, although there was a dramatic falling away in the use of the Vocabulary Tester after the first couple of weeks of the course, its subsequent pattern of usage is very similar to that of the Grammar Tester, indicating fairly low usage of testers in general rather than rejection of the Vocabulary Tester in particular. These results suggest that more lively and engaging ways of learning vocabulary, grammar and principal parts could be beneficial, perhaps coupled with activities that promote regular consolidation of these aspects of the course. However, it should be noted that the falling away in usage, here as elsewhere, can also be explained in part by a general fall in student numbers through withdrawal rather than loss of enthusiasm for a particular resource: of the 182 students who began *Classical Latin* in 2015, only 135 (74 per cent) continued studying to the end of the module (i.e. did not withdraw or defer).

Moving on now to examine student engagement with the Introducing Classical Latin site, Figure 4.8 suggests usage compatible with its intended purpose: that of enabling students to make a start on understanding key aspects of the Latin language both before the official course opening in week 1 and during the first two weeks of formal study (where it is integrated into student learning). After this initial phase, usage rapidly fell away, with only a very few students

47

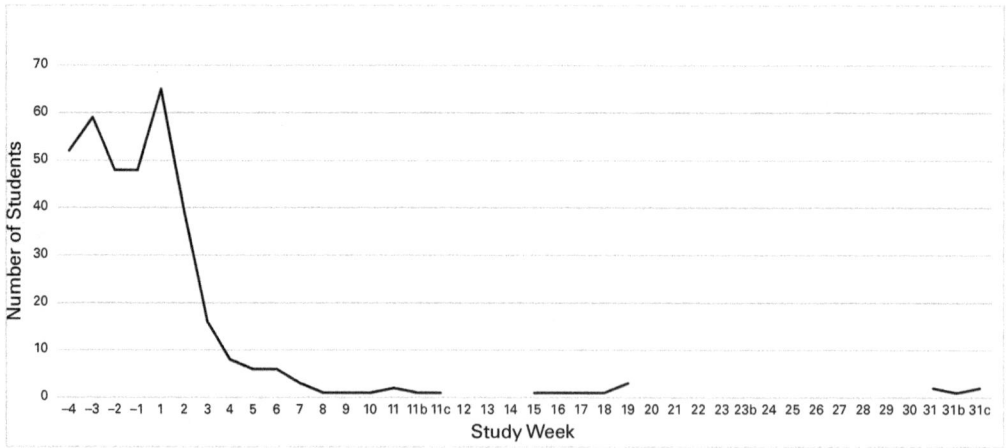

Figure 4.8 Number of students using the Introducing Classical Latin site each week. © Mair Lloyd and James Robson, The Open University.

returning to use it later in the course (including, interestingly, a handful of visits just before the final examination).

Where resources were designed in a sequence to be used at different points in the course, examining patterns of student engagement can give an impression of whether learners persisted with using them. The ten interactive Story Explorer versions of the Latin texts and their corresponding audio recordings were prescribed for use in weeks 1, 2, 4, 5, 6, 7, 9 and 10, with the final two stories in week 11. The use of each pair of resources (Story Explorer and audio recording(s)) is shown in Figure 4.9.

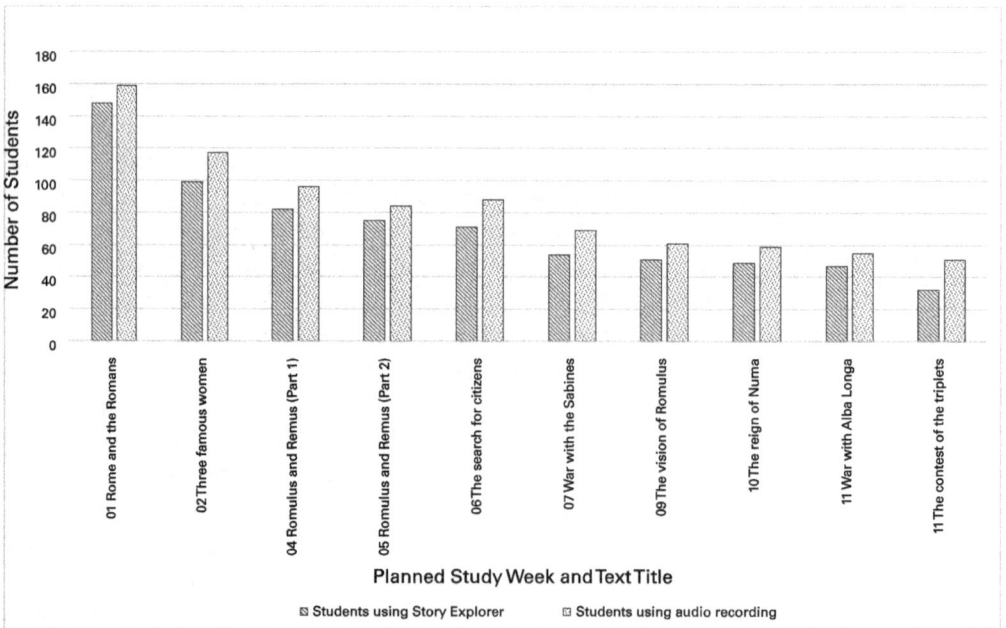

Figure 4.9 Students using the Story Explorer and audio recordings. © Mair Lloyd and James Robson, The Open University.

In this graph, the week in which the text relating to the Story Explorer and audio recording was prescribed is shown at the beginning of its title – so, for example, 'Romulus and Remus (Part 1)' was prescribed in week 4. The graph shows that the number of students using each resource died away as the course progressed, with audio recordings consistently attracting slightly more students than the Story Explorer. Again, this pattern may suggest that students become less experimental, more set in their study habits and more ruthless in their use of time as their studies progress. There is also perhaps an indication here of students feeling more confident and independent as learners once the initial stages of the course have been successfully navigated.

Student perceptions

Turning now to the end-of-module survey, there were two questions (Q5 and Q34) that cast light on student perceptions of the technology provided. Students were asked to state the extent to which they agreed with each statement by selecting a score between 1 and 5, where 1 represented 'definitely disagree' and 5 represented 'definitely agree'. The statements were:

Q5: The teaching materials and learning activities were well integrated and helped me to learn.
Q34: Overall, I was satisfied with the materials provided on this module.

The proportion of students who gave each response is shown in Figures 4.10 and 4.11.

Unhelpfully, these questions (and results) conflate printed and online materials, so it is necessary to look to free-text comments made by students in order to explore what resources they found helpful. Overall, fifty-three students commented positively on the resources and among these, eleven made specific mention of one or more of the testers, eight mentioned the online quizzes, five the audio recordings and three the Story Explorer. In total, thirty of the fifty-three specifically mentioned some form of online resource. Among other strengths mentioned were the Latin texts and the course tutors.

Since we were aware that the official, standard end-of-module survey conducted by the OU would not provide us with as much feedback as we would like on the online resources, we also

	65 valid responses (out of 182 students)
5 definitely agree	51%
4 mostly agree	45%
3 neither agree nor disagree	2%
2 mostly disagree	3%
1 definitely disagree	0%

Figure 4.10 Student responses to survey statement Q5: 'The teaching materials and learning activities were well integrated and helped me to learn.' © Mair Lloyd and James Robson, The Open University.'

	63 valid responses (out of 182 students)
5 definitely agree	65%
4 mostly agree	29%
3 neither agree nor disagree	5%
2 mostly disagree	2%
1 definitely disagree	0%

Figure 4.11 Student responses to survey statement Q34: 'Overall, I was satisfied with the materials provided on this module.' © Mair Lloyd and James Robson, The Open University.

conducted a separate, free-standing online survey (using Survey Monkey) towards the end of the study year, to which thirty-six students responded. Of these, 89 per cent (thirty-two students) rated Introducing Classical Latin as either 'very helpful' or 'quite helpful', with 47 per cent (seventeen students) claiming to have spent at least three hours using the site and another 33 per cent (twelve students) one to two hours. In addition, 50 per cent of those surveyed (eighteen students) reported using the Latin Vocabulary Tester at least once a week, and a pleasing 61 per cent (twenty-two students) were either 'extremely satisfied' or 'very satisfied' with the interactive resources on the module as a whole. Some of the free-text comments were extremely positive ('I cannot criticize the interactive resources – found them to be fantastic'), with feedback about the audio resources in particular confirming the benefits of our pedagogical approach ('The recordings of the extracts were helpful to keep the vocab in my memory . . . hearing and saying the word correctly really helped'). When it came to criticism, however, a number of students singled out the Latin Vocabulary Tester in their comments. The initial glitches on this site (which, for example, saw some correct answers marked as wrong) clearly led to some students losing their confidence – or worse, their patience – with the tester: 'I have used it a few times and found it hugely frustrating.'

Conclusions

Two aims of this chapter have been to evaluate the actual usage and perceived usefulness of the various online resources developed for the Open University module *Classical Latin: The Language of Ancient Rome* in 2015, and to articulate a range of methods by which a robust analysis of pedagogical technology can be achieved, combining multiple sources of quantitative and qualitative data in a rigorous 'mixed methods' approach. But we hope to have accomplished more than this through our research: the driving force behind this study has, after all, been a desire to inform the approach taken by us and by others in the future when designing, packaging and promoting the use of interactive resources for learners of classical languages. In our discussion, we have therefore sought to articulate ways in which the OU resources and their presentation to students not only succeeded but also fell short, while at the same time raising pertinent questions and highlighting unexpected data that our study has thrown up.

Among the provisional lessons learnt are that students might need more encouragement and reminders than we initially thought to engage with resources, and perhaps a greater explanation of their utility and/or of the learning objectives that they will potentially help learners to achieve. Indeed, if distance learners like those at the OU who are used to accessing teaching materials online need encouragement to use interactive resources, then those teaching students in face-to-face contexts may need to think particularly carefully about their strategies when trying to integrate technology into classroom-based teaching. Of course, face-to-face teaching contexts provide important opportunities for students to engage with interactive resources, too: instructors can demonstrate resources in class, for example, or use 'flipped classroom' techniques whereby online tasks completed by students in their own time are then discussed during lessons.

The patterns of use we discovered also provide important pointers for anyone looking to create interactive resources (or, indeed, simply integrate existing resources into their own teaching). Our data certainly point to two key factors when it comes to student engagement: an initial enthusiasm that subsequently waned, and last-minute examination revision – and so if limited time and funds are available for developing resources, these may be the two obvious points to target in a course. One unexpected finding concerned the differing levels of engagement with the OU resources by students depending on age. This is no doubt a topic ripe for further investigation and which is particularly important for those designing resources for younger students to consider (under 25s made up only 9.9 per cent of those studying the OU module in 2015, although this percentage is rising). It is also worth recalling that glitches in the 2015 version of the Vocabulary Tester caused considerable dissatisfaction among a vocal minority of students. So there are lessons to be learnt here about user testing in advance of release (though there is, of course, a balance to be struck between making a valuable resource available for use and making sure it works perfectly). One last point to make is the warm reception that the audio resources received from a number of students. No doubt the facility to hear (and, indeed, speak) Latin is largely underused by instructors except in the explicitly communicative classroom. Yet, as some of our feedback suggests, regular exposure to the sounds of Latin can help students to establish the phonological awareness that will enable them to learn the language more easily than if they just read words on a page.

As a coda, let us say something about the results we achieved with this cohort of students. In 2015, 68 per cent of the students initially enrolled on *Classical Latin* completed the module successfully (i.e. obtained a pass) and, of those taking the final examination, 91 per cent passed – unremarkable, perhaps, for a Latin module taught at a conventional university, but a considerable improvement on the overall pass rate (58 per cent) and the pass rate of those completing (74 per cent) the OU beginner's Latin module that *Classical Latin* replaced. To be sure, these two Latin modules differed in a whole host of ways, but a distinct element of *Classical Latin* was the extent to which technology was consistently used throughout to support students' acquisition of the language. Naturally, technology is not for everyone and there will always be students who choose to study Latin in more traditional ways – and do so successfully. But as pedagogical researchers, we are nevertheless beginning to establish evidence of the importance of the role of technology in enhancing the performance of our Latin students. The key question that remains is how this potential can be unlocked even more effectively for students both at the OU and beyond.

Note

1. See http://www.open.ac.uk/Arts/introducing-classical-latin/.

References

Gay, B. (2003), 'The Theoretical Underpinning of the Main Latin Courses', in J. Morwood (ed.), *The Teaching of Classics*, Cambridge: Cambridge University Press, 73–84.

Krashen, S. D. (1982), *Principles and Practice in Second Language Acquisition*, Oxford: Pergamon Press.

Lloyd, M. and Robson, J. (forthcoming), 'Staying the Distance: Transforming Latin Pedagogy at the Open University', *Journal of Latin Linguistics*.

CHAPTER 5
VLES, LATIN LITERATURE AND STUDENT VOICE
Elizabeth Lewis

Introduction

The use of virtual learning environments (VLEs) for education is becoming more and more popular with the rise of technology (Johnson 2016). VLEs that utilize cloud technology allow students with electronic devices in different geographical locations to view and edit the same text or document simultaneously and react to each other's responses in real time. Digital environments therefore can enable a shift from the typical student dynamics in a traditional classroom. This is due to the fact that individuals can change their behaviour online, a change described as the 'online disinhibition effect' (Suler 2004: 321), whereby people often become happier to disclose information or speak their true feelings due to increased anonymity and minimized authority (Suler 2004). To date there has been no research conducted on the use of online discussion forums in Classics teaching.

Rationale for research

I was interested in my research to utilize a live editing environment, Microsoft OneDrive, for facilitating online discussions in my A-level Latin class as part of teaching their literature set text. My research took place in an all-girls' selective school. My class consisted of four A-level Latin students, all high achieving. The class that I chose to conduct this research with had very varied vocal contributions in the classroom. Student A is a confident Latinist, previously vocal in discussions and happy to answer questions when unsure. Student B is happy to offer contributions in class and works frequently with Student A. Student C appears to offer fewer contributions in general than Students A and B, but is very happy to ask for help if unsure. Student D has been identified as a selective mute. She does not offer any responses voluntarily, and no longer than a simple one-word 'yes' in response to a question. She does not speak to any other students during lessons, but does speak to other students outside lessons. As using a regulated digital environment would provide a higher degree of anonymity for students than in the classroom, I wished to investigate the impact this would have on students' participation and collaboration from using the technology as a tool for discussion of their Latin literature A-level set text.

Technology in the classroom

Many correctly question the entrance of technology into the classroom, such as Natoli, who argues that educators 'pressured by administrative expectations to incorporate technology into instruction have begun to adopt these models only for the sake of using technology' (Natoli 2014: 37). Gibson (2001) additionally argues that in his own teaching experience, not all students will find the same type of experience with technology rewarding. However, others believe that technology has the capacity to transform the classroom, and that it can act as a powerful tool for inclusion, levelling the playing field for all types of students. For example, Standen and Brown argue that interactive software 'encourages active involvement in learning and gives the user the experience of control over the learning process' (Standen and Brown 2004: 96). They argue that this is of great benefit to people with learning difficulties, as learners can learn at their own pace and make mistakes independently, as 'the computer will not tire of the learner attempting the same task over and over again' (Standen and Brown 2004: 97). They argue that 'virtual environments create the opportunity for people with learning difficulties to learn by making mistakes but without suffering the real, humiliating or dangerous consequences or their errors' (Standen and Brown 2004: 97).

Underwood et al. (1996) also support this view in their research of integrated technological learning systems in secondary schools. The use of the technological system produced a teacher's view that 'the students like competing against themselves and that they were also happy to tackle new things because they were in a non-threatening, non-judgemental environment, and she felt that correction of errors were "not personally offensive as it often is in the classroom"' (Underwood et al. 1996: 958).

Some particular unique benefits of ICT for Latin teaching can also be noted. Hunt (2008) argues that the use of ICT for teaching Latin literature at A-level can be more time efficient, and additionally allows students to take responsibility for their own learning off site. Hunt also argues that the use of ICT can allow unique visualization and exploration of Latin texts; students can highlight and pick out words and manipulate the word order of the text, which encourages a more 'active and participatory' approach to the text (Hunt 2008: 116).

Collaborative learning and technology

Arguably, as technological innovation progresses, collaborative learning is more widely facilitated. Many value the benefit of collaborative learning in the classroom, linking it to the educational theories of Vygotsky (1978). Natoli summarizes thus: 'Vygotsky's concept of social constructivism primarily revolves around the notion that social interaction is paramount to learning and that groups can achieve more than individuals' (Natoli 2014: 38). Gibson suggests that collaborative work in the classroom helps students 'become deeply involved in manipulating information and thinking about it through processes of inquiry, critical thinking, problem solving, discussion and communication' (Natoli 2014: 42).

Paterson (2012), in his research using an interactive whiteboard with an A-level Latin Literature class, reported positive effects of the use of ICT on collaboration and discussion in the class. He presented that the use of an interactive whiteboard and wireless mouse allowed students to manipulate the Latin text in front of them and to produce an essay plan collaboratively as a class, as the mouse was passed around and students added their contributions to the document (Paterson 2012: 15). He reports that 'students felt that the high level of participation was engaging and gave several students more confidence' and that the discussion created was 'considered beneficial as it allowed students to develop their own points and learn from others' (Paterson 2012: 15). Paterson concurred with Gibson (2001), that, when a teacher used the technology of the interactive whiteboard, a shift of roles took place from being a teacher who is 'the judge of what is a good or bad argument', to a 'co-worker, a participant in the co-construction of a essay plan' (Paterson 2012: 15). Similarly, Smith (2012) investigated the impact of using web design technology on the achievement of his GCSE Latin literature group. Using the strategy, Smith (2012) believes that their learning became less teacher led, and that there was significant benefit in students being able to see the work that they had each done on the websites and to explore multiple viewpoints.

Johnson (2016) set out to investigate classroom discourse in an online learning environment and what effect this had on collaborative learning, by studying a group of teacher trainees and their instructor at a Midwestern university in the United States using the online discussion forum Blackboard for a period of ten weeks. Data analysis was conducted using Stahl's computer-supported learning methodology, monitoring online discussions and codifying responses as indexical, elliptic or projective (Johnson 2016: 1496). Johnson asserts that, due to over 10 per cent of all postings in the class (including those by the instructor) being projective entries, 'students were able to collaborate and develop meaning around the artefact prompts the instructor assigned', despite 'student geographic separation' (Johnson 2016: 1501). She further argues that 'the use of the internet, however, has been shown to support collaborative learning by providing instructors leverage in socio-cognitive scaffolding through classroom discussions and thus allowing classrooms to function as "self-improving communities"' (Johnson 2016: 1485). It is perhaps possible to question whether 10 per cent is a significant enough percentage of projective contributions to warrant Johnson's opinion, given that this percentage included instructor comments; the instructors 'consistently posed questions and encouraged students to explore new ideas and variations on the ideas they had been considering' (Johnson 2016: 1497). However, the greater value of online discussion forums may arguably lie in the enabling of some students who may offer few or no contributions in a physical classroom, but may do so in an online environment, which was an area of inquiry which I set out to investigate.

Participation

Research on online discussion forums and digital learning environments (Ferdig and Roeler 2004; Johnson 2016) also explores some interesting benefits of digital learning environments for participation. Johnson (2016) argues that online forums can alter teacher–student dynamics:

And while the course instructor may retain overall ownership of the virtual classroom, primarily by establishing expectations and creating assignments and discussion prompts, the direction of interactions are often controlled by the students who carry out the discussion, thereby providing them with a level of control and power in the class that may not be typical of the traditional classroom.

Johnson 2016: 1486

Ferdig and Roeler suggest that online discussion forums, in contrast to the traditional classroom, allow students 'time to think out structured and more in-depth responses ...

something critically important for shy members, who are then given space and time to speak up' (Ferdig and Roeler 2004: 121).

These ideas about participation, however, rely on the definition of classroom participation as a type of verbal contribution (which in an online environment thus becomes a written contribution). As Schultz (2009) argues, classroom participation is understood most often as students' verbal activity. However, Schultz cautions that narrow interpretations of the meaning of silence and a lack of verbal participation can lead to 'false assumptions about student participation in classroom activities', and that the absence of talk may lead a teacher to assume the absence of learning (Schultz 2009: 5). Schultz hence argues that classroom participation, given that it is fundamentally about contribution, should be defined as 'any verbal or nonverbal contribution in aural (spoken), visual (pictorial), or written (textual) form that supports learning for the individual student and/or other members of the class' (Schultz 2009: 6).

However, others such as Collins conversely argue that quiet behaviour is 'detrimental to learning' (Collins 1996: 9). She argues that quiet behaviour prevents children from learning to express themselves, asking questions, becoming independent learners and allowing teachers to monitor their learning (Collins 1996: 9). It remains that there is often a critical difference between what teachers believe students are learning from their assessment of students' verbal participation, and what the student may in reality be learning, and how. I was especially interested in assessing the students' participation and collaboration in discussions of the set text in the two different settings of my investigation: the physical classroom and the online environment. Given my previous knowledge that verbal participation varies hugely between students in the class, I was particularly intrigued to find out the students' opinions and perceptions using the online digital environment.

Methodology

My data collection for the investigation was made up of classroom observations, observations of online activity on the Microsoft OneDrive documents, questionnaires and interviews with the students. The short time frame of four lessons limited my findings, but I hoped still to gain insightful qualitative data during my investigation. Each discussion monitored (in the classroom or online) was focused on ten lines of the students' prescribed verse set text (Ovid *Amores* 2.5), which I set as homework for the students to analyse for rhetorical devices and literary themes. I carried out with the class two classroom-based discussions and two online discussions.

The order of the teaching sequence was as follows:

Lesson 1: Classroom discussion (approx. 20 mins) on ten lines of text set for homework (students asked to bring their paper notes). Online discussion of ten lines of set text to be completed before Lesson 2 set for homework.

Lesson 2: Follow-up classroom discussion of online document produced (approx. 15 mins). Online discussion of ten lines of set text to be completed before Lesson 3 set for homework.

Lesson 3: Follow-up classroom discussion of online document produced (approx. 15 mins).

Lesson 4: Classroom discussion (approx. 20 mins) of ten lines of text set for homework (students asked to bring paper notes).

The classroom-based discussions on the text took place at the beginning of the following lesson after the preparation homework was set. For these observations, carried out twice (Lesson 1 and Lesson 4), I undertook the role of a silent observer whilst another Latin teacher directed the discussion. I devised a template to help record elements of the discussion, distinguishing between voluntary and non-voluntary responses, as simply recording the number of times a student spoke would not provide hugely useful data for analysing participation and collaboration.

The online discussions were completed in the students' own time before the lesson, in which they made annotations on an online Word document in Microsoft OneDrive (with the Latin text and translation). The online discussions were followed up during the following lesson, with the online Word document being projected onto the interactive whiteboard. I decided to let the students work alone on the online document in their own time, and only add my contributions in the class discussions in Lessons 2 and 3, where problems with and different interpretations of the text could be discussed further. I chose to do this as I wanted to promote discussion from all students as much as possible, and I felt that my not having an immediate presence online might help facilitate this, particularly given the known vocal reticence of Student D. The use of Microsoft OneDrive does not allow for anonymity whilst users are live in the document, but it does not record which user made particular edits. Due to the small class size, keeping up total anonymity would be impossible, so I devised a system whereby students each chose a colour, and, once they had written their contributions, they would write their name in that colour at the bottom of the document to identify themselves; this thus achieved a higher degree of anonymity than in the classroom.

Data and findings

Of my findings, first I will analyse my classroom-based observations, which I carried out twice. I observed the students having a discussion for twenty minutes, led by their teacher, about ten lines of Ovid *Amores* 2.5, which they had analysed for homework. Student C was absent for the first observation, and that may have affected the contributions of the other students. Below is a summary table (Figure 5.1) of the students' relevant responses.

I found that in the first observation, as I had expected, Student A was the most vocal, offering six relevant voluntary responses in the discussion. For example, she said, 'There is juxtaposition of "tongues" next to the word "to join"'. She also answered many of the teacher's questions that were directed to the whole class. Student B was the next most vocal, offering four relevant voluntary responses in the discussion. What was particularly of interest to me was evidence of direct collaborative learning between Students A and B: Student A asked the teacher 'What is parenthesis?' and Student B answered her instead, explaining the concept which she had apparently learned in English lessons. I had also decided to record non-verbal responses such as head nodding, as to ignore these would be to ignore the participation of Student D, who as I had expected offered no verbal responses apart from a single 'yes' in response to one of the teacher's questions. The teacher made an effort to include Student D in the discussion by asking

	Response to directed individual question		Response to whole class question		Voluntary response	
	Factual question	Open-ended question	Factual question	Open-ended question	Question	Statement
Student A	0	3	8	1	3	3
Student B	1	1	8	0	1	3
Student C	ABSENT					
Student D	1 (+ 5 head nods/ non-vocalized responses)					

Figure 5.1 Summary of student responses in first classroom observation. © Elizabeth Lewis.

	Response to directed individual question		Response to whole class question		Voluntary response	
	Factual question	Open-ended question	Factual question	Factual question	Open-ended question	Factual question
A	0	0	1	1	4	6
B	0	3	1	0	2	0
C	0	0	0	0	4	1
D	0	0	0	0	0	0

Figure 5.2 Summary of student responses in second classroom observation. © Elizabeth Lewis.

her for her written notes (which Student D consented to by nodding and passing the notes), which she then read out to the class for the student. This appeared to me evidence of non-verbal participation as theorized by Schultz (2009), facilitated by the teacher. Both Students A and B reacted positively to Student D's points, with Student A saying, 'Oh that's a good point!'

Figure 5.2 is a summary of the second observation:

In this observation, as the teacher did not ask Student D for her notes, there was no evidence of her contributing to the discussion through that means; however, I did observe that she had prepared for the lesson, had annotations in front of her and was listening and being attentive to other students' contributions. These acts could, as Schultz (2009) argues, still be conceived as participation. In the second observation, there was evidence again of collaborative learning, this time between Students A and C, as Student C posed two questions to the teacher that were answered by Student A:

Student C (to the teacher): Would they have had punctuation like that in the actual Latin?

Student A: Isn't it where the caesura would be?

Student C (to the teacher): I don't really understand what Jupiter is doing here?

Student A: Isn't it talking about Jupiter's weapon?

What was particularly of interest to me in these two instances was that, though Student A attempted to answer Student C's questions, she herself posed her answers as questions, aimed towards the teacher for confirmation. For me, this highlighted the importance of the teacher as a facilitator of the discussion, as the students seemed to seek confirmation that their answers were correct.

Also interestingly, in the second observation neither Student B nor Student C actually offered any voluntary statements about the literature, only questions – acts which seemed to suggest that this discussion, set up in a flipped learning fashion, did provide opportunity for the teacher to target specific difficulties of individual students and become more of an assister in aiding students to become independent learners, as Gibson (2001) suggests. However, as Natoli (2014) argues, problems can occur using flipped learning, as some students (like Student D, who offered no responses at all) do not make queries, and misunderstandings can then become ingrained.

I will now assess my data collected from the use of Microsoft OneDrive. First, I will analyse the observation data I collected, and then the student perceptions as collected from the questionnaires and interviews to see how they correspond with my observational findings. As I had expected, the contributions of the students changed quite significantly in the online environment.

Figure 5.3 numerically summarizes the types of responses the students gave over the two uses. I categorized the responses in the framework of Johnson (2016): indexical responses being those which are relevant to the intended focus of the discussion, elliptic ones which are irrelevant to the discussion, and projective ones which extend the meaning of other responses (Johnson 2016: 1496).

In the first use of Microsoft OneDrive, the students identified themes and rhetorical devices. An example of this can be seen in Student C's response above; Student D, though silent in the classroom, offered responses such as the one shown in Figure 5.4. Originally each student was

| | Response type | |
	Projective	Indexical or elliptic
Student A	2	8
Student B	2	9
Student C	0	12
Student D	4	1

Figure 5.3 Summary of student responses in online discussions. © Elizabeth Lewis.

> **'Quid facis?' exclamo,** 'quo nunc mea gaudia differs?'
> iniciam dominas in mea iura manus!
>
> **Present tense to convey the immediacy of the exclamation to suggest Ovid's desperation and frustration.**
> *Exclamation mark is used to convey his determination at this point.*
> 'Ruling' sounds like a legal term so continues the legal imagery.
> 'my rights' (mea iura) also contributes to this imagery.

Figure 5.4 Student responses, 'Quid facis?' © Elizabeth Lewis.

identified by their responses being in a particular colour, but here they are represented by type forms. Student A's responses have a dotted underline, Student B's are in italics, Student C's are in bold and Student D's have a solid underline.

Again, in the second use of Microsoft OneDrive all the students participated, writing responses about themes and specific rhetorical devices, though notably Students A and C wrote the most extended responses on this set of lines. However, Student D still wrote extended responses such as the one shown (with the solid underline) in Figure 5.5.

Although in total Student D offered the fewest responses, the number of her responses was still significantly higher than in the classroom discussions; this was the same for Student C, who in fact offered the most online responses of any student. I feel that the appearance of increased confidence in offering responses in the online environment may reflect opinions such as Standen and Brown's (2004), that the student may have felt more control over the online learning environment and felt that it was a safer, less threatening place to offer responses. As Ferdig and Roehler (2004) argued, this may have given her a chance to speak because of the increased time online environments offer to think through responses. As I checked the document at regular intervals (once a day) whilst students were completing the homework over a week, I did, however, notice that Student D was always the last of the students to write her contributions, a fact that I feel could perhaps still display some level of 'vocal' (or written, as it were) reticence.

However, what was more striking, and what I found quite unexpected, was Student D's collaboration on the online document. There were four instances over the two uses of Microsoft

> qui modo *saevus* eram, supplex ultroque rogavi,
> **oscula** ne nobis deteriora daret.
>
> **Emphatic position of kisses to show how important her kisses are to Ovid.**
> Alliteration emphasises Ovid's yearning for kisses, especially the lengthy 'n' sounds which create a sense of longing.
> He is begging her which shows his desperation (he just wants her to kiss him as well as she kissed the other man).
> *'cruel' juxtaposes the notion of kissing and depicts his inner turmoil.*

Figure 5.5 Student responses, 'qui modo saevus eram'. © Elizabeth Lewis.

> haec tibi sunt **mecum, mihi** sunt communia **tecum** –
> in bona cur quisquam tertius ista venit?'
>
> **Alliteration of m sound to create a mournful tone showing how hurt he is over Corinna cheating. Emphatic position of 'you'.**
> *Rhetorical question* – <u>shows his confusion (he doesn't understand why she cheated on him)</u>

Figure 5.6 Student responses, 'haec tibi sunt mecum'. © Elizabeth Lewis.

OneDrive in which Student D extended the meaning of the other students' contributions, in fact providing the most projective responses of any student. For example, Student B identified that 'in bona cur quisquam tertius ista venit?' (line 32) was a rhetorical question, but offered no further analysis (shown in Figure 5.6). Student D then added, 'shows his confusion (he doesn't understand why she cheated on him)'.

There is evidence of all the students, apart from Student C, providing projective responses. In both uses of the document, Student C added the first contributions, but did not appear to return to the document to follow up on others' contributions, a finding that arguably displays that levels of collaborative learning were varied.

I was impressed that the students still strove to interpret as much meaning as possible from sections of the text, and did not 'settle' for one meaning; in many instances there were multiple ideas collated on the same lines of text. This seems to support Gibson's theories of ICT and collaborative learning, whereby technology aids students to engage in opportunities for collaboration, and provides 'a medium for creative thought, expression and knowledge construction' (Gibson 2001:42).

The discussions I had with the students about their contributions to the document, similar to the class discussion, allowed me to ask them to explain and elaborate on their points if they were not exactly clear. For example, I asked Student A to elaborate on the comment she had made online: 'The moon is personified, and often the moon is used as a symbol to represent women.' I asked her to explain to the class if she knew of any specific incidences where the moon is used as a symbol for women, which she did so successfully. I felt that having all the students' content on the interactive whiteboard led to a more equal discussion, because, although Student D did not make any verbal contributions, I felt that being able to pick up on and refer to each student's online contributions in the same way, praising and adding my own thoughts, created more of an equal participation atmosphere.

I will now analyse some of my data collected from the students themselves about the experience and how I feel it relates to my observational data. I was intrigued, given the change of verbal participation in the online environment, to find out how conscious students felt about others reading their responses, and whether they experienced any sort of 'online disinhibition effect', as I described. Therefore, on the questionnaire I posed the question 'On a scale of 1–10 (1 being not concerned in any way, and 10 being very conscious), how conscious were you of other students and the teacher reading your contributions?' As I had expected, Students A, B and C rated themselves as not being concerned, (scores between 1 and 3). Student D rated herself as 5, so more conscious than the others, which I had also expected. In the student interviews I took the opportunity to ask the students if they had any further comments on their answer to this question. Due to Student D's vocal reticence, which also showed itself during the interview, I did not manage to collect any further data on her thoughts, but Student B and Student C's responses were of particular interest:

> **Student B:** I am happy in normal discussions or on the document to put what I think because even if it's wrong other people might be able to argue with me and help me understand it more. I would be happy to do that even in a class of forty.
> **Student C:** I didn't mind, though I think I find it easier to make points online than in class.

Student B, therefore, felt that there was no difference to her participating in the online environment compared to the classroom, but she was appreciative of the opportunity in both environments for collaborative learning. Student C's response was perhaps reflective of the theories I have previously discussed, that online environments can give a voice to quieter students; it can be noted that Student C, though she was very happy to ask questions in the classroom environment, did not offer any literature 'points'. In the second use of Microsoft OneDrive, in fact, she numerically offered the most and longest responses to the poem, a finding that was very different the data I collected in the classroom observation. A comment of Student A's in the interview was also very striking (in response to the question 'Were you interested by any other students' contributions?'):

> **Student A:** It was really nice to read [Student D]'s points because obviously she doesn't contribute in class. I sat next to her in GCSE Latin and I know that she's really clever so it was really nice for us to read what she thought because she made really good points.

In my observational data I had considered whether Student D's tendency to join the online discussion last might be due to her vocal reticence, but interestingly in response to the question 'Did you prefer to make the first contribution on a particular section of text or respond to other students' contributions?' she said, 'I didn't feel strongly either way – sometimes it was easier to respond than to make new contributions though' – an answer that could reflect that it was more her response to the content that dictated when she contributed, rather than her not wanting her responses to be read by others.

Further to Student B's comment in the interview, I found other instances of the students seeing benefits in the collaborative nature of the activity. Student C showed appreciation that 'more notes' would be created for them all to use, and commented in the questionnaire, 'It was good to share work.' Student B also commented that it was beneficial to read others' interpretations of the same text.

Student engagement appeared to be high. Student B commented that 'It was really fun seeing other people type at the same time.' However, it is this novelty aspect of the technology that could diminish over time, as Paterson (2012) warns. The flipped learning aspect of the activity appeared to be positively received by the students, who all commented that it was valuable. In the interviews, responses to the open-ended question 'Was there any benefit you felt to analyzing the literature like this?' included:

> **Student A:** I felt that I understood the text more than normal doing it this way.
> **Student B:** I definitely feel like I remember the bits we did on the document more. I was looking back at some Propertius yesterday and I didn't really remember any

of it but now I still remember really well the passage we did online a couple of weeks ago.

On her questionnaire, in response to the question 'Did you feel it was beneficial in any way to draw out your own analysis on the text before being given annotations?', Student D commented, 'Yes it was helpful as it makes you think about the text more in depth than you might have otherwise.'

Student C drew out the value of the skills being practiced in the activity, commenting, 'I found it really reassuring that I can actually do the analysis on my own, because that's what we will have to do in the exam. It's really good practice because at the moment we only ever really do the analysis for ourselves on tests.'

It also appeared that students found the discussion after the completion of the online document helpful. In her interview, Student A said:

> **Student A:** I liked also having you check our points because I always get worried my points about literature aren't right so I don't write them down.

It is interesting, though, that similar to the findings of Johnson (2016) about instructors and online discussions, I felt I had acted more as a co-collaborator in the discussions about the student's findings, but in reality perhaps the students had felt that I was 'checking' or 'authorizing' their views, given my physical authority as the teacher in the classroom.

Student opinion, however, did also appear to align with research that, for flipped learning to be successful, material must be cognitively accessible and within the Zone of Proximal Development (Vygotsky 1978). Comments which support this include one from Student A, who felt that this exercise would not have been successful at the start of the year, when 'we didn't know much about Ovid and his techniques'.

Other notable comments that arose from the interviews about the benefits of the technology that I had not considered included one from Student B, who felt that the technology was beneficial to her organization, as it did not require her to physically bring any paper to the lesson. Student C also interestingly commented:

> **Student C:** I actually felt it was nicer to be closer to the text, like I know it sounds stupid, but I feel really far away from the text in class when it's on the board?

Conclusion

Undertaking this research project was very valuable for me personally, as a teacher in training, to consider the meaning of participation and collaboration in the classroom and to consider the use of digital online platforms. Though my small sample size and very short time frame limits the use of my findings greatly, I still hope that some of my findings may be of interest in this area.

It appeared to me, as Natoli (2014) expresses, that we should always be cautious against using technology 'for the sake of it', although in this area of participation and collaboration, ICT and in particular online digital platforms do seem to hold some unique benefits. As researchers have attempted to argue (Standen and Brown 2004; Ferdig and Roehler 2004), ICT can provide safe environments that can allow many different types of users to participate who may not normally have participated in the classroom. This is possibly due to how users can make repeat attempts or take as much time as they wish over responses, without judgement. I feel that this element of the online digital environment was what allowed a student in my class to be able to articulate her thoughts about literature and verbally communicate with others, which she was not able to do in the normal classroom environment. I believe that the platform possibly also allowed other students to take different roles and authority in discussions compared to how they would usually have acted in the classroom. This research helped me consider different types of participation in the classroom. Though there was a complete lack of vocal participation in the classroom by one student, it cannot be said there was an absence of learning on the student's part, as evidenced by her written contributions. This highlighted the importance to me of providing varied opportunities for students when aiming to increase participation and collaboration, as different students will thrive in different environments. It is possible that the enthusiastic student uptake in discussion could be attributed to the novelty of the new technology, and prolonged use of it may enlighten future research in this area.

This project also let me explore some thoughts about what teachers perceive to be their role in discussions, and what students perceive the teacher's role to be; for example, though I felt I was acting as a co-collaborator, a small amount of evidence from a student suggests that they perceived me to be the authorizer of whether what they said was right or wrong. Further research into this area and the use of online digital platforms at secondary level would be enlightening.

Though the students cited different benefits of using the technology, what was consistently raised across the group was the benefit of learning from each other, and the benefit of doing literature analysis by themselves initially without my input. For me, the project raised the importance of being mindful in a classroom of individual students, providing varied opportunities for participation and collaboration, and seeking student feedback on activities as part of reflective teaching practice.

References

Beeland, W. (2006), *Student Engagement, Visual Learning and Technology: Can Interactive Whiteboards Help?*, Promethean. Available online: www.mypromethean.com/uk (accessed 22 September 2018).

Collins, J. (1996), *The Quiet Child*, London: Cassell.

Ferdig, R. and Roehler, L. (2003), 'Student Uptake in Electronic Discussions', *Journal of Research on Technology in Education*, 36 (2): 119–136.

Gibson, I. (2001), 'At the Intersection of Technology and Pedagogy: Considering Styles of Learning and Teaching', *Journal of Information Technology for Teacher Education*, 10 (1–2): 37–61.

Hunt, S. (2008), 'Information and Communication Technology and the Teaching of Latin Literature', in Lister, B. (ed.), *Meeting the Challenge: International Perspectives on the Teaching of Latin*, Cambridge: Cambridge University Press, 107–120.

Johnson, C. (2016), 'Rethinking Online Discourse: Improving Learning Through Discussions in the Online Classroom', *Journal of Education and Information Technologies*, 21 (6): 1483–1507.

Natoli, B. (2014), 'Flipping the Latin Classroom: Balancing Educational Practice with the Theory of eLearning', *Journal of Classics Teaching*, 30: 37–40.

Paterson, C. (2012), 'Ancient Texts and Modern Tools: Cicero and Interactive Whiteboards', *Journal of Classics Teaching*, 25: 15–17.

Schultz, K. (2009), *Rethinking Classroom Participation: Listening to Silent Voices*, Teachers College Press.

Smith, A. (2012), 'The Use of Collaborative E-learning Technology for GCSE Latin', *Journal of Classics Teaching*, 26: 3–8.

Standen, P. and Brown, D. (2004), 'Using Virtual Environments with Pupils with Learning Difficulties' in L. Florian and J. Hegarty (eds.), *ICT and Special Needs: A Tool for Inclusion*, Berkshire: Open University Press.

Suler, J. (2004), 'The Online Disinhibition Effect', *Cyberpsychological Behavior*, 7 (3): 321–326.

Underwood, J., Cavendish, S., and Lawson, T. (1996), 'Integrated Learning Systems: A Study of Sustainable Learning Gains in UK Schools' in J. Underwood and J. Brown (eds.), *The Case for Integrated Learning Systems,* London: Heinemann.

Vygotsky, L. (1978), *Mind in Society: The Development of Higher Psychological Processes*, Cambridge, MA: Harvard University Press.

CHAPTER 6
GOING DIGITAL: THE PRINCIPLES BEHIND CYBERCAESAR
Alan Chadwick

Introduction

I've made my own Latin course. It's not that big a deal; not every Classics teacher does it, but I think that there are quite a lot of them that do. When I did my PGCE, I was lucky enough to work with a mentor who was writing his own Latin course entirely from scratch. I know of many colleagues who write their own courses. I know of many more who create resources around existing textbooks so diligently that sometimes they also, in effect, produce their own teaching course. Does the world really need another Latin course? Surely, we were at saturation point years ago? Clearly the *Cambridge Latin Course* is the market leader,[1] whilst the *Oxford Latin Course* also has its adherents.[2] *Ecce Romani*, though out of print, is followed by many. Taylor has produced several excellent textbooks for Latin.[3] *Disce Latinum*[4] and *So You Really Want to Learn Latin*[5] are used widely in prep schools. *Imperium* by Morgan has proven quite popular with some teachers.[6] Many traditionalists espouse North and Hillard.[7] In fact, you can find many interesting old textbooks on textkit.com or in the marvellous collection found at edonnelly.com/google.html. So to repeat the earlier question, why another Latin course? What makes CyberCaesar any different?

CyberCaesar teaches Latin to GCSE standard. It is both an e-learning course and a resource for blended learning. I will discuss the difference later in this chapter. As far as I am aware, CyberCaesar is the only course for learning Latin hosted entirely online. Whilst materials can be printed out for use in the classroom, this is by no means necessary, especially if students have devices in the classroom. It is also, as far as I am aware, the only course that provides instant, detailed, personalized feedback to learners. There are also a range of tools that help teachers monitor and improve pupils' learning in the classroom. In my mind, it is the effective deployment of these tools that makes CyberCaesar successful. The course does not work just because it is online; it works because the online resources make learning Latin far more engaging and enduring.

Using digital technology in education

Technology has always been used in education. Any tool used to abet or improve instruction is a form of technology. Blackboards and chalk are both forms of technology, and manufacturers of both have gone the way of Kodak[8] in adapting (or failing to adapt) to shifts in technology within the classroom environment. The use of technology in the classroom has been transformed over the last two decades. Overhead projectors are now rarely seen in the wilds of the classroom, and the AV classroom from my childhood (the only room in the school with a television) has long been replaced by the ICT room(s). However, the adoption of digital technologies within schools has been met with much suspicion. Experienced teachers chafe at the perceived imposition of devices and systems that will have no ostensible effect on learning but will instead add to burden of workload. Nor is this reaction unjustified. The OECD report on the worldwide usage of digital technologies in education states that:

> despite the pervasiveness of information and communication technologies (ICT) in our daily lives, these technologies have not yet been as widely adopted in formal education. But where they are used in the classroom, their impact on student performance is mixed, at best. In fact, PISA results show no appreciable improvements in student achievement in reading, mathematics or science in the countries that had invested heavily in ICT for education.
>
> OECD 2015: 15

Hattie, in his influential study of factors influencing achievement in schools, is equally sceptical about the use of ICT in schools to improve learning, saying:

> There is no correlation of the effect sizes with the year of study, which counters the typical claim that the effect from computers is increasing with the sophistication of the technology. Across the various meta-analyses there were no differences across grades, or ability levels of the students . . . there is no necessary relation between having computers, using computers, and learning outcomes.
>
> Hattie 2009: 220–221

Whilst the latter is admittedly an earlier perspective upon the adoption of new technologies within schools, the observation is still valid. The problem arises from the integration of digital technologies with classroom practice, enabling the teacher to realize the advantages that these technologies may bring. When a new device or framework is parachuted into a school without any due proselytizing of how teaching and learning can be transformed by such technology, any new scheme is likely to cause resentment and slow adoption. In contrast, when the benefits of adapting to the new technologies are made clear, teachers may begin to incorporate usage of the new technologies far more readily. The key is to highlight how both teaching and learning can be enhanced by utilizing digital strategies. Picardo suggests:

> In the school context, technology enables us to focus on smart work, instead of hard work, and challenges us to be open to doing things in novel ways, so long as the outcomes justify the application of technology to a particular aspect of teaching and learning.
>
> Picardo 2017: 5

In short, we need to make our deployment of digital resources part of our toolkit for achieving our teaching and learning goals. When the power of our technologies has been harnessed towards improving instruction and understanding, we are moving in the right direction. As Fullan says,

Pedagogy is the driver with student learning at its center and technology as the Formula 1 Gran Prix machine that gets the student there faster and better.

Fullan 2013: 21

Technology must be paired with pedagogy if it is to have any significant contribution to improving teaching and learning in the classroom.

The realization that technology needs to be integrated into classroom practice rather than just grafted on as an afterthought (or imposed from above) can be seen from some various theories about the application of technology to the classroom. Puentedura introduced the SAMR model (see Figure 6.1), which posits that the evolution of educational technology moves from substitution, through amplification and augmentation, to redefinition (Puentedura 2013).

As both students and teachers become familiar with technology, scope for doing extraordinary things to enhance learning begins to appear.

The SAMR taxonomy enables you to think about how the learning taking place in your classroom could be extended further through your use of technology, thereby making the learning more rich, deep and extensive.

Anderson 2014: 11

RAT is a similar model, defining replacement, amplification and transformation (Hughes et al. 2006) as the various stages of digital implementation. Although there may be some scope for disagreement with some of these assumptions (a redefinition of the practice of the translation of language may well be possible, but would it have any academic recognition at examination level?), the point of both models is to emphasize that digital technology enables previously unthinkable activities to happen in the classroom.

S	**SUBSTITUTION** Technology acts as a direct substitute, with no functional change	Enhancement	
A	**AUGMENTATION** Technology acts as a direct substitute, with functional improvement		
M	**MODIFICATION** Technology allows for significant task redesign	Transformation	
R	**REDEFINITION** Technology allows for the creation of new tasks, previously inconceivable		

Figure 6.1 The SAMR model. Image by Lefflerd distributed under a CC BY-SA 4.0 from Wikimedia Commons, redrawn by the editors.

When technology is used appropriately, it achieves two main objectives:

- It improves and streamlines processes, facilitating the completion of tasks more effectively and easily.
- It allows us to do things that would be inconceivable without the use of technology.

(Picardo 2017: 5)

An alternative model is TPACK (Mishra et al. 2006), which places technical, pedagogical and content knowledge at the confluence of the three spheres of pedagogy, subject expertise and the ability to use technology effectively (Figure 6.2).

This builds upon the work of Shulman (1986), who suggested that teaching expertise comes from the convergence of knowledge from the content and pedagogical domains. Again, the point is that knowing how to use digital technology is not enough. The challenge is to assimilate this knowledge into our existing professional practice to make teaching more powerful and learning more efficacious. If the implementation of any new technology does not seek to improve teaching or learning, either by doing what we currently do more effectively or by empowering us to realize ever more remarkable achievements in the classroom, its validity is questionable.

Background to CyberCaesar

The intention of creating my own course for teaching Latin crystallized in 2009. I had been teaching from one of the most popular textbooks, creating a variety of resources to supplement understanding, including a grammar book given to students to 'fill in the gaps'. When my school introduced Moodle, I saw some excellent opportunities to improve teaching and learning. Moodle is an open-source virtual learning environment (VLE, also known as a learning management system), that acts initially as a massive repository of resources for students. VLEs have garnered a bad reputation for themselves: Wheeler (2011) indeed

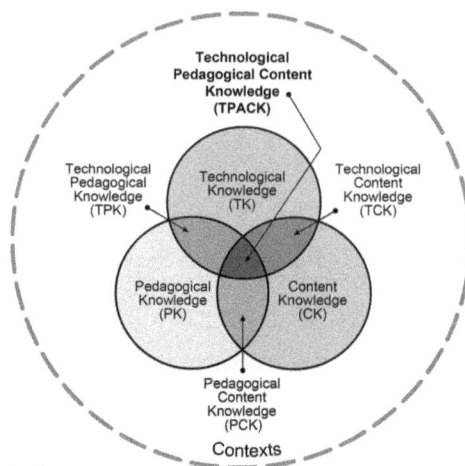

Figure 6.2 The TPACK model. Reproduced by permission of the publisher. © 2012 by www.tpack.org.

sardonically suggested that 'the institutional VLE is where content goes to die' (Wheeler 2011). But Moodle has lots of dynamic features that serve to enhance the educational experience. Whilst I thought that all the features were helpful and had potential, I was completely won over by the quiz module. For me, it was the perfect vehicle to practice accidence, syntax and translation. I developed some assessment materials for Moodle and they were extremely effective and, as a bonus, were popular with students, who enjoyed the sense of engagement. Rarely before had any pupils expressed delight in learning grammar (Latin teachers never hear the refrain, 'Hey sir, can we have another text on the imperfect passive subjunctive of ire?'), but online activities reinforcing linguistic concepts had proven to be helpful.

In addition, like all teachers of Latin, I had my own preferences for how I introduced various aspects of the subject to my students. Like all teachers of Latin, I enjoyed parts of the course that I was using, but found other aspects particularly wanting. I had always thought about writing my own course; the best course that any teacher can use is one created by oneself. The framework provided by Moodle was an ideal opportunity to organize teaching ideas, resources, materials and exercises.

Pedagogical principles

Perhaps surprisingly for a course that is so grounded in new technologies, CyberCaesar adopts a very traditional approach to the learning of grammar. Regarding language learning, attention is focused upon learning the endings of words, particularly case endings. Cases are such a profound and common aspect of the language that it is vital to immerse learners in these patterns as soon as possible. To this end, students learn and practice manipulating individual words before subsequently translating sentences exhibiting these forms. In each topic there is at least one exercise of translation from English to Latin, which is traditionally regarded as the most effective way to cement an understanding of the inflectional endings of the Latin language.

Although it takes a traditional view of grammar and syntax, CyberCaesar is also a reading course and it adopts a deductive approach to the language. The learner can encounter a new linguistic item from reading the Latin text. Over 100 stories and twenty-five sets of model sentences have been written to enrich this aspect of the course. Learners experience and practice new elements of the language in their reading. These stories have also been written to introduce learners to common details of the Roman world and to provide an overview of many of their customs, habits and ways of life.

The greatest strength and most exciting feature of the course is its use of digital technologies. The online activities aren't just an add-on but an integral part of the entire learning experience. CyberCaesar is a blended learning course; the online activities are as essential to a student's progress as conventional classroom instruction. CyberCaesar uses the 'flipped classroom' model; video lessons are available that carefully explain how a new linguistic concept functions. Online language exercises are a major asset of the course. Not only do they provide extensive assessment of any given linguistic component, they also provide clear and detailed feedback as to where a student may be going wrong. Students and teachers can chart progress via the gradebook, which provides a comprehensive overview of performance throughout the course. CyberCaesar is not a conventional course that has been copied onto a website. Rather, it has been designed to utilize technology to radically improve and enhance learning.

Structure

These are the principles that have informed the design of the course, which is itself split into three smaller sections: Basic Latin, Intermediate Latin and Further Latin. Each course is formed of twelve topics.

Basic Latin

The Basic Latin course introduces the nominative and accusative cases in topic two, the singular and plural in topic three and the present tense of verbs in topics four and five. The remaining topics then concentrate upon the genitive, dative and ablative cases, followed by the detailed analysis of the first three declensions, before concluding with the present tense of irregular verbs.

Intermediate Latin

The Intermediate Latin course focuses mainly on verbal forms, as well as adjectives, adverbs and pronouns. The first topic in this section introduces imperatives and questions, the five subsequent topics deal with all tenses in Latin, and the next two with adjectives, comparison and adverbs. The following two topics set out the passive voice and thereafter the fourth and fifth declensions, and the final two topics teach the various forms of the pronouns.

Further Latin

The Further Latin course covers all the varieties of subordinate clause that can be encountered at GCSE level. Relative pronouns and clauses are introduced to the course first, so that learners can understand the principles of complex sentences without being overwhelmed by new paradigms too early in their experience. The forms and usage of participles follow, so that students can draw on their knowledge of adjectival clauses to better comprehend how participles function in Latin. Indirect statements come next, and I felt that this was also the best place to set out the various tenses of the infinitive. The next topics explain the forms of the imperfect and pluperfect subjunctive, followed by examination of cum clauses, purpose clauses, indirect commands, result clauses, indirect questions and clauses of fearing. The final section deals with uses of the gerundive. All items of accidence and syntax for GCSE are taught by the end of this course. Vocabulary has also been consolidated (all 800 items occur in the GCSE vocabulary lists). All language requirements are covered in full.

The rationale behind this approach is simple. I have always felt that it is important for students to encounter the same types of concept in learning the language. I believe that it is vital to introduce students to the various cases and noun endings at a relatively early stage of their experience in Latin. The ability to recognize and interpret case endings is the key to acquiring any sort of mastery of Latin, and introducing all cases at a relatively early stage of development gives students the opportunity to practice them throughout their learning of the language. I have also attempted to introduce related concepts in a systematic order, hence all verb tenses appear in concurrent topics, as do adjectives and passive verbs. I wanted to deal with all the paradigms commonly encountered in reading Latin by the end of the Intermediate Latin course. I had to compromise to the degree that the forms of the subjunctive mood or the cases of participles could not be explored until much later. However, by covering all cases, tenses and other aspects of simple sentences in the first two courses, these items could be fully consolidated and understood by the learner before the introduction of complex sentences in the third course. In my experience, pupils who have followed this course throughout do not find subordinate clauses that challenging.

Approaches to learning

Narratives

The course is not just about grammar and vocabulary. As I said previously, I have written over 100 stories and twenty-five sets of model sentences as part of the course. Whilst an obvious intention of these narratives is to provide a context in which to practice reading Latin, they also deal with various aspects of Roman life. The first seven topics in the Basic Latin course are set in Herculaneum, and the remaining topics of this section are set in Pompeii. In Intermediate Latin, the first eight topics are set in ancient Rome and the final four in Roman Britain. The stories themselves deal with subjects like slavery, entertainment and warfare to generate interest in Roman society. The language of the narratives is purposefully elementary: a colleague did suggest replacing *volo* + *infinitive* in Topic 12 with *utinam* + *subjunctive*; whilst his Latin may have been unquestionably more elegant, I felt that it was educationally more valuable to stick with the former. I have attempted in writing these stories to reinforce linguistic elements that pupils have encountered only recently. This is an attempt at deliberate practice and I will refer to this later in the article. I have hyperlinked some new or unfamiliar vocabulary in these stories if I feel that this is a word that a student either does not yet know or cannot be expected to work out in the circumstances. I don't feel that it is appropriate to provide easy access to words that learners really ought to know. Instead a search function is provided for students to look up words that they may have forgotten. The idea behind this is that the process of searching may help to reinforce knowledge of the meaning of a word – the activity itself promotes more effective recall of an item.

Video lessons

Each topic in CyberCaesar contains at least one video lesson. As stated above, these video lessons have been constructed as part of the 'flipped classroom' approach to instruction. There are many different definitions of and approaches to the flipped classroom, but generally the strategy involves watching a video as part of a homework task. There are advantages and criticisms of this approach: the convenience of easily available content must be offset against the lack of the physical presence of the expert. My own view is similar to that of Sumeracki and Weinstein ('The Learning Scientists') (2018) who state that, 'there are too many degrees of freedom in the definition of a "flipped classroom"'. It could be argued that the flipped classroom has been happening ever since homework was foisted upon recalcitrant students, with the exhortation 'Go and read this chapter at home':

> The confusing thing about the idea of the 'flipped classroom' is that it is actually nothing new. Even in the traditional lecture, students are often expected to have read prior to coming to class.
>
> Sumeracki and Weinstein 2018

The only difference is in the medium; video is now preferred to the traditional book. My rationale for asking students to watch a video for homework is simple: I want them to familiarize themselves with content that we will discuss in the following lesson. Helping students to engage with material in a range of different media and circumstances can make learning more effective. Bjork and Bjork tell us that 'varying conditions of practice—even varying the environmental setting in which study sessions take place—can enhance recall' (Bjork and Bjork 2011). The video lessons are just one strand in the overall tapestry of imparting understanding of the material.

Even though I have made my own, I must acknowledge that some of the videos available on YouTube or other platforms are of very high quality. However, I don't think that it is enough just to ask students to watch a video. There is a need to make the material interactive. There is a risk that even the most interesting and compelling video can be absorbed quite passively. Everyone is capable of watching something on screen and not taking in anything. Perhaps we can call this mental truancy or, more generously, intellectual nomadism as the mind wanders from the subject matter. I try to encourage attentiveness to video content by inserting questions into the videos themselves. As pupils watch the videos, questions are triggered, assessing the student's understanding of the material. I initially used an industry-standard e-learning application published by Adobe called Captivate, but I have since turned to making online videos using presentation software like PowerPoint or Explain Everything, and I have used an open-source package called H5P to create the assessment material.

At the very least, the video lessons provide instant access to explanations of material that would not conventionally have been available. They deliver instruction for students who have missed lessons due to illness or other reasons. They afford quick support and reference to students struggling to recall or reinforce a concept. From my point of view, rather than replacing classroom elucidation, the video lessons accelerate comprehension and understanding of a new topic. It is far easier to build new knowledge on existing structures. The purpose of the video lessons is to lay the rudimentary foundations of new concepts to make long-term understanding of them more effective.

Wordlists, glossaries and flash cards

I also composed my own vocabulary lists, which I based upon the recommended wordlists of the examination boards for GCSE, but I also drew carefully upon other published vocabulary lists, notably Diederich's work on the frequency of Latin words (Raeticus 2011). I have tried to use only the most common of Latin words and vocabulary lists containing only words that are essential for understanding most of Latin literature. I have also tried to match vocabulary with a relevant grammatical topic: hence third conjugation verbs form the whole vocabulary list for topic four and verbs from other conjugations. It is vital to keep the vocabulary relevant to the grammatical material of each part of the course.

There are 200 words in the Basic Latin course, 300 more in Intermediate Latin and 300 more again in Further Latin. All items of vocabulary are listed in a glossary, which can be accessed at any point in the course by students; they can also be found in a cumulative vocabulary within each topic, which helpfully lists all the words encountered in the course so far. There are flash cards to help students retain information more effectively. Indeed, for the last few years, the only homework given to pupils has been the learning of vocabulary and endings. Pupils are advised to work for five minutes a night, every night, rather than cramming for a test the night before. Vocabulary retention is assessed on CyberCaesar through online tests. These assess not only vocabulary skills but also knowledge of inflected endings. To ensure that students learn the vocabulary thoroughly, tests on previous material are often given without notice. So far, I have been very encouraged by how effectively students have learned vocabulary.

There is also a grammar glossary in each course which is built upon the Moodle Glossary module. As well as acting as a reference guide for students, the glossary automatically links any occurrence of a term in a course to its definition. I have used this to create a dynamic reference guide. Whenever a grammatical term is used in the course, a hyperlink is created linking it back to its explanation in the glossary. Therefore, any feedback provided to students involving terms like 'accusative' or 'pluperfect' contains a hyperlink back to the glossary. It helps students understand the key terms far more readily. Instant correction of a misunderstood concept clearly helps the students train their comprehension of the subject more effectively.

Exercises

The most extensive feature of CyberCaesar is the range of exercises on each aspect of the language. The exercises (or quizzes, to use Moodle's terminology) were amongst the first things I created for the course, and they have been monitored, evaluated and rewritten according to their effectiveness. They are very flexible and versatile, enabling me to assess student performance across a range of different activities. These quizzes start at a lexical level (has the student understood the meaning of a word?), then move to a morphological level (has the student understood the ending of a word?) and finally to a syntactical level (has the student understood the usage of the word and its ending?). There are also some key skill exercises that are repeated in every topic, with the intention that repeated learning can embed these key skills. Through extended practice it is expected that learners will quickly gain mastery of the basic grammar of Latin.

One of the great strengths of Moodle is its range of plug-ins. Developers compose their own modules to extend functionality. Many aspects of the course are enhanced by these plug-ins, such as administration, activities and aesthetic appeal. I use a plug-in for the quiz module that allows me to identify if the meaning or the function of a word in a sentence is wrong. The exercises in CyberCaesar don't just determine whether an answer is correct or incorrect, they also provide immediate, detailed feedback identifying the nature of any mistakes. In this way, students can understand how to correct their answer and improve their understanding of the language. Feedback is vital, described by Hattie (2009) as the most important factor in improving learning. CyberCaesar tries to provide regular and automatic feedback to students to improve their learning. In this regard, the exercises exhibit many of the core tenets of Assessment for Learning. The feedback is more important than the grade:

> Feedback which focuses on what needs to be done can encourage all to believe that they can improve. Such feedback can enhance learning, both directly through the effort that can ensue and indirectly by supporting the motivation to invest such effort. A culture of success should be promoted where every student can make achievements by building on their previous performance, rather than by being compared with others. Such a culture is promoted by informing students about the strengths and weaknesses demonstrated in their work and by giving feedback about what their next steps should be.
>
> Black et al. 2003: 46

An exercise on CyberCaesar isn't a test. It is an opportunity for students to consolidate their understanding of the linguistic material. Students can take each exercise as often as they like. No exercise is ever the same. Most exercises have six different alternatives for each question, so that students will always experience a different assessment environment. A pupil can reformulate their answer in light of any feedback and try again. For every attempt that contains an error, there is a 10 per cent penalty. This means that when a pupil has completed an exercise, the teacher can examine progress very quickly by scrutinizing questions that have incurred several penalties. In this way the teacher can take steps to alleviate any lack of understanding of a form or concept. The teacher has time to do this because, by marking themselves, these exercises reduce the burden of marking and assessment considerably. Teachers can check course completion and progress in an exercise or over a range of activities at the click of a button.

Gamification

There are some elements of gamification in CyberCaesar. I'm sorry to use such an ugly term, but gamification has become more prevalent in many online courses today. From Easter eggs to virtual reality, many of the elements associated with computer games have been adapted for use in education:

> Educational games are a huge and growing industry, and they're being developed to help teach pretty much any topic or skill you could imagine, from history to math to science to foreign languages. When these games work—when they marry good game design with strong educational content—they provide a welcome relief to students who otherwise feel under-engaged in their daily school lives.
>
> McGonigal 2011: 75

However, it is important not to get carried away with the zeal for turning everything into a game:

> But even then, these educational games are at best a temporary solution. The engagement gap is getting too wide for a handful of educational games to make a significant and lasting difference over the course of a student's thirteen-year public education.
>
> McGonigal 2011: 75

CyberCaesar manages to hit this happy medium between engagement and irrelevance. Students can earn badges for completing certain activities within a topic. They can also unlock access to educational games by achieving pass grades in language exercises.

Approach

There is no 'one-size-fits-all' approach to using CyberCaesar; as with all school courses, it can be deployed as each teacher deems most fit to each class and circumstance. My colleagues tend to use the course in a slightly different manner to me, and that is surely a good thing. The course is versatile enough to be used in a variety of ways. I myself try to use it as a blended learning course. I try not to set any written homework. Although students can complete the exercises or translate the passages at home, I prefer that they perform these activities in the classroom, where I am on hand to provide close, one-to-one coaching should a student experience difficulty with the language. Instead, I generally set video lessons or learning activities as homework. For the latter, students are strongly advised to space out their learning over the course of a week, spending five minutes each evening on reinforcing mastery of the material.

Lessons generally begin by reviewing material either learned previously or explained in a video lesson. These principles are reinforced through classroom reading of one of the narratives on CyberCaesar. After practicing aspects of the language derived from these readings, students will then take a brief test, either on the material that was set for homework or from another topic which they have learned previously; part of our learning homework is to spend five minutes each week reviewing material (such as vocabulary, word endings or technical terminology) that has already been covered in class. This test is online and marks itself, providing feedback both to the pupils and to myself. I can gauge generally how well the pupils have performed as a group and tailor my review of the material by responding to this feedback. After this review, I relate the material that they have just covered to the material they already know and then set them to complete the language exercises online. Even though these exercises provide each student with detailed feedback, explaining where they may have gone wrong, I find that I still need to explain details of error individually to students. After this, we spend some time exploring areas of civilization, society or any other subject of interest. This is very much a superficial summary of my approach and no two lessons are alike. Quite naturally, the approach will change as the situation dictates.

Reception

Students were initially both keen and cautious to use a new course that contained all their work online. The novelty of working exclusively on computers soon wore off, but the immediacy of the course material still managed to provide interest. The use of exercise books did provide some scope for development. At first, we tried to use exercise books to chronicle progress, to carry out rough work on translations and to record aspects of grammar and Roman life. However, it became apparent that this was asking too much. Instead, I created and printed out a fill-in-the-gaps grammar book for pupils to complete as they worked their way through the course. This proved far more satisfactory, and pupils now use exercise books mainly for rough notes and ideas. Most students managed to acquire a firm grasp on the basics of accidence, and the GCSE results in Latin have improved dramatically. Those not continuing the subject to GCSE managed to gain enjoyment from learning about aspects of Roman life and improving their general knowledge about the ancient world. Recruitment to GCSE has also improved, with double the number of pupils opting to take the subject.

My departmental colleagues were also quite willing to take the plunge. Faced with an entirely new way of teaching, and daunted by the risk of something going wrong, such as the site crashing or a power cut (in fact the latter of these has occurred far more frequently than the former), it was decided that we should produce a hard copy of the course. I have created a textbook of the course in PDF format, which each user can download and which I have printed out for each pupil. CyberCaesar has managed to significantly reduce the assessment burden on the department, granting us time to produce other resources to enrich learning. It has also permitted non-specialists to teach the subject, as the feedback generated by the exercises helps colleagues interpret pupil progress more effectively.

I have been very lucky to have worked in two schools that were happy to accommodate my new approaches to teaching and learning. The senior management/leadership teams of both were extremely supportive. I was very grateful to one senior teacher in particular, who provided me with some insightful feedback that helped me develop the course further. We were very pleased to be recognized by ISI in our school inspection report for providing innovative and quality learning. I hope that this has helped to show that our approach highlights the importance of the learning experience over 'busy work'. We don't set homework just for the sake of it; every single task set for homework contributes to a planned development in subject knowledge. As the curriculum gets busier and fuller, it is vital that we ensure that students learn content and skills as effectively as possible.

Success?

The big question is, has this new digital approach to teaching and learning Latin made a difference? In stark analysis based entirely upon public examination results, CyberCaesar has made a huge difference. Results at GCSE have improved considerably since the introduction of the digital course to the curriculum. Between 2012 and 2017, 97 per cent of the students using CyberCaesar to prepare for GCSE achieved the highest A–A* grades, with 84 per cent achieving the highest possible A*. In 2018, 69 per cent achieved Grade 9 in the new GCSE and 85 per cent achieved the highest possible Grades 8–9. Students who have progressed to study A-level Latin after CyberCaesar have continued to perform exceptionally well, achieving A or A* grades at A-level.

Of course, examination results aren't everything. Students have also enjoyed using the course. In a recent survey, 100 per cent of students from the previous GCSE cohort responded that they agreed or strongly agreed with the statement that they 'enjoyed learning Latin with CyberCaesar'. They all also agreed or strongly agreed with the statement that 'CyberCaesar prepared me effectively for Latin GCSE' and that they acquired firm foundations of grammar and vocabulary in taking the course. I've also had several testimonies from current and past students, stating how much they have got from the course. One student said, 'very useful and easy to use . . . Each topic is easily split up and each exercise scales in a good progression which makes it easy to follow and understand. The lessons are very informative with memorable examples used'. Others have been extremely complimentary, from 'I really do think the entire course is wonderful' or 'It's a great website, thanks for creating it', to 'I would, indeed I have recommended it to both the tutors and fellow students'. The feedback that I have received from students shows that they appreciate the effectiveness of the course.

The way forward

CyberCaesar has been a success. Both recruitment and results have improved, teacher workload has dropped and student progress has risen. From my perspective as head of department, it was absolutely vital to ensure that the course entrenched the principles of grammar and syntax rigorously. Students who have taken CyberCaesar are far better prepared for the linguistic demands of A-level study.

However, there is still plenty of scope for further development. Aspects of Roman life are taught through the narratives in the Basic and Intermediate Latin courses, but I would like to create extra resources in this area. I would also like to develop the literature resources of the course and create activities that provide insight into the texts. I have some A-level Latin activities and resources that I need to add, and perhaps I will compose a new course just for this. I would also love to have the time to create a course on ancient Greek. Hosting the website has been an education in itself. Site maintenance can take hours every week. It has taken me the best part of ten years to get the site up to where it is now, following a succession of false starts and backward moves.

Having said that, given the opportunity, I would still do all this again. For me, this has been an amazing journey, and I have learnt much about digital technology, web hosting and computer languages, as well as how to explore and re-evaluate my professional and pedagogical standards and approaches. This has been a process of discovery. Of my many conclusions, the most pertinent one for this chapter is that course development never stops. It is always ongoing. The author of a book can make several revisions, realizing a second or a third edition until the book is abandoned or superseded. An online course can be revised or updated immediately. CyberCaesar has been the most exciting part of my career in teaching and I look forward to developing it further. Any feedback on the site is always welcome.

Notes

1. *Cambridge Latin Course* by the Cambridge School Classics Project (UK 4th Edition, 1998; US 5th Edition, 2015), Cambridge: Cambridge University Press.
2. *Oxford Latin Course* by Balme, M. and Morwood, J. (1996), Oxford: Oxford University Press.
3. *Latin to GCSE* by Cullen, H. and Taylor, J. (2016), London: Bloomsbury Academic.
4. *Disce Latinum* by Marshall, R. (1996).
5. *So You Really Want To Learn Latin* by Oulton, N. (1999), Tenterden: Galore Park.
6. *Imperium* by Morgan, J. (2013), CreateSpace Independent Publishing Platform.
7. *Latin Prose Composition* by North, M. and Hillard, A. (1913, reprinted 2013), London: Bloomsbury Academic.
8. For details, see https://en.wikipedia.org/wiki/Kodak.

References

Anderson, M. (2014), *Perfect ICT Every Lesson*, Carmarthen: Independent Thinking Press.

Bjork, E. and Bjork, R. (2011), *Making Things Hard on Yourself, But in a Good Way: Creating Desirable Difficulties to Enhance Learning*, Los Angeles: UCLA Publications.

Black, P., Harrison, C., Lee, C., Marshall, B. and Wiliam, D. (2003), *Assessment for Learning: Putting it into Practice*, Milton Keyes: Open University Press.

Fullan, M. (2013), *Stratosphere*, Toronto: Pearson Canada.

Hattie, J. (2009), *Visible Learning*, Abingdon: Routledge.

Hughes, J., Thomas R. and Scharber, C. (2006), 'Assessing Technology Integration: The RAT – Replacement, Amplification, and Transformation – Framework'. Available online: http://techedges.org/wp-content/uploads/2015/11/Hughes_ScharberSITE2006.pdf (accessed 11 August 2018).

McGonigal, J. (2011), *Reality is Broken*, Harmondsworth: Penguin.

Mishra, P. and Koehler, M. (2006), 'Technological Pedagogical Content Knowledge: A Framework for Teacher Knowledge', *Teachers College Record*, 108 (6): 1017.

OECD (2015), *Students, Computers and Learning: Making the Connection*, Paris: OECD Publishing.

Picardo, J. (2017), *Using Technology in the Classroom*, London: Bloomsbury.

Puentedura, R. (2013), *SAMR and TPCK: An introduction*.

Raeticus, C. (2011), 'Paul B. Diederich's Basic Vocabulary of Ancient and Medieval Latin'. Available online: http://hiberna-cr.wdfiles.com/local--files/downloads/DBP.pdf (accessed 19 September 2018).

Sumeracki, M. and Weinstein, Y. (n.d.). 'FAQ'. Available online: http://www.learningscientists.org/faq/ (accessed 11 August 2018).

Wheeler, S. [SteveWheeler] (26 August 2011), 'The Institutional VLE Is where Content Goes to Die #eas11' [Tweet]. Available online: https://twitter.com/SteveWheeler/status/107064421716733952 (accessed 19 September 2018).

CHAPTER 7

UNA VITA: EXPLORING THE RELATIONSHIP BETWEEN PLAY, LEARNING SCIENCE AND CULTURAL COMPETENCY

Stephen T. Slota and Kevin Ballestrini

Introduction

Humans, like other perceiving-acting organisms, are unique collections of information with unique understandings of the environment based on unique genes running through unique sets of lived experiences. No two individuals can live the same life, have the same thoughts or engage in the same interactions with their peers. Even experiences we return to at a later time in the same location with the same people doing the same thing are shaped and reshaped by in-between periods during which we explore new ideas and engage in critical reflection (see Shaw and Bransford 1977). We are biological storybooks with pages printed upon by the external world – continuous narratives that tie together existence across the space-time we occupy (something learning scientists Barab and Roth (2006) referred to as a 'life-world'[1]). Each of us is one life, *una vita*, through which questions are asked and ideas are explored to define who we are, where we belong and what story we will ultimately leave behind.

Reality

At first blush, waxing philosophic may seem misplaced in the context of a book about educational technology, but it elevates a pair of very real practical concerns regarding classroom instruction. First, our students fundamentally can't bring the same experiences to their learning that we ourselves once did to ours, nor can we comprehend what it is to be in each of their seats (bringing with them the physical, emotional, psychological and social baggage of their out-of-school lives); and second, much of our students' long-term success (in both career and life) depends on their ability to critically reflect. That makes us, teachers, responsible for (1) facilitating student exposure to multiple points of view by (2) seeking and leveraging opportunities to (figuratively) put students in another person's position, while (3) recognizing the strengths, weaknesses and relative background experiences of each learner and (4) maintaining fidelity to the psychological, emotional and cultural constructs associated with the content and skills to be taught.

This raises two important questions:

1. How does one thread the needle between expert pedagogy, contemporary learning theory, content and (often limited) technological resources while successfully attending to a wide range of student needs (i.e. TPACK: see Mishra and Koehler 2006)?

2. What does real-world implementation of the comprehensive, differentiated, experiential instruction described above look like in practice?

Although there are no one-size-fits-all responses capable of satisfying the demands of every classroom and discipline, we do have a sense for how the education of student *intention* and *attention* contributes to fulfilment of teacher and student instructional goals (i.e. tuning: see Gibson 1966 and 1969). The key lies in crafting a theoretically sound pedagogical foundation using tools that afford open-ended problem-solving, moor students to the overarching learning objectives and create a 'time for telling'[2] (Schwartz and Bransford 1998) – tools like game-based learning and its conceptual predecessor, anchored instruction.

ANCORA

Anchored instruction is a pedagogical method wherein students are presented with a realistic but fictional narrative that serves as a basis for inquiry (Cognition and Technology Group at Vanderbilt (CTGV) 1990, 1993 and 1994). The concept grew out of existing exploration-based approaches to education (e.g. Dewey 1938) and has branched into healthcare, law, finance, engineering, the military and other fields (e.g. Baker 2000, Barrows 1996, Maudsley 1999, Mills and Treagust 2003, Milne and McConnell 2001), all with the same basic goals:

1. To leverage 'generator sets' (i.e. narrative-driven situations) to *tune* student *intention* and *attention* towards invariant elements across varied contexts and experiences (Young et al. 1997).

2. To foster learners' general investigatory skills.

3. To supplement distal and proximal measurements available through direct instruction and high-stakes testing (Hickey and Pellegrino 2005).

These goals are met as teachers facilitate student identification and application of important elements related to ill-defined problems presented by and/or facing character models (Bandura 1972 and 1986). Rather than explicitly telling learners what they are expected to know, the anchor leads them to identify relevant problems and emulate relevant problem-solvers like physicists, mathematicians and biologists – a framework to incorporate prior experiences, apply learned skills and demonstrate problem-solving in richly authentic contexts (Wood 2003). It also encourages them to challenge their understanding of abstract concepts, gets them engaged in metacognitive reflection (leveraging each student's *una vita* to synthesize new and old information) and induces transfer from the classroom environment to the real world via richly authentic stories (CTGV 1990).

Fortunately, technological flexibility in storytelling (i.e. being able to utilize various media to present content) has allowed developers to take multiple paths towards constructing and implementing novel anchors. CTGV (1990) and Bank Street College (Gibbon and Hooper 1986), for instance, utilized video series (*The Adventures of Jasper Woodbury* and *The Voyage of the Mimi*, respectively) to induce inquiry and reflection about concepts like area, volume, compound fractions (e.g. gas prices, $3.98^9/_{10}$), distance/rate/time, simple machines, buoyancy, budgeting and pollution. The team responsible for *Quest Atlantis* (Barab et al. 2005) embedded their narrative in a 3D-rendered virtual world to help learners meet middle-school language arts and science objectives. Some have investigated digital and real-world simulation-based anchors, while others have migrated towards video, analog and text-based roleplaying game-based anchors (see Clark et al. 2016, Gee 2003 and Young et al. 2012).

Around 2009, the rapidly expanding number of new anchored and anchor-like materials led to an intradisciplinary debate over the ways in which narrative and performative anchor activities could and should be discussed, implemented and studied in learning environments (see Young and Slota 2017). In response, Travis (2010) introduced the phrase 'performative play practice' (later 'practomime') to describe 'playing pretend in a context where everyone agrees that playing pretend is what you do' (Travis 2010). Because practomime emphasizes particular individuals attempting to achieve particular performative goals (from a passionate peewee football coach channeling Tom Landry to a constituent giving a *Mr Smith Goes to Washington*-esque speech at a town hall meeting), and has logical extensions to activities like traditional schooling (where there are well-defined rules, goals, scoring criteria and end states with ample opportunities for playful performance), it has had important implications for the development of games and other anchor activities in both formal and informal educational settings.

Those implications (with respect to Classics education) are outlined below.

Connecting practomime and classes

Contemporary educational and linguistic research has led to a shift from grammar-based, sequential models of instruction towards models that both encourage and require sustained comprehensible input. This puts classicists in a strange position: the field has traditionally been treated as separate from modern languages, but updates to the standards have created an immediate and legitimate need to develop and implement new opportunities for students to demonstrate intercultural competency as part of their language coursework (American Council on the Teaching of Foreign Languages (ACTFL) 2017).

Thankfully, because classics content is steeped in myth, history and life in the ancient world, there has not been a persistent problem in fulfilling the 'investigation' strand of the cultures standard. There have, however, been issues in developing pedagogical tools capable of fostering richly authentic interactions between students and the cultures they are studying (e.g. ACTFL intercultural competency tool; see ACTFL 2016). Interactions with text are unidirectional by design, with no mechanism for learners to follow up on authorial intent or original context (see Bruner 1991, Gee 2004, 2010 and Slota 2014). There is also no opportunity to explore relevant situations as a means of demonstrating knowledge and application of behaviours and cultural norms – we lack everyday ancient Roman contexts to engage with, which is especially problematic when Latin educators are compared to their modern language peers.

So, given that we cannot travel back in time and space to live in the ancient world, how can we redefine what it means to interact with extinct cultures? Is it possible to create a facsimile of history that is grounded in authenticity but built with enough flexibility to allow self-direction and exploration? Can storytelling afford opportunities to investigate a culture while simultaneously belonging to the culture being investigated? Not only are these questions answerable, but their answers have roots in Rome.

Operation LAPIS

Here, we present an example of practomime in action: *Operation LAPIS*, a multi-year, text-based, alternate reality/role-playing game for Latin cultural and language education (see Slota et al. 2013).

Across 174 narrative missions, students work in collaborative teams to control an assigned Roman persona. That persona is used to weave learners through Roman history's greatest moments via the 'TSTT-interface' – a sophisticated simulation cleverly disguised as part of an existing online social media service (instructors utilize a wide selection of tools, ranging from simple bulletin board services like phpBB forums to Google Classroom or Edmodo).

Each 'episode' of *Operation LAPIS* (akin to an episodic television show) arrives in a text-based post framed as a 'TSTT immersion session' (i.e. a new piece of the narrative and a prompt to which each team's Roman must respond). Students are tasked with reading a portion of the overarching narrative (which includes predominately comprehensible Latin in addition to some embedded English) and conducting relevant background research (via information organized into a 'culturalia' section of the 'codex', much like a codex in a standard-issue, text-based role-playing game). To take an action, students must collaborate with their teammates to decide which thoughts their character should express and which behaviours they should perform inside the virtual world. Once the first act is complete, the story branches outward and the student operatives are afforded agency to direct their learning (we refer to this as a 'sandbox on rails', where students progress along a conveyor belt rail system of 1:1-aligned game and learning objectives while constructing meaning in a self-directed, inquiry-driven content sandbox).

It is not a coincidence that *Operation LAPIS* was designed as an interactive adventure. Drawing on the tenets of situated cognition and epistemology (i.e. 'knowledge as doing'; see Brown et al. 1989), it necessitates collaborative performance as a means of demonstrating learning – that is, learners work together to apply content and solve novel problems. Whereas traditional textbooks leverage linear storytelling to engage Latin learners, practomimetic curricula like *Operation LAPIS* direct them towards playful interaction and promote the integration of play-performance with their other developing skills related to the World-Readiness Standards. It is Latin as experiential, constructivist, problem based and anchored – language and culture education through a merger of real-world experiences (the students' respective *una vita*) and those of individuals from an entirely different time and place.

This culture-focused, student-centred backbone allows *Operation LAPIS* to emphasize traditional introductory Latin while offering a foundation for exploration outside the primary narrative. Within each codex are four separate sections tuned to different aspects of language learning, including: (1) a *grammatica* section that details concepts as they are introduced in the immersions; (2) *verba* for glosses of unfamiliar vocabulary in the immersions; (3) *key texts* for additional comprehensible reading material; and (4) *attunement exercises* that facilitate practice of particular Latin skills. Rather than serving as a sole instructional source that unidirectionally dictates learning, the codex flips the role of the textbook by acting as a supplement students can leverage to overcome challenges in the narrative anchor.

Perhaps the best illustration of the pracomimetic merger of storytelling and scholastic content comes when student players are introduced to one of the most popular residents of Pompeii, Lucius Caecilius Iucundus, and are tasked with fulfilling a deceivingly simple prompt: 'Dine like a Roman.'

To tell the story of their character avatars dining like Romans, students must construct an understanding of a typical Roman *cena* (dinner) and the relevant activities that might be a part of it. This includes reading the immersion prompt (in Latin), reviewing an additional key text (in Latin, which contains a wealth of opportunities for building informational reading skills) and applying prior learning about *domus Romana*, including locations of particular rooms and what function they served. There is also embedded information about Roman foods, and students are provided with a fictional story about a separate Roman *cena* (i.e. part of the anchor's generator set). Nowhere in the list of activities above (or in the background knowledge required) is the typical driver of curricular materials in a traditional Latin course, a grammatical syllabus, and that's completely by design. In a course where narrative is the primary mechanism for engagement and induction of transfer, comprehensible input helps students internalize the syntax and grammatical rules of Latin as part of their self-directed learning. One of the markers that a particular student has begun to internalize the grammar comes when, in the course of writing their collaborative contributions of the story, they ask questions about *why* an event or action occurred.

Collaborative storytelling and problem solving continue as the student groups compose short sentences describing their avatars' actions in a second highly interactive mission that occurs shortly after the Roman dinner. To construct knowledge of a typical Roman *villa*, the students are tasked with navigating the home of their main adversary, Marcus Maecenas, and avoiding his guards as they search for a hidden scroll.

The mission begins with a text-based prompt akin to every other *Operation LAPIS* immersion (Figure 7.1), but unlike other immersions, each student group has the opportunity to direct several single-action turns through which their avatar moves from room to room within the villa. Just one month after beginning formal instruction, the students find themselves

---

(2.3.b)

Vīlla of Marcus Maecēnās, Pompēiī, 79

tū in ātrium intrās. tū larārium dextrā vidēs. larārium est malīgnum. tū quoque lectum geniāle vidēs. ātrium est dēsertum. clāmōrem ē peristyliō in trīclīniō audīs.

compluvium est in mediā ātriī. multa aqua est in compluviō. luna per impluvium lucet (shines).

Prompt: find the volūmen in vīllā of M. Maecēnās. You are free to explore any area of the house that you wish, but be on the lookout for Marcus and his guards.

	villa marci - 7a
	Google Drawings
	CODEX - 2.3
	http://lapis.practomime.com/index.php/104-hud023
	episode 2.3.b
	http://lapis.practomime.com/index.php/760-ep023b

Figure 7.1 *Operation LAPIS villa* prompt. © K. Ballestrini and S. Slota.

composing short sentences (mostly grammatically correct) at the upper portions of the Novice proficiency level. Beyond the intentional repetition of particular words and phrases, a major contributor to their success is the fact that there is an immediate and achievable goal (i.e. successfully completing the mission) coupled with increased engagement (e.g. tension of avoiding the guards, extrinsic character rewards in the form of loot, a novel turn-based experience, etc.).

In the following example, these factors intersect as the instructor interacts with a trio of separate student groups (each controlling one in-game character avatar, student responses unedited):

Group 1 [G1]: Clodia ad cellam ambulat clam et volumen quaerit.
Teacher [T]: Clodia ad cellam ambulat sed spectat custodem prope tablinum et culinam. Clodia manet et tunc custos ad pedes videt. Clodia clam intrat cellam. in cellā sunt multae urnae et lectum parvum. aliquid nitidum lucet sub lecto.
Group 2 [G2]: Horatiana ambulat clam ad cubiculum et circumspectat.
T: Horatiana ad cubiculum ambulat et circumspectat. in cubiculo est lectus. tunica et toga in lecto iacent. cista quoque est in cubiculo. cista est clausa. clavem non habes. aliquid nitidum sub lecto celat.
Group 3 [G3]: Agricola intrat ad cubiculam, et quaerit clavicula.
T: Agricola cum Horatianā stat in cubiculo et quaerit clavem. Agricola clavem non invenit sed sub lectō, Agricola invenit togam fulvam! Agricola capit togam et in sacco ponit.
G1: Clodia circumspectat sub lecto et capit aliquid nitidum.
T: Clodia quaerit sub lectō et capit aliquid nitidum. est monile aeneum! Clodia monile capit et in suō sacco ponit.
G2: Horatiana ambulat clam ad Lectus Genialis, et quareit.
T: Horatiana e cubiculo in atrium ambulat. Horatiana ad lectum genialem ambulat et inspicit. lectus genialis est in atrio. lectus est ligneus et imaginem Iunonis habet. litterae 'SP' in lecto sunt. stragulum in lecto iacet. aliquid nitidum sub pulvīnō cēlat.
G3: Agricola ambulat clam ad peristylum et celat post fons. Agricola circumspectat.
T: Agricola ad peristylium clam ambulat et prope fontem se celat. luna in peristylio lucet. via est in medio peristylio. frutex in via est. lumen e triclinio venit. clamor e triclinio venit. custos in ianua stat. custos Agricolam non videt. aliquid nitidum prope fruiticum latet.

The back-and-forth continues for another fifty exchanges until, ultimately, the young Romans discover the scroll they seek inside the *tablinum*. Rather than simply memorizing the various rooms and their functions, the students have – conceptually, at least – sneaked through and interacted with a variety of spaces and objects that might have been ignored as part of a traditional vocabulary list. Moreover, because the encounter is text-based rather than digital, individual students have been given a chance to flex their imaginations in service of peer engagement, goal adoption and authentic co-authorship.

While not all immersions offer the same leeway for action, the same opportunities for intercultural analysis do emerge as part of the build-up to each immersion prompt response. At every turn, practomimetic activities and the associated narrative invite students to compare, contrast and critically examine cultures and ideas that differ from their own; this takes on a spiral structure that informs progressively more complex cultural content as the story unfolds, recurring across immersions in different residential spaces, other *cenae* and varied social situations (e.g. a recital by Publius Vergilius Maro). The immersions reach a climax when students (role-playing as their Roman avatars) are confronted with a cumulative, 'boss fight'-like challenge (e.g. standing among a tribe in northern Britannia, where the 'Dine like a Roman' prompt recurs in the form of a secondary, more challenging prompt, 'Dine like the Brigantes'), which (1) forces them to critically examine culture through both ancient Roman and twenty-first-century adolescent lenses, and (2) engage in self-reflection on perspective, historical context and what it is to be a good citizen.

There are, of course, helpful narrative elements used to tackle difficult concepts in traditional textbook series – for instance, the treatment of conquered peoples through the process of Romanization – but it is something else entirely to immerse learners in those events so they can learn culture by *doing* culture. The ability to stand on the Roman frontier and wrestle with the consequences of their decisions exemplifies how practomime fosters students' exploration of multiple possibilities, strategies and interpretations of events without real-world consequences (i.e. safe failure; see Wagner 2012). This extends to a variety of historically important moments: how would a Roman soldier react on the battlefield at Cannae when Hannibal sprung his trap? What might it have felt like to be a member of Caesar's Thirteenth when crossing into Italia and committing an act of treason against your country?

All practomimetic experiences in *Operation LAPIS* are linked through a common thread of language, culture and history in the form of the *Lapis Saeculorum*. A fictitious object, the *Lapis* serves as a metaphor for the persistent struggle between the forces of conservatism, populism and the lust for power (which defined much of the late Republic and Empire). In focusing on 79–82 CE, the students learn that the *Lapis* isn't real but immediately receive a consolation prize: looking up in the vault of the Arch of Titus, gazing upon the apotheosis on the keystone and realizing that it, in a way, is a perfect stand-in for what the *Lapis* represents. The Arch, glorifying the Roman sack of Jerusalem, deifies the individual responsible for quelling a rebellion of a people seeking to cast off the effects of Romanization; depicts the transfer of loot from the temple to Rome, where it likely funded the construction of a monstrous structure looming in the corner of your eye; and highlights the effects of leveraging the most extreme elements of populism to consolidate and solidify power. In reaching this point, the students achieve a combination of scholastic success and self-actualization – a blend of ancient and modern *vitae* to create a more informed, thoughtful and reflective learner.

Empirical data has not yet been collected and analysed for *Operation LAPIS* specifically, but pilot studies using similar practomimetic tools show promise (especially as pertaining to TPACK integration; see Slota 2014), and informal tracking data from in-house implementations provide anecdotal evidence that as intercultural competency builds, so too does language acquisition. Between 2011 and 2018, roughly 70 per cent of students who completed their first year of *Operation LAPIS* as part of a primary cohort (that is, a cohort led by one of *Operation LAPIS*'s project originators) scored at the Intermediate level on the ACTFL Latin Reading Interpretive Assessment. By the end of their second year (the approximate end of *Operation LAPIS* content), more than 85 per cent tested at the Intermediate level. That foundation eventually yielded additional success: among students who completed two more years of Latin (i.e. four years in total), 30 per cent scored in the Advanced range, and every student who opted into the Latin Advanced Placement Exam scored a three or above.

Taken together, these outcomes indicate that, at worst, practomimetic Latin instruction (as implemented by a project originator) generates the same outcomes as traditional Latin instruction, and, at best, may actually improve overall student engagement and/or induce the adoption of goals aligned to instructional standards. Whether approaching instruction from a grammar-translation perspective or one rooted in the principles of second-language acquisition theory, we believe the potential benefits warrant a more comprehensive, longitudinal study of practomime's effects on achievement, engagement, creative problem-solving and transfer.

Conclusion

Repeat opportunities to engage in richly authentic and varied simulation experiences provide students with the means to critically reflect on their past and present selves in the context of both history and the contemporary classroom environment. Pedagogical tools like *Operation LAPIS* and, more broadly, anchored instruction can help make such opportunities more widely available to our students and promote the incorporation of critical thinking, group coordination, responsiveness, reflection and intercultural competency as explicit instructional goals. After several years of successful small-scale implementation, we encourage the continued development, implementation and propagation of practomimes like *Operation LAPIS* in hopes of positively expanding our student's respective *una vita* and, ultimately, improving the quality of instruction writ large.

Notes

1. Barab and Roth (2006) defined a life-world as 'the environment for an individual described in terms of the customary ways of structuring the activities that take place within it … [it] contains those objects and (social and material) phenomena that are salient to the acting individual in part because of her current goals and intentions and in part because of her having the requisite effectivity sets. Whereas two people can share a physical space, it is a rare case indeed for two people to share a life-world' (Barab and Roth 2006: 4).

2. A time for telling, as defined by Schwartz and Bransford is the point at which learners '[notice] the distinctions between contrasting cases' and 'are prepared to be told the significance of the distinctions they have discovered' (Schwartz and Bransford 1998: 475).

References

American Council on the Teaching of Foreign Languages (ACTFL) (2016), *NCSSFL-ACTFL Intercultural Reflection Tool*. Available online: https://www.actfl.org/sites/default/files/CanDos/Intercultural%20Can-Dos_Reflections%20Scenarios.pdf (accessed 23 September 2018).

American Council on the Teaching of Foreign Languages (ACTFL) (2017), *NCSSFL-ACTFL Can-Do Statements*. Available online: https://www.actfl.org/publications/guidelines-and-manuals/ncssfl-actfl-can-do-statements (accessed 23 September 2018).

Baker, C. (2000), 'Using Problem-based Learning to Redesign Nursing Administration Masters Programs', *Journal of Nursing Administration*, 30 (1): 41–47.

Bandura, A. (1972), 'Modeling Theory: Some Traditions, Trends, and Disputes', in R.D. Parke, *Recent Trends in Social Learning Theory*, New York: Academic Press, Inc.

Bandura, A. (1986), *Social Foundations of Thought and Action: A Social Cognitive Theory*, New York: Prentice-Hall, Inc.

Barab, S., Thomas, M., Dodge, T., Carteaux, R. and Tuzun, H. (2005), 'Making Learning Fun: Quest Atlantis, a Game Without Guns', *Educational Technology Research and Development*, 53 (1): 86–108.

Barrows, H. (1996), 'Problem-based Learning in Medicine and Beyond: A Brief Overview', *New Directions for Teaching and Learning*, (68): 3–12.

Brown, J., Collins, A. and Duguid, P. (1989), 'Situated Cognition and the Culture of Learning', *Educational Researcher*, 18 (1): 32–42.

Bruner, J. (1991). 'The Narrative Construction of Reality', *Critical Inquiry*, 18 (1): 1–21.

Clark, D., Tanner-Smith, E. and Killingsworth, S. (2016), 'Digital Games, Design, and Learning: A Systematic Review and Meta-analysis', *Review of Educational Research*, 86 (1): 79–122.

Cognition and Technology Group at Vanderbilt (1990), 'Anchored Instruction and Its Relationship to Situated Cognition', *Educational Research*, 19 (6): 2–10.

Cognition and Technology Group at Vanderbilt (1993), 'Anchored Instruction and Situated Cognition Revisited', *Educational Technology*, March Issue: 52–70.

Cognition and Technology Group at Vanderbilt (1994), 'From Visual Word Problems to Learning Communities: Changing Conceptions of Cognitive Research', in K. McGilly (ed.), *Classroom Lessons: Integrating Cognitive Theory and Classroom Practice*, Cambridge MA: MIT Press.

Dewey, J. (1938), *Experience and Education*, New York: Macmillan.

Gee, J. (2003), *What Video Games Have to Teach Us About Learning and Literacy*, New York, NY: St. Martin's Griffin.

Gee, J. (2004), 'Learning by Design: Games as Learning Machines', *Interactive Educational Multimedia*, 8: 15–23.

Gee, J. (2010), 'A Situated-Sociocultural Approach to Literacy and Technology', in E. Baker (ed.), *The New Literacies: Multiple Perspectives on Research and Practice*, New York, NY: Guilford Press, 165–193.

Gibbon, S. and Hooper, K. (1986), 'The Voyage of the MIMI', *Learning Tomorrow. Journal of the Apple Education Advisory Council*, 3: 195–207. Available online: https://www.learntechlib.org/p/140364/ (accessed July 10 2018).

Gibson, E. (1969), *Principles of Perceptual Learning and Development*, New York: Appleton-Century-Crofts.

Gibson, J. (1966), *The Senses Considered as Perceptual Systems*, Boston: Houghton Mifflin.

Hickey, D. and Pellegrino, J. (2005), 'Theory, Level, and Function: Three Dimensions for Understanding Transfer and Student Assessment', in J. Mestre (ed.), *Transfer of Learning from a Modern Multidisciplinary Perspective*, Greenwich, CT: Information Age Publishers, 251–293.

Maudsley, G. (1999), 'Roles and Responsibilities of the Problem-based Learning Tutor in the Undergraduate Medical Curriculum', *British Medical Journal*, 318: 657.

Mills, J. and Treagust, D. (2003), 'Engineering Education: Is Problem-based or Project-based Learning the Answer?', *Australasian Journal of Engineering Education*, 3: 2–16.

Milne, M. and McConnell, P. (2001), 'Problem-based Learning: A Pedagogy for Using Case Material in Accounting Education', *Accounting Education: An International Journal*, 10 (1): 61–82.

Mishra, P. and Koehler, M. (2006), 'Technological Pedagogical Content Knowledge: A Framework for Teacher Knowledge', *Teachers College Record*, 108 (6): 1017–1054.

Schwartz, D. and Bransford, J. (1998), 'A Time for Telling', *Cognition & Instruction*, 16 (4): 475–522.

Shaw, R. and Bransford, J. (eds.) (1977), *Perceiving, Acting, and Knowing: Toward an Ecological Psychology*, Mahwah, NJ: Lawrence Erlbaum Associates.

Slota, S. (2014). 'Project TECHNOLOGIA: A Game-based Approach to Understanding Situated Intentionality'. Doctoral diss. Available online: https://opencommons.uconn.edu/cgi/viewcontent.cgi?referer=https://www.google.com/&httpsredir=1&article=6826&context=dissertations (accessed 23 September 2018).

Slota, S., Ballestrini, K. and Pearsall, M. (2013), 'Learning Through Operation LAPIS: A Game-based Approach to the Latin Classroom', *The Language Educator*, American Council on the Teaching of

Foreign Languages. Available online: http://www.practomime.com/pdf/tle_art.pdf (accessed 23 September 2018).

Travis, R. (2010), 'A Note on the Word "Practomime"', *Living Epic*. Available online: http://livingepic.blogspot.com/2010/01/note-on-word-practomime.html (accessed 12 July 2018).

Wagner, T. (2012), *Creating Innovators: The Making of Young People Who Will Change the World*, New York, NY: Scribner Publishing.

Wood, D. (2003), 'ABC of Learning and Teaching in Medicine: Problem-based Learning', *British Medical Journal*, 326.

Young, M., Kulikowich, J. and Barab, S. (1997), 'The Unit of Analysis for Situated Assessment', *Instructional Science*, 25(2): 133–150.

Young, M. and Slota, S. (2017), *Exploding the Castle: Rethinking How Video Games & Game Mechanics Can Shape the Future of Education*, Charlotte, NC: Information Age Publishing.

Young, M., Slota, S., Cutter, A., Jalette, G., Mullin, G., Lai, B., Simeoni, Z., Tran, M. and Yukhymenko, M. (2012), 'Our Princess Is in Another Castle: A Review of Trends in Serious Gaming for Education', *Review of Educational Research*, 82 (1): 61–89.

PART II
CLASSICS WITHOUT LANGUAGE: LITERATURE, CULTURE AND OUTREACH MODELS

CHAPTER 8
USING VIRTUAL LEARNING ENVIRONMENTS FOR CLASSICS OUTREACH
Emma Searle

Introduction

This chapter discusses the use of virtual learning environments (VLEs) to facilitate and maximize the effectiveness of student learning during long-term academic enrichment programmes, which provide opportunities to study the ancient world to school students who would otherwise be unable to do so. It focuses on the OxLAT Latin Teaching Scheme, which is one part of the broader outreach programme of the Faculty of Classics at the University of Oxford and lasts for two and a half years for each cohort, but most of the methods discussed will also be suitable for shorter-term outreach and enrichment programmes. Using the scheme's 'Online Learning Support Hub' as a case study, this chapter also demonstrates the ways in which a VLE supports the use of other digital technologies in Latin teaching and why these are particularly useful and effective in the outreach context.

Classics outreach: the state of things

'Outreach' is a general term used by many universities for all activities targeted at school students from 'non-traditional' backgrounds – the contemporary term for those who have not had the privilege of a private or other exclusive (i.e. selective) education, and are women, people with disabilities or people from socio-economic or ethno-cultural backgrounds that are historically under-represented at university level[1] – with the aim of widening access and increasing participation amongst those who have previously been largely excluded from higher education (HE) in the UK.[2] The Office for Fair Access (OFFA), the independent public body set up under New Labour's Higher Education Act (2004) to monitor and regulate 'fair access' to higher education in England, is tasked with ensuring that universities which charge 'top-up' tuition fees (currently up to a maximum of £9,250 per annum for undergraduate courses) are demonstrably working to increase participation among under-represented groups and are spending a proportion of those fees on initiatives to safeguard and facilitate equitable access to higher education through outreach work and on-course financial support.[3] Universities set their own targets in an 'access agreement', but these must be approved by OFFA, and the Director of Fair Access to Higher Education has the power to prevent any HE institution from charging fees above the basic level (currently £6,165 per annum for full-time undergraduate courses) if it cannot satisfy the regulator that it is making adequate provision.[4]

Over the past fifteen years the colleges and departments of the University of Oxford have offered numerous different kinds of events and activities, such as subject taster sessions, study days and workshops for schools, other one-off, subject-specific events, open days and summer schools (such as the highly successful UNIQ programme), often developed in response to feedback from secondary schools and sixth-form colleges, in order to support and encourage applications from students from the 'non-traditional' backgrounds outlined above. This variety and flexibility was, to a certain extent, a good thing and was successful in informing these students (and their teachers) about Oxford and about higher education in general, 'demystifying' the admissions process, providing opportunities to visit the university, developing an understanding of what it might be like to study here and encouraging all to consider applying. Our collective efforts have contributed to increasing inclusivity and diversity over the fifteen-year period (although there is of course much, much more to be done).[5]

As such, outreach work generally inspires warm-and-fuzzy sentiments in those with a social conscience. But (and there is always a but) there can also be the assumption that outreach activities, in and of themselves, are uniformly a good thing and make substantive contributions to achieving the desired outcome of a more inclusive and diverse academic community and graduate demographic, which is an assumption simply not supported by the evidence. Additionally, changes to HE organization, support and funding initiated by the Conservative/Liberal Democrat coalition government since 2010, as well as the detrimental impact of their financial and education policies on social mobility more broadly, have resulted in this reactive approach becoming a much less effective method of discharging our social responsibility. Research conducted by the Sutton Trust indicates that no outreach event constitutes a meaningful 'intervention' by itself alone: the provision of focused and sustained long-term academic enrichment schemes is crucial if universities are to achieve their widening participation aims (Sutton Trust 2008 and 2015). This conclusion and recommendation is particularly relevant to the outreach activities of university Classics and/or History and Archaeology departments (and Classics organizations more broadly). The introduction of the National Curriculum in the 1988 Education Reform Act (Department of Education 1988) dramatically reduced the number of school hours available for teaching classical subjects and categorized them as non-compulsory, causing a steady decline in the number of exam entries for Latin at GCSE/Level 2 and a shortage of Classics-trained teachers during the following two decades (Hunt 2012, Partington 2011b). After changes to make the OCR GCSE examine and recognize a more comprehensive, broader ability range so that non-selective schools could offer Latin to all their students, the number of exam entries started to increase in 2011, and by 2014 were higher than they had been in seventeen years (CSCP 2015: 7, Partington 2011a).[6] However, the high volume of content in the OCR qualification remains difficult to accommodate in the restricted timetable of the average school, particularly non-selective state schools, because the average number of teaching hours made available by schools that *were* using it was an enormous 342 hours (CSCP 2015: 14–15, 19, Stephenson 2014), far outsripping the DfE's recommended number of 120–140 guided teaching hours for a GCSE qualification (CSCP 2015: 17). Some independent schools were even allocating in excess of 400 hours' teaching time, something very few state schools would be able to do. Therefore, it remains the case that only a small proportion of students in the maintained sector has the opportunity to study the ancient world at school, and their students are thus statistically less likely to consider ancient world studies courses at degree level, a factor which results in in a disproportionate number of applications from the private sector (Lovatt 2011, Searle 2018). If a subject or area of study is not something students are introduced to as a matter of course, they are potentially denied an option for the future, an outlook on life that they might be interested in, and (particularly with Latin) the opportunity to improve their overall linguistic abilities.

Fortunately, the Faculty of Classics at Oxford recognized the need for specific objectives (and substantive, critical analysis of what the most efficient ways of achieving those outcomes might be) relatively early in the onset of the 'outreachocene' and had the necessary financial resources to establish an outreach programme in 2004 (Sandis 2009). From its inception, the aim has been less about 'raising aspirations' than recognizing and addressing the endemic structural inequality, inequity and forms of oppression in our society which deprive some of the opportunities that others take for granted, and much more about breaking the link between educational opportunities and family background so that all young people are provided with the opportunity to fulfill their potential, regardless of their background, school or where they live. 'Raising aspirations' is a patronizing and condescending phrase which elides the underlying reasons for the issues which OFFA is trying to redress (it is so much easier to attribute the relative homogeneity of HE student bodies to an individual's personal 'failing', i.e. low aspirations. Students from poor and/or black or minority ethnic (BME) backgrounds are typically just as 'aspirational', if not more so, as their more privileged counterparts; they are often simply denied the opportunities (with the right support) to realize their aspirations and so they mitigate their aspirations in the face of likely disappointment. It is not enough for outreach teams to arrive in a school, enthuse about higher education, but not provide any means to achieve it. Instead, effective outreach work requires long-term, ongoing engagement and support, the resources and opportunities for students to raise their attainment and broaden their experiences, and the reassurance that they are very much welcome and encouraged to apply regardless of whether they consider themselves to fit the perceived 'Oxford student' stereotype propagated by the media.

Overview of the OxLAT scheme

The changes to education and examinations undertaken by Michael Gove, the secretary of state for education under the Conservative/Liberal Democrat coalition government (2010–14), and continued by his successors, have made it more difficult for underfunded and under-resourced state schools to offer any classical subjects, particularly the language-based ones of Latin and Classical Greek (Hunt 2018). So although there has been an increase in the provision of Latin in the state sector, the vast majority of maintained schools are still prevented from offering it due to funding crises caused by the severe cuts to their financial resources, and a chronic shortage of staff with relevant expertise or training. With only a few notable exceptions, this is the case for nearly all state schools in Oxfordshire and its surrounding areas. Therefore, the Faculty of Classics resolved to provide free tuition in Latin language and literature *ab initio* through to GCSE examination for selected students in Years 8 and 9 (twelve- to fourteen-year-olds) attending state schools in the Oxfordshire area that have no Latin provision. The Latin Teaching Scheme started in January 2008, with the first cohort of students taking their Latin GCSE in the summer of 2010; the second cohort began in January 2010 and took their exams in the summer of 2012. Results were promising (a majority of B and C grades, with a couple of As and A*s) and several participants progressed to study Classics both here and elsewhere at undergraduate level. Due to a funding shortfall, the faculty was not able to run the scheme for a 2012–14 cohort, but in 2014, thanks to a generous grant from the Stonehouse Educational Foundation, the faculty was able to relaunch the scheme. The most recent cohort (comprising twenty-five students from fifteen schools across Oxfordshire, Berkshire and Buckinghamshire) started in January 2015 and sat their GCSE examinations in June 2017. Despite the intensity of the work, this cohort achieved absolutely stellar results: fifteen A*s, four As, two Bs and one C (not all students elected to sit the exam in the end).

This marked increase in the number of high-end grades achieved can be attributed to a more formal approach to organization and teaching (including dedicated members of staff to oversee and deliver the scheme) and the adoption of more sophisticated pedagogical tools and materials beyond the 'traditional' textbook-based approach used in previous iterations of the scheme. Lessons take place on Saturday mornings in the faculty building and are taught by two professional Latin teachers (both of whom have PGCEs in Classics and have taught in secondary schools), using the new OCR specification-specific course book *Latin to GCSE* (Taylor and Cullen 2016). The two teachers are overseen and assisted by the scheme coordinator, who fulfills the function of teaching assistant as well as undertaking communication with schools and parents/carers and other administrative duties. Essentially the scheme replicates the teaching that students would experience were they taking the subject as a GCSE option at school: the lessons are scheduled during Oxfordshire schools' term times, so we are able to provide students with a routine and learning structure that is similar to what they experience at school, albeit a more intensive and demanding one; and they are expected to consolidate their learning in class and prepare for lessons with appropriate independent study time at home each week (their amount of homework being slightly more than one would expect for any other GCSE subject). We are, however, still restricted to a radically reduced number of face-to-face teaching hours than that afforded by an in-school timetabled course. Although still more than the DfE's recommended 120–140 hours for a GCSE qualification, the 2015–17 cohort had ninety-two lessons scheduled over the two-and-a-half-year duration of the course, which resulted in roughly 184 hours of contact teaching time (each lesson being two-and-a-half hours long with a twenty-minute break).

The OxLAT Online Learning Support Hub

Analysis of the previous iterations of the scheme highlighted issues with communication and the availability of resources, and this analysis prompted a strategic reconsideration of how the students' learning could be better supported and improved. Specifically, we needed to ensure maximum efficiency and effective use of face-to-face teaching hours, a quick and efficient turnaround time between homework submission and marking, a swift method of distributing learning materials to those who may have missed lessons, and a means for students to independently progress in their learning outside of class hours. We therefore wanted some form of centralized system for storing and distributing classroom materials, setting and receiving homework, and providing access to other forms of learning materials for students' use at home.

Informed by the design and functions of other online learning tools (most schools have some form of VLE to facilitate sharing of resources and information to students and parents), we created a subsite for the Faculty of Classics area of the university's current VLE, WebLearn, and developed the OxLAT Online Learning Support Hub, which students on the scheme are able to access through their own WebLearn user accounts. The OxLAT VLE which we produced has four key functions: (1) hosting and sharing materials which help students to prepare for forthcoming classwork and the introduction of new topics, and to consolidate material and topics previously covered in class, as well as hosting supporting materials and revision resources for individual GCSE papers; (2) setting online vocab quizzes and language manipulation exercises, etc. and providing marks and feedback for students instantaneously; (3) allowing students to (re)view details of each week's homework and to upload their completed work to the system; and (4) providing a lesson plan/details of the material covered in each class, along with links to download any relevant worksheets (.pdf and .docx format). We are also able to host information about and links to other online resources, such as educational videos and podcasts on a variety of third-party platforms (e.g. OxPLORE (https:// oxplore.org) and YouTube), which are particularly popular and have helped draw students' attention to other aspects of ancient world studies beyond the study of Latin.

Blended Latin learning: consolidating classwork, and flipped learning

The OxLAT VLE has been integral in developing and delivering a 'blended learning' or 'mixed-mode instruction' method which works well and ameliorates some of the difficulties posed by teaching Latin *ab initio* to GCSE in such a tight timeframe: students work face to face with the language instructors on Saturday mornings and independently during the rest of the week by using the VLE. The system can help consolidate learning by presenting content taught in class in different formats which accommodate a range of learning styles. Links to instructional videos and podcasts are particularly useful since they allow students to (re)visit appropriate visual and audio content which covers key grammar points (e.g. cases, indirect statements, expressions of time), both during the initial acquisition period and during later revision. The VLE also supports the adoption of 'flipped classroom' learning, in order to maximize the efficiency of contact time with students by delivering learning activities electronically prior to class sessions (see Chapter 1 in this volume). We have used the VLE to post initial reading material, images and introductory videos, as well as links to audio-visual content elsewhere on the internet associated with forthcoming sessions. Such videos and audio files can be used to introduce new constructions, tenses and cases and provide students with a preliminary understanding that can be built up during face-to-face teaching time. It should be noted, however, that this method was only introduced after the students had experienced the language sufficiently to build up the cognitive schemata necessary to be able to successfully interpret the instructional videos in an independent setting.[7] Students are able to highlight any aspects of these preparatory materials which they did not understand using the VLE, and these responses can be viewed by the teachers before classes begin and addressed anonymously during the lesson. The VLE has also allowed us to host our own video and audio files, such as readings of the set texts by colleagues and graduate students, which have been very useful in helping students memorize passages from the *Aeneid* and experience and appreciate the aural effect of Virgil's Latin when it is spoken aloud.

The VLE has also expanded the use of digital technology in the classroom by our tutors. One aspect of the VLE which has been particularly successful is its facilitation of easy collation of and access to materials and resources used in class on the faculty's interactive whiteboards. Work on set texts can be saved, uploaded to the relevant section of the VLE and shared with students instantaneously. Running translations and annotations of the prescribed lines from

Virgil's *Aeneid,* Tacitus's *Annales* and Caesar's *Bellum Gallicum* are produced collaboratively by students in class and can be copied and disseminated through the VLE, and can also be reused in subsequent lessons and edited/reconfigured. Although classroom discussion remains the key to developing students' understanding of textual analysis and criticism, the collective construction of a running translation and commentary as a group helps broaden and deepen classroom dialogue. Teaching students *how* to think about the subject matter is as important as teaching them *what* the subject matter is, and the process of producing annotations/commentary during class discussion, which is created synchronously on the interactive whiteboard, achieves this. This method of working through the set texts has had particular benefits: engagement with and focus on the text is maintained throughout the lesson as the annotated text on screen is the object of joint reference; the process allows for a much more detailed and precise interrogation of the text than would otherwise be achieved by oral means alone; and the teacher and students work together and each class member's contribution is visualized as well as vocalized as it is added to the document on screen. This is effectively a visualization of the collective classroom experience, wherein the discursive element is transformed into a 'physical' visual element that can also be replicated kinaesthetically by students as they write their own annotations in their hard-copy workbooks, organizing their notes in whatever way best suits their learning style.[8] Crucially, this method of 'documenting' the class discussion allows any absent student(s) to see what was covered in the missed lesson and helps the teacher and classmates recap what they discussed. It is, however, crucial to pay close attention to the manner in which annotations are made: ensuring consistency of approach in colour, line and shape is important.

Reinforcing vocabulary and accidence learning

The use of the OxLAT VLE has also worked very well with the use of specific digital resources for supplementing the learning of Latin. One issue, which seems prevalent amongst those learning Latin, is difficulty memorizing a large amount of vocabulary and accidence. As other subjects no longer expect students to memorize information, it seems to have become the sole responsibility of language teachers to help students understand and develop the techniques necessary to cement information in their long-term memory. Students are simply not used to having to memorize large amounts of information. Here, digital resources are very useful, particularly for augmenting audio and visual memorization techniques. By using the WebLearn VLE system it is possible to create short multiple-choice quizzes and grammar exercises to assess how well students understand how to form cases and tenses, forms of pronouns and pronominal adjectives, infinitives and subjunctives, etc. Although developing these online assessments takes a significant amount of time, once in place they can be reused for each cohort and reattempted by students who wish to use them in ongoing learning and revision exercises. The system is also able to store student results automatically, providing our teachers with useful data on how individual students are progressing and a means of identifying where they need additional support.

Our VLE also links to Memrise (www.memrise.com), a web-based platform which allows teachers to create their own course-specific vocabulary lists, as well as to test vocabulary, the endings of nouns, verbs and adjectives (Walker 2015). We are also able to incorporate a competitive aspect into the use of Memrise: the group is set up with their own leader board and, like in a multi-player game, students are in competition to gain the most points and to beat their own personal best scores over the summer. This has proved very popular and has been a great motivator (not least because of the prize awarded to the top scorer in September).

Homework

Our Latin tutors are able to see all information about homework submissions, including whether or not the work was submitted late. This aspect has allowed them to more easily analyse trends in a student's performance and more easily highlight whether they might need extra help and support, not just regarding the academic content, but also in managing their time effectively in what is a very demanding course. Previous iterations of the scheme required students to hand homework in at the start of each class; it would then be marked and returned the following lesson. This lag meant that students would not receive their marks or feedback until two weeks after the topic of the homework had been covered in class. With the use of the VLE, students are required to upload their homework mid-week between classes so that it can be marked and returned promptly, and any issues, misunderstandings or mistakes can be addressed promptly before the group moves on to new grammar and content.

Permanent resource centre

The VLE also provides students with a permanent resource centre – not just an archive of what was covered in each lesson and copies of the presentations and other digital materials used in classroom teaching, but also links to other resources which cover a broad range of other aspects of the study of the ancient world, such as the languages, history and archaeology of Greece, the Near East and Egypt. This repository of further reading on particular topics, much like a digital library, allows our students to pursue their own interests and to explore other areas of potential interest, from ancient philosophy, to the development of alphabetic scripts, to the archaeology of death and burial. Several have even used the resources gathered in the further reading section of the VLE to inform their selection of a topic for their Extended Project Qualification projects, and to write their reports. This feature has proven particularly valuable for some, as the resources which we have made available are not ones to which they would normally have access at their school.

This archival aspect of the VLE has also developed our students' sense of independent learning, since they are able to access all past class information independently and to take the initiative when it comes to their own learning (a very important, transferable life skill). They feel confident that they know exactly where they should be able to find information, how to access it and what to do with it.

I emphasize again that our use of online platforms to introduce blended learning or mixed-mode instruction does not replace face-to-face teaching and learning in this outreach programme – digital technology is not used as something to replace the teacher. Rather we have used it to support and enhance traditional direct and in-person teaching and learning methods. For Latin language learning, as used by us, it is by no means an alternative to classroom teaching but a supplement to it. The method works because we require students to attend classes in person, as well as to work independently towards their GCSE.

Recommendations

In their current format, VLEs are usually a (sub)section of the institutional website which users access through their own unique login (as is the case for the University of Oxford's current VLE, WebLearn). However, there are now many VLE systems which provide access to content via Android and iOS smartphone apps, as well as via the conventional website using an internet browser (the university will soon be moving to the Canvas VLE (www.canvasvle.co.uk), which does exactly that). The popularity and success amongst our students of the Memrise learning platform, which can be accessed via a smartphone app, is consistent with the fact that many people prefer to access online content through their smartphone. One of the main benefits of moving to a VLE format which also offers access via an app is that the mandatory login to a specific site is no longer required: students can simply and quickly open the app and start working, wherever they are, to utilize time that would otherwise be lost to travel, etc. The immediacy with which students can access learning materials means that it is easier for them to find time to fit additional vocab learning and practice into their daily routine.

Whatever VLE system is used, I would advise organizing an instructional session for your students (particularly if they are not university-age students) to guide them through the platform, as it is unwise to assume a high level of computer know-how and efficiency (despite the prevalence of computers in most aspects of life). As part of the students' induction to the scheme, we include an orientation session to ensure that they know how to access the VLE site, how and where to log on and how to navigate around it. Demonstrating how the homework upload function works was particularly useful, as most students said that they would not have automatically known what all the words meant or how to navigate around the user area on their own PC/Mac to find the right file to upload.

There is, of course, the danger of a VLE simply becoming a dumping ground for worksheets and presentations, but the fact that students are required to use the VLE to submit work each week, to participate in quizzes and to access set work means that it is not simply a repository but a platform with which they have to interact regularly and to which they must contribute.

Potential issues and problems

This approach to organizing and delivering Latin teaching as part of an outreach programme incurs the same issues which affect schools, but to a greater extent since it relies more heavily on students having regular access to a computer and the internet. Although the target audience is of an age and a culture in which the internet has typically been a pervasive part of daily life, the ability for students in our targeted demographics to participate in such courses is threatened by the damaging effects of the 'austerity' agenda and the decline in real terms of wages and living standards – declines which have resulted in fewer people, particularly those in the most deprived sections of society, having regular access to a computer or the internet. Organizers of outreach programmes must also remain vigilant to the economic hardships faced by an increasing number of students. We should not assume that all students have access to devices such as iPhones and iPads or the internet at home, and the possibility of having to provide such access (and the costs involved) needs to be taken into consideration. Likewise, the fact that students must attend classes in the faculty potentially incurs travel costs which may not be within the budget of some households. The university has introduced financial assistance for those students and potential applicants who wish to attend open days and other outreach events but are otherwise prevented from doing so due to the prohibitive cost of travel. Assistance with travel costs to the faculty for participants in the OxLAT scheme is something which we consider, although as yet no applicant has requested it when completing the application form. This potential additional cost is, however, one which university departments and Classics organizations should bear in mind to ensure that the opportunities they offer are accessible to those who would benefit from them the most.

The motivation to establish the OxLAT scheme was the knowledge that the faculty could not just attempt to stimulate an interest in classical subjects by one-off or intermittent visits to local state schools, but that we also needed to provide school students with the opportunity to realize that interest if we were going to have any long-term success in getting a larger and more diverse number of young people involved in the study of the ancient world. As a supra-curricular extra, however, the scheme is not helping to establish and expand Latin provision *in* schools (though this has to remain a long-term aim). The intensity and supra-curricular nature of the scheme also means that it generally only appeals to very able and well-motivated students in the upper ability range (the best scoring As and A*s in their other GCSEs, and the weakest B and Cs) due to the extra (and heavy) workload. This, of course, does not achieve the aim of encouraging the provision of classical subjects in a comprehensive education system. Any potential ways of addressing this to make it more accessible and available to a wider ability range, and on timetable in schools, have to be considered seriously. This problem suggests a broader tension in priorities and some degree of hypocrisy on our part: we deride the fact that access to Latin is restricted to a narrow, very able group of privileged students, while simultaneously offering Latin to a small group of very able students (albeit ones attending state schools). Some might argue that something is better than nothing, but ultimately our aim is to seed enthusiasm in the hope that it will generate Latin in schools or communities which we could then support in other ways. There seems to have been some success in this aim: Wallingford School (secondary), the soon-to-open Aureus School (secondary) in Didcot, as well as several primary schools across Oxfordshire, have or are planning to introduce Latin to the curriculum, and the faculty looks forward to working in close partnership with the charity Classics for All to establish and contribute to the Oxfordshire Classics Hub.

But nevertheless, the OxLAT team looks forward to being able to help local schools introduce and embed Latin and Classical Civilization into their timetable so that even more students have the opportunity to explore this diverse and inspiring subject area.

Of course, the aim of stimulating interest across Oxfordshire, with the long-term aim of prompting and supporting schools to offer Latin in-house, is thwarted by the funding cuts to maintained schools' budgets by the Conservative government. In times of dramatically increased financial, social and educational inequality, it is all the more important that we increase our efforts to help provide students from disadvantaged social, economic and educational backgrounds with equality of opportunity and equity of educational support and enrichment. There is still cause for optimism if university departments take the initiative and offer whatever substantive opportunities they can to better support local schools, and share their expertise and resources to help ensure all children have the same opportunities as those in the privileged private sector. Hopefully the work we have done developing a blended learning or mixed-mode instruction approach can be used as an example to support and inform schools that wish to offer Latin.

Notes

1. These diverse aspects of 'background' highlight the crucial need to recognize the intersectional nature of an individual's identity, and to consider the interaction of related systems of oppression, domination and discrimination and their impact. We cannot only address one form of marginalized identity: issues relating to gender, ethnicity, sexual orientation, disability and socio-economic class cannot be observed separately or addressed in isolation but must be considered holistically. See www.ox.ac.uk/about/increasing-access for details. On the importance of intersectional outreach work, see Cullinane and Kirby (2016), Evans (2009), Lehmann (2007), Reay, Crozier and Clayton (2009, 2010) and Reay, David and Ball (2005).

2. The phrase 'Schools Liaison' is used by some colleges and departments, and at other universities, as an umbrella term covering all activities with school pupils, whether from under-represented groups or not. For overviews of widening participation policy and research up to 2007, see Spohrer (2015), Greenbank (2006), Kettley (2007) and Lovatt (2011) for Classics outreach.

3. Clarke (2004); Department for Education and Skills (2003b), 85; OFFA (2004). New Labour's Higher Education Bill (2004) sought to introduce variable tuition fees, but during the parliamentary debate of the bill (2003 to 2004) there was considerable concern (across all parties and amongst the wider public) that the amount of debt new graduates would face could dissuade some potential students from entering higher education altogether; see Sanders and Goddard (2003) and Callender and Jackson (2005 and 2008). In response, New Labour proposed to institute a regulator (OFFA) to ensure that universities and colleges took steps to mitigate such dissuasion. Although some parts of the UK did not implement top-up fees (university funding is a devolved matter for Scotland, Wales and Northern Ireland), most universities and colleges in the UK are located in England and are therefore subject to monitoring and regulation by OFFA. See Department for Education and Skills (2003b, 2004a and 2004b). Further details are available at www.offa.org.uk.

4. A copy of Oxford's own 'access agreement' with OFFA is available at www.ox.ac.uk/about/facts-and-figures/admissions-statistics/undergraduate/additional-info/access-agreement-target-categories.

5. We have increased the number of applications from students educated in the UK state sector, and in 2016 58 per cent of places went to applicants from state-maintained schools, up from 47.8 per cent in 2004 (although school type is a crude and sometimes misleading indicator of disadvantage); one in four UK students admitted in 2016 was from a low-income household and thus received additional financial support in the form of an Oxford Bursary; and 12 per cent of UK undergraduates of known ethnicity admitted to Oxford for 2015 entry were BME (not far short of the 15 per cent of UK undergraduates at other Russell Group universities, but some way short of the 20 per cent of UK undergraduates across all UK universities). A comprehensive breakdown of Oxford's admissions statistics for the period 2007–16 is available here: https://public.tableau.com/views/UoO_UG_Admissions2/Summary?%3Aembed=y&%3Adisplay_count=yes&%3Ashow Tabs=y&%3AshowVizHome=no.

    Admissions statistics for previous years are available at: www.ox.ac.uk/gazette/statisticalinformation/#d.en.6207.

    A broad overview of Classics outreach in universities across the UK up to 2010 can be found in Lovatt (2011).

6. There are now more non-selective state schools offering Latin than selective state and independent schools combined. Based on continuous data-gathering by the Cambridge Schools Classics Project, as of 2015 there are 553 non-selective state schools offering Latin, compared to 515 schools in the independent and selective state sector combined (CSCP 2015: 3). However, this statistic conceals a larger, less positive one: proportionately, pupils in the private sector are more likely to have the

opportunity to study classical subjects than those in the maintained sector, despite the fact that they only make up 7 per cent of the student population.

7. On the importance of ensuring pupils are properly prepared to respond positively to the 'flipped learning' method, see Natoli (2014). On the 'flipped classroom' method, see Bishop and Verleger (2013), Fulton (2012) and Herreid and Schiller (2013).

8. On the significance of producing annotated texts and their support of classroom dialogue, see Hennessy (2011).

References

Bishop, J. and Verleger, M. (2013), 'The Flipped Classroom: A Survey of the Research. American Society for Engineering Education', *ASEE National Conference Proceedings*, Atlanta, GA.

Callender, C. and Jackson, J. (2005), 'Does the Fear of Debt Deter Students from Higher Education?', *Journal of Social Policy*, (34): 509–540.

Callender, C. and Jackson, J. (2008), 'Does the Fear of Debt Constrain Choice of University and Subject of Study?', *Studies in Higher Education*, (33): 405–429.

Cambridge School Classics Project (2009), *A Survey of Access to Latin in UK Secondary Schools*, Cambridge: CSCP. Available online: www.exams.cambridgescp.com/ (accessed 23 July 2017).

Cambridge School Classics Project (2009), *A Statistical Report on Latin in UK Secondary Schools*, Cambridge: CSCP. Available online: www.exams.cambridgescp.com/files/ (accessed 23 June 2018).

Cambridge School Classics Project (2012), *Changing Demands in Latin and Ancient Greek Examinations 1918 to 2012*, Cambridge: Cambridge School Classics Project (unpublished report for the DfE).

Cambridge School Classics Project (2015), *Who is Latin for? Access to KS4 Latin Qualifications. An Investigation into the Viability of the DfE's Proposed Ancient Languages GCSE Subject Content (April 2014)*, Cambridge: CSCP. Available online: www.exams.cambridgescp.com/files/ ks4qualsresearch2015.pdf (accessed 23 June 2018).

Cambridge School Classics Project (2016), *Report on the DfE/CSCP Teacher Training Initiative*, Unpublished presentation at the Cambridge School Classics Project Annual Conference.

Clague, A. (2013), 'WJEC Latin Certificates', *Journal of Classics Teaching*, (28): 72–73.

Clague, A. (2014), 'WJEC Latin Certificates: Summer 2014', *Journal of Classics Teaching*, (30): 52.

Clarke, C. (2004), *Letter of Instruction to Sir Martin Harris, Director for Fair Access to Higher Education, 25 October 2004*. Available online: http://webarchive.nationalarchives.gov.uk/20100210151716/ http://www.dcsf.gov.uk/hegateway/uploads/OFFA%20final%20guidance%20letter%20October%20 2004.pdf (accessed 23 June 2018).

Cullinane, C. and Kirby, P. (2016), *Class Differences: Ethnicity and Disadvantage,* Sutton Trust. Available online: www.suttontrust.com/wp-content/uploads/2016/11/Class-differences-report_References-available-online.pdf (accessed 23 June 2018).

Department of Education and Science (1988), *Education Reform Act (Act of Parliament)*, London: Her Majesty's Stationery Office. Available online: www.legislation.gov.uk/ukpga/1988/40/pdfs/ ukpga_19880040_en.pdf (accessed 23 June 2018).

Department for Education and Skills (DfES) (2003a), *Widening Participation in Higher Education*, London: Department for Education and Skills.

Department for Education and Skills (2003b), *The Future of Higher Education (Higher Education White Paper)*, London: Her Majesty's Stationery Office. Available online: http://webarchive. nationalarchives.gov.uk/20040117000548/http://www.dfes.gov.uk/highereducation/hestrategy/pdfs/ DfES-HigherEducation.pdf (accessed 23 June 2018).

Department of Education and Skills (2004a), *Higher Education Bill (Parliamentary Bill),* London: Her Majesty's Stationery Office. Available online: https://publications.parliament.uk/pa/cm200304/ cmbills/035/2004035.pdf (accessed 23 June 2018).

Department of Education and Skills (2004b), *Higher Education Act (Act of Parliament),* London: Her Majesty's Stationery Office. Available online: www.legislation.gov.uk/ukpga/2004/8/pdfs/ukpga_20040008_en.pdf (accessed 23 June 2018).

Evans, S. (2009), 'In a Different Place: Working Class Girls and Higher Education', *Sociology,* (43): 340–355.

Fulton, K. (2012), 'Upside Down and Inside Out: Flip Your Classroom to Improve Student Learning', *Learning & Leading with Technology,* (June/July): 12–17.

Greenbank, P. (2006), 'The Evolution of Government Policy on Widening Participation', *Higher Education Quarterly,* (60.2): 141–166.

Hennessy, S. (2011), 'The Role of Digital Artefacts on the Interactive Whiteboard in Supporting Classroom Dialogue', *Journal of Computer Assisted Learning,* (27): 463–489.

Herreid, C. and Schiller, N. (2013), 'Case Studies and the Flipped Classroom', *Journal of College Science Teaching,* (42.5): 62–66.

Higher Education Funding Council for England (1998), *Widening Participation in Higher Education: Funding Proposals,* Bristol: HEFCE.

Higher Education Funding Council for England (2006), *Widening Participation: A Review,* Bristol: HEFCE. Available online: www.hefce.ac.uk/widen/aimhigh/review.asp (accessed 23 September 2018).

Higher Education Funding Council for England (2007), *HEFCE Strategic Plan 2006–2011,* Bristol: HEFCE. Available online: http://hefce.ac.uk/pubs/hefce/2007/07_09/ (accessed 23 September 2018).

Higher Education Funding Council for England (2014), *Outcomes of Access Agreement, Widening Participation Strategic Statement and National Scholarship Programme Monitoring for 2012–13,* Bristol: OFFA/HEFCE.

Hunt, S. (2012), 'Classics Teacher Vacancies 2010–11: Not Meeting the Demand', *Journal of Classics Teaching,* (25): 2–6.

Hunt, S. (2016), *Starting to Teach Latin,* London: Bloomsbury Academic.

Hunt, S. (2018), 'Getting Classics into Schools? Classics and the Social Justice Agenda of the Coalition Government 2010–2015', in *Forward with Classics: Classical Languages in Schools and Communities,* Musié, M., Holmes-Henderson, A. and Hunt, S. (eds.), London: Bloomsbury Academic, pp. 11–28.

Kettley, N. (2007), 'The Past, Present and Future of Widening Participation Research', *British Journal of Sociology of Education,* (28.3): 333–347.

Lehmann, W. (2007), '"I Just Feel Like I Don't Fit In": The Role of Habitus in University Drop-out Decisions', *Canadian Journal of Higher Education,* (37): 89–110.

Lovatt, H. (2011), 'Sitting on the Fence or Breaking Through the Hedge? Risk-Taking, Incentives and Institutional Barriers to Outreach Work Among Academics and Students', in *Arts and Humanities Academics in Schools: Mapping the Pedagogical Interface,* G. Baker and A. Fisher (eds.), London: Contiunuum, 28–42.

Natoli, B. (2014), 'Flipping the Latin Classroom: Balancing Educational Practice with the Theory of eLearning', *Journal of Classics Teaching,* (30): 37–40.

Office for Fair Access (2004), *Producing Access Agreements: OFFA Guidance to Institutions,* Bristol: OFFA.

Office for Fair Access (2010), *Submission by OFFA to the Independent Review of Higher Education Funding and Student Finance,* OFFA. Available online: www.offa.org.uk/wp-content/uploads/2010/02/OFFA-Fees-Review-submission-first-call-for-evidence-January-2010-FINAL.pdf (accessed 23 June 2018).

Office for Fair Access and Higher Education Funding Council for England (2014), *National Strategy for Access and Student Success,* OFFA/HEFCE. Available online: www.gov.uk/government/publications/national-strategy-for-access-and-student-success (accessed 23 June 2018).

Office for Fair Access (2015), *Strategic Plan 2015–2020,* OFFA. Available online: www.offa.org.uk/wp-content/uploads/2015/03/OFFA-Strategic-Plan-2015-2020.pdf (accessed 23 June 2018).

Office for Fair Access (2016), *Closing the Gap: Understanding the Impact of Institutional Financial Support on Student Success,* OFFA. Available online: www.offa.org.uk/wp-content/uploads/2016/11/Closing-the-gap-understanding-the-impact-of-institutional-financial-support-on-student-success.pdf (accessed 23 June 2018).

Paterson, C. (2012), 'Ancient Texts and Modern Tools: Cicero and Interactive Whiteboards', *Journal of Classics Teaching*, (25): 14–16.

Partington, R. (2011a), 'Latin Stages a Comeback in the Classroom', *Journal of Classics Teaching*, (23): 11–12.

Partington, R. (2011b), 'The Threat to Latin Posed by Teacher Shortages', *Journal of Classics Teaching*, (23): 12–13.

Reay, D., Crozier, G. and Clayton, J. (2009), 'Strangers in Paradise? Working-class Students in Elite Universities', *Sociology*, (43): 1103–1121.

Reay, D., Crozier, G. and Clayton, J. (2010), '"Fitting In" or "Standing Out": Working-class Students in UK Higher Education', *British Educational Research Journal*, (36): 107–124.

Reay, D., David, M. and Ball, S. (2005), *Degrees of Choice: Social Class, Race and Gender in Higher Education*, Stoke-on-Trent: Trentham Books.

Riddell, R. (2010), *Aspiration, Identity and Self-Belief: Snapshots of Social Structure at Work*, Stoke-on-Trent: Trentham.

Ryan, C. (2011), 'Chains and Controversia: Non-Judgementally Exploring the Richness of the Past with Primary School Children', in G. Baker and A. Fisher (eds.), *Arts and Humanities Academics in Schools: Mapping the Pedagogical Interface*, London: Contiunuum, 130–141.

Sanders, C. and Goddard, A. (2003), 'Rebel MPs Steadfast Against Variable Fees', *Times Higher Education Supplement*, 19 December 2003.

Sandis, E. (2009), 'The Oxford Perspective on Classics Outreach', *Journal of Classics Teaching*, (16): 3–5.

Searle, E. (2018), 'Shattering the Class Ceiling: How the Outreach Agenda Is Helping Bring Classics to the Masses', in M. Musié, A. Holmes-Henderson and S. Hunt (eds.), *Forward with Classics: Classical Languages in Schools and Communities*, London: Bloomsbury Academic, pp. 29–42.

Spohrer, K. (2015), 'Opening Doors or Narrowing Opportunities? The Coalition's Approach to Widening Participation, Social Mobility and Social Justice', in M. Finn (ed.), *The Gove Legacy: Education in Britain after the Coalition*, London: Palmgrave Macmillan, 101–115.

Stephenson, D. (2014), 'WJEC Level 2 Latin: A Teacher's Viewpoint', *Journal of Classics Teaching*, (29): 45–47.

Sutton Trust (2008), *Increasing Higher Education Participation Amongst Disadvantaged Young People and Schools in Poor Communities*, London: Sutton Trust.

Sutton Trust (2015), *Evaluating Access*, London: Sutton Trust. Available online: www.suttontrust.com/wp-content/uploads/2015/12/Higher-Education-Access-Report-1.pdf (accessed 23 June 2018).

Universities UK (2005), *From the Margins to the Mainstream: Embedding Widening Participation in Higher Education*, London: Universities UK.

Walker, L. (2015), 'The Impact of Using *Memrise* on Student Learning Latin Vocabulary and on Long-Term Memory of Words', *Journal of Classics Teaching*, (32): 14–20.

CHAPTER 9
FROM RESEARCH ON ROMAN HISTORY TO CARTOONS AND OUTREACH IN UK SCHOOLS[1]
Ray Laurence

Introduction

It would be nice to say that I planned the development of two animated films or cartoons, *A Glimpse of Teenage Life in Ancient Rome* (2012) and *Four Sisters in Ancient Rome* (2013), with the intention of presenting my research to a worldwide audience. Even with the millions of views and numerous comments – positive, negative, racist and misogynist – these two films have recorded on YouTube, I can safely say I did not really plan any of this. However, how I ended up making these films based on my research interests is worth knowing and will maybe act as a counter to the desire in some universities in the UK to manage processes that lead from research to impact or outreach.

How did this happen?

The story begins in 2011. My eldest son, aged seven, was in Year 3 at a North London primary school, and he had a project on the Romans to complete: an A–Z of anything about the Romans. This we duly did by going to the British Museum to locate objects beginning with the letters A–Z, plus a tad of Dad intervention to stick in Zosimus. His teacher then asked me to run an afternoon for the two Year 3 classes. I had a show-and-tell selection, but I also was curious about how the children would react to the idea of a Roman betrothal of a seven-year-old girl to a teenage boy: this was graphically revealed on the faces of the seven-year-old girls with respect to their perception of male teenagers at the neighbouring secondary school. Hands were raised and questions were asked, from fashionable colours to ideas about where London came from. The next year, when my youngest son was in Year 3, I went back to deliver the same classes, but I was also made aware of a syllabus that dichotomized Celts and Romans in a manner alien to even Roman archaeology in the 1990s. Primary school had been a totally new audience for me, but one that could engage with my knowledge of childhood in Rome and allow me to articulate for them the experience of their own age group 2,000 years ago.

As well as this personal or familial point of origin for the cartoons, there is another that is professional. In 2010 I had taken up a new job as professor of Roman history and archaeology at the University of Kent. Within a week of accepting the job, Canterbury City Council put forward the concept of closing its Roman Museum. The local population protested, and through the Dean of Humanities a meeting was arranged with the council, at which I explained the importance of the collection not just academically, but for schools and for one of their target audiences: families. After numerous meetings and much lobbying, the museum stayed open and a heritage group was formed, chaired by Tim Le Lean. He showed me an animation of a lecture by David Harvey (an urban geographer, of whom I am a fan) and suggested the same company might make films about my lectures.

A year later, I asked Tim to arrange a meeting with Cognitive, and a few weeks later Andrew Park, the founder of this animation studio, and his business manager, Rob Coward, knocked on my office door. A whirlwind of ideas entered my office, but most importantly they listened and took in ideas about what could be done about Rome. They left saying they would put me in touch with TED-Ed.

My idea was to make a film about Rome as the first global empire. However, I was also toying with another idea. A statistic had emerged that males were far less likely to go to university than females.[2] Also, recruitment of students is the lifeblood (i.e. money) of all university departments, and the government had announced the massive hike in fees to £9,000 *per annum*. These factors underpinned my idea to focus the cartoon on a seventeen-year-old male (the target age group for university recruitment), and I pitched the idea on this basis. The pitch was successful.

As readers can work out from this, there were several ideas colliding to create the concept for the films – not least that both my children are male, and that they were rather fascinated by the teenagers they saw as they walked to and from primary school. Hence, the first film – *A Glimpse of Teenage Life in Ancient Rome* – was written with them in mind.

The two films were released in 2012 and 2013, just a year after the book *Rome, Ostia, Pompeii: Movement and Space* was published, driven forward by Newsome, with myself as co-editor. This book was fundamental to *A Glimpse of Teenage Life in Ancient Rome*.

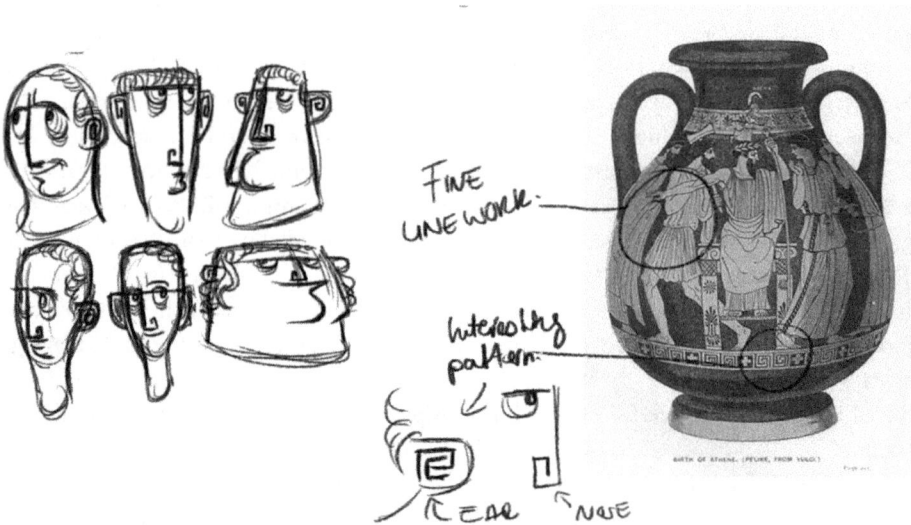

Figure 9.1 The inspiration for the imagery in the cartoon comes from linework and patterns in Greek pottery found in Italy. © TED-Ed.

Research content

The scripts of both the first film and its follow-up, *Four Sisters in Ancient Rome,* contained elements drawn from my research on at least three themes from Roman history: the life course, roads and transportation, and life in the city of Rome. It is worth spelling out the connections here, so that the presence of research in the films can be seen.

The films in both cases are based around the structure of a day in ancient Rome, with an emphasis on time moving along through the day from dawn to dusk. All of these timings are drawn from my book *Roman Pompeii: Space and Society* and a chapter on time and the city (Laurence 2007: 154–166). They trace the idea of the importance of gendered spatial arrangements, whereby once the *paterfamilias* left the house, his absence reconfigured the social relations of the house itself; this is shown through the young girls getting ready to leave the house in *Four Sisters in Ancient Rome.* Outside the house, the *paterfamilias* heads across the city with his sons and some clients.

Movement across the city is also a feature of the two films. *A Glimpse of Teenage Life in Ancient Rome* moves the participants across the city, from their house to the Forum of Augustus and then onto the Baths of Agrippa or Nero in the Campus Martius (Laurence 2009: 63–77). Nuisances are met (drawing on the paper by Hartnett (2011)) and the banning of vehicles is presented, but the animated format has its limitations, and the subtlety of banning of only heavy, large carts (rather than all carts) from dawn until the end of the ninth hour of the day (Kaiser 2011) could not be incorporated. In *Four Sisters in Ancient Rome,* the sisters are carried through the streets of the city in litters, and this allows the film to contemplate their view of the streets – so different to that of the pedestrian in *A Glimpse of Teenage Life in Ancient Rome* (see Laurence 1999: 138–139 for litters).

Underpinning both films is the central concept of betrothal of young girls to teenage boys, a topic that was discussed in a paper by Harlow and myself in which we drew on a range of sources (Harlow and Laurence 2010). I discovered from revealing the idea of arranged marriage in Rome to primary school children that they were staggered by the idea of a seven-year-old being betrothed to a teenager. Comments on YouTube point to a fundamental misunderstanding of this aspect of the film, perhaps because 'betrothal' is a term unfamiliar or rarely used in twenty-first-century teenage worlds. Thus, many commentators – i.e. the audience – misunderstand betrothal as *marriage* to a seven-year-old. One of the more exciting features of betrothal is that, unlike in Roman marriage, gifts were given by the husband-to-be to his future wife – this comes both from Roman law and from the excavation of a tomb of a betrothed girl found in Rome with a myrtle crown, jewellery and a doll. This evidence created the image in the films of the betrothed girl as being marked out as different, in that she was loaded with 'bling' (for evidence, see Harlow and Laurence 2010).

The unequal ages of the two people due to get married at some point in the future, guided by their fathers, was a theme that Harlow and I also explored in our first book *Age and Ageing in Ancient Rome: A Life Course Approach.* This book and its research inform a shaping of the families in both films that is very gendered. Lucius in *A Glimpse of Teenage Life in Ancient Rome* is not seen to have a mother; in the second film, the mother of the Domitia sisters is revealed to have died in childbirth. The complicated nature of Roman families is revealed to resist any notion of the Roman family as being composed of mum plus dad and the two kids.

This aligns the film with current work on the Roman family and, in particular, remarriage (see, for example, Rawson 2011).

A Glimpse of Teenage Life in Ancient Rome needed to be set at a particular point in time. I chose the day of the Liberalia in 73 CE (see Ovid *Fasti* 3.771–790 on the festival). The animators created the place of this day within the Roman calendar, after I sent them an image of one of the *fasti* – a real object that was dropped into the animation. This use of a real object from antiquity provides the film with a sense of authenticity, just as the characters move across a map of the city of Rome as though there is a reality to their existence. The Liberalia also allowed me to reference the rituals of growing up and the power of the *paterfamilias* over his teenage children, a power which included his control of their money and their inability to undertake business. This limitation of their agency had been discussed at some length by me and Harlow in the book *Growing Up and Growing Old in Ancient Rome* (2002: 65–78).

Words and images

Animation as a medium allows the narrator of the script and the scriptwriter to compress the content that is in the audio file. This can be seen when Lucius, his dad and his brother navigate their way through Rome. The animators created the streets full of people, the sellers of goods, the sounds of horses and even a boxing ring down a side street (the latter is located in one of Rome's narrow side streets by Suetonius (Suet. *Aug.* 45, see Figure 9.2)). The drawing takes the viewer to a point where they can imagine both the place and the thoughts of past wars and victories. Of course, Aeneas leaving Troy is totally unlike any ancient statue. This is where the film reminds the viewer that all of this is not real; you are not seeing ancient Rome but a cartoon. Similarly, to signify a cold room in the baths, a polar bear appears – it is also reminder that we are viewing not Rome or a reconstruction of Rome, but a story that explains ancient Rome in the context of the twenty-first century. This is where animation as a genre is distinct from other forms of reconstruction or visualization: whereas those seek an authority or claim authenticity, animation does not pretend to do this (see Laurence 2016 on reconstruction of the Roman Forum).

The relationship between Cognitive creating images for the animation and children drawing images is explored in *Four Sisters in Ancient Rome*. I was working on an edited volume, *Written Space in the Latin West* (Sears et al. 2013), that contained much about graffiti, and I had also come across Huntley's work on the visual images drawn by children (Huntley 2011). The similarity between these children's drawings from Pompeii and the images produced by my own children in primary school was very striking. Hence, I wanted to include the sense of ancient graffiti in the films. This was achieved in the opening scene and elsewhere in *Four Sisters in Ancient Rome*: one of the younger Domitia sisters is seen drawing an image of herself on a column as she watches the *salutatio,* in which Lucius comes to see her father with a vague hope that he may marry one of his daughters. The graffito is being drawn upon a column, just as we find columns in Pompeii to be the preferred surface for both words and images. My sense was that many viewers might know of Pompeian graffiti (reproduced in Cooley and Cooley, *Pompeii: A Sourcebook*, 2004, but now see Cooley and Cooley 2013); however, little was accessible about the context of precisely where graffiti were found and the idea of children as writers of graffiti. This also created the marvellous situation of the animator drawing a child,

TED Ray Laurence - Romans

Shot 011	Duration 08:12	Panel 1

Dialogue
Back to the Liberalia. As Lucius prepares for his brothers coming of age,

Shot 012	Duration 02:16	Panel 1

Dialogue
the shops are open as the population goes about its business, the streets are full of itinerant traders selling trinkets and people bustling from place to place

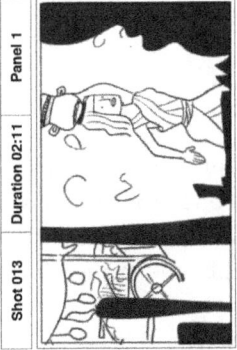

Action Notes
Montage of shots showing business of people and market traders. People walk past and see through market stalls. (Lots of panning movement and handheld camera) - Close up of market trader calling

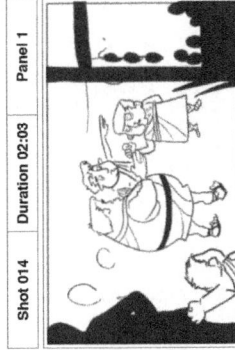

Shot 013	Duration 02:11	Panel 1

out enticing customers. - Close-up of small boy holding father/uncles hand.

Action Notes
- Pan across following woman carrying large pot on her head

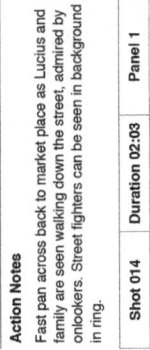

Shot 014	Duration 02:03	Panel 1

Action Notes
Fast pan across back to market place as Lucius and family are seen walking down the street, admired by onlookers. Street fighters can be seen in background in ring.

- Group of three men bargaining prices/laughing and conversing.
- Close-up of small boy holding father/uncles hand.

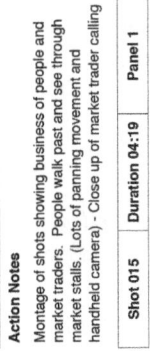

Shot 015	Duration 04:19	Panel 1

OUT

Dialogue
Large wagons are not allowed in the city until after the ninth hour, but the streets are crowded.

Action Notes
Close up of Ray Laurence narrating, but then zoom out to show he is one of the guards stopping wagons entering the city.

Shot 016	Duration 05:19	Panel 1

Dialogue
Fathers and uncles take the kids

Action Notes
We see the small boy come out of crowd and look up

Shot 016	Duration 05:19	Panel 4

Figure 9.2 Development of the images for the script. © TED-Ed.

who was herself drawing a child, and thus revealing the time depth of drawing and the use of an abbreviated two-dimensional drawing to represent a three-dimensional object.

Names, cartoons and identities

How to name your characters? It is not so easy. I decided not to make up a name, but to take a real name from Pompeii – Lucius Popidius Secundus, who we know stood in an election to be aedile (*CIL* 4.1045, 8943). This is not to make my Lucius real, but to add a degree of authenticity to his existence by having a real name of someone living at about the time of the Liberalia in 73 BCE.

All seemed fine, until in 2015 I noticed on Wikipedia that the entry for Lucius Pedanius Secundus – the city prefect murdered in 61 CE – contained a reference to *A Glimpse of Teenage Life in Ancient Rome* that said the film was completely incorrect in representing the famous city prefect in this way. Obviously the names were not the same, so I contacted Wikipedia and tweeted about the issue. Fortunately, the erroneous confusion between Popidius and Pedanius was cleared up, and the reference to the film was deleted. There is a point to this tale though: cartoons are a form of historical fiction, but within them people can see reality and consider them to be a real representation of people from the past. This only dawned on me after the film was released – the academic content behind the film was real, but the storyline of the day in the life of a person who had no existence in Rome was a fiction. Hence, cartoons position themselves as not real, but for viewers they can seem real and authentic.

One of the fundamental points of the second film was to explain Roman nomenclature and the possibility of a father calling all his daughters by the same name. This draws on the evidence of the Claudii of the 50s BCE being composed of a consortium of siblings: Publius Clodius, Cicero's famous adversary and tribune in 58 BC, his brother Appius Claudius Pulcher, plus

Figure 9.3 Developing Lucius as a moving figure. © TED-Ed.

three sisters all called Clodia. What is slightly uncertain is whether, like their brother, the sisters changed their names from Claudia to Clodia (see Syme (1986), Table 1 for details; Harlow and Laurence 2002: 39–40; and Bannon 1997 for discussion of *consortium*). The play on names and the impossibility of distinguishing Domitia from Domitia from Domitia from Domitia is only achieved through one of the Domitiae being identified as betrothed, wearing the gifts of her husband to be, and then revealing later in the film that there is another Domitia who is married and pregnant as a teenager. These distinctions were visual and thus suited the cartoon format, but they were also elements that defined the female identity and her place in the life course in antiquity.

Inserted around these main characters and their *paterfamilias* are others. The streets are full of people, but some characters have a stronger part to play. These are notably the clients, barbers and prostitutes – all stock characters found in the work of the first-century CE writers Martial and Juvenal. Alongside these, *Four Sisters in Ancient Rome* introduces a torturer, who first of all visits the barber in the Subura and then reappears later in the film, after a slave has dropped a dish and they await the investigation of this misdemeanour (a theme explored in Laurence 2009: 128–133). Underlying the torturer's identity is the inscription from Puteoli referring to the city's contract for the provision of workers for funerals and torture (*AE* 1971, no. 88; translated in Gardner and Wiedemann 1991: 24–27). The incident of the dish also plays on the story of Vedius Pollio, who was infamous for wanting to feed a clumsy slave to his lampreys in the presence of Emperor Augustus (Dio 54.23). I have been told by teachers that the animated version of the torturer can strike terror into a Year 8 class.

The blog: Lucius' Romans

After the release of the films, I did naively think, 'Job done.' However, I had reckoned without the comments on YouTube. Cognitive explained to me that these were best avoided, but later I realized that this is how the films are seen, and comments represent a form of engagement. These comments can be analysed and categorized. There are themes that repeatedly occur, and it is worth considering what they are.

Broadly, there is love and hate. There are those who write that they really like the films and ask us to please make some more. For various complicated reasons, their desires can only be fulfilled if TED-Ed commissions more films. Then there is the hate, focused often on myself as the narrator and claiming that my views on ancient Rome can be labelled as forms of 'cultural Marxism' (see, for example, Wilson 2015 for discussion).

More worrying, though, was the fact that we were tapping into an audience who wished to express racism and misogyny. We had deliberately given Lucius a tan – after all, it is clear that young men in ancient Rome sunbathed and, in any case, people in the Mediterranean do not have a white complexion (see Laurence 2009: 70 on sunbathing). Questions initially arose such as 'Why is Lucius black?' We also discovered that skin tone was analysed closely – a man riding on an elephant was identified as Hannibal, and thus too white to be North African. Nowhere did we identify whether the elephant rider was a Carthaginian or part of an army from Macedonia. This illustrates some of the jumps made by those watching the films – jumps which prefigure the debate in 2017 over the BBC's cartoon that featured a black African (see, for example, Heighton 2017).

There is also a degree of misogyny expressed in far too many of the comments with US(?) boys expressing that they want the life of Lucius and the ability to drink alcohol as a teenager. Debates over the content between males and females degenerate on YouTube into misogyny, with a view of the cartoons as a means to use history to push back against gender equality in the present. Most shocking, perhaps, was the comment 'This film is wrong, Islam created arranged marriage.' This engages with the central tenet of the film that betrothal and thus marriage required the consent of a *paterfamilias* from each family and the bride-to-be and groom-to-be. This comment shocked me more than any other, and I felt the need to provide further information about the film.

Engaging directly with the YouTube commentators would have been vastly time-consuming, so I developed a blog simply called Lucius' Romans.[3] The blog was funded initially by the University of Kent Public Engagement Fund. The blog went live in January 2016 and has featured posts on the *Ides* of each month without fail ever since. I was able to employ Julia Peters to write the initial posts on slavery, childhood and foreigners, until she explained that in April to May 2016, she was going to walk from Canterbury to Rome (we supported her to blog about that experience as another public engagement project). To fill the gap, I wrote a number of the posts for the ides of 2016 and 2017 myself, but then I enlisted PhD students such as Catherine Hoggarth and Paula Lock to write on bridges and bars in Roman culture. To provide further content and to showcase the work of the University of Kent's MA students in Rome, I took the decision that they should write a post about an aspect of the ancient city as part of their assessment. The best posts from the MA students included discussions of the Temple of Apollo Sosianus by Mark Crittenden, a statue that spoke by Freya Burford, and the temples in Largo Argentina by Josh Littel. Hence, although originally a response to the comments on YouTube, the purpose of the blog has since shifted towards a more central outreach project of the Department of Classical and Archaeological Studies that places students at the centre of the creation of content for the public.

Universities, impact and the classroom

By 2015, the films were reaching a wide audience across the world, whilst at the same time universities in the UK were becoming ever more conscious of the need to measure research that was being consumed by public audiences. Both films had been included in a highly rated Impact Case Study for the 2014 Research Excellence Framework,[4] but at that time, rather than millions of views, we could only report a few hundred thousand. Having millions of views on YouTube was seen as extremely positive in terms of measuring the reach of the films, but what was less clear was how these films changed anything in terms of their impact.

The question was how to capture a sense of what these films did for their target audience in schools. To answer this, on a routine school visit as part of Kent's outreach programme in 2015, I gave a talk and then suggested to the class at Nower Hill High School that we first discuss what they liked in the animations they watched, and then that they write a script for an animation about Rome, choosing any aspect of the topic that they were interested in. The discussion was fruitful and revealed to me that teenagers could articulate ideas about Rome themselves, and it was possible for them to produce a script for an animated film.

Building on this with further funding from the University of Kent, we set up an animation scriptwriting competition for UK schools. I located willing judges: Caroline Lawrence, the author; Amanda Hart, the director of the Corinium Museum in Cirencester; the writers of animation scripts at Cognitive; and Joanna Jones, the director of Canterbury Museums and Galleries. We publicized the competition and received around sixty-five scripts. Quality varied considerably, and formats were anything from dialogue to prose description. Any inauthenticity caused the script to be set aside. I sent the best batch on to the judges, who had the tricky task of choosing which was the best and who were the runners-up. The reaction of the judges varied from wondering about the levels of knowledge about Rome, to acclaiming the ability of teenagers to articulate their thoughts about Rome.

The writers at Cognitive were full of praise for the skilled storytelling that the winning script and the runners-up achieved. They were also really taken by a script in which the immortal line by Bregans from the *Cambridge Latin Course* appeared: 'I need to put my sunglasses on now, because I'm going to rap.' None of Cognitive's professional writers had ever heard of anyone putting a rap into an animated film before. The script itself was awarded third prize. However, Rosie Wyles and I visited St Paul's Way Trust School (Tower Hamlets) to record the rap, created by Tahirah, Sadia and Imah from Year 8, which can be listened to on the blog Lucius' Romans.[5] This take on Bregans the lazy slave is quite a remake of the *Cambridge Latin Course*'s lazy slave, with his Lemmy-style moustache from the course's creation in the 1970s.

The winning script 'A Day in the Life of a Roman Client', written by Kien Powell, has a direct connection to *A Glimpse of Teenage Life in Ancient Rome* through its picking out one of the clients as the focus of the action. The script ticked all the boxes and I met Kien at Stow School in 2016 to hand over the prize and to present a talk to his class. Kien's burning question was, 'When will the animation be made?' Easier said than done! I just could not find the budget to make a film on the scale of *A Glimpse of Teenage Life in Ancient Rome*. Again, a lucky chance meeting occurred at a secondary school parents' evening that took the film forward: I met a parent with a daughter in my son's class. I asked her how her other children were doing, and she explained that her son Malachi was pursuing an animation degree and handed me his card. I followed up to discover that Malachi James needed to do a placement and I found a small budget from the University of Kent to pay him during the placement.

By this time, I'd edited Kien's script and Malachi had come up with his main concepts and thoughts. When we met, he quite literally drew a storyboard in front of me. He also explained that he wanted to make the film in the manner of traditional animation, such as that of Hanna Barbera. In an interview with Professor Aylish Wood, Malachi explained how he felt the character of a person come together as he drew them.[6] We also decided that we would place Kien Powell, the author of the script, into the film as a key character. Malachi spent a day in my office looking at books and drawing continuously as he encountered objects and buildings that caught his eye. Later, as in the case of working with Cognitive, I sent Malachi images of apartment blocks, dress and any other details that he requested. The film, *A Day in the Life of a Roman Client*, has quite a different feel to earlier films by Cognitive, but that is a feature of animation – it seems to be deeply personal to the style adopted by the artist or company. When viewing these films, I see the personality of Malachi James and Andrew Park (from Cognitive), plus the personalities of all who work on them.

We ran the scriptwriting competition again in 2017, and again Year 8 students from St Paul's Way Trust School produced a highly original take on the Roman Empire, focusing on the possibility of migration from West Africa to the Roman Britain of the *Cambridge Latin Course*. I checked out the possibilities of West Africans being recruited into the Roman Army with Professor David Mattingly, who stressed that there was no evidence from inscriptions, but that the recruiting officers would have met West Africans in the oases of southern Libya. These, of course, coincide with the modern migration routes of the twenty-first century. At the time, I was leaving the UK and unfortunately was unable to spend time turning this script into a film. However, I did return to St Paul's Way Trust School to record the script in the words of the Year 8 students.[7] Olivia Sanchez, their teacher, explained to me how the scriptwriting competition had been incorporated into the teaching schedule and how students used the freedom of historical fiction to explore ideas about Rome in the classroom.

After Lucius?

My own work with Cognitive did not end with the film *Four Sisters in Ancient Rome*. In 2014, I met with Andrew Park to discuss our very different worlds: his of business and drawing and my own of academia. I was very excited by the results of 3D laser scanning and I interested Andrew in the development of an animated museum label based around a scanned object. We chose the scan of a Dea Nutrix, a nursing goddess, that was discovered in the nineteenth century, when what is now Lloyds Bank on Canterbury High Street was built. The find, now in Canterbury Roman Museum, had its head broken off. It was also featured in my 2012 book *Roman Archaeology for Historians*. The film was incredibly simple in some ways, but it actually reproduced a considerable amount of information about the life of the object in just 80 seconds. Cleverly, Cognitive had developed a sense of movement that allowed the object to be viewed and for its head to move.[8]

The following year, 2015, saw the fiftieth anniversary of the University of Kent. Professor Keith Mander (deputy vice-chancellor) had challenged me to explain to him in three sentences what humanities research was in the university – I failed. However, I decided this would be a topic for an animated film. I gained a budget and held meetings with staff at Kent about what they thought humanities research was and how their experience as academics varied according to where they were from – 40 per cent had migrated to the UK. The film walks a tightrope between representing the views of colleagues from across the university – on, for example, the difficulties of measuring the impact of humanities research – and continuing to be on message with the university's managers. Somehow, we did manage to include Professor Philippe de Wilde (pro-vice chancellor of research) saying in a speech bubble, unbelievably with a typo in the Flemish. Cognitive went to town in their scribing format to explain research to a wider public – although stepping away from Classics, museums and archaeology, this film encapsulates the research ecosystem of a modern twenty-first-century university.[9]

Arising from this film's emphasis on migration came another, *How immigration shaped Britain: part 1* (2016), in which the subject of migration in the Roman period was addressed, alongside the role of people from across the world in the First World War. At the time, we were in the lead up to the Brexit referendum. As usual, there was not enough money, but I solved the problem by teaming up with Hella Eckardt from the University of Reading and Julie Anderson from Kent's History Department. All three of us met with Cognitive at their offices to explain our ideas to them; they listened and highlighted our concerns. The storyboard appeared the following week – this very short film (just over a minute long) explained the concept of diversity created through migration in the Roman period, and migration to the First World War trenches by people from India and China.[10] This keyed into a new syllabus development in the UK's history curriculum – a unit on the history of migration that had proven far from uncontroversial with the UK's right-wing press.

Conclusion: was it worth it?

Over the time period 2010 to 2017 in the UK, I often met the reactions by academics at Kent and in other universities that impact and working with the public was just a distraction from the real business of research. This thinking is challenged by the impact agenda in the Research Excellence Framework (REF).[11] Yet, academics can be dismissive of even the REF in the hope that it will all go away. To a certain extent, this point of view can work for the individual, but it is damaging for their department and for the subject. Without the excitement of working to provide teachers with content to use in lessons and to engage with children studying our subject – the Roman past – there is no future for the subject in the UK. This may seem alarmist, but Classics and Ancient History are minority subjects in universities without feeders of large A-level subjects.

I have felt at times that I am an outlier engaging with the public via impact, something that other colleagues saw as being of less value or frivolous. I have to say that they are simply wrong. Academics in the UK need to engage with a wider public and, in fact, this should be a valued part of the research ecosystem in universities. Institutionally, this was worth it because the University of Kent was ranked second (to Cambridge) for impact in the 2014 REF. The ongoing impact from 2013 onwards can contribute, if my colleagues at Kent choose to use it, to REF 2021.

On a much more personal note, the experience of working with an animation company and a student animator has been a worthwhile experience, not least for the simple fact it has enriched the lives of young people I have known. Recently, my next-door neighbour, in Year 7 in Sydney, ran to tell me that his teacher had shown his class one of our films. My own son, in Year 9, explained to me in a moment of weakness that 'it was kind of cool that I had created a cartoon character'. Yet more value was gained from working with Andrew Park, Cognitive and, more recently, Malachi James – these people can draw my research, and through drawing make those ideas appear to come to life. I also gained new perspectives on how to tell a story and to make things more approachable, something that I hope crosses over into my lectures to undergraduate students.

As you will have seen from the account above, the research underlying most of the content in these films was published around the same time as the films were made. There is a sense in which I am seeing in the films my own ideas about ancient Rome transformed into cartoons that I know reached more than thirteen million people – more people than my academic books ever would.

Notes

1. I wish to acknowledge the extraordinary help, aid and friendship of Andrew Park and Rob Coward, plus innumerable others at Cognitive, based in Folkestone. Their talent and interest in visualizing

ideas was really eye-opening. I wish also to acknowledge TED-Ed, for whom *A Glimpse of Teenage Life in Ancient Rome* and *Four Sisters in Ancient Rome* were made, and who granted permission for the images to appear in this chapter. Various parts of the University of Kent funded the later films and outreach activities. I am particularly grateful to Philippe de Wilde's Public Engagement Fund; the Faculty of Humanities Research Fund; Keith Mander and the 50th Anniversary Committee; and the School of European Culture and Languages Research Fund for their unwavering support from 2010–17. Lynne Bennett, Phil Ward and Simon Kerridge deserve the warmest thanks for focusing my enthusiasm for public engagement. Aylish Wood kindly interviewed Malachi James for a blog on Lucius' Romans. That blog would not have got going without the assistance of postgraduate students and, in particular, Julia Peters and Jeff Veitch. Thanks also to Tim Le Lean, who introduced me to Andrew Park and was a sounding board for all sorts of problems and initiatives between 2010 and 2017. Malachi James's enthusiasm and knowledge of drawing needs to be recognized as well. Teachers and children at Malorees Junior School, Nower Hill High School, Stow School and St Paul's Way Trust School also shaped the work itself, as did my children Zak and Max, whom I saw first-hand discovering history for the first time in primary school.

2. *C.* 43 per cent male uptake to *c.* 57 per cent female uptake (Berry 2011). See discussion by Hillman and Robinson (2016), but compare Woodfield (2017). UCAS (2018) for latest figures suggest the figures 43 per cent male to 57 per cent female uptake are still present.

3. See https://blogs.kent.ac.uk/lucius-romans/.

4. Full submission: http://impact.ref.ac.uk/CaseStudies/CaseStudy.aspx?Id=936.

5. See https://blogs.kent.ac.uk/lucius-romans/cambridge-latin-course-corner/.

6. See https://blogs.kent.ac.uk/lucius-romans/2017/05/15/animating-a-day-in-the-life-of-a-roman-client/.

7. See https://blogs.kent.ac.uk/lucius-romans/cambridge-latin-course-corner/.

8. See https://www.youtube.com/watch?v=fC0WL-tNZjs.

9. See https://www.youtube.com/watch?v=NzbG1GcEEmQ).

10. See https://www.youtube.com/watch?v=NzbG1GcEEmQ.

11. The REF is the system for assessing the quality of research in UK higher education institutions. See http://www.ref.ac.uk/ for details.

References

Bannon, C. (1997), *The Brothers of Romulus: Fraternal Pietas in Roman Law, Literature, and Society*, Princeton: Princeton University Press.

Berry, J. (2011), *Male Access to Higher Education: A Discussion Paper*, Higher Education Academy. Available online: https://www.heacademy.ac.uk/system/files/maleaccess.pdf (accessed 23 September 2018).

Cooley, A. and Cooley, M. (2004), *Pompeii: A Sourcebook*, London: Routledge.

Cooley, A. and Cooley, M. (2013), *Pompeii and Herculaneum: A Sourcebook*, Abingdon: Routledge.

Gardner, J. and Wiedemann, T. (1991), *The Roman Household: A Sourcebook*, London: Routledge.

Gorski, G. and Packer, J. (2015), *The Roman Forum: A Reconstruction and Architectural Guide*, Cambridge: Cambridge University Press.

Harlow, M. and Laurence, R. (2002), *Growing Up and Growing Old in Ancient Rome: A Life Course Approach*, London: Routledge.

Hartnett, J. (2011), 'The Power of Nuisances in the Roman Street', in R. Laurence and D. Newsome (eds.), *Rome, Ostia, Pompeii: Movement and Space*, Oxford: Oxford University Press, 135–159.

Heighton, L. (2017), 'Mary Beard in "Misogynist" Race Row Over Black Romans in BBC Cartoon',

Daily Telegraph, 6 August 2017. Available online: https://www.telegraph.co.uk/news/2017/08/06/mary-beard-misogynistic-race-row-bbc-cartoon-us-academic-claimed/ (accessed 6 August 2017).

Hillman, N. and Robinson, N. (2016), *Boys to Men: The Underachievement of Young Men in Higher Education – And How To Start Tackling It*, Higher Education Policy Institute Report 84.

Huntley, K. (2011), 'Identifying Children's Graffiti in Roman Campania: A Developmental Psychological Approach', in J. Baird and C. Taylor (eds.), *Ancient Graffiti in Context*, London: Routledge, 69–89.

Kaiser, A. (2011), 'Cart Traffic Flow in Pompeii and Rome', in R. Laurence and D. Newsome (eds.), *Rome, Ostia, Pompeii: Movement and Space*, Oxford: Oxford University Press, 174–193.

Laurence R. (1999), *The Roads of Roman Italy: Mobility and Cultural Change*, London: Routledge.

Laurence, R. (2007), *Roman Pompeii: Space and Society*, Abingdon: Routledge.

Laurence, R. (2009), *Roman Passions: A History of Pleasure in Ancient Rome*, London: Bloomsbury.

Laurence, R. (2016), 'Review of Gorski and Packer 2015', *Antiquity*, 90: 1406–1408.

Laurence, R. and Newsome, D. (2011), *Rome, Ostia and Pompeii: Movement and Space*, Abingdon: Routledge.

Rawson, B. (2011), 'Introduction: Families in Greek and Roman Worlds', in B. Rawson (ed.), *A Companion to Families in the Greek and Roman Worlds*, Oxford: Wiley-Blackwell, 1–12.

Sears, G., Keegan, P. and Laurence, R. (2013), *Written Space in the Latin West*, London: Bloomsbury.

UCAS (2018), *2018 Cycle Applicant Figures – January Deadline*. Available online: https://www.ucas.com/file/147376/download?token=uH7rfzR6 (accessed 1 January 2018).

Wilson, J. (2015.), '"Cultural Marxism": A Uniting Theory for Rightwingers Who Love to Play the Victim', *The Guardian*. Available online: https://www.theguardian.com/commentisfree/2015/jan/19/cultural-marxism-a-uniting-theory-for-rightwingers-who-love-to-play-the-victim (accessed 19 January 2015).

Woodfield, R. 2017. 'The Gendered Landscape of UK Higher Education: Do Men Feel Disadvantaged?', *Gender and Education*, 28: 1–18.

CHAPTER 10
VASE ANIMATIONS AND PRIMARY-AGED LEARNERS
Sonya Nevin

Introduction

One of the most effective ways to approach understanding a culture that is different from your own is to study the artwork and objects that that culture produces. In the case of classical Greece, one of the most distinctive art forms is pottery, the vase. Familiar to adults from many a museum collection or reproduced image, these pots are typically made of terracotta clay and decorated with black slip showing patterns, animals, people and gods. Children at school in England frequently study 'ancient Greece' as a topic between the ages of seven and eleven. For the children between those ages, the idea of 'long ago' can encompass anything from ten years ago to the times when dinosaurs stalked the Earth. Understanding the ancient, classical past as a history of real people in real societies can therefore present a significant, though worthwhile, challenge.

Artefacts offer an excellent route into thinking about antiquity, precisely because their reality as objects confronts us with the reality of the lives of the people who made and used them. In the case of ancient Greek pottery, there is the added bonus of the images on the pots – images of all sorts of aspects of life, be it sport, parties, war, gods or worship, and further figures known through stories. By looking closely at Greek pots, or even at images of Greek pots, young children can gain enormous insight into the 'realness' of the classical past, into the sorts of images that ancient people liked to look at, and what those images suggest about the ways that those people lived and saw the world.

Nonetheless, the images on vases can often be hard for children or even adult non-specialists to digest. The repetitive colour scheme can create the false impression of sameness, and the details and overall sense of the image can be hard to interpret. This chapter introduces the Panoply Vase Animation Project, a cultural, educational initiative which helps to bridge the gap between artefacts and modern viewers. I will discuss what the animations are, what learning benefits they offer, and I will suggest some activities that can be combined with watching the animations in order to make them a particularly effective teaching tool for primary-aged learners.

The Panoply Vase Animation Project

The vase animations made by the Panoply Vase Animation Project bring the scenes on pots to life and in doing so make the scenes more approachable and make ancient pots in general more engaging. This extends the learning and inspiration that can be achieved via ancient pottery, offering an excellent route into ancient Greek culture. Animator Steve Simons and I began the project after witnessing the modest success of stop-motion animations set in the ancient world that we had made for fun. We soon heard that teachers were showing the animations in schools, a report which indicated straightaway that there was an appetite for short, accessible animations based on antiquity. We determined that if people wished to see antiquity live we should make ancient artefacts the focus. The wonderful, varied world of ancient pottery offers material to animate and on which to base our stories, and the use of actual artefacts brings viewers closer to antiquity by making the artefact the star of the show – a show intended to make antiquity accessible, engaging and understandable. Since then we have exhibited vase animations in a number of museums, made all of the animations available for free via our website (www.panoply.org.uk), carried out vase animation activities with thousands of children, and received great numbers of charming emails from teachers around the world who are delighted to have been able to use the animations in their teaching.

Creating vase animations

In the first stage of planning an animation we discuss what action and meaning is implied by the images on the pot we are working with, how we might draw that out and what cultural themes could be usefully emphasized. We then draw up our ideas in storyboards: a rough draft at first, followed by a more polished version. In making the vase animations, we take the figures on the pot and enable them to move. It is necessary to create new parts, such as limbs or pieces of clothing, so that figures can be placed in new positions. To do that we take elements from the existing vase to work with and we research contemporary images of objects on which to model the additional material. Both aspects enhance continuity. The background surface of the pot must also be prepared so that there is still a surface in place when the figures move from their original positions. The figures are then rigged so that they can be minutely controlled as if they were puppets. In some of the animations, such as *Clash of the Dicers*, the scene starts as the normal static vase scene and the figures then blink and begin to move. In other animations, the narrative begins at a point before the scene on the vase and works up to that moment before freezing into the original scene. This is the case in *Heracles and the Erymanthian Boar* in which the scene on the pot acts as a sort of comedy punchline to the myth and makes it preferable for us to tell the story and finish with the original scene.[1] The animations are short. Most are between one and three minutes long. One of our most popular, *Hoplites! Greeks at War*, is unusually long, at almost ten minutes.[2] The brevity of the animations means that they fit easily into a class without eating into much-needed time.

The animations address a number of topics. There are those featuring gods and goddesses, such as *The Procession*.[3] *The Symposium* features Medusa and a group of partying symposiasts.[4] *Clash of the Dicers* features Achilles and Ajax playing a board game at Troy.[5] *The Cheat*, *The Runners* and *Hermes' Favour* feature a fragment of a pot depicting athletes in action.[6] At the time of writing, we are creating five new animations with mythological themes as part of the ERC-funded project Our Mythical Childhood . . . The Reception of Classical Antiquity in Children's and Young Adults' Culture in Response to Regional and Global Challenges.[7] These animations are:

- *Heracles and the Erymanthian Boar*
- *Iris – Rainbow Goddess*

- *Sappho 44. Hector and Andromache. A Wedding at Troy*
- *The Gods at Home*
- *Dionysus*[8]

The animations can be located on the website by topic, project and A–Z by title. Each animation appears on its own page featuring additional information on the topic, related ancient images, links to relevant ancient literature, comments on the creation of the animation and suggested further reading and activities. This material is aimed at teachers in order to increase their confidence about delivering the topics and to give ideas for linked activities. The site also has a blog that features updates on our work and interviews, typically with academics talking about how they use vases in their research, and also with teachers, students and others doing interesting things related to antiquity.

Learning with vases and vase animations

Since the 1980s there has been increased reference to the idea of the modern world as one of visual culture or *bildwissenschaft*.[9] While this is evidently an oversimplification, there is enough truth in it to make it essential that young people develop visual literacy and learn to interpret the 'rhetoric of images', to 'read' images effectively – understanding how images work, how meanings and messages can be conveyed through images, and what sort of things to look out for to do this. Vase animations – based on real images but interpreting and moving them – can support people who are undergoing this learning process. The transition from image to alternative can help viewers to recognize the power of the original image, or rather to recognize that the image is one way but could have been another – a basic tenet of understanding the significance of an artwork appearing as it does. The animations can also help people to understand what they are seeing in the original image. The scene from which *Heracles and the Erymanthian Boar* was made, for example, can be hard to read. Heracles holds the boar aloft above the head and hands of a man in a large pot. Those familiar with the myth might readily understand that this depicts King Eurystheus hiding in fright at the sight of the beast. In talking with children and non-specialists however, it has become clear that people frequently wonder why the man is in the pot – they often wonder if he is being cooked or if he has been buried in

Figure 10.1 King Eurystheus escapes into a pot when Heracles presents the boar. Screenshots from *Heracles and the Erymanthian Boar*. © University of Roehampton.

the ground. In many cases, people fail to see the head and hands at all. By watching the animation, viewers gain a better appreciation of the dynamic between the parties in the original scene and understand that the king has jumped into the pot to protect himself. The addition of movement and the increase in understanding help viewers to engage with artefacts, to take an initial interest a step further. That act of further looking boosts the ability to see, interpret and understand. It helps that animation is strongly associated with fun and leisure, so learning with the animations can feel like an enjoyable activity, even as it stimulates thought and connections.

A word of caution might be added. As with any material, teachers should view the animations before their session in order to determine which of them are suitable for their class. None of the animations show sexual material or graphic violence. There is no film content of real people. Nonetheless, *Hoplites! Greeks at War*, *Combat*, *Amazon*, *Heracles*, *Medusa* and *Plant Food* feature stylized violence that some teachers may feel is not well suited to their class. Likewise, several of the animations (*Bad Karma*, *Procession*, *Runners*, *The Cheat*, *Hermes' Favour*, *Symposium*, *Heracles and the Erymanthian Boar* and *Dance Off*) include stylized nudity, which some teachers may prefer to avoid. All of these animations have been deemed suitable by many teachers and used successfully in teaching sessions for young children, but each school is different and as such the application of usual pre-viewing practice is advised.

Ideally, a teacher might watch the animations with their class before or after going to see pots in a museum (in some cases they can see the vase animations and their vases exhibited together).[10] Nonetheless, there is much to be gained from watching the animations as part of learning about antiquity in the classroom when museum visits are not possible. Teachers can read about the vases and their subjects on the website beforehand to gain insight into the material; they might then look at a number of vases with their class, or watch one or more of the animations together, talk about what they have seen and follow up with related activities. For these, there are a number of vase-themed colouring and further activity sheets on the website that can be downloaded. Drawing new vase scenes is another great activity, and there are downloadable sheets featuring vases from the animations with the figures removed, ready for new scenes to be filled in. There are also software packages available that enable students to work on their own simple animations with a teacher's support; making vase-themed flip books remains an effective low-tech alternative. It is also hugely stimulating to bring actual clay into the classroom, helping young people to appreciate the physical nature of pottery and pots. This can take the form of moulding damp clay, or of providing students with dried pottery shards and black paint with which they can paint their fragments. Cocktail sticks make an effective tool for scraping details into the surface. While students will likely be pleased with the results of their work, they are also likely to gain a renewed appreciation of the skill with which ancient vase scenes were executed.

In the classroom

Primary school (and other) teachers will have call to emphasize different aspects of ancient pottery with their classes. This section will draw out some of the various themes and activities that they may wish to pursue.

Where vases themselves are the topic, a teacher may wish to help their class to be more conscious of the different shapes that vases come in. To achieve this they might play a series of animations that helps to express those differences. So, for example, after looking together at some photos of vases, the class might watch *Symposium* and/or *Hoplites! Greeks at War*, animations which emphasize the round shape of their vessels – a cup and *lekanis* respectively.[11] The class could then watch *Clash of the Dicers* and/or *Well-Wishers*, amphora animations which demonstrate the contrasting, more rectangular shape of an amphora's main decorative panel. Good follow-up activities to extend this focus on shape include inviting students to trace the outline of vase shapes, or to pick a vase shape and then to draw, cut out and decorate it.

The understanding of vases and their physicality can be further extended by watching *Iris – Rainbow Goddess*, part of the Our Mythical Childhood series. This short animation, made from a High Classical *hydria*, has no clear narrative but rather explores the idea of a goddess's difference from humans by playing with her form, size and ability to fly. This animation, uniquely, has been made in 3D, rather than 2D. The viewer follows Iris as she flies around the 3D form of the vase. Technically, this raised a number of challenges: creating the vase in 3D, mapping the animation onto the 3D object and enabling movement around the object. Young students will be able to see the difference between the 2D and 3D depictions of vases, even while they may still require support in articulating that difference. Once that has been achieved, the experience of the 3D version will give them significant insight into different modes of representation and the different abilities of digital technologies. Seeing the vase in 3D helps to reinforce the concept of vases as physical objects, and the exposure of young learners to the varied ways in which objects can be recreated and represented (be it through photography, 2D or 3D imaging) will inform their understanding of science and technology as well as antiquity.[12]

On other occasions, the vase animations may be more useful as a multimedia accompaniment to teaching on ancient-world topics which are not primarily focused on vases themselves. Mythology is frequently at the heart of early introductions to classical antiquity, and the vase animations offer many options for exploring this topic. *Heracles and the Erymanthian Boar*, for example, offers a straight-up retelling of the Twelve Labours myth. *Heracles*, by contrast, combines two further myths: Heracles wrestling a water deity and his battle with the Hydra.[13] After watching the two animations together and looking at images of their vases, a teacher might ask a class to discuss or write about what they think an ancient audience might have found frightening about the different monsters they saw Heracles tackling. Which monster do they find scariest? What monster would they use to decorate something? Another monster – Medusa – appears within an animation that explores a further popular ancient-world topic, namely *The Symposium*. Medusa appears in the central *tondo* of a beautiful black-figure cup. When Medusa shuts her eyes, the symposium proceeds; when she opens them, the action freezes. Watch the animation with the class several times, challenging the students to identify the different things going on at the symposium party. Once those activities have been discussed, use the activity sheet from the project website to challenge the students to draw their own ideal parties within the circular outline of the cup.

Another topic commonly covered at primary level is the ancient Olympic Games – perfect for an accessible connection with the modern world. *The Runners* makes an excellent accompaniment to sessions on this topic. It is made from a fragment of a black-figure cup and features a series of runners in the bottom band and a horse grazing in the upper band.[14] A teacher might begin by asking students to study the image of the vase fragment, with questions exploring what movements they can see in the picture (i.e. what things the image suggests might be moving, and what it is about the image that makes it seem that those things might be moving) and what else could happen next. Then the class might watch the animation together and compare their answers to what they saw. To explore the social role of athletics and the Olympic Games further, ask the class to consider what it means that the ancient Greeks had pictures of running races on their pottery. This sort of discussion can be usefully augmented by inviting students to look at the images on their lunch boxes or pencil cases: what scenes do they have? Why are they there? What do those particular images show us? This sort of activity can reinforce children's understanding of decoration in an ancient context by helping to bridge the gap between ancient artefacts as functional yet decorative objects, and the functional, decorated objects within their own experience. Challenge the students to decorate vases or other objects showing their own favourite sports and games.

Some activities around vases and vase animations support functional literacy as well as extending visual literacy, namely writing or performing dialogues based on the vases and their animations. Most of the animations come without dialogue or language. The chief advantage of this is that it removes potential language barriers, enabling the vase animations to be used internationally; classical civilization is, after all, a global phenomenon. The absence of dialogue is also an opportunity for young people to speculate on what the figures might say to each other if they could talk. *Well-Wishers* and *Clash of the Dicers* are particularly suitable for adding dialogue. The former depicts family members bidding farewell to a young warrior; the latter depicts an argument over a board game between Achilles and Ajax. A teacher might watch the animations with the group and ask them to discuss what is happening between the characters and what visual clues make them think that. The students would then be invited to write dialogue for the figures. If the teacher thinks that it might be suitable for the class, the students might even perform their dialogue with the animation or record it and play them together. The same activity can be done with any vase, but the animations' extra movement and development can help to make the additional features more conceivable.

Rather than dialogue, the animations rely on music for their audio content. Many of them feature tracks by ancient music specialists such as Professor Conrad Steinmann of the music academy Schola Cantorum Basiliensis in Basel, Switzerland, and the Thiasos Theatre Company. *Sappho 44. Hector and Andromache. A Wedding at Troy* features a particularly special of piece of music. Professor Armand D'Angour of the University of Oxford scored the piece for us based on the rhythms and notes indicated in the surviving fragment of one of Sappho's poems (*Fragment 44*). As a result, the tune that can be heard playing throughout the animation is the same tune that the poem would have been sung to, now reperformed for the first time since antiquity. These soundtracks create an opportunity to extend students' soundscapes through the wild sounds of the *aulos* and unusual ancient rhythms. Ask students to try and describe the music on an animation such as *Sappho 44* or *The Symposium*. What does it sound like? How is like or unlike modern music? Would the animation seem different if the music was different? Test this final question by inviting the students to create new soundtracks (typically using percussion instruments) and to play those soundtracks over the muted animations.

Despite featuring ancient music, the Sappho animation departs from our usual practice by making additional use of language. Sappho's lyrics appear on screen, translated into English in one version and Polish in another, as Sappho plays the accompaniment.[15] Sappho offers us that rare thing, an authentic women's voice from antiquity, and for that reason we resolved to bring her command of words into focus. The vase from which *Sappho 44* is made is an early portrait

Figure 10.2 Sappho sings of Hector and Andromache's journey to Troy. Scene from *Sappho 44. Hector and Andromache. A Wedding at Troy.* © University of Roehampton.

vase, painted at the end of the sixth century BC, the century in which she actually lived. She appears austerely as a lone figure on a black glaze, holding a *barbiton*, a kind of deep-toned lyre. In addition to showing her play, we added smaller figures who appear and act out her poetry. Younger viewers may find it challenging to read the text and follow the movement simultaneously, but they are likely to be able to follow the narrative performed by the figures. We depicted the music-conjured figures using the geometric style, a style from an earlier generation of vase painting to that of the Sappho vase, so that they act as a visual indicator of an earlier age, a time that would have been 'long ago' even in Sappho's era.

The side-by-side appearance of figures from different eras of pottery offers an opportunity for students to explore the contrasting styles and to appreciate the way that styles of art change over time. As primary-aged learners typically lack the background information with which to contextualize the appearance of the earlier geometric figures, they are likely to benefit from seeing images of geometric-ware before they watch *Sappho 44*, and from having it explained explicitly that figures from one period are appearing in the same animation, but not on the original vase. Before watching the animation, a teacher might also ask students to look at the image of the Sappho vase and to discuss what parts of the image might move – an opportunity for them to notice details such as hands and feet, plectrum, strings and earrings. Once the animation has been watched, they might consider how accurately they guessed. They might then be asked to list differences between the Sappho figure and the geometric figures – what is it that constitutes the change in style? If the students have understood that the animated figures act out what is in Sappho's poem, it may be constructive to encourage them to consider other possibilities: can they write a poem that Sappho might sing? Can they draw a picture of geometric figures acting out that poem?

For those who are tackling the Trojan War with young students, *Sappho 44* offers an opportunity to stretch their thinking about Troy itself as an imagined environment (i.e. one

127

where things can be imagined happening before the famous war). It also offers an insight into ancient Greek relationships with the Trojan War myths – the idea of people returning to the same story to add prequel or sequel material. They may be able to think of similar examples from the modern world. This is helpful for supporting children in recognizing the ongoing creativity at work within ancient Greek culture and the long period of time that 'ancient Greece' represents. Adults working with young children who have experienced displacement through military conflict may find it constructive to focus conversations around the figure of Andromache. Andromache famously experienced painful hardships and losses. After leaving a happy childhood home to marry Hector, she was cut off from that childhood environment by the killing of her family, only for her new family to suffer the same fate. She herself was transported to an inhospitable Greece. Gently discussing Andromache is a way of exploring difficult issues to do with change and loss, as well as the importance of remembering happy times.[16] The materials that are being released along with the animation via the project website will support teachers in implementing all of these activities and discussions.

An example session

The ideas above demonstrate that there is no one way to use the vase animations in class; they can be used to reinforce any number or historical and art historical sessions. Nonetheless, here is a step-by-step guide to implementing one possible session, which emphasizes a mythology topic and image comprehension:

- Visit www.panoply.org.uk to select the animation(s) that will suit your class and to read around the topic.
- As a class, examine some modern images of Heracles. Is there anything distinctive about him? Are there any motifs that recur?
- Look together at an image of the vase featured in *Heracles and the Erymanthian Boar*. Do the students recognize the hero? What is similar or different about the way he has been depicted? What is going on in the scene?
- Watch the animation together.
- Were the students right about what was happening in the original vase scene? What was different? What was the same?
- Now challenge your students to create their own artworks based on this myth. Ask them to consider the following questions: what moment from the myth will they depict? How will they depict Heracles? Who or what else will be in their image?
- Provide materials for students to create with, e.g. ordinary plain paper, thick card to be cut and painted, standard (perhaps coloured) card that can be drawn on with pencil or felt tip, air-dry clay that can be prepped in an earlier session and painted following the animation viewing, or pre-prepared papier mâché that can be painted.
- Encourage willing members of the class to share their results in order to reinforce the variety of representations that are possible for a single myth.

The old and the new

Through watching the vase animations together with class discussions and the sorts of follow-up activities described above, children can gain a greater appreciation of ancient pottery and vases as evidence for life in classical antiquity. There is an important additional learning point that they may gain indirectly, namely antiquity's continuing influence on culture and creativity. The vase animations demonstrate that ancient objects and ancient culture continue to inspire new material, new art, in modern media. This is a message that can provide inspiration to young people in the way they think about antiquity and their own relationship with it. The ancient can inspire the new. The ancient world is not only something to be learned about, but something to which they can turn to inform their own creativity and artwork, and something which they can find their own ways of expressing. Through digital art, the vase animations offer a new way of looking at artefacts that helps us to appreciate the artefacts themselves and to consider what we wish to *do* with antiquity.

Notes

1. *Heracles and the Erymanthian Boar*, National Museum in Warsaw, 198042/a-b MNW.

2. *Hoplites! Greeks at War*, University of Reading, Ure Museum of Greek Archaeology, Accession number: 56.8.8, made with AHRC funding via the University of Oxford's Archive for Performances of Greek and Roman Drama.

3. University College Dublin Classical Museum, Catalogue number: UCD 197. This animation was made with funding from the UCD College of Arts and Celtic Studies.

4. University of Oxford, Ashmolean Museum, AN1974.344. This animation was made with funding from the Oxford University Knowledge Exchange Fund, for Classics in Communities.

5. Vatican Museum, Rome, Accession number: 344.

6. Ure Museum, Accession number: 51.4.6.

7. This project has received funding from the European Research Council (ERC) under the European Union's Horizon 2020 Research and Innovation Programme under grant agreement No. 681202, Our Mythical Childhood ... The Reception of Classical Antiquity in Children's and Young Adults' Culture in Response to Regional and Global Challenges, ERC Consolidator Grant (2016–21), led by Prof. Katarzyna Marciniak, Faculty of 'Artes Liberales' at the University of Warsaw.

8. These animations have been created from vases in the National Museum in Warsaw: 198042/a-b MNW; 142289 MNW; 142333 MNW; 142460 MNW; 142355 MNW.

9. See, for example, Kümmerling-Meibauer (2015) and Eilam (2012).

10. See Cox-Petersen and Melber (2001). Animations on display in the Ure Museum, Reading; UCD Classical Museum, Dublin; The National Museum in Warsaw.

11. *The Symposium*, Ashmolean Museum, AN1974.344; *Hoplites! Greeks at War*, Ure Museum, Accession number: 56.8.8.

12. *Iris – Rainbow Goddess* (made from National Museum in Warsaw: 142289 MNW) depicts Iris creating rainbows through her flight, and a rainbow appears as the iris of Iris's eye. This offers a further crossover teaching point exploring the use of ancient Greek words and concepts within biology and other sciences.

13. *Heracles and the Erymanthian Boar*, National Museum in Warsaw: 198042/a-b MNW; *Heracles*, Ure Museum, Accession number: 52.3.1.

14. Ure Museum, Accession number: 51.4.6. The related animation, *The Cheat*, was created for an award-winning Open University OpenLearn course: The Ancient Olympics: Bridging Past and Present. Teachers may find it helpful to look at material about the games within that course as well as the material on the Panoply website: www.panoply.org.uk/the-cheat.html.

15. A number of different languages are represented via subtitles. Many thanks to all those who helped with the translations.

16. Tackling recent war trauma through antiquity can be constructive, as seen in the recent productions of Euripides' *Trojan Women* (The Syria Trojan Women Project, UK-Jordan, 2013, www. syriatrojanwomen.org/index.html) and *Iphigenia at Aulis* (Volksbuehne Theatre, Germany, 2018) by people from refugee communities.

References

Cox-Petersen, A. and Melber, L. (2001), 'Using Technology to Prepare and Extend Field Trips', *The Clearing House*, 75 (1): 18–20.

Eilam, B. (2012), *Teaching, Learning, and Visual Literacy The Dual Role of Visual Representation*, Cambridge: Cambridge University Press.

Kümmerling-Meibauer, B. and Meibauer, J. (2018), 'Picturebooks and Cognitive Studies', in B. Kümmerling-Meibauer (ed.), *The Routledge Companion to Picturebooks*, 391–400, New York: Routledge.

Kümmerling-Meibauer, B., Meibauer, J., Nachtigäller, K. and Rohlfing, K. (eds.) (2015), *Learning from Picturebooks: Perspectives from Child Development and Literacy Studies*, New York: Routledge.

Nevin, S. (2015), 'Animating Ancient Warfare: The Spectacle of War in the Panoply Vase Animations', in A. Bakogianni and V. Hope (eds.), *War as Spectacle: Ancient and Modern Perspectives on the Display of Armed Conflict*, London: Bloomsbury Academic, 335–352.

Nevin, S. (2015), 'Animations of Ancient Vase Scenes in the Classics Classroom', *Journal of Classics Teaching*, 16: 32–37.

Nevin, S. (2016), 'Animating Antiquity: An Interview with Classical Scholar Sonya Nevin and Animator Steve K. Simons', *Thersites: Journal for Transcultural Presences and Diachronic Identities from Antiquity to Date*, 3. Available online: http://www.thersites.uni-mainz.de/index.php/thr/article/view/30.

Painter, C., Martin, J. and Unsworth, L. (2014), *Reading Visual Narratives: Image Analysis of Children's Picture Books*, Sheffield: Equinox.

Painter, C. (2018), 'Multimodal Analysis of Picturebooks', in B. Kümmerling-Meibauer (ed.), *The Routledge Companion to Picturebooks*, New York: Routledge.

Sylva, K. and Lunt, I. (1982: 1994), *Child Development. A First Course*, Oxford: Blackwell.

Wetterlund, K. (2008), 'Flipping the Field Trip: Bringing the Art Museum to the Classroom', *Theory into Practice*, 47 (2): 110–117.

CHAPTER 11
SKETCHUP AND DIGITAL MODELLING FOR CLASSICS
Matthew Nicholls

'There is a satisfactory and available power in every one to learn drawing if he wishes, just as nearly all persons have the power of learning French, Latin or arithmetic, in a decent and useful degree.'

Ruskin, *The Elements of Drawing*, 1.3.

Introduction

In recent years the representation of the ancient past using digital reconstructions has become a commonplace of television documentaries, museum and archaeological site guides and computer games, and is becoming increasingly common in academic projects. By 'digital reconstruction' I mean here a three-dimensional (3D) model of a structure, space or environment created inside a computer using modelling software. Such models can then be used to generate a still image or animation, as well as many other possible outputs, some of which we will encounter later in this chapter.

My own reconstruction work is chiefly concerned with the city of Rome as it appeared in the imperial period. My work on individual structures, which began with the city's public libraries, has grown over time into a model of the entire city of Rome as it appeared around 315 CE. Researched and created from a wide range of archaeological, literary, numismatic, epigraphic and artistic evidence, this model contains hundreds of thousands of separate elements, including many buildings with interior and exterior detailing good enough to sustain ground-level 'exploration'.

Research applications of this work include the study of sight lines within and between monuments, and the effects of solar illumination at different times of day and year (Nicholls 2016, 2018; Russell 2014). This chapter is chiefly concerned with its teaching applications, however, and these are almost limitless. I use still or moving images from my digital models to illustrate lectures, articles and book chapters, public and outreach talks, field trips to Rome, and more. On large screens I 'walk' or 'fly' around the model in real time with students. Since 3D model content of this type is becoming ever easier to share, or to adapt to new forms of use, I have also made elements available in online 3D sharing platforms where users can explore buildings for themselves, used it as the basis for a free massive open online course (MOOC) which has now been taken by 27,000 people, experimented with 3D printing and virtual reality, licensed the model for adaption in television documentaries, smartphone apps and a computer game, and more. The overall point is that 3D content, once made, can be used, shared and explored in many different ways that lend themselves to imaginative use in teaching contexts.

Figure 11.1 The Colosseum and its surroundings, looking towards the Esquiline Hill. © Matthew Nicholls, University of Reading, 2018.

Digital reconstructions of this sort, therefore, have enormous potential for research and teaching in a field like Classics. As I intend to show here, they can now be created in software that is cheap and user-friendly enough to be amenable to use by the non-specialist. This brings digital reconstruction within the reach of research and teaching projects that do not have the resources for professional-grade software or expertise. My own background, for example, is in Classics. I am a researcher and educator in ancient Roman history, not a professional in the field of digital visualization. I created much of the work described in this chapter without any formal training, using free or cheap software – in particular, the free 3D modelling software SketchUp – that will run on most standard computers.

It follows that other academics and teachers could do the same, and further, that their students could be taught to create models of their own, as I describe below. Though it is certainly helpful to begin with an aptitude for visualizing 3D forms, and a certain facility with computers, these are not essential. A skilful or patient modeller can always reach new levels of accuracy and detail, but a very simple model can itself be a useful illustrative or teaching tool, and almost anyone can learn to make such models in software like SketchUp in a relatively short period of time (hence the epigraph from Ruskin with which this chapter opens).

Though I would like to encourage readers to experiment with their own models, it is also the case that huge online repositories of free content now make it easy to use this sort of material in teaching without having to create it for oneself. As well as my own work, there are many other ancient world 3D reconstruction projects to explore, like Rome Reborn, the Digitales Forum Romanum project of the Humboldt University in Berlin, Byzantium 1200, Virtual Amarna and many more. SketchUp's own integrated '3D Warehouse' contains millions of user-generated models, all of which can be freely downloaded and edited. At the time of writing, these free models included over 150 versions of the Colosseum in Rome, and nearly

90 versions of the Athenian Acropolis. The quality of these models varies widely, of course, but many excellent models are available. Specialist 3D platforms like SketchFab contain millions more models, freely explorable within any internet browser on desktop and mobile devices, or in virtual reality headsets. These include models made by users, but also many contributed by an increasing number of museums and galleries, bringing high-quality annotated models of world-class artefacts into the classroom for virtual handling.

Digital reconstruction is predominantly a visual domain, of course, but other sensory inputs and outputs are increasingly possible. 3D printing is becoming commonplace in schools and universities, allowing for the production of tangible physical versions of buildings, vases or statues. Virtual reality, delivered through a headset, brings proprioception and movement stimulus as well as proper stereoscopic 3D to a user's immersive experience of architectural environments: the effect can be very striking, adding in particular an instant intuitive appreciation of scale that can be hard to gauge on a flat computer screen. It is already possible to put a class of students into an immersive 3D environment to explore in real time – I have experimented with the Roman Forum space and with ancient theatre buildings – and as virtual reality equipment becomes more widespread, with the games industry driving technological innovation, this should become cheaper and easier to do. Augmented reality, on the other hand, allows a model to be projected into a real-world space such as a classroom tabletop via the screen of a smartphone or tablet (try, for example, free apps like Augment and Kubity). Meanwhile, experiments with auditory and even olfactory modelling are allowing other senses to supplement sight.

Using digital models in teaching

If we limit ourselves for the present to using only standard current classroom technology – reasonably up-to-date computers, a projector or digital whiteboard and perhaps tablets – digital models still offer tremendous potential for teaching topics in (say) ancient architecture. Different levels of engagement are possible. At the simplest level, digital 3D content of the sort outlined above can simply be used to produce illustrative material, in the form of still pictures or animations, to use alongside other imagery like photographs or ground plans. Digital models have particular advantages even at this relatively basic level of engagement, because they can provide a vivid and accessible proposition of the appearance of an ancient space or building, which can be more intuitively comprehensible for some students than the traditional 2D ground plans or black-and-white line drawings often used to illustrate ancient architecture.

A digital 3D model is particularly useful in this way because an almost infinite variety of images can be generated by positioning the virtual viewpoint or 'camera' anywhere in the space around or within it. The same model can, therefore, generate both a scaled plan view and a 3D view in which elements of height, depth and volume are visible, thus combining the advantages (and mitigating the heuristic limitations) of planimetric and perspectival views. Animated sequences like fly-throughs can be automatically generated by moving the 'camera' through space, or around an object, and parameters like lighting, colour and transparency can all be controlled.

This ability to control and change viewpoint brings us to a deeper level of engagement with ideas about space and architecture. A model in SketchUp can be explored and edited on the screen, while the apps named above allow a digital object at least to be spun, positioned and scaled. Navigating and manipulating digital models in this way, whether on a computer or a hand-held device, is immediately more engaging than just looking at images, and can encourage students to think critically about ways of viewing and perceiving ancient objects, buildings or spaces, working out how ancient visitors used, moved through or experienced them. This sort of approach complements current directions in scholarship on ancient cities and architecture, in which an emphasis known as the 'spatial turn' is being placed on how ancient spaces were experienced, considering, for example, questions of movement, appearance, sight lines, topography, social interactions, streetscapes, processions and performances of various types. The scope of a digital model for visualizing an ancient building or space from any point of view, and for moving through it, enables these sorts of questions to be considered both accurately and intuitively; simply put, we can step 'into' an ancient space and look around (acknowledging always the limitations of whatever model we might be using), a mode of investigation which is not possible in other media. Within the same model, we might for instance contrast a conventional plan or overhead view with the ground-level experience of a visitor, considering how buildings might have been designed, how ancient writers might conceptualize or describe them, how they actually appear on the ground or function in practical terms, and how they relate to their surroundings and to each other when seen from a distance. We can also set buildings in their wider context of landscape and neighbourhood, generate plan views, transparencies, elevations and sections relatively easily from the same base model, superimpose ancient buildings onto modern map views, and so on.

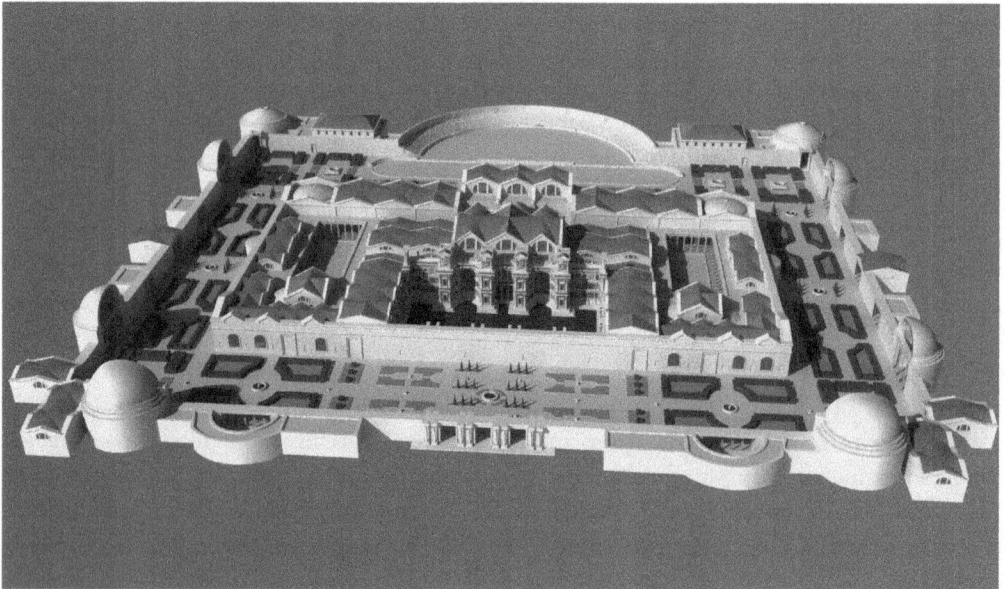

Figure 11.2 Digital model of the Baths of Diocletian in Rome. © Matthew Nicholls, University of Reading, 2018.

These types of enquiry or activity are possible with ready-made content from the sources named above, but a still deeper level of engagement comes when students make their own digital models; I describe my own experience of teaching students to do so below. The process of making one's own reconstructions necessitates a complete consideration of the structure or space in question, as gaps in knowledge, evidence or thought quickly become evident when they show up as blank spaces in the model. Every click of the mouse becomes a decision point, grounded where possible in evidence or, where that is not possible, in reasonable conjecture. The task of making a digital model therefore encourages critical thinking about the reconstruction process as a way of handling incomplete evidence, making hypotheses or arguments about the past and representing those visually. This is a valuable complement to the traditional textual modes of research and assessment in a discipline like Classics, which embraces numerous visual subject areas in material culture, architecture and art history, but typically asks students to make hypotheses and arguments in a written form like an essay. The methodological similarities and differences inherent in a visual reconstruction exercise can be illuminating, as we will see.

An endless range of activities becomes possible with a class of students who are able to generate their own models, or to discover and explore ready-made 3D content: they could be asked to make a building model from a textual description, fresco, archaeological ground plan or coin image; to think about the different experiences of a building from different points within or outside it; to visualize elements of an ancient itinerary like Ovid's or Martial's tours of Rome; to experiment with the effects of colour and lighting, crowds and empty space, stillness and movement; and no doubt to invent – as my students have frequently done – creative investigatory or presentational uses for digital model content that had not occurred to their instructor.

How are such digital models made?

A variety of modelling software is available, adapted to different sorts of task and user. Readers might find their own favourites, but my work is largely done in SketchUp, an elegant and simple 3D modelling program. Elsewhere in this volume Jessie Craft discusses his excellent work using *Minecraft* (see also Craft 2016). While *Minecraft* uses the placing of ready-made building blocks to create structures – like digital Lego – SketchUp is essentially a drawing tool, using lines to create bounded 2D and 3D shapes that can exist in any form and combination, enabling its users to create an almost infinite variety of 3D digital content at whatever level of detail they wish. The basic toolset is simple enough: a line tool draws a line between two points chosen with mouse clicks inside the modelling environment; a closed loop of coplanar lines creates a 2D surface (a square, say, or a circle); these can be 'push-pulled' or extruded into 3D shapes (a cuboid or a cylinder), which can then be further extended, partitioned, coloured, moved, sectioned, scaled, rotated, duplicated and so on. Images can be imported into the program, including ground plans to use as references for modelling or as 'textures' (a brick pattern, say, or plaster) that can be painted onto surfaces to enhance a model's appearance.

Using this basic toolset, even an inexperienced user can generally create simple but useful models very quickly. Conversely, almost any amount of time and effort can be invested to produce larger and more detailed results: my own model of Rome has been around a decade in the making, and work continues. Here, for example, is a SketchUp model of the Temple of the Deified Claudius in Rome. It requires an understanding of the evidence for the building from preserved remains, published archaeological ground plans, literary descriptions and so on, and the interpretative reconstruction of those remains, but this sort of knowledge is already within the domain of the ancient historian or archaeologist with an interest in Roman architecture.

In terms of modelling skill and time, the simple schematic model on the left took approximately five minutes to make using only a subset of the simplest drawing tools in SketchUp (line, erase, push-pull, move, paint bucket). The more detailed model to the right took several days' work and uses a wider repertoire of tools and actions, but all still within the user-friendly native toolset of the free version of the software. Either could be useful for classroom explorations, as a stimulus for questions like: what is the view of the complex from below? Can you tell that it contains a temple? How does the view change as you 'climb' the monumental stairs? The simpler model could be made by many students within an hour or so of starting to use the software for the first time. When I teach SketchUp workshops, I tend to see beginner students – from primary school to undergraduate level – racing ahead of my tuition to explore what the different tools do; later on, when we get to more complex functions, the pace settles down.

This is because, like *Minecraft* modelling, SketchUp is relatively easy and (importantly) fun to use from the outset. Professional-grade software like AutoCAD or 3DS Max can generate more complex and sophisticated models, but comes with a correspondingly steep learning curve. I suggest that for non-specialist use in the context of teaching a subject like Classics, a free and simple tool like SketchUp is ideal because it is not off-putting to the complete beginner; in fact, I – and many of my students – have found that it is actually annoyingly addictive.

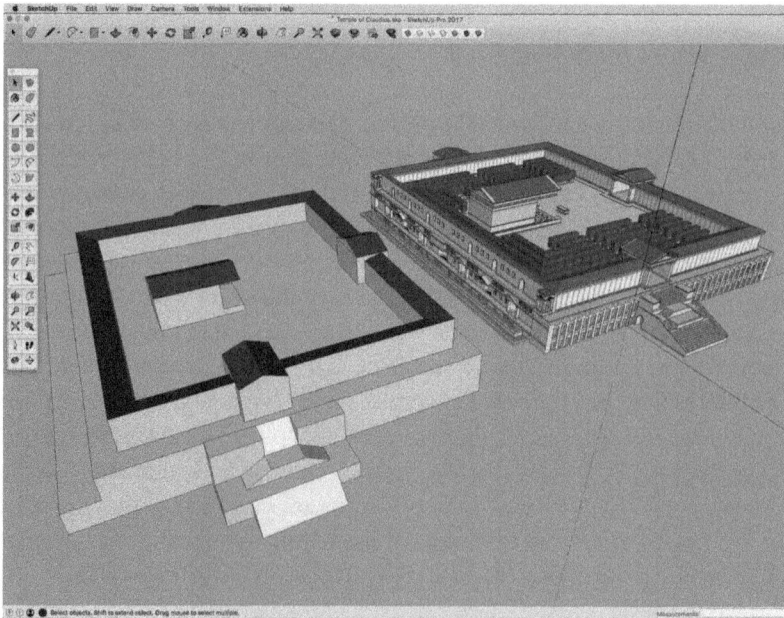

Figure 11.3 A model of the Temple of the Deified Claudius in Rome, made and viewed in SketchUp. © Matthew Nicholls, University of Reading, 2018.

Beginners encouraged by this chapter to try digital modelling might well find the same: the rewards of success come early and often enough to encourage persistence to higher levels of competence and fluency.

As SketchUp has become a popular tool with millions of users worldwide, it is well supported by online resources, including the 3D Warehouse mentioned above, plug-ins, extensions and tutorials to support a user's development. It can also import and export a very wide variety of file formats, which means that content made there can be reused in lots of other digital contexts, including all those suggested above, and vice versa.

Though SketchUp is capable of producing very detailed results – it is used by many architects, landscape designers and cabinet makers, for example – it has limitations. It could not hold my entire model of Rome, which I create and export in smaller subunits and assemble in more complex and expensive software like Lumion and Cinema 4D. These are able to deal with massive models, and to 'render' still or moving images by simulating the effect of light and shade on the various natural and man-made surfaces in the city, achieving a more convincing appearance. For most uses, however, and certainly for beginners or as part of a larger educational project, tools like SketchUp are more than sufficient.

Teaching students to make their own models

My own experience of learning to create digital models as a non-specialist suggested that I might be able to involve students in making similar models of their own. I was encouraged to do this by students at the University of Reading who saw pictures of my model that I used in my lectures (that first, fairly simple level of engagement described above) and wanted to know how I had made them; when I described the process, they asked if they could try for themselves. This opportunity to develop a new style of teaching seemed worth taking for a number of reasons.

Firstly, it seemed likely that it would be tremendous fun for both educator and students, which is not a negligible consideration. I like making 3D models: the software is enjoyable to use, the results are very satisfying and it offers an avenue for visual and creative expression that is not always possible within the conventional disciplinary confines of a Classics degree. It seemed likely that students would find the same, and this has in fact proven to be the case, shown anecdotally in the fact that the classes are always a pleasure to teach, and more formally by strong expressions of positive feedback during and after the course, and by the quality of the submitted work. Many students are attracted to studying the ancient world in the first place by their experience of computer games, films, documentaries or museum exhibits which make use of digital reconstruction, and I discovered a strong appetite to find out more and to have a go for themselves.

Secondly, offering a course of this type fitted with certain pedagogical aims of my department and university, which are keen to get students actively involved in 'enquiry-based learning'. Towards the latter stages of their degree, our aim is to encourage students to develop their own research topics and the skills, problem-solving abilities and knowledge needed to address them, with the lecturer acting more as a facilitator than (only) as a source of information. The goal is to encourage initiative and to deepen the students' acquisition of knowledge, since it is acquired in projects of their own devising. A task like researching and creating a digital model of an ancient building lends itself very well to this sort of approach because it is very open-ended: as I hope the material above has started to show, and as we will see below, digital models come in a wide variety of types and can be used to address many different sorts of questions, so an important initial step is for students to determine what sort of model they wish to make and why.

Thirdly, an exercise of this type necessarily introduces a number of new skills and aptitudes that are highly distinctive within a Classics degree. Many of these – not only the use of the digital modelling software itself, but also the associated skills of image research and manipulation, file management and visual presentation of material – are valuable 'transferable' digital skills that are important for a non-vocational discipline like Classics to be able to demonstrate in at least some of its teaching; several former students have gone on to make use of this distinctive experience in their first job interviews (and sometimes first jobs) after graduation. The necessarily visual learning style is also unusual within a Classics degree and appeals to a wide variety of students, including those with some learning disabilities who are able to flourish in a non- or at least not solely verbal form of assessment.

I therefore decided to create an undergraduate digital modelling module (at Reading, a 'module' is a unit of undergraduate study, typically worth 20 of a year's total of 120 credits, and often taught in the course of one or two terms' instruction). The module was based on creating digital reconstructions of buildings from the Romano-British town of Silchester, local to Reading and excavated by our own archaeology department over recent decades. Silchester was inhabited from at least the first century BC to around the sixth or seventh centuries CE. It began life as the stronghold of an Iron Age British tribe, and then became a regional Roman capital in southern Britain, at an important junction point in the island's road network. At its height it was an important town, with impressive public buildings (a forum with a basilica, a bathhouse, an amphitheatre), an imposing wall circuit with entrance gateways, and a large number of houses whose furnishings, including impressive mosaic decorations, survive and are displayed in our town museum.

A town like Silchester thus offers a good basis for a digital reconstruction module because a lot of information is readily available, from Victorian and Edwardian excavation plans and publications, to the museum artefacts and standing remains of the walls and amphitheatre, to more modern and intensive excavations. The site is compact, but contains a wide variety of building types, with good comparable examples from elsewhere in the Roman Empire to help supplement the foundations which survive at Silchester – all interesting, but none so vast or known in such detail that making a model becomes a daunting task for a beginner. There is a decent, if dated, single-volume guide to the site (Boon 1974) with just enough information on each building type to give students a good start, and a well-developed body of more detailed scholarly literature, including a meticulous compilation and mapping of all excavation data (Creighton 2016). Since finding and assessing the usefulness of the available evidence is a fundamental part of creating a digital reconstruction, this well-defined body of material is an excellent starting point. To avoid wear and tear on fragile Victorian pull-out maps and journal articles, I arranged for the library to make scanned copies available in our virtual learning environment (VLE); otherwise, all the necessary material was readily and immediately available.

The module, Digital Silchester, is taught in two-hour classes in a computer lab on university PCs running a free educational licence of SketchUp. A free in-browser version of the software has now removed the need to install anything on networked machines; any computer with an internet connection can run it, including students' own laptops, though a proper three-button mouse vastly improves the user experience.

Students are encouraged to download and experiment with the software before the start of term, but no prior knowledge or experience is assumed. We start, however, not with software skills, but with introductory lectures about the historical context of the site and the Romans in Britain. We then move on to questions of methodology, tools and goals. At an early stage in the module I tend to ask students about their ambitions for the digital models they will be creating, and their initial answers are fairly uniformly variations on the concept of 'realism'. But that is a rather more labile quality than might be supposed. In general, the students aim at first to create the sort of photorealist impression of verisimilitude that computer games and television reconstructions can display. This is possible to do within the software we use, but one aim of the module is to encourage a more critical interrogation of this frequently encountered mode of visual interpretation, in the same way that we train classicists to be critical readers of texts. Documents like the London Charter seek to establish ground rules for the practice and 'ethics' of digital reconstruction, given its potential for creating images with a high superficial degree of convincingness, and it is important to include a similar element of methodological reflection in a module taught within the disciplinary context of Classics, Archaeology or Ancient History.

Questions worth asking include: does apparent verisimilitude necessarily equate to accuracy or intellectual rigour? How do we link what we show in the model to what we know from our research? What, in fact, do we know about the site? What do we not know? Can and should we represent in our models doubtful or variant interpretations of the evidence? We also think about ways of presenting digital reconstruction: what sort of information do we actually want to convey, and how might this be affected by styles of presentation? The software can generate whatever we wish: a 'photorealistic' mode of presentation certainly, but also something more like a graphical illustration, or a cross-section, partial transparency, cutaway or plan. We could choose to show a scene inhabited and full of furniture and the clutter of daily life, if we are interested in investigating questions of social history; or, like my Rome model, empty, as an architectural maquette, if we are more interested in architectural and topographical questions. We could show a building 'realistically' (that is, from the ground-level perspective of an ancient visitor), but we might find it more useful to choose an 'unrealistic' viewing mode, such as an overhead view with the roof removed, like a dolls' house, to reveal the interior. We could aim for multiple different viewing possibilities, including different camera positions and different types of content (e.g. people, furniture, roofs, colours, periods of time, annotation labels) on layers that could be turned on and off, or animated in sequence. All of this works much better if planned carefully in advance, before starting to make the model, so it is important to begin by asking what kinds of claims to authenticity or reliability these different types of model make, and how they present information to their audience. This discussion helps to build a degree of visual critical literacy in students, which they can bring to bear on visual material they encounter elsewhere in their studies.

After covering these questions, we move into masterclass-style SketchUp workshops on practical modelling techniques. I connect my computer to a projector so I can show the students how to use various tools within the software as they follow along. I also reinforce important points, or address student requests, with short narrated screen-grab videos in our VLE to make the most efficient use of classroom time. Towards the end of the module I try to allow time for troubleshooting work on students' individual models.

The assignments for the module consist of a small interim model with written commentary, to be handed in at the mid-point of the term and worth 20 per cent of the overall mark, and a larger model with commentary due at the end of term, worth the remaining 80 per cent. The split in the value of the two pieces was intended to force early engagement and competence with the software: while a student can sometimes scrape a passing mark if they leave work on an essay to the last minute (though one is loath to admit it), a similar attempt to put off any digital modelling practice until very late in the course would be disastrous.

The written commentary element is intended to encourage a scholarly and thorough approach to the modelling process, and to remind students that, as discussed above, the module is not a beauty contest: though well-made and well-organized models often do appear visually attractive and convincing, the task at hand is to research and propose something about the site of Silchester in a way that passes muster within an ancient world degree, where evidence is always the foundation for argument. The written commentary, which I suggest should function as the 'footnotes' to the model, therefore justifies and explains the choices made in putting the model together: sources of evidence, grounds for conjecture where necessary, comparative material and bibliography consulted, and so on. This was an important part of making this an academically credible module, sitting naturally within an Ancient History or Classics degree programme, and in securing the agreement of internal quality assurance and external examiners: the emphasis is on evidence, argument and analysis as much as on technical software skills, and it is possible to score a high mark for a visually simple but clever and well-argued model.

The model for all students' initial small assessment is of a single structure that I pick. I tend to use the so-called 'church' at Silchester, which is small and fairly simple to model, but admits of an interesting variety of approaches and modes of presentation. The images here show that students can already see the potential of the software for displaying different ways of interpreting and explaining a building by this mid-point of the module.

The choice of structure for the second, larger assignment is left to the student, fulfilling the principles of enquiry-based learning. As the examples here show, students are able to create extremely convincing and impressive work after ten weeks of instruction. Ability levels naturally vary, but at the top end of the scale I have awarded higher marks in this module than in any of my other teaching, while – somewhat to my surprise – I have not yet come across a case of complete inability to produce a competent result. Students enjoy SketchUp, grasp the inherent flexibility of digital content and produce a wide range of imaginative presentations from their models that exceed the brief I give them. I have received animations of change over time, sample lesson plans from an aspirant teacher, 3D printouts, superimpositions of reconstructions on the excavation trench at the site, detailed diagrams of the timber jointing in a Roman roof, and more.

Overall, students have responded very well to the challenge of learning a new way of investigating the ancient world, and seem to have enjoyed doing so. The intuitive user interface of SketchUp has been an important element in the success of the module, but I hope to have shown that some of the principles and modes of enquiry involved can be adapted to other sorts of content, including ready-made online material. The inclusion of 3D digital content develops valuable digital skills, but also encourages new approaches to the traditional questions of evidence and presentation, deepening critical engagement with the way the past is studied and presented.

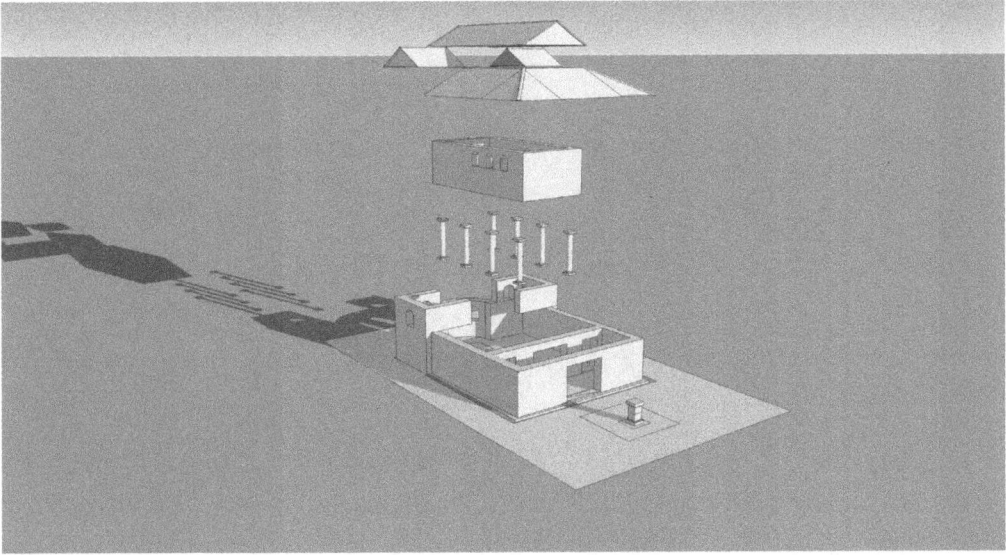

Figures 11.4a and 11.4b Different views of the so-called 'church' at Silchester, from student models made and viewed in SketchUp. Images courtesy of third-year undergraduate students George Jukes and Philip Smither.

These questions, and tools, are readily adaptable to a wide variety of pedagogical contexts. We can put ourselves, and our students, in the position of a worshipper at the Panathenaia, a gladiator in the Colosseum, an actor on the stage of the Theatre of Pompey, a visitor to the Roman Forum or the inhabitant(s) of a house in Pompeii, Athens or Silchester; or we can simply 'pick up' and explore artefacts that are now kept behind glass in London, Paris or New York. The technological tools necessary to do this have never been so easy to use, or so freely

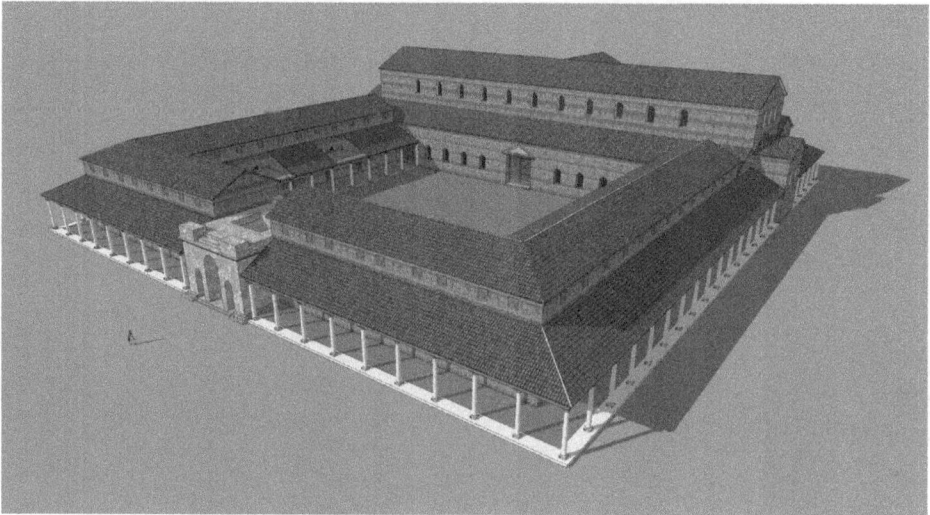

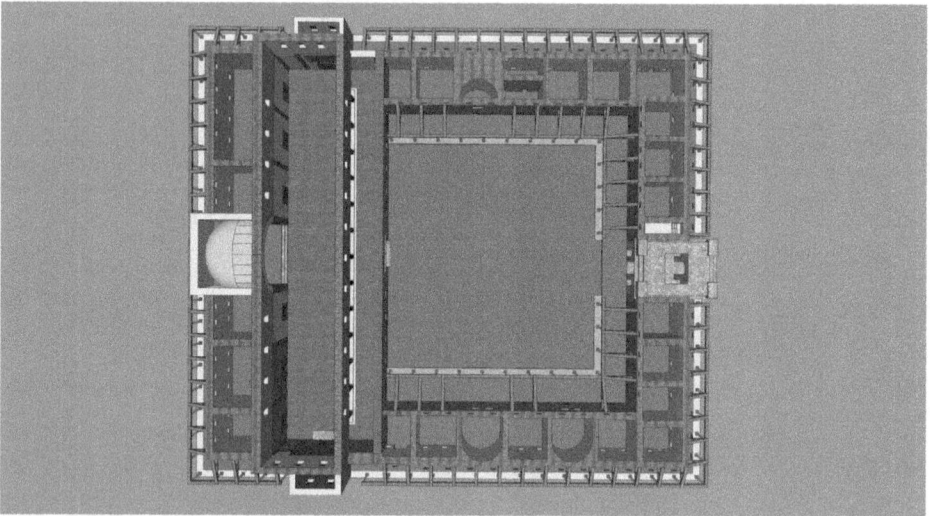

Figures 11.5a and 11.5b The Forum-Basilica at Silchester, from a student model made and viewed in SketchUp. Images courtesy of third-year undergraduate student George Jukes.

and widely available. Classics as a discipline has long been in the vanguard of innovative digital approaches to scholarship, and there is great potential to share these benefits with our students as users and co-creators of worthwhile digital content.

References

Boon, G. (1974), *Silchester: The Roman Town of Calleva*, London; David & Charles.
Craft, J. (2016), 'Rebuilding an Empire with Minecraft: Bringing the Classics into the Digital Space', *The Classical Journal*, 111.3: 347–364.

Creighton, J. with Fry, R. (2016), *Silchester: Changing Visions of a Roman Town. Integrating Geophysics and Archaeology – The Results of the Silchester Mapping Project 2005–10*, Britannia Monograph Series, 28, London: Society for the Promotion of Roman Studies.
Nicholls, M. (2016), 'Digital Visualisation: Ancient Rome, and Beyond', *British Academy Review*, 27 (February 2016): 41–44.
Nicholls, M. (2018), in Leoussi, A. and Heuser, B. (eds.), *Famous Battles and How They Shaped the Modern World: From Troy to Courtrai, 1200BC – 1302 AD*, Barnsley: Pen & Sword: 81–92.
Ruskin, J. (1857), *The Elements of Drawing*, 2nd edn.
Russell, A. (2014), 'Memory and Movement in the Roman Fora from Antiquity to Metro C', *Journal of the Society of Architectural Historians*, 4 (73): 478–506.

Links (correct at time of writing)

Ancient world 3D modelling projects:

- https://www.virtualrome.org – the author's Rome digital modelling project.
- https://www.romereborn.org – another 3D model of ancient Rome.
- http://www.digitales-forum-romanum.de – 3D models of the Roman Forum at different time periods.
- http://www.byzantium1200.com – a 3D model of Byzantium.
- http://www.amarna3d.com – a 3D model of ancient Amarna in Egypt.

Online resources:

- https://www.futurelearn.com/courses/rome – the author's free five-week interactive online course on Rome, using the digital model elements and real-world footage.
- https://www.theguardian.com/higher-education-network/2014/feb/18/winner-university-of-reading-teaching-excellence – *Guardian* article on the Rome and Digital Silchester projects.
- http://www.londoncharter.org – establishing internationally recognized principles for the use of computer-based visualization by researchers, educators and cultural heritage organizations.

Digital tools and software:

- https://sketchfab.com – repository of free 3D content.
- https://www.kubity.com – platform for sharing 3D models, including those made in SketchUp.
- https://www.augment.com/portfolio-items/university-of-reading/ – free tool for augmented reality, here describing the author's use of the tool with ancient Rome 3D content.
- https://www.sketchup.com – free 3D modelling software.

CHAPTER 12
iPAD TECHNOLOGY AND THE LATIN CLASSROOM
Caron Downes

Introduction

Whilst I tell my classes that 'Latin doesn't change', I strongly believe that our teaching of it can, and should, change to develop with the technology available to us. Teaching Classics allows us to combine the old and the new in one classroom.

Having trained in a school that was an Apple Training Centre, I have been incorporating iPads into my lessons since the start of my teaching career, often with just one iPad in the room displayed on the screen in my classroom via Apple TV. In the face of comments such as those by Ofsted's chief inspector Amanda Spielman[1] that mobile phones have 'made the challenge of low-level disruption even worse', and that she is 'yet to be convinced of the educational benefits of all day access to "Snapchat" and the like', it can seem easier to remove technology from classrooms. Spielman concluded her comments on the subject by saying that she believes 'the place of mobile phones in the classroom seems to me dubious at best' and by backing head teachers who decide to ban phones completely. However, I believe that, used effectively, technology can add value to the activities and outcomes of a lesson, which is in addition to the benefit of teaching the next generation how to use technology responsibly.

Initial thoughts

For two years, I led on the introduction of a 1:1 iPad scheme that equipped all students and staff with an iPad for use in lessons. As part of my role as the 'Leader of e-Learning', I have had the chance to incorporate technology into my lessons with all of my classes at some point. This has been with the sole purpose of finding out what enhances my teaching or the learning of my students. I have also been able to assess the value that students place on such activities. I have not thrown out books and pens; my students use their iPads alongside the traditional methods to record, analyse and share their learning.

During my Initial Teacher Training, my mentor encouraged me to teach in innovative ways; during my school placement I experimented with role-playing activities, team-based lessons, treasure hunts, a range of games and many more ideas. The habit has stuck, and years later I still try to teach using varied and creative methods. One such lesson last year involved me dressing up in a CSI suit and encouraging my students to investigate a 'crime scene' that I had set up in my classroom. The clues around the classroom were designed to teach my students the background to, and the key plot events of, the Greek tragedy *Medea*. In a staff meeting held shortly after the lesson, colleagues talked about my outfit and the excitement of the students passing my classroom. One teacher pronounced that, 'as fun as it may be, some of us do not have the time to run around playing dress-up because we are busy helping the students to actually learn something'. At first, the comment upset me; I have always prided myself on teaching lessons that the students enjoy but also learn from, and I thought my aims in this lesson were achieved. However, the comment made me question my methods further: am I 'running around playing dress-up' in vain? Are my students 'actually learning something' from my lessons? Do the students value the lessons? Are they even enjoying these activities?

With these thoughts in mind, I began looking into active learning techniques[2] to try to encourage my students to take greater control of the lessons. Active learning became a focus of research in America in the 1980s, when it was concluded that students learn best by doing; Bonwell and Eison define active learning activities as 'instructional activities involving students doing things and thinking about what they are doing' (Bonwell and Eison 1991: 1). In the UK, many authors (Kyriacou 1992, Halsall and Cockett 1998, Kyriacou and Marshall 1989 and Wolfe 2006) outline active learning strategies as those which allow pupils to have some level of input in their learning compared to those which are 'teacher-centred, didactic, prescriptive and expository teaching, in which the pupils are passive receivers of information' (Kyriacou and Marshall 1989: 1). Kane develops this definition further, saying that active learning activities 'seek to encourage independent, critical thinking in learners' (Kane 2004: 276). I hoped that with more input into the lessons the students would see a greater purpose to them. So, whilst I continued to dress-up during some lessons, I took more time to share the intentions of the activities clearly with the students and recorded their thoughts about the activities both before and after my lessons.

Methodology

For the sequence of lessons for this study, I decided to use the app Explain Everything, as I felt this would allow me to use technology and active learning activities within the lessons. The app allows text, audio and photographs to be recorded alongside a series of slides or a video. After we have completed the learning on a particular topic, my classes record short films on a section of the topic, which we annotate with the notes they have made during previous lessons. As the app is easy to use, I felt that the pupils were able to take the lead on the production of the video, thus combining technology and active learning techniques. From reading Drew and Mackie (2011), I understood that it is important for the teacher to maintain control of the lesson to ensure the pupils still achieve the learning goals. They write that 'the pupil may be in the driving seat but this is a dual-control vehicle where the teacher enables the pupil to become more active through a symbiotic pedagogical relationship, with the teacher moving through a continuum of support and challenge from facilitator to coach, speaker to listener (though in the last instance the teacher can slam on the brakes)' (Drew and Mackie 2011: 14). By keeping some control of the lesson, the teacher can make sure that the pupils are all learning the intended content from the activities that the pupils have selected. I felt that, by using the app, I could maintain the right amount of control whilst allowing the pupils to take a lead on discussions. I have found that my students value and enjoy this process and find it useful to review their work in an interactive manner that they can watch later as they revise for exams. I wanted to learn the opinions of pupils in my exam classes to understand how they perceived active learning strategies when meeting content that formed part of their examination specification; I therefore looked into the views of my Year 12 and Year 10 classes.

With my Year 12 classes, I have used Explain Everything to create a revision video for the Greek theatre module. In September, at the start of the course, I always begin with students researching the different parts of an ancient Greek theatre, and building their own model theatre. We then photograph the model theatre and annotate the image as a group. In the following months, lessons focus on reading and annotating the scripts of the plays, of which students need to have an in-depth knowledge for the exam. I often found that students struggled to see the texts as plays that would have been performed. For this reason, I wanted to find a way to re-establish an appreciation of the visual elements of plays.

After revision for their mock exams, when students should have a thorough knowledge of the texts but are often only thinking of the plays as a text to be studied and not for an audience to watch, I turn the focus back to the visual elements of the plays. We start with discussions of exam questions on the visual elements of the plays, with essay plans created in a shared document. We also watch extracts of Greek tragic plays on YouTube, as well as returning to the video introducing Greek theatre produced by the UK's National Theatre to show students images of theatres and the style of masks worn by the actors.

Through group discussion, the students select key scenes from their plays and focus on those scenes that would have included a variety of visual elements when performed originally. Once again, their notes are recorded on a shared document. For homework, students create their masks so that they are ready to act in a subsequent lesson. The mask-making tends to be something that is very popular with students, and they often take the time to work together in the art department. I usually allow one fifty-five-minute lesson for students to act out up to five scenes and to record the scenes on an iPad.

The following lesson (I prefer to use a double lesson of two hours), we import the recorded scenes to the Explain Everything app. Using just one iPad projected using the Apple TV, we discuss and annotate the scenes. Students use their annotated texts from throughout the year to contribute ideas to the notes. By using a wireless keyboard, the students can pass the burden of being the 'note taker' between them, so that everyone is able to annotate and contribute equally. Once the notes are completed, we save the file as a video and share it in the class Microsoft OneNote[3] for students to refer to whenever they need. I end the series of lessons by having the pupils plan an essay as a class, with notes saved in a shared document displayed on the projector, ready for them to write an essay in timed conditions for homework.

With my Year 10 classes, I have used Explain Everything to produce an annotated video of a Roman sacrifice. This is one of the more complex topics for students who have not studied it before, as there are a number of Latin words for students to learn – particularly of the different jobs taken by attendees of the ceremony – so I usually take three fifty-five-minute lessons for this topic. At the start of their course, the group will have met the topic briefly and filmed a basic Roman sacrifice. In the first lesson we return to their notes and the group works together to produce an outline of the events on the board.

In the second lesson, I encourage the students to use the iPads to search for images of sacrifices and then to annotate them using their notes on the Explain Everything app. At the end of the lesson, the students show each other the results of their work and discuss the images.

In the final lesson, we collate their notes, the video and the images produced in the previous lesson. I put the videos of the sacrifice into the Explain Everything app, and the students work together to order the events and annotate the videos (see Figure 12.1). For homework, they answer some examination-style questions based on Roman sacrifices.

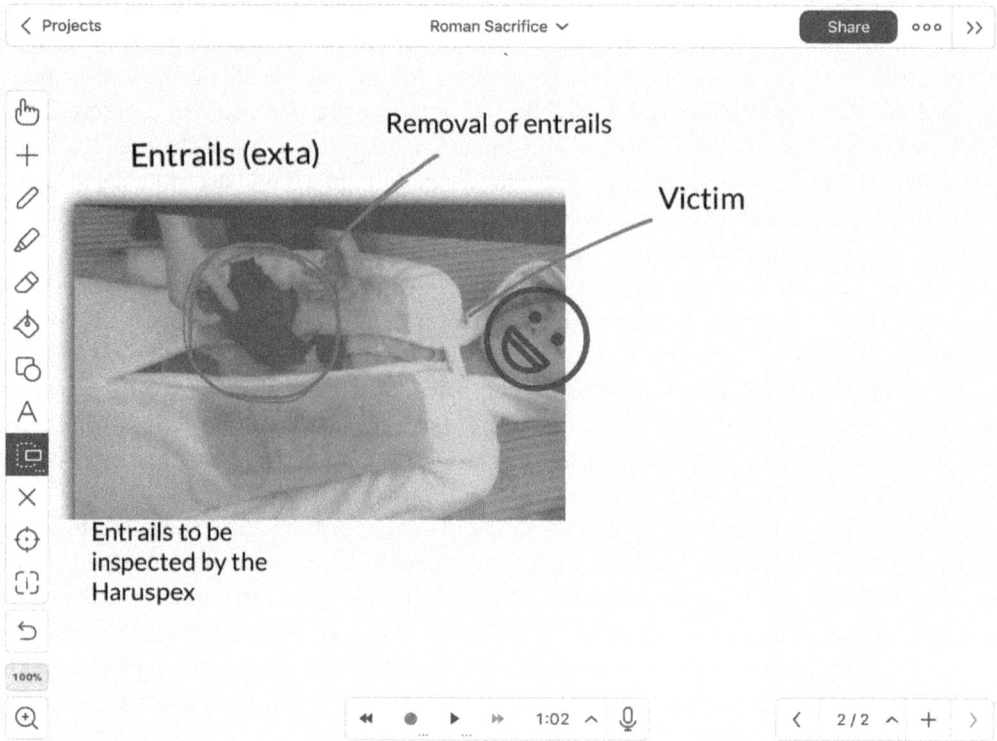

Figure 12.1 Screenshot of the Year 10 video with annotations in the Explain Everything app. © Caron Downes.

Further examples

With younger classes, usually in Year 7 or 8, I do not tend to dedicate so much time to recording videos of events, instead using only a single lesson to allow students to draw together their learning on a particular topic, such as Roman food or bath houses. With these topics, I have run lessons where students might host a 'dinner party' of their own or design their own set of bath houses to present to the rest of the class. I photograph the finished product and, in the following lesson or for homework, I ask students to annotate the images with key Latin and English terms. When working with classes in which students each have their own iPad, I would ask students to annotate the image for homework via the OneNote app, and then to review their work and create one final annotated image in the following lesson. This would draw together their learning on the topic whilst giving them a visual representation of their knowledge to revise at a later date.

Pupil feedback

As part of my master's in education research, and afterwards, I have taken the time to investigate the views of my students through interviews, observations of their comments and records of pupil opinions written by the classes at the end of each lesson. These insights have helped me to develop my teaching further and to confirm that students do find the use of Explain Everything and active learning motivating and valuable.

In line with the views in Kane's (2004) research, the case study of my own students showed that they were interested in the content and activities of the lessons. The students seem to have found the content interesting because they thought more, and in a different way, about what they had been studying all year. One Year 12 student commented that the lessons made her 'think a lot more about what the characters were saying . . . [and] how they would have acted it out'. Another felt that they had 'engaged with the text a lot more' when considering how to act it out and annotate it in class. In our previous lessons, we had only briefly discussed how the stories would have been acted out, so the focus on the texts as plays had allowed the students to reconsider the texts and to remind themselves that they were originally written to be performed. My own observations of the group mirrored their comments, as I often noted that they were focused and asking questions during lessons. I was also impressed by their efforts between the lessons (e.g. coming to ask about a scene or to talk about an idea they had). I recorded that my weakest student came to see me later in the day, 'excited about the scenes', and to recommend that we use Meeting Room Two because, as she correctly pointed out, it has 'a plain backdrop like the Greeks would have had'.

With my Year 10 class, I noted that the students were '*so* excited when using their iPads' and that 'the use of the iPad and the Explain Everything app seemed to be exciting to the students'. Whilst the students have access to iPads in all their lessons, it is not common that they are able to work so collaboratively, nor do I use Explain Everything in many of their lessons. I am pleased that the technology is motivating from the start of an activity, but I am more interested in how it enables the students to learn more about the topics they are studying. The Year 10 students claimed that annotating the video had encouraged them to think further about the topics we were studying.

One of my key motivations for the study was to see whether pupils valued the active learning lessons that I teach. Whilst I believed that pupils learn from a variety of activities, I had concerns that pupils in exam classes were more focused on taking notes from more traditional, expository-style lessons. Previous research has shown that the activities 'should not be gimmicks' (Kane 2004: 284) and teachers should try to avoid falling into the false sense of security that pupil engagement leads to their learning (Halsall and Cockett 1998). With these thoughts in mind, I produced lessons that I believed would require the pupils to engage actively with the content and to create a valuable revision resource, albeit in a different format to the notes they are used to taking in lessons.

One Year 12 student commented that the lesson in which they created their video 'was probably the most important one' (over the acting out of the scenes). She went on to explain that it allowed her to look back at all the work they had done – the notes on a theatre and each of the plays – and to see how everything fitted together. Other students agreed with her comments, and one added that they 'had to use our own knowledge to annotate the films, so we were thinking back through everything that we had learnt', and even went further, claiming that 'it was nice to input our own thoughts at the end'. My students have used their videos when revising; I felt that, by returning to the videos at a later date, the students felt they were a valuable resource. After the lessons, one commented that having my input into their video notes was important because 'whatever we write down is what we will take for making notes and essays in the future'; so they thought that the notes were valuable enough for them to use during revision. I was most pleased that the students felt the collating of notes in the video from their folders and playscripts 'helped us to add to the scenes the points that we missed when acting them out'. The Year 10 students cited activities where they learnt new content and added to or reviewed their notes as being particularly valuable. They were all positive about the annotated video that they produced by the end of the lessons, writing that it would 'remind them later about the key participants and their roles', that they had 'enjoyed it' and that it had allowed them 'to review all of their notes'. This is what I believe makes the technology so valuable for teaching: it allows us to build on the notes and activities that we already use as part of our teaching, and can draw all of their notes into a format that can be kept to review later.

Active learning encourages pupils to engage with the content more actively, but also allows the pupils to drive their own learning and consider the content rather than being the passive receivers of information. As Wolfe points out, this 'requires pupils to utilise higher-order thinking skills, such as synthesising and evaluating information, not just information memorization and recall' (Wolfe 2006: 78). These activities should allow the pupils to remember the information more successfully. It is difficult to study the impact of active learning on students' memory, or whether activities like these have an impact on their exam results. It is difficult to tell how much the active learning activities alone impact on the pupils' ability to remember information when they have been taught the content through a combination of both active and passive learning over the course of the year. However, I was still interested to see whether my students believed that the activities had helped them to remember the content that they were studying, and I have noted that students often refer to their videos during discussions when planning essays at a later date. Previous research into the effectiveness of active learning strategies on pupil learning (Wolfe 2006, Watkins 2008 and Atkinson 1999) suggests that there is persuasive evidence that people learn best by doing. So, by actively engaging in the lesson, I hope that my pupils are able to remember more of the content that they have met. Certainly, my pupils commented that 'the active lessons will probably stick in our heads better', a sentiment which one furthered by saying that she thinks she 'remembers things better when I get up and use the texts'. One also said that that the use of the 'iPad will help me to remember what happened during the lesson', as it brought together their notes from previous lessons.

As Latin and Classics are not usually popular subjects at my school, I was interested to see whether the students would find that active learning techniques helped them feel more motivated to study Classics further. From their comments and actions, the students clearly enjoyed the lessons.

After deciding on the scenes they were going to use and the roles they were going to play, the Year 12 students seemed more excited about the activities later in the week. The students would talk to me about the lessons when they saw me around school, something that they had not done before. Jocasta and Electra had spent a great deal of time on the homework activity that I had set (to decorate their masks ready for the recording of the scenes) and even came to show me their masks when they had finished. I noted that they arrived 'very excited' and 'burst into my classroom wearing their new masks. They could not wait to show me the paintwork and explained that they 'had painted them together so that [they] would match because they are the Chorus and the Chorus always wore the same'.

When asked about what they had learned, all the students could comment or write down new knowledge they had gained after each lesson. This act of referring back to their notes to retrieve information they have forgotten has become a popular theme for teachers to encourage in students, and these lessons are no different, but they do allow the pupils to record their findings in a different medium.

Whilst the lessons did not always cover new ground for the Year 12 students, they did write about the greater clarity and understanding they had of the conventions and acting of the plays. Something which I noticed in my own observations was that the students were 'now pulling together their ideas on the staging from different sources as making references to notes, videos and plays we have seen on stage'. I also found that they had shown an understanding of new 'ideas about the staging, props (particularly their impact with so few of them), and the way the masks would have looked'. One pupil commented that she thought she had learned most when editing the video, as she 'returned to the images of the theatre that we had annotated' some months before. Another student also thought that 'going back through the information again and watching the videos on it' had been valuable. From my own observations, I found the lessons had consolidated 'previous note taking' and noted in particular that 'comments from students seem to suggest that the videos have given new understanding about how the theatre would have looked and been laid out'. During my discussions with students, one said that playing the different characters 'helped us to understand all of the plays better' as all of the students had taken a role in each of the scenes, and so had played five different roles.

Conclusion

Whilst not the focus of my original research, spaced practice and 'dual coding' have re-emerged as popular topics for educational research. Spaced practice is the reviewing of content at regular intervals so that students have the chance to forget and then relearn the information. William James suggested that, rather than cramming information, by reviewing 'the same thing on different days in different contexts, read, recited, referred to again and again, related to other things and reviewed, [it] gets well-wrought into mental structure' (James 2005), which should help students to learn content more thoroughly. Dual coding is the use of a combination of verbal and visual material when reviewing a topic. Research suggests that, by having the information in two formats, both words and images, it is easier for students to recall it later. The drawing together of previous learning into a video format seems to utilize both of these practices, and certainly seemed to benefit my pupils.

My original research took place when my school had a very limited ICT infrastructure. We had to make do with limited access to iPads, and the WiFi would often drop connection during a lesson – a fact that made displaying work via Apple TV a challenge. Therefore I can appreciate that some may find it difficult to implement the use of technology in lessons regularly; certainly it was the only suggestion for improvement from the students' feedback. However, by persevering, we were able to create the videos and to share them with the class for them to view later in a format that is more flexible than group work usually allows.

Seeing the excitement of my Year 12 class as they walked through school wearing their masks (see Figure 12.3), and hearing comments like that of one Year 10 student ('well, I preferred the religion lessons much more all round, because I enjoyed it and therefore I learnt more'), has helped me to see that, for these classes at least, my innovative lessons using active learning techniques are valued and enjoyed by my students. I shall continue to gather the feedback of my students, but for these classes at least, it seems I do not need to pack away my CSI suit and iPad just yet.

Notes

1. Transcript of Amanda Spielman's speech at the Wellington Festival of Education, 21 June 2018, is available online: https://www.gov.uk/government/speeches/amanda-spielmans-speech-at-the-wellington-festival-of-education (accessed 15 October 2018).

2. Active learning techniques are those that encourage pupils to have a greater level of input in their learning compared to more didactic, expository teaching.

3. Microsoft OneNote is a computer program and app that allows teachers to gather notes (handwritten or typed), drawings, clips, etc. from one class. These OneNotes can then be shared with the pupils in the class; in this way it is similar to using Google Classroom.

References

Atkinson, S. (1999), 'Key Factors Influencing Pupil Motivation in Design and Technology', *Journal of Technology Education*, 10 (2): 4–26

Halsall, R. and Cockett, M. (1998), 'Providing Opportunities For Active Learning: Assessing Incidence and Impact', *The Curriculum Journal*, 9 (3): 299–217.

James, W. (2005), 'Talks to Teachers on Psychology'. Available online: https://www.gutenberg.org/files/16287/16287-h/16287-h.htm#XII__MEMORY (accessed 24 September 2018).

Kane, L. (2004), 'Educators, Learners and Active Learning Methodologies', *International Journal of Lifelong Education*, 23: 3, 275–286.

Meyer, R. and Anderson, R. (1992), 'The Instructive Animation: Helping Students Build Connections Between Words and Pictures in Multimedia Learning', *Journal of Educational Psychology*, 4: 444–452.

Watkins, C. (2008), 'Active Learning Is Better Learning', *Managing Schools Today*, 18.

Wolfe, K. (2006), 'Active Learning', *Journal of Teaching in Travel & Tourism*, 6 (1): 77–82.

CHAPTER 13
'JUST-IN-TIME LEARNING': USING HAND-HELD VOTING DEVICES IN THE UNDERGRADUATE LECTURE ROOM
Helen Lovatt

Introduction

A sea of faces rises up in front of you, gazing blankly ahead or looking at their open laptops, leaning sideways to whisper to a friend, perhaps smiling and nodding if you are lucky, or looking puzzled, annoyed or bored if you are not. Lecturing is an odd form of teaching, in that it can be remarkably one-sided. Particularly in large groups, it is hard to gain an insight into what students understand and what they have yet to fully grasp. It is hard, too, to tell how engaged they are: we carry out evaluation surveys or ask students to write down three things they have learnt at the end of a lecture, but are they really paying attention?

University lectures are here to stay, at least for the foreseeable future. It is the most efficient way of giving students the contact hours that they feel result in value for money, the face-to-face engagement with research stars that is the big selling point of university. Lectures are also an essential part of research-led teaching: if the material has not been published yet, or written, then presenting it orally has been and still is an effective way of communicating it to students. But sitting and passively listening for fifty minutes or even two hours is a skill many current undergraduates do not possess. What can a single lecturer in possession of a large group of students do to engage and involve them, to interact with them individually without being overwhelmed?

There is an additional problem in the rise of anxiety among the student population.[1] In the past, we might have asked simple questions to the room, with the hope that many would raise their hands or simply respond. Now many students are reluctant to talk in the classroom, even in small groups, and many have problems even attending lectures.

Just-in-time teaching

'Just-in-time teaching' is a phrase used to describe teaching in which teachers gauge the understanding of students in real time to influence how they teach classes, rather than sticking rigidly to pre-prepared plans or materials (Novak et al. 1999). In university physics courses, students were set questions to prepare in advance and send to teachers. Teachers then assessed their responses shortly before the lecture and adapted the teaching accordingly (Crouch and Mazur 2001). These techniques generally use online quizzes or the submission of formative assessment, but they can also be applied to interactive classroom technology (Stowell and

Nelson 2007). Discussion and evaluation of these methods began in STEM (science, technology, engineering and maths) subjects, but has now been expanded to humanities courses (Dallaire 2011, Simkins and Maier 2010, Cookman 2010). Electronic response systems have also been used successfully in conjunction with a pedagogical framework taken from just-in-time teaching (Sun et al. 2014). Discussion-based learning and the flipped classroom are not really new concepts in higher-level university Classics teaching, where the seminar is a key element of teaching provision.[2] In seminars, students discuss pre-prepared material in relatively small groups, and seminar tutors get to know their existing levels of understanding and their problems and difficulties, before helping students to resolve them and improve. However, electronic response systems and just-in-time teaching also allow these methods to be used in large group lectures.

There have been a number of studies of electronic response systems in university teaching in various disciplines, but not Classics: Blood and Neel (2008) used student response systems (SRS) in a graduate-level special education class and reported improved content mastery and self-reported engagement in the lectures which used SRS, as well as a high preference for the system from the students. Ghosh and Renna (2009) report a pilot project at the University of Akron in which an electronic personal response system was used in combination with peer discussion, with very favourable student evaluations. Addison et al. (2009) found no measurable improvement in mean exam performance among students using clickers in a large-class introductory biochemistry course, but a higher proportion of students were in the highest achievement category, and students gave high approval ratings for the SRS for increasing their participation and engagement in lectures. Zou and Xie (2018) compared two different flipped classroom models in two groups from an upper-intermediate English as a foreign language class, one of which involved peer instruction and SRS, and found that the latter improved language learning. Sun et al. (2014) compared clickers with online polling in a pilot study involving six instructors and 209 students at a US university across a range of disciplines. They found that 'plenty-of-time teaching' was an improvement over just-in-time teaching, and that online polls allowed students to engage in more depth with questions and allowed staff to prepare more effectively for well-targeted teaching.

Electronic response systems

There are a number of methods available that allow students to answer questions or vote on issues remotely and/or anonymously, both in lectures and as distance learners. These are sometimes called 'electronic response systems'. I came to this topic through the use of voting keypad technology such as TurningPoint. This requires keypads ('Keepads', sometimes also known as 'clickers') for everyone in the room, software integrated with PowerPoint and a pre-prepared questionnaire. It is fiddly to set up and time-consuming to make sure all the keypads are handed out and returned. My experience has been with TurningPoint, but the results of the evaluation process should also be useful for thinking about other electronic response systems and their pedagogical effects.[3] Electronic response systems allow students to see their answers and those of others in real time and assess their own opinions and thoughts against those of others, while remaining anonymous.

Context

I have now used TurningPoint in three modules: a first-year literature survey module, a second-year project module, and a second- and-third-year option module. I was not initially interested in using a technological solution to interaction, since I already keep interactions going orally and by asking students to write down thoughts on Post-it notes. I first tried TurningPoint when I inherited a second-year project module from a colleague who had run it in previous years (Dr Lynn Fotheringham). The Independent Second Year Project allows students to engage with the Classical world in a non-essay format. The early sessions explain the purpose and aims of the project, which has a strong focus on communicating Classics to wider audiences. There were TurningPoint questions already set up in the PowerPoints for the lectures. The project module had fairly leisurely two-hour sessions, where it was a struggle to fill the time with material relevant to all students since they were all working on different areas, but we had to meet the university's minimum contact hour requirements. I decided to learn how to use the technology, and was asked by the university's learning technology team to discuss what it was like to use for the first time. I therefore decided to develop my own questions and experiment with the possibilities in order to give more meaningful feedback. I did this in a large first-year ancient literature module that same semester, in which we were at that time running two one-hour lectures per week. In both sessions I had some problems making the technology work reliably and organizing the different elements, and I underestimated how much time these activities would take.

Personal voice and engagement

In the first session of the project module the voting technology was used to find out what students had experienced before, essentially using it as a show of hands. We also asked what different social media platforms people used regularly, in a later session about networking and employability. In the first session, I asked students whether they had experienced hostility about their choice of degree course, and what sorts of attitudes to Classics they had encountered. This is an example of a question that benefitted from being anonymous: in the same session in the following year, without the keypads, students were reluctant to raise their hands and the interactive element was less successful and engaging (although we could have asked students to write down their experiences of hostility on Post-it notes and then have read them out, maintaining anonymity that way). Gathering personal experiences is a good use for this technology, and the social media use survey gathered useful data that helped us to understand how our students interact with various communities (over the years, fewer are using Facebook and more are using Instagram, for instance). This data can be saved and kept for comparison in future years.

Testing preconceptions, prejudice and concept change

The first-year literature module was a large group of about 100 students in a tiered lecture theatre, who were required to discuss passages frequently as part of the lectures. The first one-hour lecture in the week introduced the texts and issues, and the second one consisted mainly of discussion activities. I used the TurningPoint keypads in several lectures, but most memorably to discuss Cicero's portrayal of Clodia in the *Pro Caelio*, and to explore truth and fiction in Tacitus's and Suetonius's accounts of the emperor Nero. In both lectures, I used questions as a framing device at the beginning and end of the lectures to see whether students' opinions had changed.

In the discussion lecture on the *Pro Caelio*, I performed *Pro Caelio* 32, asked students to vote on how convincing the argument was (is Clodia really key to the case?), spent some time analysing the rhetorical tactics in the passage, with contributions from the students, and then asked them to vote again. Later I asked them whether 'Clodia was a slut', with the options: 'Yes definitely', 'Yes probably', 'Maybe', 'Not likely', 'Definitely not' and 'Don't know'. I was hoping that a long discussion of Roman attitudes to women and Cicero's tactics in the *Pro Caelio* might shift students from 'Yes definitely' to 'Don't know', but I was disappointed to find that mostly students maintained their initial prejudices. I think it would have been a more effective pedagogical activity if I had allowed time to discuss their reasons, or used the voting as a means of starting discussion rather than closing it down.

With Tacitus and Suetonius, I was trying to encourage students to read both sources critically and especially to explore the effects of the generic differences between history and biography. I asked students how much they believed in both authors: 'All of it. It's all true', 'Maybe some of it is true', 'No smoke without fire', 'There must be a kernel of truth', 'It's all fiction' and 'We just don't really know'. Many more were inclined to believe Tacitus than Suetonius. We then looked at the two authors' representations of Nero in the theatre, and Nero as performer, and also the way each presented Nero's possible involvement in the Great Fire of Rome. I attempted to bring out the ways that Suetonius's adoption of more outrageous stories does not necessarily mean his account contains less truth and to show the continuities in the way both accounts use rumour and insinuation. Students were still much more inclined to believe Tacitus than Suetonius, but there were more sceptical students who felt that 'We just don't really know'. What this exercise mainly revealed to me is that students have strong pre-existing opinions and it is very difficult to change them, even in the situation where you will be marking their essays. It struck me that the voting technology might serve to reinforce opinions rather than change them, since students would see that many people agreed with them and not the lecturer. The voting processes also took up a great deal of time in a one-hour session and removed valuable discussion time. I decided that the technology might be better used in two-hour sessions where there was more room for reflection and discussion.

Quizzes and discussions

In the following year, therefore, I tried the keypads in a two-hour lecture in a module on Virgil. The module had previously consisted of twenty one-hour lectures and five two-hour seminars, but because of curriculum changes this needed to be expanded to thirty hours, which I chose to do as ten two-hour lectures and ten one-hour lectures. I used the keypads to go into more depth in the two-hour lectures, which each focused on a book of the *Aeneid* (the one-hour lectures tackled themes and receptions). Since the two-hour lectures started at 9.00 am, I decided to use the voting as a way to ease people into the lectures and to wake them up, to put them in a positive frame of mind to contribute later on in the lecture. The lectures used to begin with a summary of the book from me. The students were supposed to have read the book in detail before the lecture. I now designed quizzes for each book to bring out interesting details about the poem and reflect on its complexity, particularly focusing on narrative order, imagery, surprising elements, such as the transformation of Aeneas's ships into nymphs, the complexities of divine machinery and the mechanics of epic causation. Pressure of time in designing the classes meant that I did not do as much in the later parts of the lecture with the keypads as I would have liked, but students suggest that voting activities would also be a good way of consolidating points made in the lecture and summarizing the material tackled.

The voting does affect the flow of the lecture, since it is necessary to stop reading, writing or discussing, activate your device (if you are not already using it) or change app, log in and vote. Some students found this interruption irritating. However, the variety of activities is likely to be useful in itself, since offering a variety of activities and assessment as part of an active learning strategy tends to improve student engagement (Suskie 2009: 67).

The module was taken by sixty-eight second- and third-year students, many of whom had read the *Aeneid* before. In the first session, I spent some time checking their current levels of knowledge and understanding, as well as their opinions about the politics of the poem. The polarized nature of debate about the *Aeneid* made it a particularly good text to debate and discuss, and about which to gather people's opinions. In the first lecture, I used the interactions to find out about previous experience of learning the *Aeneid* and existing knowledge and understanding. Screenshots of PowerPoint slides with the actual percentages of answers from the lecture show the results.

Figure 13.1 shows the varied backgrounds of those taking the module, information which they might have volunteered by a show of hands, but about which they might have felt unable to be honest.

Figure 13.2 shows that approximately the same number of people who had studied Virgil at school had some knowledge of his life and context, but that others guessed wildly. Only 48 per cent were able to correctly identify in which century he lived. Subsequent questions (Figure 13.3) addressed issues and ideas which I wanted to complicate in the module:

It was interesting that so few people felt absolutely sure that the *Aeneid* was not a poem of praise for Augustus.

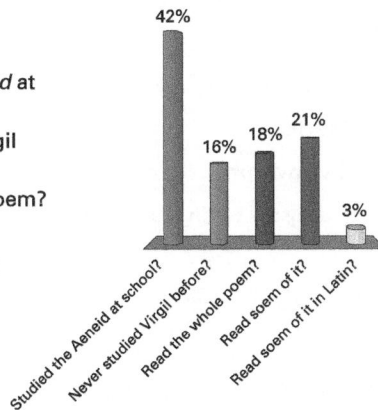

Figure 13.1 Students' prior knowledge of the *Aeneid*. © Helen Lovatt.

Where did Vigil come from?

A. Pisa
B. Carthage
C. Rome
D. Mantua
E. Verona
F. Naples

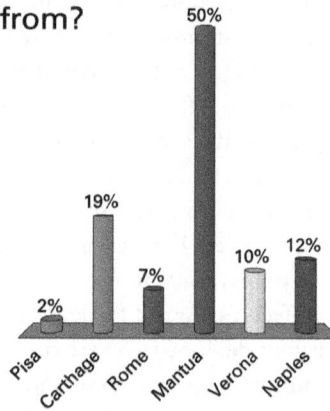

Figure 13.2 Students' prior knowledge of Virgil. © Helen Lovatt.

The *Aeneid* is a poem of praise for Augustus. Do you agree?

A. Yes
B. No
C. Sort of
D. Don't know

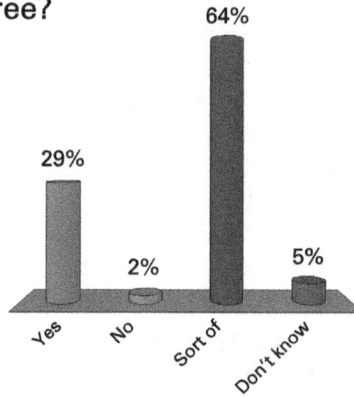

Figure 13.3 Students' perceptions of the *Aeneid* as a praise poem. © Helen Lovatt.

The following examples show some quiz questions in Book 4, but without the student response rates. This first question led to an interesting discussion about how imagery in Book 4 portrays Dido.

- What is Dido not compared to in a simile?
  - A maddened Maenad
  - Diana among her nymphs
  - A deer wounded by a Cretan shepherd
  - A tigress
  - Orestes

The below question raised the issue of divine and rational causation, brought out by the extraordinary intervention of Juno at the end of Book 4, and the multi-layered nature of epic narrative. It was also possible to talk about Dido's role as embodiment of the city and state of Carthage and the different ways that men and women commit suicide in different ancient texts.

- What causes Dido's actual death?
  - Hanging
  - Fire
  - The word
  - Juno

Student evaluation of module

As part of the evaluation of the module, I designed a questionnaire specifically on the use of the voting technology. Of the sixty-eight people on the module, twenty-six filled in the questionnaire (a 38 per cent response rate). The results of the questionnaire were strikingly positive: 100 per cent of respondents enjoyed using the keypads and felt that the voting technology made the lecture more engaging. All but two of the students (92 per cent) found the two-hour Wednesday lectures, which included voting, more engaging than the Thursday ones, although two people pointed out in the qualitative comments that having more time to explain and go into depth was also a factor. In my experience of student feedback across our modules more generally, two-hour lectures evoke a mixed reception: the majority of students like the opportunity to go into greater depth (and the efficiency of not needing to move around campus so much), but a significant minority find two hours too long to focus.

I suggested some possible benefits and asked for other thoughts:

- 92 per cent felt voting technology allowed them to participate without embarrassment;
- 62 per cent felt that they could give honest answers about their levels of knowledge;
- 27 per cent found it fun to find out what other students think; and
- 19 per cent felt that they stayed more focused on the lecture materials because they knew they might have to answer questions about it.

The other suggestions mainly focused on the quizzes, which they found motivated them to do the reading before the lecture, and were useful for revision purposes and bringing out parts of the text that they might otherwise have overlooked. They also stated that the voting process stimulated discussion and reflection.

On the other hand, I offered some possible disadvantages and asked for other thoughts:

- 42 per cent felt that the multiple choice questions ran the risk of oversimplifying complex issues;
- 35 per cent felt that voting could be a distraction from learning; and
- 12 per cent felt that voting was (or could be) a waste of time.

The qualitative comments tended to focus on the effectiveness of the question design for the quizzes rather than the use of the voting technology itself. Some questions did not have clear correct answers, a fact which some students found irritating. It is important to differentiate between asking for opinions or interpretations, and asking trivia questions with right or wrong answers. There was a high level of knowledge of the text, so it was a challenge to find factual questions that might catch people out. If the questions were pitched too low, the students found the process boring; if the questions were pitched too high, those without prior knowledge of the text were distressed by their lack of knowledge. Sometimes the questions were too complicated and were difficult to read on the PowerPoint. The importance of question design is discussed in Anthis (2011).

Of those who answered the question about whether I should use the keypads in this module again in future, 100 per cent said yes, and 82 per cent felt they should be used more widely in university teaching. Students suggested that they could be used more to sum up what had been learnt in lectures, and to start discussions and reflect on them. One student's final comment was: 'It's wicked. Spread the word! BIGUP' – an answer which suggests voting technology is likely to be very popular with students, if used thoughtfully to enhance learning.

The biggest surprise for me was how useful the process was in starting discussion and involving more students in whole-class discussion. A successful quiz question that got people talking to each other could lead to a discussion of why they answered in the way they did and what surprised or intrigued them about an aspect of the poem, and those who were often silent at the back were much more inclined to participate in discussion.

In the formal university evaluation of the module, the scores were around the university average, both for module evaluation (Virgil average: 78.4 per cent; university average: 78.9 per cent) and teaching evaluation (Virgil average: 84.4 per cent; university average: 85 per cent). Since the university reversed its scale from one (highest) to five (highest) since the previous time the module was taught, it is hard to compare previous evaluation scores, and there are many different variables in the comparison (e.g. lecture time, group size, cohort ability). The evaluation comments included three positive comments on the use of the interactive classroom technology, and two negative comments (that it was a waste of time). The negative comments came from a student who had not previously studied the *Aeneid* and felt that in that twenty minutes 'we could have been taught some helpful information', an answer which suggests they prefer a more didactic teaching style. One comment that 'others in the group seem passionate and knowledgeable and obviously enjoy the module but in comparison I feel left behind' did make me wonder whether the fact that the quiz answers were on display could make those who repeatedly did worse than average in the quizzes feel alienated, even though others did not know that their answers were incorrect. This might suggest that it would be better to focus on 'concept test' questions, where there is no clear correct answer, so students can then justify their decisions to each other and enter into discussion of the issues.

Conclusions

This experiment certainly showed that interactive voting technology is very popular with students, if used carefully. It can be used to break down social barriers and to empower students to join in discussion. However, as with all technology, how one uses it matters. Questions require careful design. Pace, timing and integration into the lecture structure all take time and effort. Whether it really delivers greater learning benefits than oral questions or asking students to write down answers to questions on Post-it notes or another equivalent methodology is less clear. Once all in the classroom – teachers and students – are familiar with the process, it can certainly improve engagement and help retain attention.

Perhaps most beneficial is the necessity to think very hard about what you are trying to achieve in the session and in the discussion. The main uses are:

- finding out about levels of knowledge;
- finding out about students' personal experiences;
- testing preparation and existing knowledge;
- revealing common misconceptions;
- encouraging students to challenge their prejudices;
- giving a starting point for discussion;
- summing up learning.

A couple of unforeseen effects: waking students up in the morning, improving the social interactions of the class, getting a wider range of students involved in classroom discussion in big lectures (although learning students' names, dividing them up into groups and then nominating individual students to respond for each group can also work well for this purpose). Once we know more about students' prior knowledge, this then raises the challenge of appropriate differentiation in large group lectures, so that all students are included and supported in university teaching.

In short, then, after my initial reluctance, I am convinced that there are significant benefits to be gained from allowing students to vote in big lectures, and it is worth putting in the effort to learn to use the technology, and to design interactions to maximize engagement without being reductive.

What next?

It is now much easier to use apps such as Kahoot! or Socrative. Both require an internet connection for the lecturer and a device connected to the internet for the student (laptop, tablet or mobile). It is now the case that in my university (The University of Nottingham) students are expected to have an internet-enabled device in their lectures in order to fill in the student evaluations of teaching (which are done online during a class). If warned in advance that they will need a method of going online, they will mostly be able to do this (and if not, they can work in pairs, or borrow a device). Kahoot! is discussed elsewhere in this volume. Socrative is more flexible and varied: you can do various different interactive activities, for instance a space race, an exit ticket, or set up questions in real time during a class.

One benefit of clickers or keypads is that all students who attend are guaranteed to have them. In all the sessions where I used the TurningPoint system, all but two students participated in the voting, in classes of 60–100 students. Participation rates in the university's online student evaluation surveys are often below 50 per cent, and rarely higher than 75 per cent. Attendance at classes using the keypads was also much better than average, with an 80 per cent attendance rate which continued to the end of the module. Evidence of student approval from this and other studies suggests that they enjoy interactive student response systems, whether clickers or online systems, and that this motivates them to attend and participate in classes. The next challenge is to integrate these technologies with the flipped classroom, peer instruction and effective differentiation for students with different levels of prior knowledge and ability. The most problematic barrier is staff overload: so many different elements are now expected of academics to produce popular and effective teaching (PowerPoints, online materials, online reading lists, interactive apps) that teaching development can become extremely time-consuming and less flexible.

Notes

1. In a US context, with references: https://theconversation.com/1-in-5-college-students-have-anxiety-or-depression-heres-why-90440 (The Conversation 2018). In an NUS survey from 2015, eight out of ten students said they had experienced mental health problems: https://www.theguardian.com/education/2015/dec/14/majority-of-students-experience-mental-health-issues-says-nus-survey (*The Guardian* 2018).
2. For the flipped classroom in Latin teaching, see Natoli (2014) and, in this volume, Natoli and Gilliver.
3. Some discussion of the benefits of Socrative for very large lectures: https://telimedblog.wordpress.com/2014/10/10/a-case-study-of-socrative-employing-students-smartphonestablets-to-create-an-interactive-lecture/ in medicine; and in philosophy (TELiMed 2014), http://blogs.nottingham.ac.uk/talkingofteaching/2014/spacetech-fisher/ (Fisher and Pearhouse 2014). A very helpful overview of various different ways to use Socrative: https://catlintucker.com/2014/01/my-favorite-mobile-apps-2-socrative-lesson-ideas/ (Tucker 2014).

References

Addison, S., Wright, A. and Milner, R. (2009), 'Using Clickers to Improve Student Engagement and Performance in an Introductory Biochemistry Class', *Biochemistry and Molecular Biology Education*, 37: 84–91.

Anthis, K. (2011), 'Is it the Clicker, or is it the Question? Untangling the Effects of Student Response System Use', *Teaching of Psychology*, 38: 189–193.

Blood, E. and Neel, R. (2008), 'Using Student Response Systems in Lecture-Based Instruction: Does It Change Student Engagement and Learning?', *Journal of Technology and Teacher Education*, 16: 375–383.

Cookman, C. (2010), 'Using Just-in-time Teaching to Foster Critical Thinking in a Humanities Course', in S. Simkins and M. Maier (eds.), *Just In Time Teaching: Across the Disciplines, Across the Academy*, Sterling, VA, 163–178.

Crouch, C. and Mazur, E. (2001), 'Peer Instruction: Ten Years of Experience and Results', *American Journal of Physics*, 69: 970–977.

Dallaire, D. (2011), 'Effective Use of Personal Response "Clicker" Systems in Psychology Courses', *Teaching of Psychology*, 38: 199–204.

Fisher, A. and Pearhouse, I. (2014), 'LectureTools, Socrative and Dynamic In-class conversation'. Available online: http://blogs.nottingham.ac.uk/talkingofteaching/2014/spacetech-fisher/ (accessed 29 September 2018).

Ghosh, S. and Renna, F. (2009), 'Using Electronic Response Systems in Economics Classes', *Journal of Economic Education*, 40: 354–365.

Natoli, B. (2014), 'Flipping the Latin Classroom: Grounding Classics Pedagogy in the Theory of eLearning', *Journal of Classics Teaching*, 30: 37–40.

Novak, G., Patterson, E. et al. (1999), *Just-in-time Teaching: Blending Active Learning with Web Technology*, Upper Saddle River, NJ.

Pace, D. and Middendorft, J. (2010), 'Using Just-in-Time Teaching in History', in S. Simkins and M. Maier (eds.), *Just in Time Teaching: Across the Disciplines, Across the Academy*, Sterling, VA, 153–162.

Simkins, S. and Maier, M. (eds.) (2010), *Just-in-Time Teaching: Across the Disciplines, Across the Academy*, Sterling, Virginia.

Stowell, J. and Nelson, J. (2007), 'Benefits of Electronic Audience Response Systems on Student Participation, Learning, and Emotion', *Teaching of Psychology*, 34: 253–258.

Sun, J., Martinez, B. and Seli, H. (2014), 'Just-in-Time or Plenty-of-Time Teaching? Different Electronic Feedback Devices and Their Effect on Student Engagement', *Educational Technology and Society*, 17: 234–244.

Suskie, L. (2009), *Assessing Student Learning: A Common Sense Guide*, San Francisco.

TELiMed (2014), 'A Case Study of Socrative: Employing Students' Smartphones/tablets to Create an Interactive Lecture'. Available online: https://telimedblog.wordpress.com/2014/10/10/a-case-study-of-socrative-employing-students-smartphonestablets-to-create-an-interactive-lecture/ (accessed 29 September 2018).

The Conversation (2018), 'One in Five College Students Have Anxiety or Depression. Here's Why'. Available online: https://theconversation.com/1-in-5-college-students-have-anxiety-or-depression-heres-why-90440 (accessed 29 September 2018).

The Guardian (2018), 'A Majority of Students Experience Mental Health Issues Says NUS Survey'. Available online: https://www.theguardian.com/education/2015/dec/14/majority-of-students-experience-mental-health-issues-says-nus-survey (accessed 29 September 2018).

Tucker, C. (2014), 'My Favourite Mobile Apps'. Available online: https://catlintucker.com/2014/01/my-favorite-mobile-apps-2-socrative-lesson-ideas/ (accessed 29 September 2018).

Zou, D. and Xie, H. (2018), 'Flipping an English Writing Class with Technology-enhanced Just-in-Time Teaching and Peer Instruction', *Interactive Learning Environments*. Available online: https://www.tandfonline.com/doi/abs/10.1080/10494820.2018.1495654 (accessed 29 September 2018).

CHAPTER 14
TEACHING ANCIENT GEOGRAPHY WITH DIGITAL TOOLS

Scott Lawin Arcenas

Introduction

Familiarizing students with the geography of the ancient world is one of the most difficult challenges faced by teachers of classical history, languages and literature. Recent increases in the accessibility of historical maps (both digital and in print) have made it easier for students to learn about the physical spaces occupied by the ancient Greeks and Romans.[1] Even the best possible maps, however, misrepresent the ways in which historical actors experienced and conceptualized those spaces. Consequently, students often develop anachronistic understandings of life in the Greco-Roman Mediterranean.

In this chapter, I introduce a digital tool that provides both teachers and students with an opportunity to develop historically accurate understandings of space, time and connectivity in the ancient world: ORBIS: The Stanford Geospatial Network Model of the Roman World. The chapter comprises four parts, in addition to this introduction. Part 1 discusses the ways in which maps misrepresent pre-modern geography. Part 2 introduces ORBIS, with particular attention to its user interface. Part 3 provides three examples of the many ways in which teachers and students can use ORBIS both in classroom settings and at home. Part 4 concludes by clarifying one possible point of confusion and discussing three of the characteristics that make ORBIS such a useful teaching tool.

Traditional maps

Even the best maps fundamentally misrepresent the geography of the ancient world.[2] Consider, for example, how Figure 14.1, a historical map generated using Antiquity à-la-carte, represents Rome, Alexandria and Augusta Treverorum (modern Trier).

By depicting the three cities cartographically, the map implies that Rome was much closer to Augusta Treverorum than to Alexandria; that the distance from Rome to Alexandria was always the same; and that the distance from Rome to Alexandria was the same as the distance from Alexandria to Rome.

At first glance, these implications may seem reasonable. Closer examination, however, reveals that they are substantially misleading. From a Roman perspective, Rome was much closer to Alexandria than it was to Augusta Treverorum. Rome was closer to Alexandria in September than it was in March. And Rome was often much closer to Alexandria than Alexandria was to Rome.

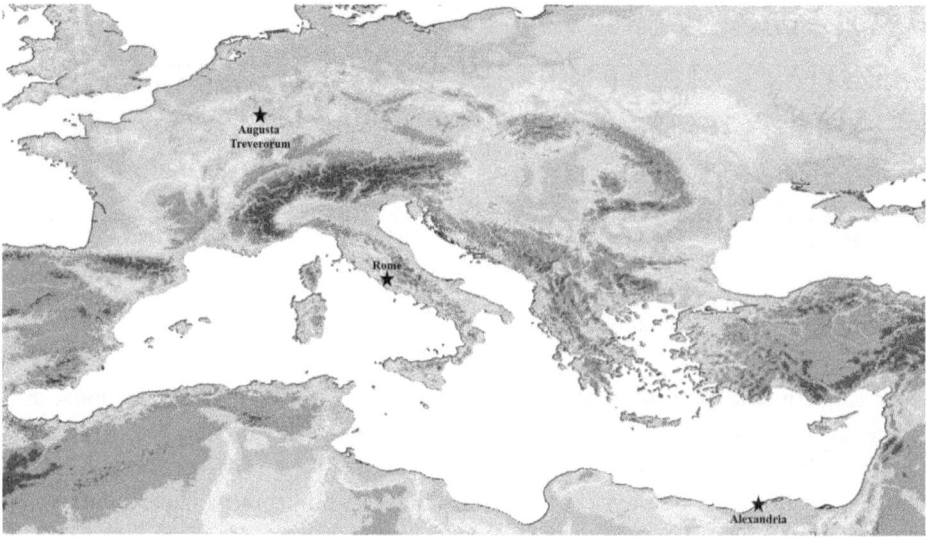

Figure 14.1 Alexandria, Augusta Treverorum and Rome. Source: Antiquity à-la-carte. By permission through a Creative Commons Attribution 4.0 International License (CC BY 4.0) (accessed 10 July 2018).

To account for the incongruity, we need to recognize four key insights concerning connectivity (a broad category that encompasses travel, transportation and communication) in pre-modern societies:

1. Connections tended to occur along a limited network of more or less strictly defined routes.
2. Cost – in terms of time and money – rather than distance was the most significant variable in determining the level of connectivity throughout the network.
3. Sea and river routes tended to be more efficient connectors than land routes.
4. The cost of connectivity varied substantially depending on a range of conditions: for example, seasonal shifts in wind patterns, predation and direction of travel.

Due to the combination of these four factors, Romans tended to conceptualize geography in relational rather than absolute terms.[3] When, consequently, the time came to undertake a journey, Romans tended not to ask themselves how many miles lay between their point of departure and intended destination (i.e. the absolute distance), but rather how long it would take and how much it would cost (i.e. the relational distance).

Understanding the ways in which Romans conceptualized geography is a necessary condition for understanding almost any aspect of Roman society. In the paragraphs that follow, therefore, I introduce a digital tool that provides teachers with an opportunity to familiarize both themselves and their students with this key topic.

Introducing ORBIS

ORBIS: The Stanford Geospatial Network Model of the Roman World is a product of collaboration between a group of classicists and information technology specialists at Stanford

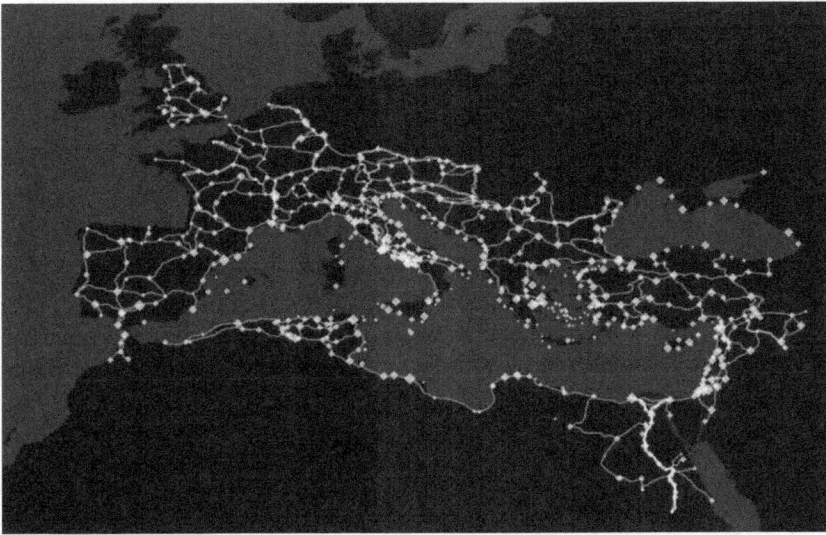

Figure 14.2 Nodes and edges of the ORBIS Network (terrestrial and fluvial only). Source: ORBIS (accessed 08/10/18).

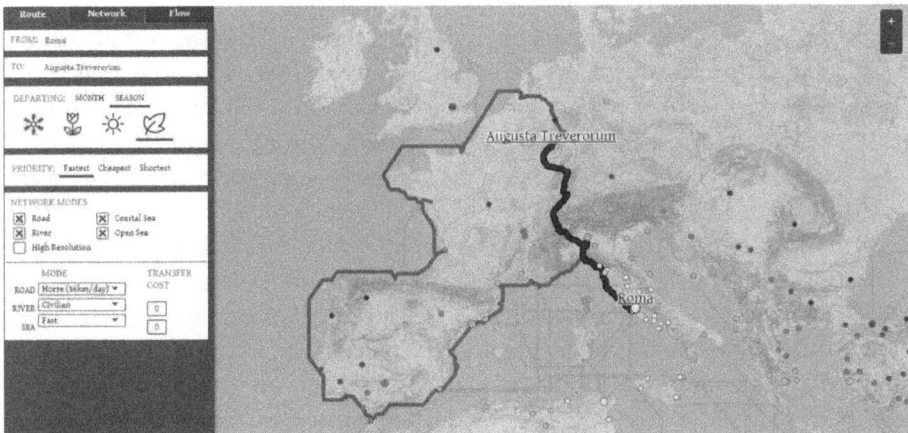

Figure 14.3 Travel and transportation between Augusta Treverorum and Rome. Source: ORBIS (accessed 08/10/18).

University.[4] At its most basic level, ORBIS is a geospatial network model that comprises 844 nodes, each of which represents a city, promontory, pass or crossroads somewhere in the Roman Empire; and 1,292 edges, each of which represents a sea, land, river or canal route between two nodes.[5]

Collectively, these nodes and edges allow ORBIS users to calculate the cost (in terms of both time and expense) of travel throughout the Roman transportation network, and then to interact with these estimates using three different tools.

The first tool is a route planner that will feel natural to anyone familiar with Google Maps, Waze or any other twenty-first-century navigation app. A key feature of this tool is the ability

Origin	Destination	Priority	Season	Time cost (days)	Monetary cost* (denarii/kg)	Distance travelled (km)	Linear distance^ (km)
Rome	Augusta Treverorum	fastest	summer	21	28.6	1,411	611
Augusta Treverorum	Rome	cheapest	fall	61	7.2m	7,024	611

* Cost estimates are per kilogramme of wheat, using a wagon for overland transport.
^ Linear distances calculated using Google Maps, between Lat/Lon coordinates provided by Pleiades.

Figure 14.4 Costs of connectivity between Augusta Treverorum and Rome. © Scott Arcenas.

to customize routes according to a variety of different parameters, such as time of year or direction of travel. Users can, for example, specify that they want to find the fastest route from Rome to Augusta Treverorum during the summer, riding a horse on all overland routes and using a relatively fast ship by sea. Alternatively, they can specify that they want to ship goods from Augusta Treverorum to Rome by the cheapest route, during the fall, travelling by wagon on land and using a relatively slow ship by sea. (See Figure 14.3–4.)

The second option is a network tool that calculates and visualizes the cost of connectivity throughout the entire network. More specifically, it allows users to designate one node as the central reference point for a given simulation, to specify the parameters under which the simulation will occur, to simulate the cost of connectivity throughout the network given the specified parameters, and then to visualize the results in a variety of ways: for example, a network cartogram (Figure 14.5) or isochrone map (Figure 14.6).[6]

To clarify, network cartograms arrange the network under consideration around whichever node has been designated as central, with each node's position determined by the cost of connectivity between it and the central node. In Figure 14.5, for example, Rome has been designated as the central node, and the following parameters are assumed: travel begins in July, uses all available forms of transportation and occurs along the most efficient (i.e. speed-optimized) route from each of the other nodes to Rome; terrestrial, fluvial and maritime travel occur via foot, civilian transport and a relatively fast ship, respectively; and transferring from one mode of transportation to another does not incur any costs. Accordingly, each node's position is determined by the time cost of travel from it to Rome, given the aforementioned parameters.

Isochrone maps divide the nodes that comprise a given network into groups, based on the time cost of travel between each of them and whichever node has been designated as central. They then visualize the division by splitting a map of the territory under consideration into zones, with each zone corresponding to the area(s) occupied by one of the aforementioned groups.

In Figure 14.6, for example, the small ovoid centred on Rome (though it appears to be centred on a patch of sea just to the east of Sardinia, which provides yet another example of the distortions introduced by cartographic depiction) represents the set of locations from which one could travel to Rome in under a week, assuming the same parameters as Figure 14.5. The next zone (which encompasses, for example, the Balearic Islands and the Peloponnese)

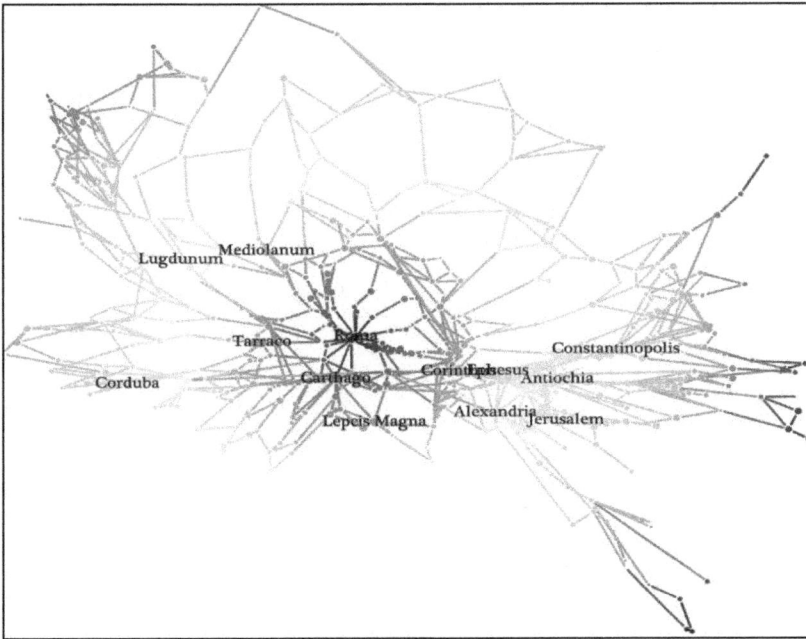

Figure 14.5 Network cartogram of time cost to Rome. Source: ORBIS (accessed 08/10/18).

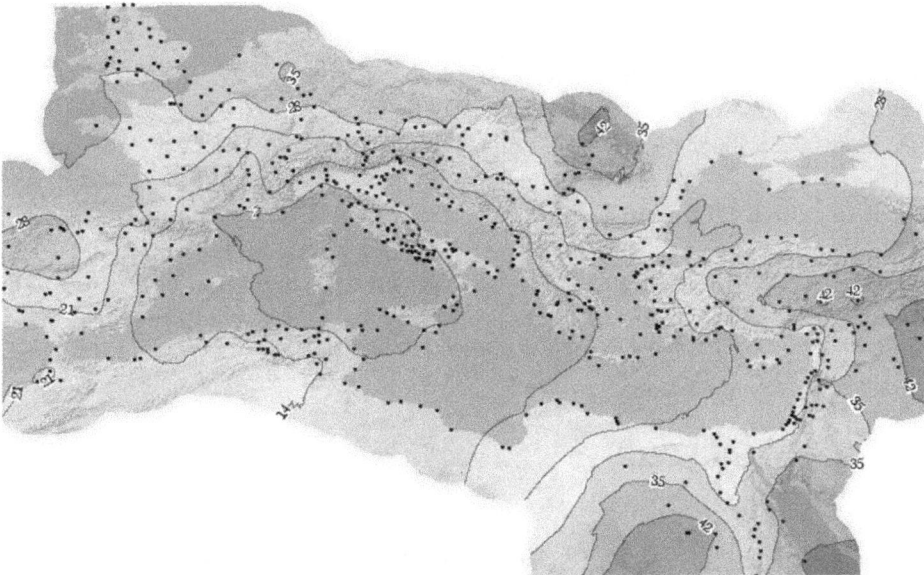

Figure 14.6 Isochrone map of time cost to Rome. Source: ORBIS (accessed 08/10/18).

represents the set of locations from which one could travel to Rome in under two weeks. And so on, and so forth.

The third option, called the flow tool, also allows users to designate a central node for a given simulation and specify the parameters under which the simulation will occur. It then calculates the most efficient route between the central node and each of the others, given the

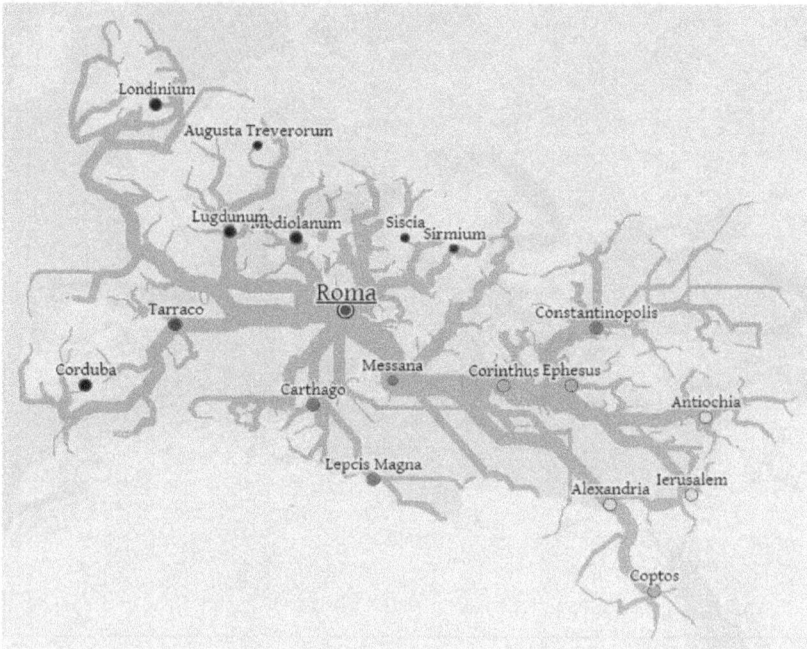

Figure 14.7 Minard diagram of fastest routes to Rome. Source: ORBIS (accessed 08/10/18).

specified parameters, and visualizes the relative frequency with which each edge is employed by varying the thickness of the lines that represent them.

Consider, for example, Figure 14.7, which assumes the same parameters as Figures 14.5 and 14.6.

At one extreme, the relatively thick line between Rome and Messana represents the fact that this was a trunk route, along which almost all traffic bound from the eastern half of the empire would travel. At the other extreme, the lack of any overland connection between Lugdunum and Mediolanum indicates that the road between these two nodes was not employed by any of the routes under consideration. Rather, the routes from Lugdunum and its subsidiary nodes invariably go by way of Massalia.

Teaching with ORBIS

Since its launch in the spring of 2012, I have used ORBIS as a teaching tool with groups ranging from students at middle schools in the San Francisco Bay Area to teachers and professional scholars at the Society for Classical Studies Annual Meeting. I am also planning to use ORBIS in several of the courses that I am teaching at Dartmouth College during the 2018–19 academic year.

In the section that follows, I briefly introduce two ORBIS-based exercises that I have found to be particularly effective, as well as one exercise that I am particularly excited to try this coming year. The first and second exercises are designed for use in a course on Roman history, although I have used both of them to good effect in other contexts. The third is designed for use in a course on Alexander the Great. I am confident, however, that it could be easily adapted for use in courses on many other topics in pre-modern history.

Exercise 1

I begin the first exercise, which is designed for use in the first half of a Roman history course, by introducing both the route planner and the network tool and then using them to demonstrate the four insights discussed in Part 2. In a seminar at Duke University, for example, I used the route planner to estimate costs associated with six trips between Rome, Alexandria and Augusta Treverorum (Figure 14.8); and I used the network tool to generate two network cartograms which visualized the time cost of travel to Rome using all available forms of transportation (Figure 14.5) and travelling exclusively by road (Figure 14.9).

To demonstrate the first insight – i.e. that connections tended to occur along a limited network of more or less strictly defined routes – I explain the visualizations generated by both the route planner and the network tool (e.g. Figures 14.3, 14.5–6 and 14.9). To demonstrate the second – i.e. that cost, rather than distance, was the most significant variable in determining the level of connectivity throughout the network – I compare the speed- and expense-optimized trips from Rome to Augusta Treverorum (Figure 14.8, Rows 1–2) to the distance-optimized trip between the same two nodes (Figure 14.8, Row 3). To demonstrate the third – i.e. that sea and river routes tended to be more efficient connectors than land routes – I emphasize the tight clustering of Mediterranean ports at the centre of the first network cartogram (Figure 14.5) and conduct three comparisons: between the speed-optimized trip

Origin	Destination	Priority	Time cost (days)	Monetary cost* (denarii/kg)	Distance travelled (km)	Linear distance^ (km)
Rome	Augusta Treverorum	fastest	33	25.17	1,464	611
Rome	Augusta Treverorum	cheapest	83	8.39	6,148	611
Rome	Augusta Treverorum	shortest	48	47.16	1,347	611
Rome	Alexandria	fastest	14	1.45	2,332	1,213
Rome	Alexandria	fastest (overland)	138	125.83	4,756	1,213
Alexandria	Rome	fastest	21	2.88	2,588	1,213

Unless otherwise indicated, all estimates assume the following parameters: departure in July, using all available forms of transportation; high-resolution mode disabled; terrestrial travel by foot, fluvial travel by civilian transport and maritime travel by fast boat; and no transfer costs.

* Cost estimates are per kilogramme of wheat, using a wagon for overland transport.

^ Linear distances calculated using Google Maps, between Lat/Lon coordinates provided by Pleiades.

Figure 14.8 Costs of connectivity between Alexandria, Augusta Treverorum and Rome. © Scott Arcenas.

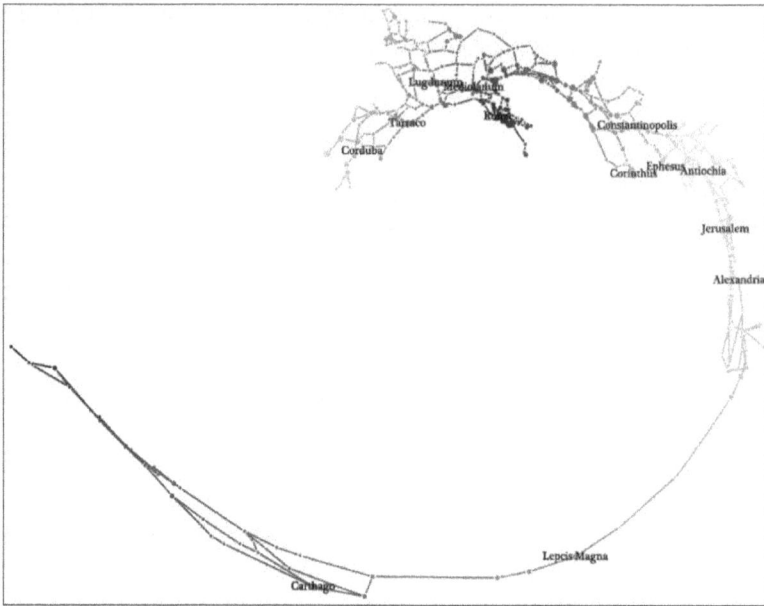

Figure 14.9 Isochrone map of time cost to Rome (overland routes only). Source: ORBIS (accessed 08/10/18).

from Rome to Augusta Treverorum (Figure 14.8, Row 1) and the speed-optimized trip from Rome to Alexandria (Figure 14.8, Row 4); between the two trips from Rome to Alexandria, one of which used all available forms of transportation (Figure 14.8, Row 4) and the other of which avoided travel by sea (Figure 14.8, Row 5); and between the time cost of travel to Rome using all available forms of transportation (Figure 14.5) and travelling exclusively by road (Figure 14.9). To demonstrate the fourth insight – i.e., that the cost of connectivity varied substantially depending on seasonal shifts in wind patterns, direction of travel, etc. – I conduct two comparisons: between the speed-optimized trip from Rome to Alexandria (Figure 14.8, Row 4) and the trip from Alexandria to Rome (Figure 14.8, Row 6); and between the time cost of travel to Rome using all available forms of transportation (Figure 14.5) and travelling exclusively by road (Figure 14.9).

Next, I ask students to consider how contemporary Americans use navigation apps, with particular attention to both the similarities and the differences between modern and Roman navigational practices. To give just three examples of responses that this question has elicited, students have recognized that, like Romans, users of Google Maps optimize for speed (when using the default settings) or a combination of speed and expenditure (with the 'avoid tolls' feature activated); that, just as during the Roman era, twenty-first-century travel speeds vary substantially depending on a range factors, such as method of travel, nearby concerts or sporting events and rush hour traffic; and that, unlike the Romans, contemporary Americans tend to conceptualize large bodies of water as obstacles to rather than facilitators of connectivity.

My next step is to divide students into small groups and provide each of them with a set of historical questions designed to be answered using ORBIS (together with, of course, the historical knowledge they have acquired during the course thus far). I have, for example, asked students to explain the eventual separation of the Roman Empire into eastern and western halves; to explain why first-century BC Romans saw the spread of piracy throughout the Mediterranean as an existential threat; to estimate the size of the Roman Empire in experiential terms; and to discuss the ways in which analogous estimates by Roman individuals would have varied depending on factors such as their gender, occupation and status.

Finally, I ask the members of each group to present their findings, being certain to provide specific examples in support of their claims. To give just two examples, one group tasked with explaining the significance of piracy used the route planner to obtain two sets of estimates vis-à-vis the time cost of travel between roughly a dozen large ports – one with all available forms of transportation enabled, the other considering only terrestrial and fluvial routes – and then compared the two, to illustrate the huge impact that restrictions on maritime transportation would have had on connectivity around the Mediterranean. Another group, assigned the same task, used the network tool to compare the economic cost of transportation to Rome with maritime transportation enabled on the one hand, and disabled on the other, and then leveraged the comparison to show that, if the increased risks associated with piracy increased the cost of shipping goods by sea to even one-third the cost of transporting them by land – and they argued persuasively that such may indeed have been the case – the results would have been ruinous. In both cases, the comparison provoked animated and perceptive discussion concerning, for example, the importance of maritime transportation to Rome's ability to project power around the Mediterranean, the economic consequences of predation and the ways in which both governments and private individuals responded to predation and other, similar threats.

To conclude, I would like to emphasize three of the most significant pay-offs that this exercise generates. First, it familiarizes students with the ways in which Romans – and, by extension, other ancient peoples – conceptualized and experienced geography. Crucially, moreover, it does so more effectively than any other method of which I am aware. Based on feedback from my students, I attribute the relative efficacy of this exercise to a combination of three factors: the intuitive user interface of the route planner, which helps students feel confident using ORBIS right away; the striking visualizations generated by the network tool, which convey complex ideas both more efficiently and more fully than any lecture, reading assignment or discussion; and the comparison to app-based navigation, which consolidates the lessons learned during the first half of the exercise by emphasizing both the basic similarity (insights 1–3) and the striking differences (insight 4) between ancient and modern ways of thinking about space.

Second, this exercise familiarizes students with the fundamental influence that geography exerted on the development of Roman society – and, by extension, other ancient societies. In so doing, it provides students with a powerful new tool with which to answer the many historical questions they will encounter both inside and outside the classroom.

The third and final pay-off that I would like to emphasize is that this exercise forces students to re-examine how they think about not only ancient societies, but also the society in which they live. One of the first times that I used this exercise, I was trying to convey just how different geography looks once we start to conceptualize it in relational rather than absolute terms. To a Roman senator, I explained, the empire seemed much bigger than the whole world seems to us; whereas we could hop on a plane and be in Sydney tomorrow, he would have needed roughly three weeks to make it just from Augusta Treverorum to Rome, travelling on horseback overland and on a fast ship by sea. Furthermore, the empire would have seemed even larger to the many Romans who lacked the financial resources necessary to pay for faster-than-foot transportation. For them, the same journey would have required roughly seven weeks of constant travel, not to mention the more than twenty-four weeks they would have needed to make it all the way to Alexandria.

In response to my comparison, one of my students argued that, while it may be accurate vis-à-vis the minority of people alive today who can afford to buy a plane ticket to Australia, it fails to account for the much larger number who cannot. For them, she persuasively argued, the world might not be quite as vast as the Roman Empire was to its inhabitants, but it is much larger than my comparison implied. This perceptive observation led to an animated discussion of, among other topics, the ways in which wealth and other types of privilege shape conceptions of space in the modern world and the extent to which we should think of geography relationally rather than in absolute terms – a discussion that many of my other students subsequently identified having been particularly instructive.

Exercise 2

I begin the second exercise, which is designed to be used after the first, by reminding students of what they have already learned concerning the geography of the ancient Mediterranean and its impact on the development of Roman society. Next, I challenge them to imagine that, at some point during the first millennium BC, both the city of Rome and all of its citizens had been transported to somewhere near our current location, and then to consider how the geography of the surrounding area would have affected the ways in which the transplanted society developed. Working with Stanford undergraduates, for example, I asked them to consider how the geography of coastal California would have affected a quasi-Roman society that had been transported to Palo Alto *c*. 500 BC, just after the establishment of the Republic.

In my experience, this prompt invariably generates energetic discussion. Among the aforementioned group at Stanford, for example, a consensus rapidly emerged that – due, as one student persuasively argued, to the extraordinarily low cost of connectivity in the San Francisco Bay Area – our transplanted Romans would have rapidly consolidated control over their immediate surroundings and then, taking advantage of the (higher, but nonetheless still relatively low) cost of connectivity along the coast in both directions, established an empire that occupied the whole Pacific coast of North America by the end of the second century. Disagreements arose, however, concerning the extent to which the Romans would have penetrated the interior, due to the difficulties involved in travel and, especially, transportation through the Sierra Nevadas, Cascades and other inland mountain ranges.

This very short exercise, which requires less than half an hour of class time, generates numerous pay-offs. By way of conclusion, I would like to emphasize two of the most significant. First and foremost, it reinforces the lessons learned during the first exercise. By using local geography, moreover, with which students have first-hand experience, it conveys these important concepts on a more visceral level.

Second, by situating fifth-century Romans in a counterfactual geographic context, this thought experiment forces students to grapple with one of the most important methodological problems faced by historians: when attempting to explain historical phenomena on a macro scale, how much agency should we assign to geographic factors? And how much to human factors? Crucially, moreover, discussion along these lines tends to emerge organically from the thought experiment, which allows students to discover the methodological dilemma for themselves.

Exercise 3

After the death of Alexander the Great in 323 BC, the vast empire that he had accumulated over a dozen years of near-constant campaigning rapidly disintegrated. Existing scholarship attributes the disintegration to a variety of factors, including Alexander's failure to designate a successor, the structural weakness of Macedonian kingship, and Alexander's failure to unite the disparate societies that he had conquered.[7] In the third exercise, which is designed for use in a course on Alexander the Great that I am teaching at Dartmouth College in the fall of 2018, I will use ORBIS to propose an alternative explanation that emphasizes the crucial role played by geography.

After discussing existing scholarship on Alexander's death and its immediate aftermath, I will introduce my students to ORBIS and use the network tool to emphasize the vital role that the low cost of connectivity across the Mediterranean played in both the establishment and the maintenance of the Roman Empire. I will then ask them to create a rudimentary network cartogram that represents connections among a selection of important nodes throughout the territory conquered by Alexander, based on travel times reported by Arrian (whose *Anabasis of Alexander* they will have read) and the other Alexander historians, as well as extrapolations from those reports. I should emphasize that I do not expect the cartogram to be at all precise – merely to be accurate in very broad terms.

Next, I will ask my students to compare the cartogram that they have created to the Roman transportation network as visualized by ORBIS, and to keep the comparison in mind as we discuss the disintegration of the Macedonian Empire after Alexander's death. Finally, I will ask them a set of questions designed to help them consider the impact of geography on the tortuous geopolitics of the early Hellenistic period: for example, are there any conditions under which Alexander's vast conquests could have remained intact after 323 BC? If so, what are the necessary conditions? In accounting for the way in which events unfolded, how much weight should we assign to geographic factors, as opposed to cultural factors or the actions of individual men and women?

To conclude, I would like to emphasize three of the most significant pay-offs that I both hope and expect this exercise to generate. First, like the other two that I have already discussed, this exercise will familiarize students with both (1) the ways in which ancient societies experienced geography and (2) the ways in which geography influenced the development of those societies. In so doing, it should help them (re-)examine both the particular events that we cover in the course and pre-modern history more broadly with new and more perceptive eyes. It should, for example, help them recognize the sharp constraints that geography put on the scale at which pre-modern societies were able to operate, in the absence of modern transportation and communications infrastructure. On a more specific level, comparing the time cost of travel in the Macedonian and Roman Empires should help them appreciate the full scale of Alexander's conquests and recognize that the territory he briefly occupied was even larger than historical maps would lead us to believe. This is due to the fact that the territory conquered by Alexander lacked a unifying connector like the Mediterranean. Consequently, the time cost of travel from one side to the other would have been much higher than that of an analogous journey in the Roman Empire, even though cartographic depictions seem to imply that the two would be roughly comparable.

Second, this exercise introduces students to two useful skills that are too often neglected in humanities classrooms: data visualization and intersocietal comparison. In so doing, it substantially improves their ability to both formulate and answer historical questions.

Third, this exercise introduces students to one of the most innovative and successful digital humanities projects concerning the classical world. In so doing, it provides students who are fascinated by both technology and Classics with a model of what they can accomplish by pursuing both interests simultaneously.

Conclusion

By way of conclusion, I would like to clarify one possible source of confusion and emphasize three of the characteristics that make ORBIS such an effective teaching tool. First, the clarification. At the beginning of this chapter, I argued that traditional maps (whether in print or online) misrepresent the geography of the ancient world. In so doing, I may have seemed to imply that teachers ought to avoid using them. Accordingly, I would like to clarify that this is emphatically not the case. Rather, my point is that teachers ought to use traditional maps together with tools like ORBIS that will help students recognize the substantial disjuncture between the ways in which maps represent geography and the ways in which historical actors conceptualized and experienced it.

Finally, a few words on some of the characteristics that make ORBIS such an effective teaching tool. First, the close resemblance between the route planner and popular navigation apps like Google Maps allows students to use and become comfortable with ORBIS almost instantaneously. Second, the network and flow tools allow both teachers and students to easily create visualizations that communicate extremely complex concepts on an almost intuitive level. Third and finally, ORBIS both (1) documents all of the interpretive decisions and (2) makes publicly available all of the code that underlies the network model. In so doing, it provides students with both the information necessary to conduct independent research projects and a model for responsible research practices in the digital age. Together with the project's unparalleled ability to familiarize students with both the ways in which ancient societies experienced geography and the ways in which geography shaped those societies, these three characteristics make ORBIS an invaluable contributor to any classroom.

Notes

1. The standard (and best available) print resource is the *Barrington Atlas of the Greek and Roman World*. Among the best digital tools are Pleiades (https://pleiades.stoa.org/), Antiquity à-la-carte (http://awmc.unc.edu/wordpress/alacarte/), Google Earth Pro and the Barrington Atlas of the Greek and Roman World app for iOS.

2. The *Oxford English Dictionary* defines geography as: 'The field of study concerned with the physical features of the earth and its atmosphere, *and with human activity as it affects and is affected by these*' (emphasis mine). In this chapter, I use geography in the latter, rather than the former sense.

3. For application of the classic absolutist–relationist distinction to spatial history, see esp. White 2010.

4. Walter Scheidel was the primary investigator. The other core contributors were as follows: on the IT side, Noemi Alvarez, Karl Grossner, Elijah Meeks and Ashley Ngu; from Classics, Scott Arcenas, Federica Carugati, Dan-el Padilla Peralta and Jon Weiland.

5. For a more detailed discussion of this and the following, see the ORBIS website: http://orbis. stanford.edu/.

6. Like many other digital tools, ORBIS relies heavily on colour and motion to convey complex ideas visually. The figures employed in this chapter have been selected and adapted to function as printed images in black and white. Readers should be aware, however, that the visualizations they can generate using the ORBIS website will be substantially more effective.

7. For a useful discussion, with bibliography, of Alexander's death and its immediate aftermath, see Cartledge (2004).

References

Cartledge, P. (2004), *Alexander the Great: The Hunt for a New Past*, New York: Overlook Press.

Talbert, R. (ed.) (2000), *Barrington Atlas of the Greek and Roman World*, Princeton: Princeton University Press.

White, R. (2010), 'What Is Spatial History?', Spatial History Lab Working Papers. Available online: https://web.stanford.edu/group/spatialhistory/cgi-bin/site/pub.php?id=29 (accessed 7 August 2018).

PART III
USING TECHNOLOGY IN THE ANCIENT LANGUAGE CLASSROOM

CHAPTER 15
BRIDGING THE GAP BETWEEN STUDENTS AND ANTIQUITY: LANGUAGE ACQUISITION VIDEOS WITH *MINECRAFT* AND CI/TPRS
Jessie Craft

Introduction

For over a decade, teachers have been seeking to supplement their curricula with compelling and meaningful technology. In recent years, a surge of K–12 Latin teachers having been trying to find ways to discuss culture in the target language. This paper will describe an innovative way to combine the vastly played video game *Minecraft* with Latin classroom language and culture needs using technology and second language acquisition methods. The author will elaborate on some of the theoretical underpinnings of CI (Comprehensible Input) and TPRS (Teaching Proficiency through Reading and Storytelling) and discuss the central reasons for using *Minecraft* as the medium to deliver information in the target language. He will present some of the best practices for implementation in class along with some accompanying activities, and along the way will include tips and cautions for the recreation of this pedagogical method.

Teaching a language can be difficult at times, especially when there is often a great deal of pressure to discuss culture. As is the case in the Latin classroom, these conversations about culture often occur in the class's native language and not in the target language (TL). Subsequently, the opportunity for students to further advance in their language acquisition is diminished. In recent years, many Latin educators have been turning to more modern methods for teaching Latin and are, in many ways, treating Latin like a living language. The results are that students are beginning to *acquire* the language as opposed to *learn* about it, as is typical in classes whose primary focus is solely on grammar and translation methods. What I provide and what I am proposing in this chapter is a way to teach students about the wonderful and varied culture of antiquity while simultaneously fostering second language acquisition. To achieve this end, I create videos which show, using *Minecraft*, and discuss, in level-appropriate Latin, various cultural aspects of ancient Rome and ancient Greece, all of which are couched in the principles of CI and TPRS.

What is *Minecraft*?

Minecraft is a video game, originally made for the computer, and it is perhaps best likened to Lego. To play the game, one selects an avatar and enters a randomly generated 3D world full of trees, animals, hills, mountains, lakes, rivers, villages and villagers. In *Minecraft* everything is square, or at least composed of squares, making construction a bit easier initially, until one wishes to make a circle or build something at an angle. The primary goal of the game is to build houses, cars, cities, pixel art and so on. The game also includes a multi-player option, so people can team up to build things together in the 3D virtual space and in real time. Roughly four years ago, the makers of *Minecraft* saw the educational potential of the game and created *MinecraftEdu*, a version of the game built specifically for teachers, with mods allowing teachers to create in-game assignments, patrol and control students' behaviour and interactions, and physically demonstrate learning objectives to students in ways never before possible.

What are CI and TPRS?

Comprehensible Input[1] is often abbreviated as CI, but there are those who would see that abbreviation lengthened by adding another 'C' for 'Compelling', as the basics of the pedagogy work like this. First there is 'Input', which refers to any way one might acquire the target language (TL); listening and reading are the primary ways to acquire the TL, though not the only ones.[2] 'Comprehensible' refers to the students' ability to understand the TL message in terms of vocabulary, grammar and context.

With CI there is often an acceptable target percentage range of comprehension associated. That range is typically from 95–98 per cent comprehension:[3] students should understand this percentage range of vocabulary, grammar and context. This range, for most teachers, also includes glossed words provided in parentheses to the side or bottom of the page, images depicting and thus aiding in the understanding of certain words or phrases, or derivatives – derivatives, for some teachers, belong to the percentage of the unknown. The 2–5 per cent which is unknown to the student should be comprehensible from the context or be an easily recognizable derivative. In theory, the 95–98 per cent of the input is what is used to carry across meaning and reinforce previously acquired vocabulary and grammar, thereby creating or strengthening a mental representation of the language. The remaining 2–5 per cent, which rests just above the student's present ability, exists in Vygotsky's Zone of Proximal Development (1980) and thus acts to impart upon the student new language constructs.

As Krashen (2011) suggests, the input must also be compelling to students. 'Compelling' means that the students are so interested in the story or its presentation that they do not realize that they are reading a school text or in another language, and there are several ways to achieve this. Some authors fill their stories with intrigue and twists;[4] some make their stories about the very students listening;[5] some teachers become method actors by passionately gesticulating, widely varying the tone and inflection of their voices and using props;[6] and others use colourful videos and images to catch the eye of students and fill in understanding gaps.[7]

Teaching Proficiency through Reading and Storytelling (TPRS)[8] is a method based on CI that seeks to utilize stories to impart the TL to students. Typically, TPRS is broken down into three components: establish meaning, storytelling and reading. 'Establish meaning' means to ensure that the story about to be told is comprehensible. One way to establish meaning is to pre-teach students any targeted vocabulary, grammar or context that will appear in the story. Some pre-teaching methods are traditional vocab lists, Quizlet, Kahoot!, composition, alternate stories,[9] circling,[10] PQA (personalized questions and answer)[11] and TPR.[12] Meaning can also be established during the storytelling. When new words, grammar or context are encountered for the first time during the story, the teacher can write the new material on the board with its L1 counterpart. Using the class's native language in this instance is not thought to hinder TL acquisition

(Piantaggini 2016). Each time the targeted word, grammar or context occurs in the story, the teacher can point to it on the board slowly and purposefully, making sure that all students are comprehending and following along. Finally, the audio-visual aspect of videos infuses lots of comprehensible meaning into a scene or sequence of scenes while staying in the TL.

The need for materials for the CI/TPRS class

With the present resurgence of oral Latin and the subsequent turning of teachers to more modern philosophies and pedagogies like CI and TPRS, many educators have found themselves in a predicament. For the Latin language there is a great need for reading and listening material that is comprehensible and compelling, but much of what is available (textbooks and authentic texts) is often above students' reading level,[13] contains too much vocabulary or contains too few repetitions of grammar or vocabulary. In recent years, several teachers have taken it upon themselves to begin creating level-appropriate, comprehensible and compelling material: novellas,[14] audio recordings[15] and videos. Some teachers have even created Facebook groups,[16] websites[17] and podcasts,[18] in which they share their material and discuss with other teachers the current best pedagogical practices and advice on how to create material appropriate for twenty-first-century students. These groups of teachers and professionals are generally very supportive and encouraging. Often it is here where teachers and professionals network, finding readers and editors for each other's material.

Why *Minecraft* and why videos?

As discussed earlier, there is a great need, according to CI principles, for the TL input to be compelling. The need for student buy-in is high to ensure student participation and TL acquisition. One thing I have done with my videos to help increase buy-in and make the content compelling is to use *Minecraft* as the medium. Of course, the term 'compelling' is rather subjective – what is compelling will often change from class to class, even within the same school – but a quick look at *Minecraft*'s sales figures will quantify, to a certain extent, the general likeability of the game among pre-teens, teens and even adults.[19]

What makes *Minecraft* so appealing to students is their familiarity with the game and its relatability. Over the past four years I have always asked my Latin I classes who has played or knows the game, and every year the answer is nearly a constant 100 per cent, and almost all of these students report positive, pleasant experiences with the game. Through their direct or indirect contact with the game, my videos become relatable to students, thereby allowing me to speak to them on their level. *Minecraft* is the bridge over which I bring the Roman world to my students.

The videos themselves bring with them a sense of relatability which helps the instruction and acquisition processes, but more importantly, videos help to establish meaning with images. The circumlocutions necessary for explaining more complex or abstract ideas do not occur until the language learner has achieved a certain linguistic proficiency, and depending on the complexity of the idea, this might not happen until an intermediate or advanced proficiency has been acquired. As discussed previously, the students' native language may be used to establish meaning. However, for those teachers who wish to use a more immersive approach, or simply wish to eliminate the use of any languages other than the TL, images – whether still or video – are a great way to establish meaning. These images also have the advantage of enabling students, typically, to arrive at the meaning of a word or phrase more quickly than most circumlocutions and more quickly than having to pause to look at a word wall, the board or notes. Obtaining the meaning of a word or phrase from its visual representation permits the student to remain in flow.[20] A video which is visually stimulating and familiar to the student, as well as comprehensible and compelling, can immerse the learner in the context of the story, allowing the viewer's subconscious mind to handle all the secondary lexical/grammatical information. Students take cues and can establish meaning subconsciously by observing the scenery. Furthermore, images allow the storyteller to reduce vocabulary, thereby limiting some of the mental fatigue of the students and ultimately keeping them better focused on acquiring the language in the current activity.

Implementation

Since I began producing these videos in December of 2016, teachers and professors have come up with many ways to effectively use the videos in their language classes. After hearing from many of them and comparing what they do with what I do and with what I intended for the videos, I have determined that there are two basic categories of use: language acquisition and non-language acquisition. For this chapter, I will only describe the most common procedures for implementing these videos in class in terms of language acquisition uses.

If the videos are to be effectively used as language acquisition tools, there are a few things which must be secured prior to showing the videos in class or having students watch them on their own. First, one must determine the desired outcome of the video: what is its desired role in acquisition? Does the video seek to teach students something new, perhaps, about culture? Is the purpose of the video to help students acquire targeted language components? Should the video do both? If the video is to teach students something cultural or historical, then the majority of the language, if not all, needs to be easily understood – this could mean 98–100 per cent comprehensibility. If the video is to help students acquire targeted language components, the video must still be comprehensible, but more importantly, there must be a suitable number of repetitions of the desired vocabulary or structure in meaningful contexts; seeking the golden mean is optimal, as too many repetitions can become tedious. Of course, a combination of the two will satisfy imparting new cultural/historical information and granting students ample practice with targeted language structures to ensure some demonstrable amount of acquisition.

Because one of the fundamental principles behind CI/TPRS, and thus these videos, is comprehensibility, students should have previously acquired or be able to intuit 95–98 per cent of the vocabulary. The intuition of this vocabulary can be done through the video itself, which uses images and sounds to help establish the meaning of words and phrases. One way to ensure that a majority of – and preferably all – the students will experience the video at this targeted comprehension percentage is to show videos using close to all – or solely – previously acquired vocab. Although it will be somewhat challenging to find videos which fit your specific needs, if they supply a transcript of the video, you can then copy it into a word frequency tool like Voyant Tools.[21] From there you can determine the occurrences of each word and pre-teach the vocabulary to your students accordingly. The most common practice is for teachers first to screen the video, taking note of all the words unknown to their students. Then they create word lists, Quizlets, Kahoot!s or simplified short stories comprised of the targeted vocabulary, and they have students work with these new words prior to showing the video. How long prior to showing the video is up to the teacher: some prefer that students acquire these words and thus will work to incorporate the new words into their day-to-day curriculum well in advance. Other teachers may present the new words a day before, or that very same day. It is at this point that the video should be mostly comprehensible to students and should now act to reinforce the new vocabulary students were just exposed to. Although I have spoken only about vocabulary thus far, the same advice applies to grammar as well.

Once students have been exposed to and/or acquired enough vocabulary or grammar, they are ready for the first iteration of the video. Ballestrini (2017) suggests that for the '[f]irst viewing: play through video, check for comprehension'. To elaborate on this, I would suggest telling students your intentions. They will watch once without subtitles so they can take in the scenery, listen to the narration and see how the two work together. There will be Latin subtitles in the second viewing. Telling students what to expect and when to expect it allows them to mentally prepare a necessary framework for the information they are about to receive and the type of energy they will need to put forth in paying attention. As Ballestrini (2017) suggests, after the first viewing I do an informal comprehension check. I ask questions in the TL about what happened, careful to not confirm or deny what the students offer up. The point is for me to determine from those who speak approximately how much they were able to get from just the video. I never associate a grade with these informative assessments – this needs to be a low-stakes activity to keep students engaged in the subconscious acquisition. After my TL questions, I briefly switch to English to inform the students that we are now going to watch the video again with Latin subtitles – this is the students' cue to ready themselves mentally and to prepare paper and pencil for note taking.

The second showing is one of the most important ones. First, the motive for showing the same video or having students reread the same passage is backed up by research in neuroscience. For the development of associative memory, a key element in language acquisition, research has demonstrated that multiple interactions with the same material helps learners to lighten the load which was put on the brain during a first encounter with, say, a text, thus allowing the brain to dedicate more resources to the region of the brain which creates associative memories (Dennis et al. 2015). Any subsequent showings give students the opportunity to listen and read with less strain. The images serve to help establish the meaning behind the words, and the oral component serves to help students acquire the language through a more natural method – both of which are ultimately scaffolding for interpretive reading, which is performed through the reading of the Latin subtitles and, later, of a handout without the aid of the scaffolding. In this and subsequent showings, students are creating stronger associative memories of the words and phrases, and thus a longer lasting and more complete mental representation of the language, by simultaneously hearing the words spoken and seeing them visually represented while they read. The viability of the image-to-word connection has support in the direct method of language teaching,[22] as well as in the neuroscience of associative memory (Suzuki 2005). Based on these principles, I present images of objects and actions accompanied by the words in the TL, creating a direct connection between the word and the object and foregoing the use of English as the intermediary filter. Hearing the words spoken while reading them is a powerful combination which has serious positive implications on second language acquisition and literacy skills.[23] Since the goal in my Latin class is for students to improve their reading/interpretive proficiency by means of listening activities, imagery and extensive reading, the second viewing is a culmination of all three, where students work to bring it all together.

After the second showing, I may administer or perform some sort of assessment to determine what students have understood through the language. There are several common types of low-stakes assessment to give at this point. To name but a few, I may ask a series of True/False questions in the TL; if there were multiple characters in the story I could ask a series of 'Who did X?' questions; or I might present students with the option of writing an English summary (sometimes in Latin) of what happened. After the second showing, I may even engage students in a conversation, an activity which has been shown to have a profound impact on language acquisition (Sénéchal 1997). I could start and guide the conversation with questions like: What happened in the story? What were your favourite parts? What did you hear a lot of? What still gave you difficulty?

Third viewings are rare in my class, but there are some teachers who use this practice *in lieu* of reading a transcript. Bartlett and Jergen (2017) ask if their students would like to watch a third time – often they do – and they give their students a choice of 'Latine' or 'Anglice'. They report that when students select 'Latine', they like to give a running translation of the video. Other teachers may use the third showing as an ultimate way to establish meaning using English subtitles. However, what I prefer is to read a transcript of the video. If possible, I find it best to do the first two showings on one day and towards the end of class.

I start the next class with an image taken from the video that students describe in Latin. When everyone has finished, we have an open discussion in Latin about the image, with students offering what they wrote. Depending on how many new words there were in the story, we may do a review of them – calling out each new word and its English meaning, depicting each of the new words or some such activity – and then students will read through a script of the video. Usually, I give a graded comprehension quiz at this point. Because these videos and the other activities done in class are meant to help students improve their reading comprehension proficiency, it is important to administer some form of assessment at this point. If students' scores fit the 80/80 guide[24] (i.e. if 80 per cent of students score an 80 out of 100 or higher on the graded assessment) then we move on to the next story.

Although this most recent description details the original intent of the videos, there is another acquisition-based way to use them in class. Alessandro Conti (Veronensis 2017), a Latin educator in Italy, often uses my videos as 'brain breaks' for his students. Brain breaks are a way to break up the monotony of an activity and to stimulate the brain by doing something new and invigorating (Desautels 2015), and they may be done at varying intervals (Walker 2016). When Conti has decided it is time to take a break from the vigorous work of second language acquisition, he may offer students a brain break in which they will sit back, relax and watch one of these videos. Because the videos are suited for a proficiency level often lower than Conti's own students, they can watch and comprehend with relative ease. They can enjoy the imagery and laugh at my attempts at humour, all while staying in the TL. So, even though the difficulty of the language is often below their proficiency, the repetition helps to reinforce the vocabulary and grammar they have been working to acquire in class. After the video, Conti returns to teaching his students at their usual vigorous level. In my upper-level Latin classes, I occasionally administer a comprehension check after these brain breaks, but students are not threatened by this because they were watching the video with approximately 100 per cent comprehension and were often enjoying themselves. In these upper-level comprehension checks, I rarely have anyone make less than 100 per cent; if I do, the student may have missed half a question or a whole question, but thus far never more than that.

Movie talks are another great way to take any video and make it relevant and comprehensible for your own class. First, view the video a time or two to get the full gist of the clip and to determine how it can be used in class – perhaps the video lends itself well to giving more repetitions in vocabulary or a recent grammar concept, or maybe a targeted cultural topic is being shown. Once you have an idea of the video's content and how the scenes support vocabulary, grammar and/or a cultural concept then present the video to the class. For first-timers, one might consider writing out a planned script of sentences and questions with time stamps from the video. Once you are ready to press play, mute the audio. For this video, you are the narrator. You can therefore adapt the text completely to your students' level and needs, either on the spot or beforehand. As the video plays and you narrate, you can also pause the video to do some PQA to make the video interactive for the students. This is a great way to 'check the temperature', for you can instantly determine who is tracking or who is struggling. This allows you to address any immediate concerns and get the class back up to the targeted 95–98 per cent comprehension rate.

Results and feedback

Using these videos in class has been overall a great success. I have found, and many teachers have reported to me, that students were very eager to participate in these activities and were willing to tolerate multiple viewings of them. Students often react with great visible joy when it is time to put on a video, and they become silent of their own accord when the video starts. Krashen's Affective Filter Hypothesis (1982) can help to shed light on the increase in participation and engagement. His hypothesis states that high motivation, high self-confidence and low anxiety are conducive to second language acquisition, while their opposites are detractors and inhibitors. The students are motivated to engage in this kind of activity, first because it is a video, and by now most students have come to see videos as a break from traditional learning; and second because the video is made with *Minecraft*, a game which nearly all students have or currently play, usually with great joy and fond memories. This makes the material more relatable to students, thereby increasing motivation and also confidence. Students' eagerness and self-confidence thereby diminish their anxiety about the activity. To further reduce anxiety, all the students know that I do not plan to trick them with any of the questions that will follow, that I will cover all vocabulary prior to or during the showing, and that we will watch and discuss the video multiple times so that if they missed something in the first iteration they may catch it in the second. As a result of all of these factors, my students are confident that they will demonstrate high proficiency on any comprehension checks. All of this translates into excitement for these compelling and comprehensible videos, which in turn translates into language acquisition.

Along with experiencing an increase in participation, students are demonstrating increased proficiency in listening and reading comprehension. Sometimes during – though mostly after – the video, students can be heard mimicking select words or phrases from the video, e.g.

'Salvete plurimum!', 'Nomen mihi est Magister Craft', 'Hodie de _____ discetis', 'Ecce, finis fabulae' and 'Valete!' Getting students to take command of even a few phrases in the TL and freely recite them is a great way to foster a positive learning environment and to invite other students to join in. During reading activities, some students have commented, 'Hey, this is that part of the video where Magister Craft did X'. This demonstrates that students interact more with the text by connecting it to the mental visual representations they acquired during the viewing. To date, I have not personally had a single student fail one of my comprehension checks after any of my videos. Instead, grades tend to average around 85 per cent (alpha grade B), and the number of students who performed at 90 per cent or higher (alpha grade A) greatly outweighs the number of students in the 60–79 per cent range (alpha grade range D–C). These grades are considerably higher compared to texts of a similar difficulty which are not accompanied by a visual representation or an audio recording of the text. Before creating and using videos in class, the results of comprehension checks for the same readings (now video transcripts) trended as follows: approximately 10 per cent scored a 0–59 out of 100 (alpha grade F), 70 per cent scored a 60–79 (alpha grades D–C), 15 per cent scored an 80–89 (alpha grade B) and 5 per cent scored a 90–100 (alpha grade A). Although these preliminary data are taken from a year and a half of using videos in class, the trends are clear, consistent and promising.

Because the videos are published on YouTube, people are allowed to anonymously like or dislike the videos, and if they feel inclined they may leave a comment, though this is not anonymous per se, as that person's YouTube alias shows next to the comment. Here is a sampling of some typical comments which are really testimonials to the efficacy of using videos to foster second language acquisition:

> I love this video. It has help me with Latin vocabulary that I use in class. My teacher was very impressed. Also I love your videos you are my favorite YouTuber.
>
> Dave Da Rave 21, *Forum Romanum* video

> Thank you! This is great practice for basic Latin. The video offers useful context clues to help pick up vocab.
>
> Andrew Benson, *Forum Romanum* video

> The best channel about Latin culture and language! Please don't give up to make videos.
>
> Thank you for your videos! I recently started learning Latin and your videos helps me to understand the language by ear.
>
> Кузьма Симонов, *Septem Reges* video

> For someone beginning to learn Latin or brushing up on Latin after many years without practice (such as myself), your video is fantastic. The enunciation is slow, clear, and expressive. Mirabile auditu! Also, nice Minecraft build!
>
> Andrew Benson, *Naumachia* video

> Salve, Magister Craft! Iamdudum tibi gratulari volebam! Nunc quidem id facio: Pelliculae tuae mihi discipulisque meis maximo emolumento sunt! Gratias! Vale!
>
> Beatus Helvetius Salodurensis, *Mythology: Diana* video

Conclusion

Presenting students with videos which tell stories in Latin is a unique way to foster second language acquisition. The videos use *Minecraft*,[25] which has been shown to resonate positively with students, thereby securing some buy-in. If presented in the right way, the videos become less stressful, low-stakes activities in which students tend to be more engaged and relaxed, which in turn usually leads to better language acquisition than merely reading through a text. Although more empirical data with control groups is needed to better quantify to what degree these videos are aiding students in language acquisition, the preliminary small sets of empirical data accompanied by anecdotal data indicate the likelihood of promising results.

Notes

1. Stephen Krashen is often credited with popularizing CI, but Krashen readily admits that he was not the one to invent this term. In his 2017 article 'Who Invented Comprehensible Input?', he cites several figures in first language and second language acquisition who used the term before him.

2. Total physical response is a method created by James Asher (2009) in which language is learned through a combination of oral communication and physical reaction. Teachers may give students commands or communicate simple ideas and students will demonstrate comprehension through a physical response using a part or all of their bodies.

3. See Schmitt et al. (2011). Although this article seems to prefer a larger range of 90–100 per cent covered vocabulary, the origins for the 95 per cent come from Laufer (1989), and the origins for the 98 per cent come from Hu and Nation (2000).

4. See, for example, Demuth and Rath's *Tres Fabulae Horrificae* Latin stories.

5. See, for example, Buczek's *Iter Mirabile Dennis et Debrae: A Latin Novella* Latin story.

6. See *Justin Slocum Bailey in day 2 of Express Fluency Latin Class.* Available online: https://www.youtube.com/watch?v=C_Qhf7Nu8-w (accessed 29 August 2017).

7. See Reka Fazekas (n.d.), Home [Reka Fasekas], available online: https://www.youtube.com/channel/UCkxukeH2GPwf0sHArSUR1bA (accessed 29 September 2018); and Jessie Craft (n.d.), Home [Divus Magister Craft], available online: https://www.youtube.com/channel/UCTtKmPD0_Qo9Uy932ZGKFhA (accessed 29 September 2018).

8. Blaine Ray is credited with having invented TPRS, but Lichtman (2018) masterfully and precisely lays out all of the fundamental principles behind TPRS, as well as a detailed discussion, including examples, of the implementation of this method and its various forms and iterations.

9. Alternate stories involve putting all the new vocabulary on the board with their L1 meanings, and then attempting to create a story on the fly with students. As each new vocabulary word is encountered and entered into the story, the teacher should repeat each preceding vocabulary word with its accompanying storyline.

10. Bex (n.d.) suggests: 'Begin by making a statement in the target language. The statement should contain only ONE new target structure (vocabulary term or phrase), and the rest of the statement should be completely comprehensible to students (previously acquired vocabulary, cognates, and proper nouns). Follow it up with yes/no, either/or, and open-ended questions, and restate/recast the original statement after the answer to each question is given.'

11. PQA is quite similar to circling, except that the goal is to involve the students and their interests in the TL questioning. The teacher will ask a student a simple question about, for instance, their likes. The student will provide, most likely, a one-word answer. The teacher then recasts the student's information in a properly formed TL statement. Then the teacher will repeat that statement in the

form of a question now posed to the rest of the class. The teacher might say, 'Class, does Paul like books or worms?' The class will reply, and the teacher can recast that statement and so on.

12. TPR is when the teacher expresses something (usually a command) in the TL and the students react with some whole-body action. For instance, when I teach my Latin I students the word *surgite*, I have them repeat the word and stand up from their desks. Some practitioners of TPR will use the method with words other than commands, e.g. *amat* or any variation of it is rendered by putting one's hands together in the shape of a heart. Extending TPR to more than just commands is great for doing periodic comprehension checks during a story. The teacher can stop at a specific or random moment and ask students to 'show' the meaning of the word. In doing so, you can better troubleshoot who is missing what. This is also great because it allows for more time to be spent in the TL by not having to resort to the class's native language to establish meaning – using the native language to establish meaning is definitely acceptable and often encouraged, but some teachers prefer to associate the TL with physical or abstract things directly and not indirectly through the filter of the students' native language.

13. By reading level what is intended is not to be confused with translating, for translating is not reading. Reading refers to a person's ability to view words in a specific sequence, extract information from each word in real time and understand the information such that the reader can visualize what is being communicated.

14. See, for example, *Cloelia* (Arnold 2016); *Pluto: Fabula Amoris* (Ash and Patrick 2016); *Tres Fabulae Horrificae* (Demuth and Rath 2017); *Itinera Petri: Flammae Ducant* (Patrick 2015); *Iter Mirabile Dennis et Debrae* (Buczek 2016); and *Piso Ille Poetulus* (Piantaggini 2017).

15. See (or hear), for example, Sonitus Mirabilis, available online: http://www.steppingintoci.com/sonitus-mirabilis.html; Musaeolum, available online: http://www.musaeolum.com/ (accessed 29 September 2018).

16. See, for example, the following Facebook social media discussion fora: Teaching Latin for Acquisition; Teaching Latin to the Littles- Elementary Latin Teachers; Latin Best Practices: The Next Generation in Comprehensible Input; Latinitium; Legonium; Latinum; Latin and Greek Course & Audiobook Catalogue; and Magister Craft.

17. See, for example, https://magisterp.com/, http://johnpiazza.net/, http://latintoolbox.blogspot.com/, http://www.latinahilara.com/, http://pomegranatebeginnings.blogspot.com/, http://indwellinglanguage.com/latin/, http://todallycomprehensiblelatin.blogspot.com/ and https://latinbestpracticescir.wordpress.com/.

18. See, for example, http://quomododicitur.com/, https://infororomano.blogspot.com/, http://sermonesraedarii.podomatic.com/ and http://www.musaeolum.com/.

19. As of February 2017, *Minecraft* confirmed over 122 million copies worldwide sold across all consoles (PC, Mac, Playstation, Xbox and mobile devices) (*Minecraft*, 2017a). Furthermore, *Minecraft*'s sales statistics webpage shows that around 9,000 copies (on PC and Mac alone) are sold in a twenty-four-hour period (*Minecraft*, 2017b).

20. Csikszentmihalyi (1990) described 'flow' as that moment when a person becomes so engaged in and focused on an activity that they seemingly forget their current surroundings and situation. Krashen (2011) applies Csikszentmihalyi's idea of flow to language acquisition and the compellingness to language learners of a particular topic found in oral discourse or reading.

21. See http://voyant-tools.org/.

22. The direct method, sometimes called the natural method, was developed in the early twentieth century in response to the then-dominant grammar-translation method. The direct method seeks to keep all communication in the TL and to utilize realia or natural context to establish meaning for language learners.

23. See, for example, Teaching Strategies (2010); Bredekamp et al. (2000); Fountas and Pinnell (1996); and Guignon (2016).

24. Credit is due to Bob Patrick for this handy guide.

25. Although *Minecraft* is the medium I use for my videos, there are several others who produce videos which can be used to great effect in class. Daniel Pettersson of Latinitium has produced a few animated and several audio-only videos which are great for advanced- to superior-level learners. ScorpioMartianus is another YouTuber who produces excellent videos, in which he acts out parts or uses a computer program to give viewers Latin tours of Italy and even the solar system; his videos are probably best suited for intermediate to advanced levels. Lance Piantaggini has produced a few excellent novice-level videos, and although his videos are not animated, he draws pictures on a whiteboard as he tells his stories to aid in comprehension. Ysmael on YouTube has made a video using images of ancient art, which would be appropriate for advanced-level learners. Anthony Gibbons of Legonium uses images of Lego creations to help tell his stories at the novice level. His work is not on YouTube but can be found at www.legonium.com.

References

Allen, W. (1989), *Vox Latina: A Guide to the Pronunciation of Classical Latin* 2nd Edn, Cambridge: Cambridge University Press.

Arnold, E. (2017), *Cloelia: Puella Romana*, CreateSpace.

Ash, M. and Patrick, B. (2016), *Pluto: Fabula Amoris*, CreateSpace.

Asher, J. (2009), *Learning Another Language Through Actions*, 7th edn, Los Gatos, CA: Sky Oak Productions.

Ballestrini, K. and Little, S. (2017), *The Standards for Classical Language Learning: Inspiration and Application*, Paper presented at CANE's Annual Meeting, Exeter, NH.

Bartlett, E. and Jergen, J. (17 October 2017), Personal message, Facebook Messenger.

Bex, M. (n.d.), 'The Comprehensible Classroom'. Available online: https://martinabex.com/teacher-training/essential-strategies-for-tprsci-teachers/how-to-circle/ (accessed 29 September 2018).

Bredekamp, S., Copple, C. and Neuman, S. (2000), *Learning to Read and Write: Developmentally Appropriate Practices for Young Children*, Washington, DC: National Association for the Education of Young Children.

Buczek, C. (2016), *Iter Mirabile Dennis et Debrae: A Latin Novella*, Unknown: CreateSpace.

Craft, J. (2016), 'Rebuilding an Empire: Bringing the Classics into the Digital Space', *Classical Journal*, 111.3: 347–364.

Csikszentmihalyi, M. (1990), *Flow: The Psychology of Optimal Experience*, New York: Harper Perennial.

Demuth, J. and Rath, R. (2017), *Tres Fabulae Horrificae*, CreateSpace.

Dennis, N., Turney, I., Webb, C. and Overman, A. (2015), 'The Effects of Item Familiarity on the Neural Correlates of Successful Associative Memory Encoding', *Cognitive, Affective, & Behavioral Neuroscience*, 15(4): 889–900.

Desautels, L. (2015), 'Energy and Calm: Brain Breaks and Focused-Attention Practices', *Edutopia*. Available online: https://www.edutopia.org/blog/brain-breaks-focused-attention-practices-lori-desautels (accessed 29 September 2018).

Fountas, I. and Pinnell, G. (1996), *Guided Reading: Good First Teaching for All Children*, Portsmouth, NH: Heinemann.

Guignon, A. (2016), 'Reading Aloud: Are Students *Ever* Too Old?', *Education World*. Available online: http://www.educationworld.com/a_curr/curr081.shtml (accessed 29 September 2018).

Hu, M. and Nation, I. (2000), 'Vocabulary Density and Reading Comprehension', *Reading in a Foreign Language*, 23: 403–430.

Krashen, S. (1982), *Principles and Practice in Second Language Acquisition*, Oxford: Pergamon.

Krashen, S. (2011), 'The Compelling (Not Just Interesting) Input Hypothesis', *The English Connection* (KOTESOL), 15, 3: 1.

Krashen, S. (2017), 'Who Invented Comprehensible Input?', *The International Journal of Foreign Language Teaching*, 12.

Laufer, B. (1989), 'What Percentage of Text-lexis Is Essential for Comprehension?' in C. Lauren and M. Nordman (eds.), (316–323), *Special Language: From Humans to Thinking Machines*, Clevedon, England: Multilingual Matters.

Lichtman, K. (2018), *Teaching Proficiency Through Reading and Storytelling (TPRS) An Input-Based Approach to Second Language Instruction*, London: Routledge.

Minecraft (2017a), Twitter Announcement. https://twitter.com/Minecraft/status/836214707602210816 (accessed 22 February 2017).

Minecraft (2017b), Statistical Bulletin. https://minecraft.net/en-us/stats/ (accessed 22 February 2017).

Patrick, B. (2015), *Itinera Petri: Flammae Ducant*, CreateSpace.

Piantaggini, L. (2016), 'Assumptions and Definitions: Establishing Meaning'. Available online: https://magisterp.com/2016/05/12/assumptions-definitions-establishing-meaning/ (accessed 12 May 2016).

Piantaggini, L. (2017), *Piso Ille Poetulus*, CreateSpace.

Sénéchal, M. (1997), 'The Differential Effect of Storybook Reading on Preschoolers' Acquisition of Expressive and Receptive Vocabulary', *Journal of Child Language*, 24 (1): 123–138.

Schmitt, N., Jiang, X. and Grabe, W. (2011), 'The Percentage of Words Known in a Text and Reading Comprehension', *Modern Language Journal*, 95 (2011), 26–43.

Suzuki, W. (2005), 'Associative Learning and the Hippocampus', *Psychological Science Agenda*, American Psychological Association.

Teaching Strategies (2010), *Research Foundation: Language and Literacy*. Available online: https://teachingstrategies.com/wp-content/uploads/2017/03/Research-Foundation-Language-Literacy.pdf (accessed 29 September 2018).

Veronensis, A. (18 October 2017), Personal message, Facebook Messenger.

Vygotsky, L. (1980), *Mind in Society: The Development of Higher Psychological Processes*, Cambridge, MA: Harvard University Press.

Walker, L. (Producer) (23 October 2016), 'Give Your Students a "Brain Break" with Annabelle Allen', Episode 004, TeachersThatTeach.com. Available online: http://www.teachersthatteach.com/podcast/ (accessed 29 September 2018).

CHAPTER 16
ON STAGE AND SCREEN: 'BIG BOOK' LATIN AND DIALOGIC TEACHING

Steven Hunt

Introduction

The data projector, along with the interactive whiteboard, has been almost ubiquitous in British school classrooms now for over a decade, since the roll-out of educational technology during the Blair government of 1997–2010. However, training has been patchy and resources – aside from the generic ones provided with smartboards – have been generally restricted in the Classics classroom to the use of the digital resources created by the Cambridge Schools Classics Project. These resources include video documentaries, drag-and-drop interactive activities and fully interactive Latin texts, identical in every way to those in the commonly used school textbook *Cambridge Latin Course*. This chapter comprises an investigation into how a novice Latin teacher uses the CLC Explorer Tool and the data projector to move beyond merely projecting the text of the stories on the screen, towards a delivery of high-quality dialogic teaching and thereby the enhancement of all students' learning.

The teacher remains central to the Classics classroom, even when the computer is an integral feature. However, the computer has changed the organization of the classroom (Cole and Griffin 1987), and the interactive whiteboard (IWB) has had a big impact on the nature of teacher–student interactions (Mortimer and Scott 2003). The Classics classroom is not immune to these changes, as I have previously noted (Hunt, S. 2013 and 2014). This chapter is an investigation into how a beginning teacher uses screen-projected Latin text on the IWB in the school classroom. I have chosen four particular episodes from an observed lesson. I recognize that the sample of episodes in this study is small. Nevertheless, I feel that the sample is representative of the very many other observations of lessons which I have undertaken throughout the year in classrooms across the UK, in which beginning teachers have taught Latin to students using screen-projected text. The subject of this study reveals the teacher as orchestrator of the class, in which he seeks to build knowledge and understanding through the Vygotskian idea of social collaboration (Vygotsky 1978). The screen-projected text seems to encourage new pedagogical practices, such as the teacher's physical positioning in the classroom, his integration of different kinds of media, his recognition of the power of perceptual saliency and his developing confidence in the use of dialogic teaching approaches. While the study investigates the e-CLC digital resources developed by the Cambridge School Classics Project, I believe the findings are transferable to any screen-projected texts, and it is my hope that they inform not only current teacher practice but also the development of future resources. For reasons of space, I have not discussed the teacher's use of the e-CLC word analysis facility (the 'Explorer Tool'); this is specific to the e-CLC.[1] However, in the discussion that follows, I make some observations about how this and other textual analysis resources might be developed in projected Latin text resources to support teaching and learning more generally.

Latin and technology

Latin teaching using technology has a long history. Fifty-five years ago three linked articles appeared in the first volume of *Didaskalos*, the journal of the Joint Association of Classical Teachers, which between them prompted discussion of how new technologies might support the teaching and learning of Latin (Lee 1963, Sargent 1963, Morris 1963). The authors' interest in technology reflected concerns that traditional pedagogical practices were increasingly unattractive to students in a competitive curriculum, and they also reflected an interest in the developing field of communicative approaches to modern language teaching and how they might be employed in the Classics classroom. *Didaskalos*'s pioneering spirit[2] was marked by an article the following year in which Classics teachers Buckle and Ellwood described how their experiments with audio-visual techniques improved their students' motivation and attainment (Buckle and Ellwood 1964). William Thompson, lecturer in education at the University of Leeds, welcomed this enterprising method of teaching Latin and anticipated further experimentation. He looked with optimism to the future, saying:

> For an experimental course it seems wise to try and fit the method to an existing text book. But it is already clear that the ultimate ideal must be the production of a special text book.
>
> Thompson 1964: 80

Sidney Morris, lecturer in education at the University of Birmingham, was similarly alert to the possibilities, writing in his teaching methods book *Viae Novae*:

> Recent developments in linguistics, in modern language teaching and in electronic equipment have made possible the application to Latin teaching of several new techniques which share in common Comenius' *dictum: omnis lingua usu potius quam praeceptis discitur.* Audio-lingual and audio-visual techniques, the tape recorder and the language laboratory, programmed courses and teaching machines now offer new resources to the Latin teacher, resources which, if wisely used, can make a valuable contribution to Latin teaching.
>
> Morris 1966: 15

However, Thompson and Morris's hopes that technology would improve pedagogy have been rather slow to flourish. While the 1960s and 1970s signalled the desire for change,[3] and technology has been able to provide support for it, audio-lingual approaches to teaching Latin still do not seem to be widely evident in the classroom in the UK.[4] Despite anxiety about the effectiveness of the grammar-translation approach in terms of student motivation, attainment and enrolment, this traditional approach seems to have persisted. Two causes, perhaps, for this: the teachers' adherence to grammar-translation and reading comprehension course textbooks;[5] and the alignment of curriculum and pedagogical practices with the national examination system.[6] The written translation of English to Latin and Latin to English is still the predominant requirement in the examination hall,[7] with the result that written translation has largely become both pedagogy and assessment.[8] Change in pedagogical approaches is happening, however. I would argue that, within the boundaries set by examinations and course books, technology is encouraging the development of more interactive pedagogical approaches, and that these will begin to challenge the dominance of traditional methods.

The most obvious manifestation of this type of change can be observed by the interactions teachers make when teaching from a projected digital text on an IWB. It seems to be but a small change from using the printed book alone, but I believe it is making a big difference in supporting teachers in pursuit of a more dialogic approach to teaching.

The e-CLC text

I hold that the observations I make in this chapter are entirely transferable to other projected texts, but I should point out the particular design features of the e-CLC Latin texts. The printed CLC narrative is fifty years old and a product of the thinking of its time. While I believe that the CLC texts remain impressive as a learning resource, the e-CLC is very much additional material for a printed course which had been designed for reading and discussing in English. Indeed, Wilkins, the developer of the linguistic scheme of the CLC, had ruled out other communicative approaches, stating, 'the terminal objective [of learning Latin] is a single skill, the literary reading skill' (Wilkins 1969: 186). Furthermore, he argued that the lexical density and complex subordination of original authors and their 'aesthetically stylized literature' rendered the teaching of Latin 'abnormal' (Wilkins 1969: 186) compared to that of modern foreign languages. Instead, arguing that the subject specificity of Latin pedagogy should recognize the importance which grammar played, he envisaged a linguistic scheme of reading materials composed in a graded sequence of stages into which a 'passenger' grammar should 'migrate inside the material' in such a way that 'significant patterns are rehearsed up until the point that habits are formed in the learners' (Wilkins 1969: 192). Wilkins's (1970) arguments in favour of a broadly Chomskian generative grammar approach were hugely influential over the CLC's content and linguistic sequence. Later editions of the CLC have included more explicit grammar exercises, in response partly to other theories of language learning[9] and partly to teacher feedback,[10] but it retains the inductive approach: through classroom discussion in English of the graded sequence of narratives, the student learns *about* the Latin language *through* reading the Latin language.

Research into the use of the e-CLC has focused on personal computers, in particular the use of the Explorer Tool – a digital dictionary and text analyser. The picture is mixed. The accelerated learning of vocabulary and language acquisition is said to have motivated students and improved the accuracy of translation (Laseron 2005a, Lister 2007), but students seem to have remained unconvinced that they were doing 'real work' (Laserson 2005b). Teachers seem to be becoming more discriminating in usage (Hunt, S. 2016), but doubts are raised by them about students' comprehension of grammar (Hunt, F. 2018). A recent Facebook thread[11] displayed some forty-two comments of sharply divergent views – was the interactive text a cheat or a boon? But the increasingly common use of screen-projected e-CLC texts has received little attention apart from my own previous studies (Hunt, S. 2008 and 2016). I hope that this chapter will redress the balance.

The Big Book and dialogic teaching

I suggest that the way Latin teachers use projected Latin texts is pedagogically analogous to the 'Big Book' shared book reading technique used in primary schools. In this technique the teacher uses large-print, illustrated books ('Big Books') in whole-class teaching activities to provide opportunities for the students to learn contextualized language and vocabulary together with each other. Research at the University of Cambridge has shown that a successful approach to such co-constructed learning is through what has become known as the dialogic teaching approach (Alexander 2004). Three features of dialogic teaching are:

1. The *elicitation* of knowledge from the students.

2. The *marking of knowledge* to the students as important (using 'keywords', the 'royal we').

3. The *recasting* of student responses (such as improving phrasing or introducing technical terms). (Edwards and Mercer 1986)

Further refinements of the dialogic approach include the idea that every answer should lead to another question and that error-making offers 'potential for a rich dialogue of possibility' (Alexander 2004). While such elements of the dialogic approach can obviously occur with students using traditional printed textbooks, I argue that the use of projected text provides the teacher with a richer vein of teaching and learning opportunities. I hope that the following commentaries on four classroom transcripts of dialogue between a beginning teacher and his students demonstrate what I mean.

The study

The story is 'Domitilla cubiculum parat - I' from CLC Book Two.[12] In the printed CLC text, there are a number of features which assist the students in comprehending the material. These all follow standard approaches to helping students learn strategies for reading comprehension: the visual stimulus to set the scene (original carving of four slave hairdressers arranged around the seated *domina*); the text genre (the text is laid out as a conversation between members of the *familia*); and the meaning conveyed in the narrative itself.[13] The e-CLC Big Book text does not have the visual stimulus, but otherwise it is the same.

I have chosen four episodes from an early part of the lesson, where the story begins. The coding for the transcripts is as follows:

1. *Italics* represent original Latin text and its translation into English;

2. Text in [CAPITAL LETTERS] represents actions of the teacher or students; and

3. Underlined words are those to which the teacher or student give tonal emphasis.

Students' names have been changed. The transcripts are by kind permission of the teacher.

Before the transcripts below begin, the teacher has asked the students to recall the nominative, accusative and dative cases of the first three declensions and the terminations of the present, imperfect and perfect active verb. These have been written on an adjacent whiteboard and act as a silent scaffold throughout the lesson.

Episode 1

Teacher: [FACING THE CLASS, READING THE TITLE IN THE BOOK, HELD IN HANDS] It says 'Domitilla prepares the bedroom'. There's a picture at the top of the page. What can we see in the picture? [PAUSE] Basically, Domitilla is an old slave. Here she's telling Marcia to tidy up. But what's in the <u>picture</u>?

Freddy: There's four <u>hairdressers</u>.

Techer: Who's the hairdresser? [POINTING TO THE WORD *ORNATRIX* ON THE IWB] *Ornatrix*. Domitilla – Domitilla is the <u>hairdresser</u>. [FACING THE CLASS] What activities was Domitilla doing around the house? Benjamin, what was Domitilla doing around the house?

The teacher initiates discussion about the text with a reference to the visual material in the printed CLC to activate the students' cognitive processes. Because the e-CLC Big Book does not have the same visual stimulus as the printed CLC, the teacher provides the link between the contextual clues in the printed CLC and the e-CLC Big Book. Is there an unstated suggestion that the students are 'allowed' to use both? In observation, students seem to move freely and easily between the two, and a dialogic space is opened up between the projected text and the textbook, teacher and students. The teacher does not ask the students to 'translate', but instead asks *what was happening* in the story: a small change in emphasis, but one which establishes a positive affect among the students – the activity is for reading, finding out and learning together, not for assessment.[14]

Episode 2 (lines 9–12)

Benjamin: Er, was she, like, *cleaning the floor*?

Teacher: She was *ambulabat – she was walking* [PAUSE] *lente –*

Benjamin: I don't know what this is. Is it *slowly*?

Teacher: [FACING THE BOARD AND INDICATING *LENTE*] *She was walking slowly*, cleaning . . . yes, she was going round the house doing the chores, doing it *slowly*. [FACING THE CLASS] What does this show about her?

Benjamin: She was a bit reluctant?

Teacher: Why do you think she was <u>reluctant</u>? She's a hairdresser, so she might be quite . . . she wants to make everything perfect, but doing easy jobs doesn't please her – later down on line 11 [POINTS TO THE RELEVANT LINE ON THE IWB], *it's not right for a hairdresser to sweep the room*, and the old woman – she doesn't think she should be doing these chores.

The teacher uses repetition and his tone of voice to add perceptual saliency when he physically draws attention on the e-CLC Big Book to important language features. The first example ('slowly') is to reinforce the students' knowledge of the important adverb *lente*. He also points to the word on the screen to ensure that the students see the Latin word as well as hear the English meaning, combining visual and aural links. The second example ('reluctant') confirms that the student understands the direction of the narrative. It also anticipates a reason as to why the word 'reluctant' is apposite. The teacher maintains a running commentary: these 'think-alouds' aid continued understanding of the narrative and provide further contextual clues.

Episode 3 (lines 11–13)

> Teacher: Line 11 [FRAMES BEGINNING AND ENDING OF THE SENTENCE ON THE IWB] – *ego ornatrix sum . . . non decorum ornatricibus cubiculum verrere.* What is she **saying**?
>
> Chloe: *I am a hairdresser. It's not right for a hairdresser to clean the bedroom.*
>
> Teacher: Almost! It's not quite there!
>
> Chloe: Is it *to sweep up*?
>
> Teacher: I'm not too worried about the *verrere* – think back to the *leonibus* [SAID WHILE POINTING TO *ORNATRICIBUS*, STANDING AT A POINT MIDWAY BETWEEN THE IWB AND THE WHITEBOARD].
>
> Chloe: *It is not right for hairdressers.*
>
> Teacher: [FRAMING OF PHRASE *CONSILIUM CEPIT* WITH PEN CIRCLE] What is Domitilla doing <u>here</u>? [PAUSE] She has a <u>light bulb</u> moment – she's thought of something – she's <u>seized</u> on something . . . Any idea? She's sick of the cleaning. What can she be thinking of? . . . What was Domitilla's <u>idea</u>? Is she going to make <u>someone else</u> do it for her?

The teacher uses a great deal of physical movement at this point. He uses his hands to frame the sentence on the e-CLC Big Book to draw students' attention to the requisite sentence; he steps back to occupy a space between the e-CLC Big Book and the ordinary whiteboard on which notes have been previously made, while he draws the students' eyes to the recently discussed grammar; he returns to the e-CLC Big Book to circle the phrase *consilium cepit*. Each action is accompanied by an elicitation ('What is she saying?'), a recall ('Think back') or an anticipatory statement ('She has a light bulb moment'). The last statement is repeated in various forms to elicit the appropriate response.

Episode 4 (lines 13–14)

> Ahmed: [SEMI-QUESTIONING] She might make <u>someone else</u> to do the work(?)
>
> Teacher: [CONFIRMING] She's going to get someone else to do the work for her. What's she doing – [POINTING TO THE WORD] *festinavit* – what did she do?
>
> Ahmed: *She ran.*
>
> Teacher: *She hurried* [POINTING TO THE PHRASE AND 'HOLDING IT'] *quam celerrime.* Is it normal <u>hurrying</u>?
>
> Ahmed: *Very quickly?*
>
> Teacher: *<u>Quam celerrime</u>* – as quickly as *possible* . . . *simulat* [POINTING] –
>
> Ahmed: – *suddenly* –
>
> Teacher: – *as soon as . . . intravit* –
>
> Ahmed: – *she enters* –

[TEACHER STANDS AWAY FROM THE BOARD]

> Teacher: Think about the <u>verb</u> . . . If you see the <u>ending</u> [POINTING TO THE LETTER *V*] <u>v</u> or <u>u</u> or <u>s</u> or <u>x</u> – it <u>means</u> . . .?

Ahmed: Perfect.

Teacher: What does that [POINTING TO THE TERMINATION -*VIT*] mean? *Enter<u>ing</u>*
... *not enter<u>ing</u>?*

Ahmed: *Enter<u>ed</u>.*

[TEACHER RETURNS TO THE BOARD]

Teacher: *As soon as* <u>she entered</u> *the kitchen*, what happened? *Lacrimis se dedit.*

Ahmed: [REFERRING TO THE GLOSS IN THE PRINTED CLC] *She burst into tears.*

In this episode the teacher moves between different media and signals the change by his different positioning between the IWB, the other whiteboard and whether or not he faces the class. This positioning away from the IWB and facing the students accentuates the moment when the teacher expects the students to recall previously learnt material ('Think about the verb'); meanwhile, his position close to the IWB and pointing to the termination -*vit* focuses attention on this morphological element. The teacher raises the students' phonological awareness of particular morphological elements and common Latin phrases by repetition and strong intonation ('<u>v</u> or <u>u</u>' and '*quam celerrime*').

Discussion

Physical use of space

Hall and Higgins (2005) noted that the presence of an IWB tended to make teachers even more prone to teach from the front. While these episodes confirm this, nevertheless the teacher used the space at the front of the classroom in ways which signalled different forms of cognitive processing. For the elucidation of the story, he positioned himself by the board to indicate or annotate relevant items comfortably. On other occasions, he positioned himself away from the board and took up a *metacognitive stance* where he consolidated a significant linguistic point.

Flexible and improvisatory teaching

The teacher still treats the text as a narrative in which the students will learn the language through reading the language. The teacher may treat the text *inductively*, as before, using internal and external clues to scaffold learning. They may choose to pick on a small number of grammar features to avoid cognitive overload. In other practices, teachers use texts *deductively*, employing pre-reading strategies such as front-loading vocabulary or discussing the socio-cultural background, before asking students to translate the stories independently into English.[15] Jewitt et al. have noted that the traditional design space and the new resources afforded by the IWB can 'create a tension for teachers as their design of texts for learning oscillate between print-based design principles and digital-multimedia design principles of the screen' (Jewitt et al. 2007: 315). The IWB has been said to allow more teacher improvisation and flexibility (Smith et al. 2005). While the CLC and e-CLC use the same texts, the Big Book approach seems to offer the teacher more pedagogical opportunities and flexibility. The e-CLC Big Book becomes an *object of joint reference* for the class, and forces the teacher to move beyond the idea of the *text as test* towards the idea of the *text as a stimulus* for whole-class learning (Mercer et al. 2010). Such an approach shows appreciation of students' contributions and helps them construct knowledge through dialogic interaction.

Interactions between teacher and student

Mercer (1995) noted that the IWB did not seem to change the standard 'initiate, respond, feedback' format of teacher–student interaction, but in this study it does seem less dominant. The use of think-alouds scaffolds learning, and conceptual and analytical framing reinforce the meaning and the grammar. The nature of these interactions is through dialogic talk. Because the e-CLC Big Book is easy to use and is an object of joint reference for the whole class, the pace of activities and of teacher–student interactions is fast. There is continuous interplay between modalities: the printed CLC text, the ordinary whiteboard and the e-CLC Big Book. Jewitt et al. (2007) have noted that more effective use of the board has been reported when interaction is expanded beyond the board to include students, teachers and other concrete and text-based resources. The teacher is able to get students to focus directly on the particular point of reference by physically drawing attention to the relevant section of the text. The teacher may point to, bracket or block out an individual word or phrase on the screen while saying it at the same time. The combination of visual and auditory perceptual salience improves cognitive processing. In all, I suggest that there has been a decisive movement away from the replication of traditional teaching practices using the printed text alone. The Big Book e-CLC has promoted an almost physical and performative pedagogical approach which, together with its emphasis of the dual modalities of seeing and hearing the written word, encourages a more dialogic teaching approach to meaning-making and grammatical exposition.

Further thoughts

There are other affordances of the IWB and e-CLC resources[16] in the teaching of Big Book texts which I have not mentioned in this study. However, from observations elsewhere, the choice and sequence of use of the other resources of the e-CLC seems to replicate those in the printed CLC. This is not surprising. As Jewitt et al. (2007) say:

> The IWB enables the worksheet to migrate comfortably onto the screen, leaving the pedagogy of the worksheet unchanged [and a] consequence of this is that the multimodal potential of the screen can remain dormant and unexplored.
>
> Jewitt et al. 2007: 315

Is it time for the teacher to look at 'purposeful ways of using the IWB after initial excitement has worn off' (Kennewell and Higgins 2007)? Of course, there is nothing inherently wrong with having teachers use the resources in a pedagogically reserved fashion. But the problem I have noted is that the CLC test is often surrounded by visual stimuli inserted not just to add interest and vitality to the story, but also as aids to its interpretation. The e-CLC Big Book lacks them and suffers as a result.

I feel that future resources should embrace all the possibilities which the IWB affords. Course books and resources need to consider the implications not just of teacher–student interactivity, but also the possibilities of more integrated multimedia and the use of multi-modal approaches to learning a language – even a dead one – through a multi-literacies approach to language learning.

First, increased support in the interactive texts. A digital analyser such as the e-CLC's Explorer Tool needs to be considered not just in terms of how much it replicates a dictionary definition but in how much it assists a young learner. For example, the e-CLC Explorer Tool has two functionalities: it indicates the dictionary definition of any word clicked on and it analyses the word (generally) in terms of gender/number/case (for nouns and adjectives) and tense/person/number/mood (for verbs). Further recommendations might include: more assistive functions such as word or phrase highlights in the text itself, more specificity in the meaning of the word or identification of other similarly patterned phrases or words within a text. It should be easy to annotate the text, to save it and to print it off for reference (Hennessy 2011).

Second, increased accessibility to multimedia resources. The digital text should have *as a minimum* the same number and type of external contextual clues as the printed text (e.g. visual prompts and vocabulary glosses). Ideally it should have hyperlinks to other media (including audio-visual resources) which support or extend learning. These should appear para-text so that they do not obscure or replace the text.

Third, increased use of multi-modal resources. This means moving away from merely 're-inscribing traditional ... languages teaching [into the] digital lab' (Lotherington and Jenson 2011), and thinking about the possibilities of Web 2.0 and how it might allow for students to produce their own authentic learning content.[17] An argument much along the lines of Wilkins's (1969) reported above could be made against this – 'But that's not what we do in Latin!' Two counter-arguments: learning and assessment are not the same things;[18] and we could choose to assess students in different ways which reflect other learning approaches.[19] In any case, it could be argued that teachers should capitalize on students' appetites for more participatory and creative learning activities through Web 2.0 than can be achieved through relatively traditional and formal modes of learning in the classroom.

It is clear from this study that the IWB and the e-CLC Big Book are merely tools for use in any sort of teaching. They do not govern the way in which a teacher teaches. However, the teacher in this study has developed some new and emergent pedagogical practices which harmonize with the possibilities that the e-CLC Big Book affords. I hope that this chapter provides further stimulus for discussion, trialling and training of dialogic approaches with other text-based resources in the Latin classroom.

Notes

1. The text analysers Perseus and the Electronic Pocket Oxford Dictionary are also publicly available.
2. McMillan recognizes the role of Sharwood Smith in breaking the 'historical inertia' of Latin teachers. The formation of the Joint Association of Classical Teachers (JACT) and its journal *Didaskalos* 'gave

legitimacy to the trials of new materials carried out under their auspices, thus defeating informal barriers sufficiently to introduce some movement into the system' (McMillan 2016: 31).

3. See the pamphlet *Re-Appraisal* (1962) for the problems then facing the teaching of Classics.

4. See Lister (2007).

5. Compare the 'un-textbooking' and 'un-desking' movements in the United States.

6. See Mansell (2007) for the growth in high-stakes accountability through assessment, and Oates (2014) on the importance of high-quality textbooks to ensure assessment compliance.

7. The UK examination boards allocate at least 50 per cent of their marks towards translation from Latin to English, English to Latin and English comprehension of Latin (OCR GCSE: 50 per cent (OCR 2018b); OCR A-level: 50 per cent (OCR 2018a); WJEC Level 1 (WJEC 2018a) and Level 2 (WJEC 2018b): 67 per cent; EDUQAS: 50 per cent (EDUQAS 2018)). For the GCSE examination, the total is a legal requirement.

8. For an early example of how attitudes to translation have changed, see Buckle and Ellwood (1964), who note their decision to cease all English–Latin translation. Bullock-Davies (1970) suggested the replacement of students' translation into and from Latin with the study of original authors in multiple translations. Karsten (1971) recommended the use of comprehension questions as being capable of more sustained investigation into not just the meaning but also potentially the intent and interest of the author and audiences. With the introduction of the Latin GCSE examination in 1988, translation into Latin became optional and was soon withdrawn due to low uptake. The education reforms of the coalition government have reintroduced translation into Latin (or simple parsing of grammar) with the aim of improving academic rigour (see Hunt S. 2018a). Discussion of the value of English–Latin translation can be found in Brink (1962), Melluish (1962), Mortimer and Roberts (1967), Sharwood Smith (1977: 27–47), Forrest (1996: 13–17), Lister (2007) and Hunt, S. (2016).

9. See Nunan (2011) for an overview of these approaches. For language input, see Krashen (1981, 1982); for output, see Swain (1985); for consciousness-raising tasks, see Ellis (2001); and for focus on form teaching, see Gibbons (1989).

10. See Hazel (1975) for a broadly positive early view, with reservations. For the gestation of CLC, see Forrest (1996), Gay (2003) and Story (2003).

11. See, for example, www.facebook.com/groups/LatinTeacherIdeaExchange.

12. CLC Book 2, p. 26, UK fourth edition; CLC Unit 2, p. 26, US fifth edition.

13. Kramsch (1996) identifies three types of clues which support comprehension of a story in another language: contextual clues, genre clues and textual clues. In this case, the contextual clues are the image and the narrative setting with familiar characters; the genre clue is the form of a dialogue, setting up student expectations of short questions and answers using first- and second-person verb endings; and the textual clues are contained within the narrative meaningfulness – the impact of what one person says on another.

14. See Hunt, S. (2016) for this important distinction.

15. Such approaches run against the grain of the pedagogical approach preferred by the authors of the CLC, but are commonplace.

16. Other resources include drag-and-drop exercises, audio and video links, dramatizations, grammar explanations and vocabulary testers.

17. See the New London Group (1996), which recommended greater participation and moving beyond the oral/written binary of second language learning.

18. This seems to be an argument reflected in advocates of communicative approaches to teaching Latin in the United States. See Hunt, S. (2018b).

19. In my teaching career from 1987, several different examination elements have come and gone, including oral Latin recordings and coursework/portfolios.

References

Alexander, R. (2004), *Towards Dialogic Teaching: Rethinking Classroom Talk*, Cambridge: Dialogos. Available online: http://www.robinalexander.org.uk/dialogic-teaching/ (accessed 20 September 2018).

Brink, C. (1962), 'Small Latin and the Classics', in T. Melluish (ed.), *Re-Appraisal: Some New Thoughts on the Teaching of Classics*, Oxford: The Clarendon Press, 6–9.

Buckle, P. and Ellwood, R. (1964), 'An Experiment in Audio-Visual Latin Teaching', *Didaskalos*, 2: 68–77.

Bullock-Davies, C. (1970), 'Translation in the Classroom', *Didaskalos*, 3(2): 336–347.

Cole, M. and Griffin, P. (1987), *Contextual Factors in Education: Improving Science and Mathematics Education for Minorities and Women*, Madison: Centre for Education Research.

EDUQAS (2018), *EDUQAS Latin GCSE Specifications*. Available online: http://wjec.co.uk/qualifications/latin/latin-gcse/eduqas-gcse-latin-spec-from-2016-e.pdf?language_id=1 (accessed 20 September 2018).

Edwards, D. and Mercer, N. (1986), 'Context and Continuity: Classroom Discourse and the Development of Shared Knowledge', in K. Durkin (ed.), *Language Development in the School Years*, London: Croom Helm.

Ellis, R. (2001), *Task-Based Language Teaching and Learning*, Oxford: Oxford University Press.

Forrest, M. (1996), *Modernising the Classics*, Exeter: University of Exeter Press.

Gay, B. (2003), 'The Theoretical Underpinning of the Main Latin Courses', in J. Morwood, *The Teaching of Classics*, Cambridge: Cambridge University Press.

Gibbons, J. (1989), 'Instructional Cycles', *English Teaching Forum*, 27 (3): 6–11.

Hall, I. and Higgins, S. (2005). 'Primary School Students' Perceptions of Interactive Whiteboards', *Journal of Computer Assisted Learning*, 21: 102–117.

Hazel, J. (1975), 'Grammar and the CLC. A Practical Problem', *Latin Teaching*, XXXV, 2.

Hennessy, S. (2011), 'The Role of Digital Artefacts on the Interactive Whiteboard in Supporting Classroom Dialogue', *Journal of Computer Assisted Learning*, 27: 463–489.

Hunt, F. (forthcoming 2018), 'An Investigation into Students' Use of the CLC Explorer Tool on Tablet Computers in the Classroom', *Journal of Classics Teaching*, 38.

Hunt, S. (2008), 'Information and Communication Technology and the Teaching of Latin Literature', in B. Lister (ed.), *Meeting the Challenge*, Cambridge: Cambridge University Press, 107–120.

Hunt, S. (2013), 'The Development of Teaching and Learning Through the Use of ICT in the Latin Classroom', *Journal of Classics Teaching*, 28: 24–28.

Hunt, S. (2014), 'Digital Instructional Technology in the Classroom: Plaything or Catalyst for Pedagogical Development?', *Journal of Classics Teaching*, 29: 42–47.

Hunt, S. (2016), *Starting to Teach Latin*, London: Bloomsbury Academic.

Hunt, S. (2018), 'Getting Classics into Schools? Classics and the Social Justice Agenda of the Coalition Government 2010–2015', in A. Holmes-Henderson, S. Hunt and M. Musié (eds.), *Forward with Classics!*, London: Bloomsbury Academic, 9–26.

Jewitt, C., Moss, G. and Cardini, A. (2007), 'Pace, Interactivity and Multimodality in Teachers' Design of Texts for Interactive Whiteboards in the Secondary School Classroom', *Learning, Media and Technology*, 3 (3): 303–317.

Karsten, D. (1971), 'Teaching Comprehension', *Didaskalos*, 3 (3): 492–506.

Kennewell, S. and Higgins, S. (2007), 'Introduction: Special Edition on Interactive Whiteboards', *Learning, Media and Technology*, 32 (3): 207–212.

Kramsch, C. (1996), *Context and Culture in Language Teaching*, Oxford: Oxford University Press.

Krashen, S. (1981), *Second Language Acquisition and Second Language Learning*, Oxford: Pergamon Press.

Krashen, S. (1982), *Principles and Practice in Second Language Acquisition*, Oxford: Pergamon Press.

Laserson, T. (2005a), 'The Cambridge Latin Course Online – the Learner's Perspective', in B. Lister (ed.), *Meeting the Challenge: European Perspectives on the Teaching and Learning of Latin*, Cambridge: Cambridge University Press.

Laserson, T. (2005b), 'To What Extent Can Electronic Resources Enhance the Study of Latin? An Evaluation, with Particular Reference to the Learner's Perspective', Unpublished Thesis for the Masters in Education, Cambridge.

Lee, W. (1963), 'Modern Language Teaching and the Teaching of Classical Languages', *Didaskalos*, 1 (1): 123–132.

Lister, B. (2007), *Changing Classics in Schools*, Cambridge: Cambridge University Press.

Lotherington, H. and Jenson, J. (2011), 'Teaching Multimodal and Digital Literacy in L2 Settings: New Literacies, New Basics, New Pedagogies', *Annual Review of Applied Linguistics*, 31: 226–246.

Mansell, W. (2007), *Education by Numbers: The Tyranny of Testing*, London: Politico's Publishing.

McMillan, I. (2016), 'Transformatio Per Complexitatem: The 20th Century Transformation of Latin Teaching in the UK', *Journal of Classics Teaching*, 32: 25–32.

Melluish, T. (1962), 'Latin Inquiry', in T. Melluish, *Re-Appraisal. Some New Thoughts on the Teaching of Classics*, Oxford: The Clarendon Press, 42–47.

Mercer, N. (1995), *The Guided Construction of Knowledge; Talk Among Teachers and Learners*, Clevedon: Multilingual Matters.

Mercer, N., Hennessy, S. and Warwick, P. (2010), 'Using Interactive Whiteboards to Orchestrate Classroom Dialogue', *Technology, Pedagogy and Education*, 19 (2): 195–209.

Morris, S. (1963), 'Classics Teaching: A Select Bibliography and a Note on Recent Research', *Didaskalos*, 1 (1): 145–150.

Morris, S. (1966), *Viae Novae: New Techniques in Latin Teaching*, London: Hulton Edcational Publications.

Mortimer, E. and Scott, P. (2003), *Meaning Making in Secondary Science Classrooms*, Maidenhead: Open University Press.

Mortimer, M. and Roberts, J. (1967), 'The Narrow-Minded Linguist', *Didaskalos*, 2 (3): 100–114.

New London Group (1996), 'A Pedagogy of Multiliteracies: Designing Social Factors', *Harvard Educational Review*, 66: 60–92.

Nunan, D. (2011), *Task-based Language Teaching*, Cambridge: Cambridge University Press.

Oates, T. (2014), *Why Textbooks Matter*, Cambridge: University of Cambridge Local Examinations Syndicate.

OCR (2018a), *OCR A Level Latin Specifications*. Available online: http://www.ocr.org.uk/ Images/220734-specification-accredited-a-level-gce-latin-h443.pdf (accessed 20 September 2018).

OCR (2018b), *OCR GCSE Latin Specifications*. Available online: http://www.ocr.org.uk/ Images/220702-specification-accredited-gcse-latin-j282.pdf (accessed 20 September 2018).

Sargent, M. (1963), 'Audio-Visual Techniques of Language Teaching: The Theoretical Basis', *Didaskalos*, 1 (1): 133–144.

Sharwood Smith, J. (1977), *On Teaching Classics*, London: Routledge and Kegan Paul.

Smith, H., Higgins, S., Wall, K. and Miller, J. (2005), 'Interactive Whiteboards: Boon or Bandwagon? A Critical Review of the Literature', *Journal of Computer Assisted Learning*, 21: 91–101.

Story, P. (2003), 'The Development of the Cambridge Latin Course', in J. Morwood (ed.), *The Teaching of Classics*, Cambridge: Cambridge University Press, 85–91.

Swain, M. (1985), 'Communicative Competencies: Some Roles for Comprehensible Input and Comprehensible Output in its Development', in S. Gaas and C. Madden, *Input in Second Language Acquisition*, Rowley: Newbury House.

The Classical Association (1962), *Re-Appraisal. Some New Thoughts on the Teaching of Classics*, Oxford: The Clarendon Press.

Thompson, W. (1964), 'An Experiment in Audio-Visual Latin Teaching – II', *Didaskalos*, 2: 78–80.

Vygotsky, L. (1978), *Mind in Society*, Cambridge, MA: Harvard University Press.

Wilkins, J. (1969), 'Teaching the Classical Languages – I', *Didaskalos*, 3 (1): 168–197.

Wilkins, J. (1970), 'Teaching the Classical Languages: Towards a Theory – II', *Didaskalos*, 3 (2): 365–409.

WJEC (2018a), *WJEC Latin Level 1 Certificate Specifications*. Available online: http://wjec.co.uk/ uploads/publications/WJEC%20Level%201%20Certificate%20in%20Latin%20Lang%20and%20

Roman%20Civilisation%20and%20Lang%20-%20Spec%20(2009).pdf?language_id=1 (accessed 27 July 2018).

WJEC (2018b), *WJEC Latin Level 2 Certificate Specifications.* Available online: http://wjec.co.uk/uploads/publications/WJEC%20Level%202%20Certificate%20in%20Latin%20Lang%20and%20Roman%20Civilisation%20and%20Lang%20-%20Spec%20(2009).pdf?language_id=1 (accessed 27 July 2018).

CHAPTER 17
USING ANNOTATIONS IN GOOGLE DOCS TO FOSTER AUTHENTIC CLASSICS LEARNING
Roger Travis

Introduction

This chapter presents an overview of a learning activity the author developed for his advanced courses in classical literature. Students use the comment function in Google Docs to annotate an online document shared with them by the instructor; this document, common to the whole class, becomes both a metaphorical learning space where asynchronous social learning can occur and, more importantly, a specimen of authentic classical scholarship within which continuous formative assessment of the students' growing skills naturally takes place. The chapter concludes that the activity presented balances digitally enhanced pedagogy with the traditional transmission of classical learning.

The problem: authentic classics learning

'Authentic learning' generally refers to pedagogical practices that allow students to explore concepts and develop skills in contexts relevant to their interests outside the immediate classroom (Herrington 2006, Rule 2006). In the teaching of classical literature, the fostering of engagement with ancient texts and of mastering the skills of classical scholarship through self-motivated, active learning can take many different forms, but most of them work best at the introductory level. At that stage, it is possible to blend formal modes of instruction with much less formal ones: on the one hand, the student begins to see the various ways Greek and Roman culture continue to inform our modern one through studying the Latin inscriptions that linger in our public spaces; on the other, they create dank memes in Latin or Greek and put their growing skills to work in the service of their peers' amusement.

At more advanced levels of classical instruction, whether taught in the original ancient language or in translation, authentic learning becomes attenuated. Students who have attained those levels have chosen to study classical literature through a personal motivation that makes the study of classical texts relevant in and of itself. Even for those passionate students, however, the learning practices of reading and recitation, of critical discussion and the writing of interpretative papers can seem divorced from real-world application in a way analogous to what occurs in the mathematics classroom when a student advances to the study of calculus. Field trips and dank memes give way to litotes and allegory, just as baseball statistics give way to differential equations. Authentic learning, with its benefits for interest and mastery, falls by the wayside.

A learning activity designed to afford students the opportunity to practice classical scholarship as it has been practiced since the Musaion in Alexandria therefore seems like a potentially helpful element of an engaging learning environment for the study of classical literature. This chapter presents such an activity. The author believes it would work well either as the central student practice and formative assessment of an advanced course or as a supplement to a more traditional learning environment.

Why commentary?

'Google Docs annotation', as the author has named this activity, for want of a less ungainly phrase, takes not only its inspiration but also, *mutatis mutandis*, its very form from the earliest days of classical scholarship – indeed from a time long before Classics existed as a discipline (for an excellent account of the earliest days of classical scholarship, see Reynolds and Wilson 2014). The scholiasts of the Ptolemaic Musaion in Alexandria showed the way to the humanists of the Italian Renaissance, and they in turn passed that way on to us: the scholarly reception of classical texts builds most essentially upon the scholar's efforts at elucidating the notable and challenging elements of the writing passed down to them.

This elucidation, recorded from the very beginning in the margins of the precious papyri upon which classical authors were transmitted, by its nature turns a Classics student's curiosity and beginning insight into a communication with their peers. Done in a well-designed learning environment like the Musaion – or a classroom (whether real or virtual) configured for authentic, active, social learning – the student's abilities as an interpreter of the text and its culture, indeed of the humanities as a whole, advance rapidly. Moreover, a peer looking over the student's shoulder, as it were, and receiving the communication of the scholia they make, can easily and accurately assess the progress the student has made towards mastery of fundamental concepts, whether grammatical or more broadly cultural in nature.

For example, just as the Alexandrian scholia on the first words of the *Iliad*, 'μῆνιν ἄειδε' ('sing the wrath'), seek to explain why the bards began their epic from the wrath of Achilles – sometimes by means of exegesis almost as far-fetched as undergraduates occasionally employ – a student in the author's Homer course might use a Google Docs comment to put in the margin of the text of *Iliad* 1, shared with the whole class, something like, 'Why begin with Achilles' anger? Isn't this the story of the Trojan War?' Another student might reply, 'I was wondering that, too. Take a look at the Wikipedia article about the *Iliad* that the professor assigned, especially this part', providing a hyperlink to get the first student and any subsequent readers of the document right to the relevant passage.

In both cases, the scholars involved have drawn upon the work of others and left behind evidence of their scholarship. The classical text excited inquiry and provoked thought, research and scholarly communication. The ancient scholiast practiced and developed his skills through annotation, just as the modern Classics scholar does in preparing a commentary; the modern Classics student can do the same. Above all, by doing what professional classicists do, and leaving behind a record of their work to stand as a collaborative commentary upon the text they have studied, the student engages in authentic, problem-based learning that develops their skills even as it captures their natural interest in doing something with real application and even significance (see Natoli's chapter in this volume).

Nuts and bolts

Google Docs annotation begins with a classical text pasted into a new Google Doc. Most classical authors are available through texts both in the original Greek or Latin and in English, either in the public domain or usable under a Creative Commons Share Alike licence. The English translations available have shortcomings, some of them serious: in particular, the frequency of archaism and the unavailability of poetic translations for poetic texts can be vexatious. The author has made extensive modifications in some cases and thrown up his hands in others; the signal consolation to be had in the face of an inadequate translation upon which to base the Google Doc lies in the expedient of assigning a better translation, on paper, with which students may compare the translation in the Google Doc. Annotations arising from student curiosity as to discrepancies in translation often provide the liveliest kind of scholarly discussion, with all the attendant benefits for social learning.

Once the text exists as a Google Doc, the instructor can easily frame it to scaffold student understanding by putting the assignment at the top and seeding the text itself with a few comments. These 'pre-annotations' by the instructor serve three important purposes:

1. They point the way towards the way key themes, tied to the course's learning objectives, appear in the ancient text.

2. They provide the student with examples of advanced, even professional annotation to be imitated; and

3. They show the instructor and the student both to be members of the interpretative community: the student's own annotations, and replies to the annotations of others, have visibly equal status as Google Doc comments, manifesting the fundamental authenticity of the activity.

To continue with the simple example of a Google Docs annotation of *Iliad* 1, the beginning of the Google Doc that will serve in an important sense as the virtual classroom for the activity might look like the following, to which I have in brackets appended notes the reader may find useful. Note that the full Google Doc of this first reading comprises the first 100 lines of the book. I give here only the first line.

Reading 1

Assignment

1. Read the translation at the bottom, unless you have a strong aversion to reading a translation first. After that point, refer to the translation only as a last resort. [This item has a link to the translation, given at the bottom of the document. Pedagogical philosophies will differ, of course, on this part of the assignment, but the author finds it useful in building the student's sense of professionalism: in the real world, we all consult translations.]

2. Read a sentence aloud, in Greek.

3. Construe the sentence. Autenrieth's *Homeric Lexicon* [Autenrieth 1877] should be an invaluable resource, as should Benner's commentary [Benner 1903]. [Links to these resources are given in this item.]

4. Annotate that sentence and reply to other students' annotations on it.

5. Move on to the next sentence.

6. Repeat steps 2–5 until you have spent about two hours on these steps.

7. Scan the priming material. [Here the author links Chapter 1 of Albert Lord's *The Singer of Tales* (Lord 2000). In the course from which this assignment comes, the author places emphasis on oral formulaic theory in the interpretation of Homer. The reader may, of course, elect a different emphasis; the importance of adducing scholarly secondary material, however, even if the material falls into what we might call the 'aspirational' range for the student, cannot in the author's opinion be overstated. This contact with professional classical scholarship greatly increases the authenticity of the activity.]

8. Amplify your annotations and respond to the annotations of others based on your response to the priming material.

   a. Spend about two hours on this step.

Iliad 1

μῆνιν ἄειδε θεὰ Πηληϊάδεω Ἀχιλῆος

The shading on the text represents an attempt to simulate what the Google Doc begins to look like when the instructor and students make their annotations, the darker shades indicating that students have commented, for example, both on ἄειδε ('sing') and on ἄειδε θεὰ ('sing, goddess'). To the right of the text, the first of those annotations, and the replies to it, might read something like:[1]

Student 1:[2] [on μῆνιν] Why begin from the wrath?
Instructor: [half an hour later] Old, good question. How do we start to answer it?
Student 2: [perhaps an hour later than that] In medias res, right? The same way an Avengers movie starts with an action scene!
Instructor: [the next morning] Where's that from? *In medias res* I mean.
Student 3: [perhaps online at the same time] Horace *Ars Poetica*. So, much later, but does that make it less true?
Student 1: [coming back to the assignment, perhaps, the next day] But it doesn't explain it. Looks like the ancient Greeks themselves had a bunch of different explanations. Check out this chapter from the Cambridge Companion [linking to Scodel 2004, provided as background material in the course reading list].

The interface of Google Docs, with its 'comments' functionality, makes both annotation and replying to others' annotations simple. It is equally straightforward to click on any highlighted word, phrase, sentence or even paragraph to bring the comments on it to the fore. The 'reply' window then becomes available, and indeed even tempting.

With the help of the above example, we can take a closer look at three essential aspects of the activity: the assignment, the flow of the resulting discussion and the possibilities for assessment of the activity.

Assignment

To anchor a brief exploration of the aims of the assignment as given above, it will help to quote the section of the course's syllabus that provides general instructions for the annotation activity:

Annotations may include:

- Renderings of phrases and clauses. (Do **not** think of this as translation, please. Our objective is **reading**, not translating.)

- Grammatical observations. (What case? What tense? What mood? What kind of clause?)

- Cultural observations. (Who is this guy? Who is that gal? Why would the bard say that about a battle?)

- Links, links, links for all the above. Wikipedia is always good; scholarly articles are always better. Best of all is when you link, and then summarize what you read at that link.

The assignment as given in my example from *Iliad* 1 is, of course, only one of a potentially infinite number of different ways to frame the activity. In order to mix familiar classroom scaffolding with the authentic learning at which the activity aims, this assignment attempts to accomplish three purposes:

1. Put the student in the position of a commenting scholar or scholiast – most importantly, through ensuring that the student knows the sense of the passage just as the scholar does;

2. Give the student (mostly) free rein in exercising their curiosity and interest, as they choose what words, phrases and passages to annotate; and

3. Facilitate discussion among students and instructor to build a collaborative, scholarly community of practice.

The provision of a translation to assist in accomplishing the first of the ends has proven invaluable. As noted in brackets in the example, this step may not suit every advanced Classics learning environment, but the sense that everyone in the 'room' knows what is occurring in a given passage – a goal which can be elusive even in advanced courses – can be produced quite easily by assigning an English translation. That sense makes the authenticity of the annotations activity much deeper, since the student makes their comments and replies from a broader and more scholarly range of choices: annotations will still often involve pleas for help in construing a given aorist, but it must be noted that the longest-bearded classical scholar will occasionally, in print, do the erudite equivalent of pleading for help in construing an aorist.

The broad range of possibilities envisioned, albeit in a rather colloquial way, in the course's syllabus instructions, serves to bring the activity down to a level manageable for the plurality of the author's students at a large public university. In other classroom contexts, a different approach, making more explicit the scholarly philosophy behind the activity, could work well. Providing so much choice makes the activity student-centred as well as authentic; in practice, the instructor will probably have to provide some scaffolding on the fly to prevent references to the recent fortunes of sports teams, for example, but at least in the author's classroom comparisons to superhero movies are most welcome in that ancient heroic literature lies deep at the heart of comics culture.

At the same time, the links in the assignment itself to scholarly works (in this case Autenrieth and Benner), as well as the occasional seeding of links to scholarly articles in the instructor's own annotations, ensure that the student's free range also has models for directing them towards the learning objectives. Some of the best annotations arise from a stimulus of 'superhero' interest towards a fuller understanding of a phrase in Greek or Latin, or of a literary trope. The example above of the beginning of *Iliad* 1 attempts to demonstrate how this pedagogical dynamic works, as one sort of authentic learning seamlessly becomes another, modern cultural skill transferring to classical cultural skill.

To this end, the assignment does its best to set up a free flow of discussion by requiring that students reply to their peers' annotations. In this respect, Google Docs annotation (like many other kind of activity made possible by networked digital learning environments, such as wikis – of which Google Docs annotation might in fact be considered a species) possesses a significant superiority over older, monographic forms of commentary. As part of a scholarly collective, guided by the instructor, these commentators are able to develop their scholarly skills at a remarkable pace thanks to the infusion of the active authentic learning of the annotations themselves with the social learning of discussion right there in reply.

Flow of discussion

The example of discussion above, in the *Iliad* 1 sample, is admittedly utopian: it presumes three highly engaged students and an instructor with a good deal of time on their hands. The author can attest that only a few of the exchanges in any given course will resemble the one simulated above, but he can also attest that such exchanges *do* occur with a good deal of regularity, even within a class struggling with the ancient text. The scaffolding of the activity with the assignment and the seeded pre-annotations can, of course, be varied to match the needs of the class: the author has employed it successfully in a bare-bones format with graduate students who have a good working knowledge of classical commentaries.

The instructor's role in the activity has three notable aspects:

1. Correcting errors and answering questions;
2. Treating the student as a scholar; and
3. Teaching and enforcing the difficult distinction between scholarly and non-scholarly sources.

The first of these is the simplest, but the author has found it best performed with as light a touch as possible, especially in light of the second aspect of the instructor's task. To produce the sense of a scholarly collaborative, corrections are best made as suggestions, and questions answered with advice on where the student may go to find the information sought. It is often helpful to remember that frequent feature of scholarly commentaries, the adduction of parallel passages, which can serve to aid a student both in understanding the sense of a difficult passage and in internalizing the scholarly practice embodied in the annotation activity.

This mode of accomplishing the traditional and essential task of ensuring the student has the correct understanding of the material necessary to the practice of good scholarship leads naturally into the complementary principle that the instructor can foster the authentic learning inherent in the activity most effectively when they treat their students in a collegial way, as fellow scholars. Asking questions the way one would of a peer, and providing helpful scholarly resources as one would when conversing at the lecture of a visiting scholar – or indeed when reading over a colleague's own monographic commentary – both involve the student in the enterprise of real scholarship. Every humanities instructor knows the wonderful feeling of hearing a student make an observation that strikes the instructor as 'publishable'. That sort of incipient insight occurs with great frequency in the Google Docs annotation activity introduced in this chapter.

By the same token – or perhaps inscribed upon its obverse – the instructor has the opportunity, in guiding the discussion in reply to student annotations, to clarify the boundary between scholarly and non-scholarly secondary material in a unique and very helpful way. By encouraging the student to adduce links to online sources, the assignment described here inevitably promotes their initial indiscriminate treatment. This consists not only of Wikipedia articles but also of the many freely available study guides as acceptable secondary sources for scholarship in an advanced Classics course.

Wikipedia actually serves the instructor very well here, because not only are the vast majority of the Wikipedia articles on classical topics well written and well edited, but they all feature scholarly notes, some of them quite extensive. A simple suggestion that a course at the advanced level requires using those notes propels many students a crucial step forward in their scholarship. The next move, of advising the use of JSTOR, where available, and of online handbooks like the *Oxford Classical Dictionary*, where available, along with modelling in the instructor's own annotations and replies how such bibliographic resources should be deployed, begins to join the class's collaborative commentary to the broad, onrushing flow of classical scholarship. Assigning reading from collections like the *Cambridge Companion to Homer* (Fowler 2004) can help to bridge any gap students may feel between classroom and library.

Assessment

One of the virtues of Google Docs annotation is the wide variety of ways in which the instructor can use it to assess student progress towards learning objectives. From simply counting the number of annotations and replies towards a quota, to sampling a few of a student's contributions to conducting an in-depth evaluation of developing Classics skills, the digital trail created by the activity persists and allows both the instructor and the student the opportunity to go back at any time – including after the formal end of the course – to measure their progress. In fact, the collaborative commentaries created by the activity serve as a sort of mini-portfolio that might, provided anonymization safeguards were taken, be extracted to become a portable record of a student's achievement and skills.

For reference's sake, the learning goals and learning objectives provided in the syllabus of the author's advanced course in Homer are as follows:

A. Goal: Linguistically informed knowledge of Greek epic practice.

Objective: Describe the works at the granular level of their Greek texts; summarize the works' achievement with respect to their original Greek texts.

B.   Goal: Linguistically informed knowledge of the cultural background of Greek epic practice.

Objective: Describe the cultural background; identify and summarize its key elements.

C.   Goal: Skill at analysis of Greek epic practice in the original Greek.

Objective: Produce a culturally informed analysis of a key passage.

D.   Goal: Skill at linguistically informed analysis of the role of epic trans-historically in Western culture.

Objective: Produce a comparative analysis of ancient Greek and modern epic activity.

Progress towards each of these objectives can be measured through the annotation activity. The student – aware of them from the beginning of the course, just as a professional classicist is indeed aware of the very same objectives in composing a commentary – works ideally to annotate so as to demonstrate and develop the specified skills. An annotation glossing the significance of Achilles' wrath, for example, can show progress towards goals A–C, while an annotation about the Avengers, especially supported with scholarly secondary material concerning the mythic roots of graphic novels, can demonstrate growing mastery of goal D.

On the practical level, depending on the context the author has used a variety of assessment methods for the Google Docs annotation activity. The simplest is to require that the student make five original annotations and reply to the annotations of other students five times per assignment. In this case, extra credit is awarded for annotations that exceed 100 words. This approach has the advantage of allowing for self-reporting by the student and promotes the activity's sense of authentic learning and of student-centred learning by placing trust in the student's responsible conduct as a member of the class's community of scholarly practice. If any doubt should arise concerning the student's honesty, the evidence of their contributions is there in the Google Docs, easily accessible to the instructor.

At the opposite end of the spectrum, the instructor may evaluate the student's annotations as they would a research paper. Providing a rubric for annotations could prove useful in this case, but might also obstruct the development of the student as an independent scholar. In any event, a comment made at the end of each unit in a course, treating the student as a colleague in the collaborative commentary and going so far as to thank them for their contribution while also assigning a grade for the annotation activity, balances the pedagogical necessity of grading with the pedagogical imperative of providing a learning environment that fosters the development of real-world skills.

Conclusion

The Google Docs annotation activity here described treads a line between the exigencies of the modern, digitally enhanced classroom and the passion all classicists feel to introduce their students to 'real Classics'. The author hopes that the reader will experiment with different ways to frame the activity so as to achieve the best balance for their own students. He hopes, too, that if the reader should adopt the activity, they would be kind enough to report back to him, in the interest of developing a community of practice around Google Docs annotation like the ones the activity seeks to foster around the classical texts annotated.

Notes

1. These annotations are the work of the author, for reasons of his students' privacy.
2. Student names are visible in the Google Doc.

References

Autenrieth, G. (1891), *A Homeric Lexicon*, New York: Harper and Brothers. Available online: http://www.perseus.tufts.edu/hopper/text?doc=Perseus%3atext%3a1999.04.007 (accessed 13 July 2018).

Benner, A. (1903), *Selections from Homer's Iliad*, New York: Irvington. Available online: http://www.perseus.tufts.edu/hopper/text?doc=Perseus%3Atext%3A1999.04.0083%3Abook%3D1%3Acard%3D1 (accessed 13 July 2018).

Fowler, R. (2004), *The Cambridge Companion to Homer*, Cambridge: Cambridge University Press.

Herrington, J. (2006), 'Authentic e-Learning in Higher Education: Designing Principles for Authentic Learning Environments and Tasks', Keynote address at World Conference on E-Learning in Corporate, Government, Healthcare, and Higher Education (ELEARN) 2006. Available online: https://www.learntechlib.org/p/24193/ (accessed 13 July 2018).

Lord, A. (2000), *The Singer of Tales*, 2nd edn, Cambridge, MA: Harvard University Press.

Reynolds, L. and Wilson, N. (2014), *Scribes and Scholars: A Guide to the Transmission of Greek and Latin Literature*, 4th edn, Oxford: Oxford University Press.

Rule, A. (2006), 'The Components of Authentic Learning', *Journal of Authentic Learning*, 3 (1): 1–10.

Scodel, R. (2004), 'The Story-Teller and His Audience', in R. Fowler. (ed.), *The Cambridge Companion to Homer*, Cambridge: Cambridge University Press, 45–56.

CHAPTER 18

PROJECT-BASED LEARNING, TECHNOLOGY AND THE ADVANCED LANGUAGE CLASSROOM

Bartolo Natoli

Introduction

Over the past thirty years, pedagogical theory and practice in second language acquisition (SLA) have seen a shift away from a traditional, teacher-centred model of instruction to a more active, learner-focused model. One of the major manners in which this shift can be seen is the increase of Project-Based Learning (PBL) in the language classroom, an approach that has been shown to improve language skills, content learning, real-life skills and sustained motivation in learners. However, nearly all published research on PBL has been focused on modern language instruction and not on the teaching of classical languages. Therefore, this chapter seeks to address this dearth of scholarship by detailing how PBL was used to construct and deliver an undergraduate advanced Latin course at Randolph-Macon College in the fall of 2015, a course that culminated in the learner construction of a fully searchable, online database of text-commentaries on the letters of Marcus Cornelius Fronto.[1] First, a brief overview of current PBL theory and research in SLA instruction is given, the chief value of which will be as a comparison with the situation of classical language instruction. Then, a detailed discussion of the implementation of PBL in the Randolph-Macon course will be provided, including a reflection on the qualitative and quantitative results of the course.

One of the most basic challenges facing any teacher, regardless of instructional level, is how to keep content and delivery exciting and engaging, while maintaining a level of academic rigour and expectation that pushes learners to higher levels of critical thinking. Moreover, methods that give learners the chance to produce meaningful material and to share that material with others are also coveted, as they can show learners how far they have come and can leave a lasting impression on them, a transformative experience that they can take with them after the class itself has long ended. Finally, if instructors can do all this and find a way to incorporate digital pedagogies into the methodology, they may well have found the Holy Grail of teaching.

In the summer of 2015, as I was gearing up for my fall slate of classes, I was faced with a similar situation and set out to explore ways in which I could refashion the methodology of one of my classes to provide more relevant, higher-level learning activities in which learners could actively produce material rather than passively receive it, all the while thinking about ways in which technology could be used to augment these activities. To that end, I chose my advanced undergraduate Latin seminar on Roman epistolography as the testing ground and decided to move the structure of the course from the more familiar translation seminar to one founded on the tenets of PBL. The course would feature a series of projects as its basis, in which learners would produce a full-text commentary on a selected letter of both Pliny the Younger and of Fronto, complete with an apparatus criticus. The Fronto text commentaries would then be uploaded into an open-access, fully searchable database of Fronto's letters that the students themselves would help create: www.frontoonline.com.

In this chapter, I will outline the basic structure of that course, the projects assigned, the learning outcomes, student evaluations and personal reflections, including plans for future adaptation of the PBL methodology in my advanced Latin courses. However, before delving into the details of the class, I will first set the foundation for the analysis of the methodology of the course with a brief discussion of what is meant by PBL, both in theoretical terms and practical applications.

Principles of Project-Based Learning

Simply stated, PBL is a student-centred pedagogy aimed at creating deeper and more relevant learning experiences through the active exploration of authentic problems and the development of student-engineered solutions to those problems. On a theoretical level, however, PBL is based on two conceptual foundations: the Deweyan concepts of experiential learning (i.e. pragmatism) and Vygotskian ideas of socio-cultural learning and cognitive apprenticeship. For Dewey, learning happened through experiences gained in actively exploring an environment. This process of active exploration had five basic characteristics (Dewey 1916, Eggen and Kauchak 2006):

1. learners are involved in a real-world experience that interests them;
2. within this experience, learners encounter a problem that stimulates thinking;
3. in solving the problem, learners acquire information;
4. learners form tentative solutions to the problem; and
5. learners test these solutions. The application helps the learners validate their knowledge.

Such experiential explorations, according to Dewey (1916), were far more effective for the construction and acquisition of knowledge than anything one could gain from books and lectures.

Vygotsky (1978, 1986), in turn, also worked with the ideas of experiential education, but paid particular attention to how social interaction helped to amplify knowledge acquisition. Perhaps the most familiar of Vygotsky's ideas is the Zone of Proximal Development; however, just as important is his notion of cognitive apprenticeship, an 'approach to instruction in which students work with an expert to learn both how to perform cognitive tasks and why they perform certain tasks in certain ways' (Eggen and Kauchak 2006, Lave 1990). For example, think about the way we learn tasks such as driving, cooking or even writing our names for the first time. First, we watch someone who is skilled perform the task and then we try to perform it ourselves under the expert's direction. In addition, the experts describe their thinking out loud as they model the process, and they guide the learner through the process with questioning. This is the essence of cognitive apprenticeships.

These concepts of experiential learning, socio-cultural learning and cognitive apprenticeship lie at the heart of PBL – learners are faced with a real-life, relevant problem and are tasked with working together to solve it under the guidance of an expert. As such, learners learn by doing, by experiencing and not by passive reception. In particular, one of the first things people tend to think about when presented with the term is: 'How is this different from what we are doing now?' We do projects in many of our classes as a way of differentiating instruction. Students seem to like them. So why do we need anything new? However, PBL is not just simply doing projects in the traditional sense. Traditional projects are entirely teacher-centred and teacher-designed: teachers set the parameters for the project and outline exactly what students must do. Then, at the end of the project, students present it to the teacher or class as a type of summative assessment of what they have learned.

On the other hand, PBL puts the theories of Dewey (1916) and Vygotsky (1978) to use and places the power in the hands of the learners: although the instructor initially asks a question or poses a problem, the learners themselves work together to figure out how to answer or solve it and then put their ideas to the test. After this initial foray, they revise their approaches based upon the outcomes – their experiences – and attack the problem again. At the end of the project, learners present their original research in the form of a public, published product. As opposed to the traditional project model, PBL is inherently social and constructive, giving learners opportunities to approach learning in meaningful and differentiated ways.

As I set out to apply PBL theory to my Latin class, I took my research one step further in search of explicit instructions for how to accomplish this. For, although the theory behind PBL was fairly clear, a set of concrete and practical steps for constructing a course based in PBL principles would be helpful. Such a practically facing document was developed in 2015 by the Buck Institute for Education (BIE),[2] a non-profit organization that 'creates, gathers, and shares high-quality PBL instructional practices and products and provides highly effective services to teachers, schools, and districts'. Larmer, Mergendoller and Boss, all members of BIE, drafted guidelines for PBL instruction, dubbed 'Gold Standard PBL'.[3] Their Gold Standard approach is in keeping with the Deweyan and Vygotskian principles of PBL and also provides a clear, concise roadmap for how to implement such theoretically sound PBL in the classroom. According to Gold Standard PBL, there are seven essential design elements that outline the necessary structures for maximizing student learning and engagement:

1. Challenging problem or question;
2. Sustained inquiry;
3. Authenticity;
4. Student voice and choice;
5. Reflection;
6. Critique and revision; and
7. Public product.

Firstly, the problem at the heart of the project must be challenging enough to require sustained inquiry and be authentic enough to prove worth the significant time learners will spend on it. If a project is assigned with a problem that is too small or seems too abstract or pointless to the learners, they will either not be motivated to invest time and effort into developing a solution, or they will solve the problem too quickly to engage with any real depth of learning. Secondly, the problem must be student-centred in that learners should have the ability to choose the problem they will solve and the methods by which they will solve it. Moreover, ample time for metacognitive reflection and multiple opportunities for critique and revision must be provided. As with any project-based problem, the solution is not always clear at the outset of the project and learners must have the chance to engage in trial and error, and to reflect upon what the next steps should be. Finally, and perhaps most importantly, the fruits of the learner's labour must be showcased via the creation of a public product. The public product provides extra motivation for the learner and confirms the importance of the project. Taken together, these seven design elements create a practical, pedagogical playbook for instructors to effectively apply the Deweyan and Vygotskian learning theories in the classroom.

Project-Based Learning in the Latin classroom

Now that the principles of PBL have been elucidated, both from the theoretical roots and the course design elements, let us turn to the application of these principles in the Latin classroom. As mentioned at the outset of this chapter, this class was an advanced undergraduate Latin seminar on Roman epistolography. This fourteen-week course met twice a week for ninety minutes in the fall of 2015 and had a rather diverse student make-up. There were eleven students in the class: two seniors, one junior, seven sophomores and one freshman. Moreover, they represented eight different majors: chemistry, business, French, English, archaeology, Classics, Greek and Latin.

Course goals and assessment plan

The goals of the class were fairly traditional and left quite a bit of room for PBL activities. As identified on the course syllabus, the class goals were:

1. To develop learners' Latin reading and comprehension skills through careful translation of assigned and unseen passages;
2. To review the basic morphology and syntax learned in earlier Latin classes, while introducing learners to new forms and syntax as they arise;
3. To enhance command of Latin vocabulary;
4. To introduce learners to the socio-literary and performance contexts of Roman epistolography; and
5. To introduce learners to basic professional activities of classicists.

Likewise, the assessment plan linked to each of these goals was somewhat traditional, although the emphasis on projects made up a larger percentage of the overall grade:

- Homework/parsing and translation: 15 per cent
- Article commentary/online discussion board: 15 per cent
- Test 1 (Cicero): 15 per cent
- Test 2 (Pliny): 15 per cent
- Group project: 15 per cent
- Final project: 25 per cent

Course design

In order to help the students work towards the mastery of the course goals, the course activities were scaffolded throughout, and the course schedule itself was divided into thirds, each third punctuated by either a test or a project, or both. In the first four weeks of class, learners were exposed to the basic concepts of ancient letters through an examination of Cicero's letters. Topics covered in this portion of the course explored the basics of ancient epistolography:

- How did ancient letters work?
- What materials were used to create them?
- How were letters transported and by whom?
- How were letters conceived of in theoretical terms?
- What were the major epistolary commonplaces?

At the end of this month, learners took a traditional test on these foundations, in which they were asked to translate seen Ciceronian passages, parse grammatical forms and answer an essay prompt dealing with the analysis of a seen epistle of Cicero.

In the second five weeks of class, learners expanded their view from the more practical and political letters of Cicero to the more overtly literary and organized ones of Pliny the Younger. During this portion of the course, learners were introduced to the idea of letters as social performance, as literature and as being aimed at multiple levels of audience. Again, as with the Cicero section, learners were given a traditional test at the end of this section. On the test, learners were asked to translate seen passages of Pliny, parse grammatical forms and answer an essay prompt dealing with the analysis of the literary nature of a seen letter of Pliny. In addition to this traditional in-class assessment, learners were also given a project on Pliny to complete (see below).

Finally, the last five weeks of the class were devoted to the exploration of the lesser-examined letters of Fronto – so unexamined that a student commentary actually had to be constructed for the learners, as there was no commentary on the market that was appropriate for undergraduates. During this portion of the course, learners built upon their knowledge of epistolary commonplaces and persona creation in order to analyse the manners in which Fronto, Marcus Aurelius and Lucius Verus attempted to communicate with one another and consciously construct their individual personae, both for private and public consumption. At the end of this final third of the class there was no test, but a final project for learners to create.

Adding projects to the curriculum

Thus far, the Latin class outlined is quite traditional: a topic-based, scaffolded seminar peppered with various types of assessments to serve as benchmarks along the way. It is to this basic structure that two larger projects were added. The first of these projects was a group project on a selected letter of Pliny; the second, an individual project on a selected letter of Fronto. In both of these projects, learners were asked to create the following documents for their assigned letter:

1. A fully edited text complete with an apparatus criticus;
2. An English translation of the text;

3. Notes and commentary on the grammatical, syntactical and literary dimensions of the text; and

4. A short (*c.* 200–300 words) introduction to the text.

The group project on Pliny was assigned during the second third of the class and was designed to serve as a trial run from for the final, individual project on Fronto. Learners were divided into groups of two or three by the instructor and were tasked with selecting a letter – or portion of a letter – between ten and twenty lines in length from the corpus of Pliny the Younger. Learners were allowed to consult any commentaries or texts of Pliny for ideas about what aspects of their letter to discuss, provided that any references were cited properly. No class time was devoted to these projects, and learners were to work on their projects outside of class using Google Docs and Dropbox for sharing files and collaborative writing. They were given four weeks to complete their project. During this four-week time period in which the learners were completing their projects outside of class, in-class discussions focused on the traditional textual analysis of assigned letters of Pliny, supplemented by the reading of scholarly articles on various aspects of Pliny's epistolography, and lectures on skills such as how to read and develop a stemma and apparatus criticus. All the skills and knowledge the learners would need to successfully develop a text-commentary were covered by these in-class activities.

After the learners had completed their group projects and had turned them in digitally via email, they were allowed to begin work on their individual Fronto projects. They were to complete the same assignments they had for the Pliny project, but this time on their own. Learners worked with me to identify a suitable letter of Fronto – 20–30 lines in length – using van den Hout's text-commentary. From there, learners had four weeks to craft their own text-commentary, complete with an introductory essay, an apparatus criticus, an English translation and notes aimed at undergraduate learners. These projects were due by the end of the final exam period.

Once all of the text-commentaries were received, I proceeded to grade them and also edit them for publication, contacting learners for clarification or suggestions for improvement. This round of editing was done during the three-week winter break. After all of the projects had been edited, I employed a student assistant, who had also been a participant in the class, to help me upload all of the commentaries to the website: www.frontoonline.com. This website went live in the spring of 2016 and was made open to the public.

Connecting PBL theory and classroom practice

Now that we have reviewed the course structure and how projects played such a great role in the class, let us return briefly to the theory with which we began this chapter in order to elucidate how exactly the course design aligned with the theoretical principles. In particular, let us cast our minds back to the seven design elements of Gold Standard PBL, for both the group and individual projects in my Latin class sought to align themselves with these elements. First, the problems with which the learners were presented were both authentic and challenging in nature, as the development of means to make ancient texts more accessible to learners and the general public is one of the major tasks of the modern classical philologist; moreover, the texts of Fronto are particularly challenging, since no student-centred text-commentaries exist.

Secondly, the projects represented a sustained inquiry rooted in student voice and choice. A total of eight weeks – nearly two-thirds of the class – were dedicated to the projects, and learners had to make a considerable effort and dedicate a great deal of time outside of class to complete the project. In order to motivate the learners to do this, they had the ability to choose their own topics, how they would divide the workload, the timeline for completing the project and the topics that were worth noting in their own commentaries. Thirdly, there was ample opportunity for learners to reflect on their projects and to receive feedback from their peers and instructor. As mentioned above, the group project was designed to provide a trial run at writing a text-commentary, and learners could receive feedback and reflect on how to improve for the individual project. Finally, there was a clear product in the creation of a public, online database accessible to anyone with an internet connection. Because of this, learners experienced a higher level of motivation and the depth of their learning was greatly augmented.

Therefore, it is clear that the design of the course was well rooted in the Gold Standard PBL structure and aligned well with the precepts of Deweyan relevant and experiential learning, as well as with Vygotskian social and metacognitive learning. However, the aspect of the course that made these all more accessible and possible was the inclusion of technology. Collaborative software, such as Google Docs and Dropbox, provided a powerful platform on which to do much of the social and metacognitive learning. Likewise, the creation of digital commentaries and the ability to share them via a website exponentially augmented the relevant learning and the public product aspect of the projects; these would not remain locked in the instructor's filing cabinet for no one to see, but would instead be publicly available to all and, perhaps, would become a resource for those looking to study Fronto.

Outcomes

Although it clear that the course design for this Roman epistles course was well rooted in PBL theory and sought to align itself with the principles of Gold Standard PBL, the question of the effectiveness of the approach also has to be explored. Therefore, to assess the level of success for the PBL approach to the course, both quantitative and qualitative evaluations were undertaken. Quantitatively, learner performance on the two major tests and the periodic pop quizzes was analysed. In addition, learner final grades were tabulated to give a more holistic idea of learner performance. Qualitatively, learner perceptions of the class were recorded via both traditional course evaluations and through individual interviews administered a few weeks after the end of the course. All of these metrics point to the conclusion that the inclusion of PBL methodologies provided an extra level of motivation and interest for the learners, while still maintaining a level of rigour in the learning of Latin grammar, syntax and socio-literary concepts.

Quantitative results

As mentioned above, two major tests were administered to the learners at the end of the first third (Cicero) and second third (Pliny) of the course. Each test represented 15 per cent of the overall course grade and aimed at collecting data on learner knowledge of Latin syntax, morphology and vocabulary, proficiency in translating seen Latin passages and ability to analyse Latin texts (course goals 1–4 above). Therefore, the tests were divided into three sections:

1. A seen translation portion consisting of two seen passages (30 per cent);
2. A parsing portion consisting of words selected from the two seen passages (40 per cent); and
3. An essay prompt on another seen passage (30 per cent).

Learners were given a ninety-minute class period in which to complete each assessment.

In general, the learners performed quite well on the two tests, attaining mastery level (i.e. 80 per cent) on all sections (Figure 18.1).

Learners performed best on the seen passages (92 per cent average), followed by the essay prompt (86 per cent average) and parsing (82 per cent average). The class average on the tests as a whole reached 86 per cent. Such learner performance seems to confirm that, although the PBL methodologies employed in the class differed from the traditional grammar-translation seminar style, learners still performed well when assessed on their knowledge of and proficiency in Latin grammar, syntax and translation.

The relative effectiveness of the PBL methodologies is also shown through a comparison of the quantitative results from this class with a grammar-translation seminar in the following semester (Figure 18.1). This class featured many of the same learners as the PBL class, and the results were similar. In the grammar-translation course, learners scored an average of 84 per cent on traditional tests, including an 89 per cent average on seen translation, 80 per cent on parsing and 84 per cent on essay prompts. When compared together, learners performed slightly better in all categories in the PBL course than in the grammar-translation course.

Such a trend can be seen in the pop quizzes on sight translations, as well. These quizzes consisted of a 30–40 word sight passage that learners were asked to translate. Unfamiliar vocabulary was provided. The pop quizzes were given at two- to three-week intervals and were unannounced. The aim of the quizzes was to gauge the extent to which the learners had internalized new syntax, morphology and vocabulary introduced in the course, and not just how well learners were memorizing passages studied in class. Overall, as with the two tests, the learners performed well, reaching the mastery level (86 per cent average) as a class. Moreover, this score was higher than that achieved by many of the same students in the grammar-translation course (84 per cent average).

	Sight pop quiz average	Total test average	Seen translation	Syntax analysis	Essay prompts
Roman epistles (2015) n=11	86%	86%	92%	82%	86%
Roman elegy (2016) n=7	84%	84%	89%	80%	84%

Figure 18.1 Quantitative course evaluations. © Bartolo Natoli.

Although admittedly imprecise and uncontrolled, the quantitative scores from these two classes point to some important correlations in learning outcomes. First, learners achieved a mastery level on all assessments, a fact that indicates that the goals of the course were met successfully. Secondly, a comparison of the quantitative scores of the PBL class with a subsequent grammar-translation course seems to show that the PBL methodologies employed were as effective, if not more so, as the grammar-translation methodologies, as learners in the PBL course performed slightly better than in the grammar-translation course in both seen and unseen assessments.

Qualitative results

In addition to the quantitative results provided by the seen tests and unseen pop quizzes, qualitative data were also gathered in order to gauge student perceptions of the effectiveness of the course and, in particular, of the PBL methodologies employed throughout the course. Two instruments were used to gather the qualitative data:

1. Traditional end-of-class evaluations; and
2. End-of-class, individual interviews with learners.

Taken together, the qualitative results from these instruments were overwhelmingly positive, as learners not only enjoyed the PBL methodologies employed in the class, but also reported increased motivation and content relevance.

The end-of-class evaluations were administered during the first ten minutes of the final class day. The instructor was not in the room, and ten of the eleven students were present to complete the instrument. The instrument asked learners to rate a variety of aspects of the course, including course structure, instructor effectiveness, their predicted grade and the overall rating of the course. Despite the variety of their predicted grades,[4] learners nearly unanimously rated the course and instructor at the highest levels. The course structure was rated a 4.9/5.0, the instructor effectiveness at a 4.9/5.0 and the overall course a perfect 5.0/5.0. All of these data paint a picture of a course learners thoroughly enjoyed and felt worked well for them.

Further qualitative data derived from learner interviews provide more depth to this picture and isolate particular aspects that learners identified as being beneficial and motivating. In general, the learners commented on how much they enjoyed the authentic, challenging nature of the projects and the fact that they were published for all to see and use. One student, Mary,[5] a Greek and Latin double major, stated:

I really liked that I got to go meticulously through the Latin. I had to know every single part of it. So, I actually got to know the Latin instead of just glossing over it. By working through my project, I felt like I learned how to actually be a Classicist.

Similarly, Brandon, a political science major, commented on the authentic nature of the projects and how working on a real problem gave him a deeper sense of confidence:

One thing I enjoyed about the project is that I felt like we were doing the same kind of things the highest level of Latin scholars are doing now. We got to create a commentary on something that no one has done before. It made me feel that, even though I am only in college, I am better than that. It was a cool feeling.

Finally, Christian, a biology major, spoke to the individual and relevance angles of the project, highlighting the importance of learner voice and choice:

I really liked the opportunity to get intimate with the text. It was mine. Only I was doing it. My thoughts. My opinions. My own translations. Making the commentary decisions myself that the teacher normally makes for us.

However, as positive as the learners were about the PBL portions of the class throughout their interviews, they also pointed to manners in which those portions could be improved. In particular, learners discussed how they would like to add more projects to the course design and would like to see it more integrated into the fabric of the class. Catherine, a biology major, suggested more guidance on the selection of letters:

I would have liked to have the letters we picked to go for the project to be more connected to the class. My letter wasn't from Fronto to Marcus Aurelius, but from Fronto to Antonius Pius. So, when I started, I misinterpreted part of the letter because I didn't recognize that.

Gabriella, a first-year Classics major, pointed out a lack of feedback in the project, stating:

I would have liked to see the final product. Like how my commentary actually worked in practice. Did I do a good job? Were there types of words I should have included that I didn't because I had read the text so many times?

Finally, Madison, a Latin major, addressed the ways in which the projects could have been more integrated into the class discussions:

I wish we would have tied it more into the class. I mean, we did learn a lot about Fronto and about letters, but I think it would have been nice to bounce ideas off of other people in class more. Perhaps add a few days into the schedule to facilitate or workshop our letters in class?

Taken together, these qualitative results emphasize the fact that learners overwhelmingly liked the PBL aspects of the class, and many of their suggestions for improvement included an increase both in the number of projects and in the integration of those projects into the class. When these qualitative results are combined with the quantitative data, a more complete picture emerges of a course that was able to provide the rigour and depth of a traditional undergraduate grammar-translation seminar, all while providing relevant, authentic, motivating projects for the learners to complete. Such PBL methodologies thus served not only to deepen the research learners completed and to heighten the types of learning with which they were engaging, but also to stoke the spark of imagination within the learners and motivate them to work harder than they otherwise would have done. What is more, those methodologies led to a deeper appreciation of and love for the ancient world within each of the learners.

Reflections and conclusions

At the end of the semester, and after all of the class evaluations and interviews were completed, I had a chance to reflect on this class from the viewpoint of an instructor. I found myself agreeing with many of the learners' comments; I hold this to be one of the most successful classes that I have had the pleasure of teaching, and most of the success of the class I attribute to the PBL methodologies employed throughout. Learners were, indeed, more motivated and produced more thoughtful analyses of Latin texts and engaged in higher levels of learning than in more traditional classes that I had taught. More importantly, they invested more of themselves in the content and took the lead in all the classes; it became truly learner-centred, and I played the role of facilitator as they themselves explored what the world of Roman letters had to offer.

However, as positive a learning experience as this class was, the shortcomings identified by the learners in their interviews were valid. Because of the limited class time provided by a semester-long class, some of the projects were not as well integrated into the daily class discussions as I would have liked. Moreover, suggestions for increased peer or public feedback on their commentaries – particularly on their final, individual commentaries – are also a welcome addition and fit quite nicely into the theoretical framework of PBL. Therefore, in subsequent iterations of this course, I have identified some changes to make the projects more integrated and feedback more prominent in the design of the course.

In particular, one modification that could address these issues is the creation of a course divided into halves. The first half would run traditionally in class, but learners would be tasked with the creation of an original commentary on a text due at the mid-point of the class. During the second half of the class, the main textbook would become the commentaries created by the learners. In such a design, the basic benefits of a PBL methodology would be maintained, but these would also be amplified by immediate and personal feedback for the learners. Learners could experience first-hand how well their commentaries fared and with which portions of their creation their fellow classmates struggle. Such an experience would not only improve any subsequent attempts at commentary creation by the learners, but it would also make them more sensitive – and, perhaps, more sympathetic – to issues arising from commentaries published by professionals in the field.

Aside from the issues of integration and feedback in the class, there is one last shortcoming – or, more accurately, one missed opportunity – that I would seek to add to subsequent iterations of this project. The creation and publication of original, digital commentaries provides a unique opportunity for learners to practice the twenty-first-century skill of coding webpages. In this course, due to lack of class time and learner prior knowledge, a drag-and-drop webpage was used (weebly.com) and only one student got an opportunity to upload the commentaries into the page.[6] However, in future iterations of the course, it would be a great idea to provide learners with the opportunity to code their work into a website using HTML or XHTML, or perhaps to open the possibility for interdisciplinary work with computer science programmes in the creation of a professional database with Python, Structured Query Language (SQL), *vel sim.* Such an opportunity would allow learners not only to further their mastery of the content of Latin language and literature, but also provide them with another marketable skill for use in a variety of contexts outside the classroom.

Yet, even with these shortcomings, I consider my 2015 class on Roman epistles to be an unqualified success. This has much to do with the addition of PBL methodologies to a traditional undergraduate grammar-translation seminar. The infusion of PBL into the course design resulted in heightened learner motivation, interest and depth of learning, all while maintaining the appropriate level of academic rigour. Quantitative analysis of learner performance showed the class performing at a mastery level in all areas and even outperforming a subsequent class taught in a more traditional fashion. Qualitative analysis of learner perceptions of the class revealed a high level of learner satisfaction with the class and a desire to do more. Moreover, the use of technology and the creation of digital commentaries accessible by the public at large served to further amplify the benefits of the PBL methodologies. At the outset of this chapter, I mused that if an instructor were to create a course that had high academic rigour and relevant content, produced high levels of learner motivation and incorporated digital pedagogies, that instructor would have found the Holy Grail of teaching. Well, while I may not have found the actual Holy Grail of teaching, this course – and the effects it had on learners and instructor alike – came pretty close.

Notes

1. See www.frontoonline.com.
2. See http://www.bie.org/about.
3. See http://www.bie.org/blog/gold_standard_pbl_essential_project_design_elements.
4. One learner who completed the evaluation did not fill in their predicted grade. The spread of those who did fill in their predicted grades was nearly identical to the actual final grade spread in the course. The true grade spread was four As, five Bs and two Cs.
5. Learners have been given pseudonyms in order to preserve anonymity.
6. At the end of the course, one of the learners was hired as a student assistant and tasked with uploading the commentaries to the webpage.

References

Dewey, J. (1916), *Democracy and Education*, Free Press.

Eggen, P. and Kauchak, D. (2012), *Strategies and Models for Teachers: Teaching Content and Thinking Skills*, Pearson.

Hung, W. (2008), 'The 9-Step Problem Design for Problem-based Learning: Application of the 3C3R Model', *Educational Research Review*, 4(2): 118–141.

Larmer, J., Mergendoller, J. and Boss, S. (2015), 'Setting the Standard for Project Based Learning: A Proven Approach to Rigorous Classroom Instruction'. Available online: http://www.bie.org/blog/gold_standard_pbl_essential_project_design_elements (accessed 15 October 2018).

Lave, J. and Wenger, E. (1990), *Situated Learning: Legitimate Peripheral Participation*, Cambridge, UK: Cambridge University Press.

Ravitz, J. and Blazevski, J. (2014), 'Assessing the Role of Online Technologies in Project-based Learning', in *Interdisciplinary Journal of Problem-based Learning*, 8(1): 65–79.

Tamim, S. and Grant, M. (2013), 'Definitions and Uses: Case Study of Teachers Implementing Project-based Learning', in *Interdisciplinary Journal of Problem-based Learning*, 7(2): 2–101.

van den Hout, M. (1999), *A Commentary on the Letters of M. Cornelius Fronto. Mnemosyne Supplement 190*, Leiden: E. J. Brill.

Vygotsky, L. (1986), *Thought and Language*, Cambridge: MIT Press.

Vygotsky, L. (1978), *Mind in Society: The Development of Higher Psychological Processes*, trans. M. Cole, V. John-Steiner, S. Scribner and E. Soubermain, Cambridge, MA: Harvard University Press.

CHAPTER 19
IN THE CLASSROOM WITH MULTI-MODAL TEACHING
Lisa Hay

Introduction

This chapter will look at the possibilities and practicalities of integrating ICT into a typical, mixed-ability Latin classroom, whilst acknowledging the challenges this can pose. Starting with the observation that technology has fundamentally altered how teachers and students alike are interacting with the world around them and that it has opened up network-based learning to all, the intention is to demonstrate how altering classroom practice to include multi-modal approaches not only produces better-quality outcomes for all students but also encourages them to be become independent and enquiring individuals.[1]

Teaching Classics, and in particular Latin, can be a challenge. Often, teachers are working alone and trying to deal with constant reform in education systems, coupled with pressures from management and targets to meet. Online resource-sharing on sites such as Steve Jenkin's The Classics Library, however, has enabled the widespread sharing of resources and facilitated pedagogic discussion. Facebook groups (from The Journal of Classics Teaching to the Latin Teacher Idea Exchange) mean that teachers can debate the merits of publications and materials with ease. Many Classics departments themselves boast a formidable online presence, often with far greater reach than other departments in their respective establishments, through Twitter, Instagram, YouTube, Pinterest and other sites and applications. As departments, we are connected to an extent we could never have predicted, and for many Classics teachers, collaboration with colleagues across the globe is a normal aspect of their teaching career.

Whilst the teachers are engaged in collaborative learning, many of our students are also engaging in similar network-driven learning. They are actively engaged online, seeking out material in response to their own interests, creating online communities around their subject areas and engaging in debate on all manner of subjects. They are also creating content on a daily basis, with many students even creating material based on their study of Latin: there are whole informal online communities dedicated to Caecilius from the Cambridge Latin Course, for example, along with popular memes (humorous images or text spread online, usually with variations around a core wording or theme) around the theme of 'Caecilius est in horto'. At the time of writing, I am aware of some of my students creating additional stories about characters from their textbook on the blogging site Tumblr, and a sixth-form Twitter account of student-created Latin limericks based on the texts they have been reading. Every class in Year 11 and above has a WhatsApp or Snapchat group for sharing resources and assistance. All of this was created without any teacher input. This active engagement outside the classroom contrasts with the traditional passive models of the student within a classroom.

Substantial research has been carried out into multi-modality and multi-literacies, including new and digital literacies, since the New London Group coined the term in 1996. A classroom rooted in transformative and interactive practice can not only enable students to develop into analytical learners engaged with knowledge on a deeper and more personal level, but also better prepare our students for a world which is changing rapidly and where the ability to manoeuvre critically through an international and diverse digital universe is a necessity. As Cope and Kalantzis commented in 2009:

> The kind of person who can live well in this world is someone who has acquired the capacity to navigate from one domain of social activity to another, who is resilient in their capacity to articulate and enact their own identities and who can find ways of entering into dialogue with and learning new and unfamiliar social languages.

> Cope and Kalantzis 2009: 164

The use of ICT in the classroom, where students can explore these domains in a curated environment and develop these skills, is crucial for subjects in the twenty-first century.

Acquiring adequate technology is one of the biggest issues facing teachers, especially those in establishments where budgets are tight. Whilst almost all UK schools have some accessible computer labs that may be pre-booked for sessions (98 per cent of all English secondary schools were reported as having dedicated computer labs by BECTA in 2004), this is far from ideal for integrating ICT in the most effective manner. Where technology is not used regularly and flexibly, it is more difficult to integrate it fully into students' learning and it remains a novelty or is used simply to replicate a task that could be completed as effectively in another manner.

One of the ways in which ICT can be effectively integrated is through the use of tablet computers, which are a particularly useful tool in language teaching and learning. They allow students to directly interact with and manipulate language and language elements in ways that once were only possible using laboriously created card-sort-style activities. Students are increasingly used to content with which they can interact, from commenting on blog posts to uploading 'reaction' videos, and so increasingly this kinaesthetic type of activity promotes greater enthusiasm and deeper participation. As one Year 10 student at my school commented, '[It] keeps your attention longer. You are more likely to focus if you are physically touching something.'

Tablets can also be networked in a variety of ways, and function as camera, video, notebook, whiteboard and textbook. Once the technology is acquired, however, maintenance can prove to be another challenge for schools. There are internet connections to consider, network access, updates to software and compatibility. These potential frustrations often combine with teachers' lack of confidence in using these resources to make full integration of ICT into lessons seem, frankly, not worth the trouble.

In my experience, with the exception of a few outlying enthusiasts, the main reasons students have the edge on teachers in proficiency is in their willingness simply to interact with technology with confidence. When teachers would call the ICT department to assist in solving a problem, students will scroll through menus themselves and happily try to reach a solution. They may or may not succeed in solving the problem, but they have no fear in trying. This behaviour is to be encouraged and emulated by us. Learning how to pre-empt and fix common issues gives the teacher confidence, and by publicly embracing the role of learner we can positively model the acquisition of proficiency.

It is also necessary to consider the practical issues that may arise from setting homework that can only be completed using technology. This has the potential to highlight social and financial differences between students (the digital divide), and also certain other issues – there are many students whose obsessive-compulsive disorder (OCD), for example, may prevent them from being able to touch shared equipment.[2]

In researching effective multi-modal teaching using ICT in the classroom, I gathered written feedback from students in Years 7 to 10, and recorded my Year 9 and Year 10 students talking about their experiences using ICT in the classroom, as well as observing many hours of students working with a range of technology. One of the interesting trends I have noticed in the last few years is how students' responses to ICT change from Key Stage 3 to Key Stage 4. In general, the younger students value the ways in which ICT allows them to explore and understand, to manipulate resources and create their own learning. By the time students reach a later stage in their education, they seem to have become exam-orientated and the ICT they value is that which enables them to memorize important information, such as vocabulary. The performative nature of examinations changes what is perceived as effective learning, and many students begin to feel that without demonstrating an assessed outcome, no learning has taken place.

However, the benefits of using the technology available far outweigh any challenges. It is clear that technology has the power to motivate students in a wide range of ways. As Cox states:

> Evidence from studies in education has shown that the main aspects of pupils' motivation are an enhanced sense of achievement, increase in self-directed learning, enhanced enjoyment and interest, enhanced self-esteem, and an increased commitment to the learning task ... Research into the effects of using ICT on pupils' motivation has shown it can influence the pupils to stay longer on a task, to show a greater commitment to learning, to find their schoolwork more interesting and consequently to improve their learning.
>
> Cox 1999: 33

Cox's findings are confirmed by my own interviews with Year 9 students, who referred to the fact that technology for them sped up their learning and allowed them to complete tasks in an efficient manner. As one student put it, if you are struggling through a task slowly and not enjoying it, 'you are not going to remember it anyway'.

Deaney et al. (2003) further found that interactive courseware (software designed specifically for educational use) was particularly popular with students, and also that ICT helped to overcome some of the difficulties they experienced in the production of work, for example in scribing by hand. There is also the potential for ICT in languages to be used to support certain students' needs more effectively. Some of these students may have specific identified special educational needs (SEN), such as dyslexia or a visual processing disorder, which can be differentiated for successfully using ICT. This can be as simple as changing font sizes or colours, or providing vocabulary assistance to targeted students through tools such as the Cambridge Latin Course online Explorer Tool, which provides the complete vocabulary for a story when a word is clicked, and allows students to focus on the ways in which the words are combined and the deeper meaning of the text, or simply on producing good-quality English sentences in their finished work in order to improve their literacy. As one of my Year 9 students said, 'I have found [online dictionaries] remove the fear over learning all of the vocabulary and give you time to work on translation', which seems to reinforce the theory that language proficiency can be accelerated through supportive ICT.

Developing resilience and a growth mind-set (Dweck (2012) characterized this as a belief that proficiency can be gained through effort rather than through innate talent) towards learning is a priority in education in general, but something we must be particularly aware of in languages. Fixed mind-sets tend to develop earlier around languages and maths. These subjects traditionally emphasize the performance of acquisition of a set of knowledge, and assessment is norm-referenced. Students make statements which reinforce this idea of innate talent, with some people simply being 'no good at languages', or conversely focus on grades and attainment, giving up as soon as they hit challenges which confirm their negative attitude or dent their pride in their own excellence. Fixed mind-sets develop later in subjects where assessment objectives are perceived as more varied and students do not feel direct comparison with their peers (e.g. technologies, English, arts). This fixed mind-set can even prevent students from perceiving their own learning. It was very disheartening to hear from one of my Year 8 dyslexic students who is achieving well beyond her target level of progress in Latin that she 'can do [Latin] today but ... probably won't be able to do it tomorrow'. When probed further, she explained that Latin was for 'clever' people. Through intervention, she has started to recognize her own successes, and indeed has opted to continue her Latin studies further up the school, but it has been a challenge for her to change her perception of how a student succeeds in this subject.

With the media frequently reinforcing elitist stereotypes about classicists (see Hunt 2014 and Goddard 2013 in JCT for some useful articles examining some of the biased and unrepresentative portrayals of the subject) we have a huge responsibility to ensure all our students can see their own progress and feel secure that Latin is a subject accessible for them, whatever their background and prior attainment. Effective use of ICT can help students to see their learning in terms of progress by creating individualized learning pathways. This could be through using applications such as Memrise, where vocabulary learning is a process rather than a test and rewards are given for effort expended rather than simply for the correct response.

Indeed, it was notable that my students who had used the most ICT in their Latin (Year 9 students) displayed the most characteristics of growth mind-set and resilience when discussing their learning. They frequently referenced the fact that they repeatedly tried tasks until they succeeded, which was something they simply would not or could not do on paper. One of my students commented that she 'continue[s] until I have reached my goal and that helps it stick because I do it again and again'.

ICT can also assist the teacher in creating an immersive and responsive classroom environment, where 'the interest of students may be maintained continuously by impulsive presentations ... facilitating emotional identifications, active participation and retrieval of information from the memory later on' (Benedek and Molnár 2014). Whilst a skilled storyteller will be able to elicit emotional responses from their students with words alone, this is still a directed response. An original and individual response to an authentic piece of evidence can be more powerful, and the context of an active and dynamic whole-class discussion can help to forge strong links in the minds of students. Students can be dropped into, for example, Pompeii using Google Street View or ancient Rome using Google Earth. They can then explore the town independently by virtually wandering down the ancient streets, or carry out scavenger hunts, taking screenshots of their discoveries. These can then be used as the basis of archaeological enquiry by using further resources to work out the significance of what they have found. Applications such as Kahoot![3] and Socrative[4] give the teacher the ability to engage the whole class swiftly in an impromptu debate through surveys and quick questions as a lesson develops in unexpected ways (see Lovatt's chapter in this volume). Responses can then be projected onto the whiteboard as they come in, or shared online through a real-time online classroom forum, and students can think and respond throughout the lesson as more information causes their opinions to develop. One of the benefits of these slower-paced discussions is to remove the standard initiate-respond-evaluate structure of most classroom discussions which, even when open-ended questions are posed, generally only allow a single student one opportunity to respond, leaving other students passive. ICT can remove the teacher from the role of directing the discussion and allow students to respond to one another, engaging higher-order thinking skills to challenge and question one another. Anonymity to peers through, for example, Socrative, can also prompt a wider range of responses and help to engage students who may feel unable to contribute in front of the whole class.

Emotional response can be used within games and challenges of a more competitive nature. The greater depth of engagement creates deeper learning. Kahoot! is an online application where a teacher can create a multiple-choice quiz easily, or use one of the many created by other users. These can be used as a fast way of recalling factual knowledge and are particularly effective when students work as a team, creating a learning opportunity in place of a straightforward test. This can be further developed through the 'ghost' mode, which allows students to revisit the same quiz at a later point in the lesson and play against their own prior scores, aiming to improve and beat themselves rather than each other. As an extra bonus, the data on student responses can be downloaded by the teacher immediately and used to inform their lesson. It also helps the students to identify their own revision priorities and become more independent learners who are responsible for their own progress. This is corroborated by feedback from my Year 9 students, one of whom stated, 'you remember [information] because you're happy you got it right or because you really want to win next time so you know what to revise if you get it wrong'.

As changing theories of education challenge traditional assumptions about effective learning strategies, ICT can give us the freedom to adapt to the needs of individual students. As Pachler states:

> Given the variety of preferences among pupils about the learning environment and their interactions with it, teaching approaches and methods need to be varied. New technologies offer one of many possibilities to provide varied learning opportunities.
>
> Pachler 1999: 12

Some of these needs may be met by reimagining the entire classroom dynamic. Dwyer (1996) states that, in a teacher-centred setting, learning is often seen as the transfer of ideas from the expert to the pupil: typical lessons focused around repetition and private learning. Technology can be used to remove the teacher-figure from these activities, creating a non-threatening environment in which 'failure' becomes a part of learning, as there is no longer a person to 'impress'. In an educational environment where the ability to fail constructively is a skill to be learned, removing barriers to achieving this is a key concern for teachers. Many students find the permanency of 'errors' in an exercise book a source of anxiety, as confirmed by one of my Year 9 students who found that, 'if I get a new book I can't write anything down wrong. Even if I get it wrong I just leave it. I cannot have a mistake in the front of my book . . . and I don't like crossing things out . . . I just leave it. With the iPads you can just start again'.

In student-centred models, on the other hand, 'collaborative, often team-based experiences in these classrooms help students to become deeply involved in manipulating information and thinking about it through processes of inquiry, critical thinking, problem-solving, discussion and communication . . . It becomes more difficult for the teachers to maintain control of what actually occurs . . . In this setting, technology takes on the vastly different role of a tool rather than a tutor' (Gibson 2001: 42).

This model can be arranged in a variety of ways. Tools such as the Sorting Words online activities on the Cambridge Latin Course website can be used by students to identify patterns. As students sort, for example, nouns into nominatives and accusatives, each failure becomes a step towards working out the patterns of endings. By the end of the task, the students have thought much more deeply about the words and are much more likely to be able to recognize them again. This works best when students are allowed to work at their own pace and with the freedom to collaborate with one another. Once the teacher abandons the concept of instruction with every task controlled and assessed, students are free to explore aspects of the content of the lesson. Students could, for example, pick up on the 'cheeky slave' character (such as Grumio in the *Cambridge Latin Course* textbooks), find some examples of ancient stereotyping and report back to the class. Ideas and questions can become much more challenging when students have access to an infinite textbook. As Gibson states, '[technology] often stimulates teachers to present more complex tasks and material' and 'can motivate students to attempt harder tasks' (Gibson 2001: 50–51). Effective Latin teaching is often a blend of multiple theories, deployed strategically. The repetition of tasks and rote learning has traditionally been a key aspect of learning parts of Latin language. I shall leave aside the arguments for whether this style of language learning is more effective than more organic language acquisition for the moment. The fact is that in the UK national examinations framework, students are examined in a way which requires some rote learning to have taken place, and effective vocabulary recall can be enhanced by some forms of memorization. ICT can create a more efficient environment for this to take place. Apps such as Memrise[5] (an online learning community which takes keywords, vocabulary or other material to be memorized and creates a blended series of learning and testing tasks which are repeated until students automatize their responses) encourage consistent learning patterns with integrated testing. It is also easy for a teacher to track students' progress by creating a group for the class and monitoring the data they produce. Walker (2016) investigated the utility of Memrise with her Year 11 students, concluding in addition that the convenience of the mobile app allowed students to learn in the most effective manner, freed from their own misconceptions surrounding revision. However, this type of application can create problems for some SEN students whose literacy needs put a barrier in place for these kinds of type-in tests, where the computer is unable to differentiate between an error in knowledge and an error in spelling. Quizlet,[6] an online flashcard-creation site, can resolve this, as students can create flashcards that link vocabulary to pictures rather than words, and they mark themselves as correct rather than relying on the machine.

These programs also encourage students working at all levels to continue to make effort. Vocabulary preparation becomes a task where effort and time spent is rewarded with progress, rather than a single test with a mark that can be compared with peers. Instant feedback on word sorts and selection tasks can also prevent errors from becoming ingrained. Students do not have to wait for the teacher, but can continue to work until they have independently gained mastery.

There is also the scope for greater immersion in the language and culture when students are working with technology. In terms of language acquisition, the greater the amount of target-language text that students can read, the swifter their understanding of the language can develop. Tools such as the Explorer Tool on the Cambridge Latin Course website,[7] or the apps SPQR[8] or Perseus[9] for non-confected Latin, allow students to click words to discover their meaning without having to spend time laboriously looking up vocabulary in dictionaries. Online or electronic dictionaries such as the Electronic Pocket Oxford Latin Dictionary and nodictionaries.com[10] can fulfill a similar function. This allows the students to engage with the content and the meaning more easily, and to develop skills of translation that are based on context and understanding rather than just on grammar. As one of my Year 10 students remarked when discussing the Cambridge Latin Course Explorer Tool, 'It doesn't feel like a story after a while when you just use the book.'

This immersion also aids in vocabulary retention as students usually find words easier to work out in context than in isolation. For example, students automatically translate phrases such as *per vias Alexandriae* correctly, although they may get *per* wrong in a traditional vocabulary recall test. This has been confirmed by the responses of my students, one of whom stated, 'If I see the same word repeated with the same action or object then I know what it means.'

Standard comprehension can also be examined in a different manner. Using Socrative, for example, responses to questions can be anonymously projected on the board and then students can discuss the merits of each and how others can be improved.

The scope of a lesson can also be reconsidered. ICT creates the ability to reach beyond the classroom and continue a meaningful dialogue with students and their families: perhaps a tweet or email to showcase some excellent work from a student; a complete video uploaded to YouTube or Clickview[11] for students to watch when there was only time for a clip in the classroom; or links to articles following on from questions arising in the classroom. This can easily be extended further. Time at home can be used to prepare for lessons, or even for students to create their own content to teach other students (see Gilliver's chapter in this volume). By using applications such as ShowMe,[12] an online video-creation application, it is easy for students and teachers to put together short videos combining clips, stills and basic animation together with narration. Latin students can use this very effectively to model skills such as chunking a sentence or putting together a commentary on a section of literature. Students can also work collaboratively outside of the classroom to prepare work, for example using Google Classroom[13] or through a class wiki. Most schools will have some form of online virtual learning environment (VLE), but unless it is mobile friendly and to some extent free from teacher curation, students will engage with the functions in a limited manner, as they have many other methods of communicating more naturally with their peers.

A multi-modal model lesson

Before the lesson begins, the teacher checks that students have completed the time allocated to learning vocabulary on Memrise and sends the student group a brief email congratulating them and reminding them of the minimum time expectations for the following week. Some students have also shared a starter Kahoot! quiz on the work from the previous lesson with the teacher, who briefly checks it.

Once the lesson is underway, the students run their Kahoot! with the class. If there are any significant errors, they pause to explain the idea to their peers. At the end of the quiz, the winners are congratulated, but all the students are reminded that they will be playing the quiz again at the end of the lesson so they should note down anything they need to revise. Whilst the students are doing this, the teacher downloads the data gathered by the Kahoot! to see which students might need some assistance during the lesson and also to gauge if any extra whole-class activities need to be inserted.

This lesson is a continuation of the previous work. Students have been working on Stage 17 of the *Cambridge Latin Course*, the first chapter set in the city of Alexandria and introducing the genitive case. The teacher projects the model sentences from the start of the stage onto the interactive whiteboard. Students have time to look closely at the pictures and remind themselves of the content, which they translated in the previous lesson. Whilst discussing Alexandria, the teacher is careful to have students retranslate the genitive phrases, and also to mention the different nationalities present in the city. When translating sections, the teacher uses the whiteboard to demonstrate the process using word order, drawing linking lines to make it clear. This is then saved and can be used again if necessary.

Today the students will be investigating the cultural tensions in the city of Alexandria. Whilst they are doing this, the teacher will also be ensuring that they are meeting the genitive in context. The students individually log in to the Google Classroom set up for this class. They have a Word document saved there which they can all edit together and collect information on cultural tensions. The document contains a simple table with sections labelled 'cultures in the city', 'buildings' and 'occupations', and room for further sections to be added by the students. The class also knows that, whilst they cannot delete content added by others, they are free to agree or disagree, using green text to support and red to contradict. Any content which is not linked to an existing point is simply added in black text. Students begin to add in ideas from the model sentences and from the previous lesson when they looked at the founding, layout and occupation of Alexandria, with any student free to also search online for additional material.

After roughly ten minutes, the teacher sends a question via Google Classroom to all users. Everyone is asked whether they think that Alexandria was a pleasant place to live, and all students are expected to submit a response in the next few minutes. They are also able to see each other's responses and to reply to each other. It is important to note that there is no expectation for the tablets to replace actual discussion between the students; instead they allow the students to discuss verbally with their neighbours and virtually with students on the other side of the room. The teacher is not only monitoring work via the tablet but engaging with the class in the normal face-to-face manner.

The students then examine the story 'Tumultus' on pages 78 and 79 of the CLC. This story sees the protagonist Quintus make his way through the city with an Egyptian slave boy towards the shop he has bought for his freedman Clemens. On the way, they encounter an angry mob and seek refuge with a Greek craftsman. Greeks and Romans, however, are the targets of the Egyptian mob and the story ends with the craftsman's house ransacked and the Egyptian slave boy murdered. It is a dramatic story, but one rooted in complicated social dynamics. The teacher calls up a fly-through video reconstruction of the city for context, whilst the students add information to the shared document, if relevant (it could be interesting to work into the lesson the *Assassin's Creed: Origins* video game educational walkthrough of the ancient city!). The first part of the story is then projected onto the interactive whiteboard from the Explore the Story tool online (see Hunt's chapter in this volume). The class works together to translate the beginning of the story, where the characters make their way into a part of the town near the harbour and become increasingly aware that there are only Egyptians in this part of the city. The words are clicked on by the teacher when the class cannot recall the meaning, bringing up the vocabulary. This translation is carried out swiftly, comprehension questions drawing out the underlying tension, and there is plenty of discussion of the meaning of the narrative.

Once the class has reached this point, the teacher poses two questions: 'Does the Egyptian boy have a valid reason for being concerned?' and 'Does Quintus make the correct decision in your opinion?' The students use their own iPads to read swiftly through the remainder of the text and form their opinions based upon the characters' interaction in the final section.

Another question comes up from Google Classroom via the forum for all users: 'Are the Egyptians right to be angry about the Greeks and Romans in their city?' Following this, the class comes together to try to draw some initial conclusions about the tensions in Alexandria. There are plenty of cultural avenues to explore here, and plenty of modern comparisons to be drawn out.

The second part of the story needs to retain the violence of the riot and the shock of the murder, and so speed and drama are important. There is a video re-enactment of this section available, which the students watch together on the whiteboard whilst using the Explore the Story tool to gain any vocabulary assistance needed. At the end, in groups of three, the students write up a summary of the story into Socrative. The finished versions are projected, and the class decides which parts convey the story the best. The final version is collated by the teacher (this can be printed out for exercise books, or added to the online Google Classroom).

It is time to draw the lesson to a close. Students add any final details to the collaborative document and answer the final question: 'What one thing would you do if you ruled Alexandria to diffuse the tensions?' A student group is tasked with preparing a starter on the material from this lesson, focusing on the tensions in Alexandria. They opt to produce a paper-based crossword using the online creator Discovery Education Puzzle Maker.[14] The rest of the class is reminded to carry out their minimum Memrise work (although most will exceed it).

The lesson ends with the Kahoot! quiz being replayed, with students aiming to improve on their previous result. Any student managing to do so earns a merit. After the lesson, the teacher adds the video of Alexandria to the department YouTube channel, checks the collaborative document and tweets a link for the class to a recent news report of unrest over cultural tensions.

ICT, and in particular a multi-modal approach to teaching and learning, has the potential to transform the Classics classroom. By utilizing the resources available, we can not only harness the motivational power of technology, but use it to create much more effective, immersive and engaging lessons.

Notes

1. Many thanks to the students of Hitchin Girls' School, and in particular my Year 9 Latin class (2017–18) and Year 10 Latin class (2017–19) who supplied most of the comments included in this chapter.
2. For further information, see www.ocdaction.org.uk.
3. See https://kahoot.it/.
4. See https://www.socrative.com/.
5. See https://www.memrise.com/.
6. See https://quizlet.com/.
7. See https://www.cambridgescp.com/.
8. See http://romansgohome.com/.
9. See http://www.perseus.tufts.edu/hopper/.
10. See http://nodictionaries.com/.
11. See https://www.clickview.co.uk/.
12. See https://www.showme.com/.
13. See https://classroom.google.com/h.
14. See http://www.discoveryeducation.com/free-puzzlemaker/.

References

Benedek, A. and Molnár, G. (2014), 'ICT in Education: A New Paradigm and Old Obstacle', in A. Leist and T. Pankowski (eds.), *The Ninth International Multi-Conference on Computing in the Global Information Technology*, Sevilla: IARIA, 54–60.

Condie, R. and Munro, B. (2007), *The Impact of ICT in Schools: Landscape Review*, The British Educational Communications and Technology Agency.

Cope, B. and Kalantzis, M. (2009), 'Multiliteracies: New Literacies, New Learning', in *Pedagogies: an International Journal*, 4: 164–195.

Cox, M. (1999), 'Motivating Pupils Through the Use of ICT', in M. Leask and N. Pachler (eds.), *Learning to Teach Using ICT in the Secondary School*, London: Routledge.

Dweck, C. (2012), *Mindset: Changing the Way You Think to Fulfil Your Potential*, London: Robinson.

Dwyer, D. (1996), 'The Imperative to Change Our Schools', in C. Fisher, D. Dwyer and K. Yocam (eds.), *Education and Technology: Reflections on Computing in Classrooms*, San Francisco: Jossey-Bass.

Dwyer, D. Ringstaff, C. and Sandholtz, J. (1990), 'The Evolution of Teachers' Instructional Belief and Practices in High-access-to-technology Classrooms', Paper presented at the American Educational Research Association, Boston, MA.

Gibson, I. (2001), 'At the Intersection of Technology and Pedagogy: Considering Styles of Learning and Teaching', *Journal of Information Technology for Teacher Education*, 10, 1 and 2.

Goddard, C. (2013), 'What Does the Media Think of Us?', *Journal of Classics Teaching*, 28: 54–55.

Hunt, S. (2016), *Starting to Teach Latin*, London: Bloomsbury Academic.

Hunt, S. (2014), 'What do the Media Think of Us? [Part 2]', *Journal of Classics Teaching*, 29: 19–20.

New London Group (1996), 'A Pedagogy of Multiliteracies: Designing Social Futures', *Harvard Educational Review*, 66 (1).

Pachler, N. (1999), 'Linking School with Home Use', in M. Leask and N. Pachler (eds.), *Learning to Teach Using ICT in the Secondary School*, London: Routledge.

Walker, L. (2016), 'The Impact of Using Memrise on Student Perceptions of Learning Latin Vocabulary and on Long-term Memory of Words', *Journal of Classics Teaching*, 32: 14–20.

APPENDIX I
GLOSSARY OF TERMS

ACTFL American Council on the Teaching of Foreign Languages.

A-level Advanced Level is a UK national qualification in specified subject areas taken by students aged 17–18. The A-level is often used as a matriculation requirement for entry to university courses.

AS-level Advanced Subsidiary level is a UK national qualification worth about half an A-level.

AV Audio-visual.

BBC British Broadcasting Corporation.

BECTA British Educational Communications and Technology Agency.

BME Black and Minority Ethnic (used to refer to members of non-white communities in the UK).

CfA Classics for All, a British charity which seeks to support the expansion of classical subjects in non-fee-paying schools.

CPD Continuing Professional Development.

CSCP Cambridge School Classics Project is the producer of the *Cambridge Latin Course* (see below).

CLC *Cambridge Latin Course* (Latin course book).

CUCD Council of University Classics Departments.

DfE Department for Education (UK).

EAL English as an Additional Language.

EDUQAS A UK examination board which is part of WJEC. It sets Latin GCSEs.

EBacc English Baccalaureate is a UK national accountability measure based on students' examination results across five subjects which must include English, mathematics, science, a humanity (including geography, history, ancient history – but not classical civilization), and a modern or ancient language (including Latin or classical Greek).

GCSE General Certificate of Secondary Education is a subject-specific UK national qualification taken by students at age 16. Students generally take 8–9 GCSEs in a range of subjects usually including the five EBacc subjects. GCSEs in Latin, classical Greek, ancient history and classical civilization are offered.

HE/HEI Higher Education/Higher Education Institution, such as a university.

IB International Baccalaureate is an international qualification set by the IB programme in Geneva. It is taken by students aged 17–18 and consists of a range of subject-specific assessments.

ICT Information and Communication Technology.

INSET In-Service Training (see CPD).

IT Information Technology.

IWB Interactive Whiteboard.

MOOC Massive Open Online Courses.

MAT Multi-Academy Trust.

MFL Modern Foreign Language.

OFFA Office for Fair Access.

Ofsted The Office for Standards in Education, Children's Services and Skills is a non-ministerial department of the UK government. The services Ofsted inspects or regulates include state schools, independent schools and teacher-training providers, colleges and learning and skills providers in England.

OCR Oxford and Cambridge and RSA examinations board. The board sets GCSE and AS/A-level qualifications in Latin, classical Greek, classical civilization and ancient history.

OLC Oxford Latin Course (Latin course book).

OU Open University.

PBL Project-Based Learning.

PGCE Postgraduate Certificate in Education (Scottish equivalent is the PGDE – the Postgraduate Diploma in Education). Until 2010 this qualification was essential for teaching in the UK state sector.

PISA The Programme for International Student Assessment is a worldwide study by the Organization for Economic Co-operation and Development (OECD) in member and non-member nations of fifteen-year-old school pupils' scholastic performance on mathematics, science and reading.

SEN/SEND Special Educational Needs/Special Educational Needs and Disability.

SRS Student Response Systems.

UK United Kingdom.

US United States.

VLE Virtual Learning Environment.

WJEC Welsh Joint Examinations Council. Sets Latin qualifications at Certificate Levels 1 and 2.

APPENDIX II
COMPARISON OF UK AND US
EDUCATIONAL SYSTEMS

UK school types:

State schools are free, maintained by the state and open to anyone. State secondary schools (for ages 11–18) and primary schools (for ages 4–10) may be run by the local authority, or by other groups ('free schools' and academies') on behalf of the state. Most secondary schools are non-selective by intake ('secondary moderns' and 'comprehensives') and a few are academically selective by examination ('grammar schools'). They are all funded by general taxation. Some academies link together into multi-academy trusts (MATs). Free schools and academies are allowed to vary their curriculum beyond the national curriculum.

Independent schools, including public schools (of ancient lineage) and other private schools, are all fee-paying and often academically selective by examination. These and preparatory schools are not bound by any national curriculum or standards.

Preparatory schools are private, fee-paying schools for students up to age eleven or thirteen whose purpose is to prepare them for the entrance examinations of specific independent secondary schools.

US school types:

Public schools are free, maintained by the local government and funded by local, state and federal government funds. Public schools are required to abide by certain state and federal standards, and teachers must have appropriate licensure. Students attend a public school based upon where they live.

Magnet schools are public schools that specialize in certain areas (e.g. technology, arts or science). As public schools, magnet schools are free, but are operated by school districts. Students are admitted into magnet schools either based upon academic achievement or via random lottery.

Private schools are private, fee-paying schools and receive no government funding. Because private schools do not receive any government funding, they are not bound by any national curriculum or standards. Students are admitted by application.

Charter schools are a hybrid between public and private schools. Like public schools, charter schools are free. However, like private schools, students are admitted via application. Any organization can apply to the state government to open a charter school. If the application is accepted, the charter school can receive government funding for a specified period of time. However, if the state government is dissatisfied with the charter school, their charter can be revoked and the school closed.

	UK				US		
Age of student (years)	School year name	Key Stage name	School type	National examination	School year name	School type	National examination
4–5	Reception		Primary		Pre-Kindergarten (PreK)		
5–6	Year 1	KS1	Primary		Kindergarten (K)	Primary/ Elementary School	
6–7	Year 2				First Grade		
7–8	Year 3	KS2			Second Grade		
8–9	Year 4				Third Grade		
9–10	Year 5				Fourth Grade		
10–11	Year 6				Fifth Grade		
11–12	Year 7	KS3[1]	Secondary		Sixth Grade	Middle School	
12–13	Year 8				Seventh Grade		
13–14	Year 9				Eighth Grade		
14–15	Year 10	KS4			Ninth Grade	Secondary/High School	
15–16	Year 11			GCSE[2]	Tenth Grade		
16–17	Year 12	KS5	Sixth-form college[3]	AS level	Eleventh Grade		Preliminary Scholastic Aptitude Test (P-SAT)
17–18	Year 13			A level[4]	Twelve Grade		Scholastic Aptitude Test (SAT)

[1] Some schools only have a two-year KS3 in Years 7–8.

[2] Students in some private schools take the International GCSE (IGCSE). State school students are not allowed to take it as it has not been validated by the UK Qualifications and Curriculum Authority.

[3] There is a variety of educational establishments at this stage, including sixth forms attached to secondary schools, stand-alone sixth-form colleges and further education colleges often for vocational studies.

[4] Students in some private schools take the Pre-U qualification. Some students take the International Baccalaureate (IB) examination.

INDEX

Index

Index